HONG KONG IN THE SHADOW OF CHINA

HONG KONG IN THE SHADOW OF CHINA

SHADOW OF CHINA

Living with the Leviathan

RICHARD C. BUSH

BROOKINGS INSTITUTION PRESS
Washington, D.C.

Library of Congress Cataloging-in-Publication data

Names: Bush, Richard C., 1947– author.
Title: Hong Kong in the shadow of China : living with the Leviathan / Richard C. Bush.
Description: Washington, D.C. : Brookings Institution Press, 2016. | Includes bibliographical references and index.
Identifiers: LCCN 2016017498 (print) | LCCN 2016028869 (ebook) | ISBN 9780815728122 (paperback : alk. paper) | ISBN 9780815728139 (epub) | ISBN 9780815728146 (pdf)
Subjects: LCSH: Hong Kong (China)—Politics and government—1997– | Democratization—China—Hong Kong. | Business and politics—China—Hong Kong. | Political participation—China—Hong Kong. | Political Culture—China—Hong Kong. | BISAC: POLITICAL SCIENCE / Political Ideologies / Communism & Socialism. | POLITICAL SCIENCE / Political Process / Elections.
Classification: LCC JQ1539.5.A91 B87 2016 (print) | LCC JQ1539.5.A91 (ebook) | DDC 320.95125—dc23
LC record available at https://lccn.loc.gov/2016017498

9 8 7 6 5 4 3 2 1

Typeset in Garamond Premier Pro

Composition by Westchester Publishing Services

For my siblings

Nancy Ellen Bush Frenkel

Susan Thompson

Paul Harris Bush

Contents

Acknowledgments

In most cases, the acknowledgments section of a book recognizes people and institutions only. In this case I feel obliged to acknowledge my debt to a place—Hong Kong. My family lived there from 1960 to 1965 (my parents were missionaries), which were my years for secondary school. Because I went to a British school with a very British curriculum, I learned nothing about China in my classes. But more than any other reason, the experience of living in a Chinese society for five formative years led me to devote my professional career to the study of China. Without my Hong Kong experience, I am sure that my life would be very different and probably a lot less interesting. So I owe Hong Kong a lot, and this book is but a small and partial repayment of the debt I owe.

But there are others to whom I am indebted as well. First of all are the donors who have made this book possible: the generous individuals in Taiwan and elsewhere who made donations to the Chen-fu and Cecilia Yen Koo Chair in Taiwan Studies, which I hold, the Smith Richardson Foundation, and the Taiwan Semiconductor Manufacturing Corporation (TSMC) Education and Cultural Foundation. I am grateful to Allan Song at Smith Richardson and Morris Chang at the TSMC Education and Cultural Foundation for their sustained encouragement of my work.

Colleagues at Brookings have been unstintingly supportive. Strobe Talbott has set a shining example of how to combine administration and scholarship.

Martin Indyk and Bruce Jones, the previous and current directors of Brookings' Foreign Policy Program, have given me strong encouragement for this project, as have colleagues in the John L. Thornton China Center. In particular, I have drawn on the many conversations Jeff Bader and I had over the years about Hong Kong and how the U.S. government should and should not attempt to promote democracy overseas. My staff and colleagues in the Center for East Asia Policy Studies have been consistently supportive. Of that group, my greatest appreciation goes to Maeve Whelan-Wuest, my research assistant since early 2015. She has assisted me in countless ways: relentlessly searching for the data I needed to make my analytical points, combing through each draft of each chapter with a fine-toothed comb, and generally making it easy to stay in "the zone" of thinking and writing. Michael O'Hanlon, Stephen Young, former U.S. Consul-General in Hong Kong, and an anonymous specialist reviewed the manuscript and made many good suggestions (I alone am responsible for the mistakes that surely remain).

Many other friends and colleagues have made invaluable contributions to my understanding of Hong Kong's past, present, and future. Hong Kong has an outstanding group of scholars who have done exceptional work on an array of relevant issues, but regrettably much of that work is unknown and unrecognized in the West. Those Hong Kong scholars who have had the greatest impact on my thinking include: John P. Burns, Jean-Pierre Cabestan, Johannes Chan, Joseph Y. S. Cheng, Anthony B. L. Cheung, Michael C. Davis, Brian C. H. Fong, Leo F. Goodstadt, Richard Weixing Hu, Lau Siu-kai, Christine Loh, Percy Luen-tim Lui, Sonny Shiu Hing Lo, Ma Ngok, Suzanne Pepper, Ian Scott, Alvin Y. So, Yue Chim Richard Wong, Wilson Wong, Ray Yep, Rikkie Yeung, and Simon N. M. Young. I have also had the good fortune of enjoying the friendship and counsel of the individuals from Hong Kong who were Brookings visiting fellows from 2002 to 2015: Nelson Cheng, Richard Hu, Francis Leung, Simon Shen, Injoo Sohn, James Tang, Wilson Wong, Ray Yep, Chris Yeung, Rikkie Yeung, Zheng Hao, and Zhu Wenhui. Many others in Hong Kong, too numerous to name, opened their doors and their minds to me, and I am very grateful for their kindness. Officials at the U.S. Consulate General and in the Hong Kong Special Administrative Region government were always gracious in illuminating key issues. Other current and former Hong Kong hands who have been generous with their time and friendship include George Chen, Frank Ching, Michael DeGolyer, Steve Yui-sang Tsang, Richard Vuylsteke, Anna Wu, and Ted Zimmerman. Yun-han Chu, Larry Diamond, and Andrew Nathan have long been my gurus on democratization (and other subjects).

Sadly, two individuals who contributed a lot to American policy toward and understanding of Hong Kong will not have an opportunity to read my book. Congressman Stephen J. Solarz, who was my former boss, died in 2010. Nancy Bernkopf Tucker, a good friend and professor at Georgetown University, passed away in 2012.

As always, the members of my extended family have been immensely supportive. I dedicate this volume to my sisters and brother. It was in Hong Kong that we were last together before scattering to the four winds.

Note on Romanization

The Romanization of Chinese names is often an unstandardized jumble, especially for people connected with Hong Kong. Individuals who moved to Hong Kong in the last thirty years from the rest of the People's Republic of China generally use the *pinyin* system that is tied to standard Chinese (*Putonghua*, or Mandarin in the West). Chinese who came to Hong Kong in earlier periods or were born in the city are mostly Cantonese, that is, they come from the province of Guangdong, which borders Hong Kong to the north. The Romanization of their names reflects their Cantonese origin and native dialect, which is mutually unintelligible from *Putonghua*. There are a couple of systems for Romanizing Cantonese names, and individuals are also free to exercise their individuality in how they "spell" their names. To make things more complicated, many people in Hong Kong also have an English-language given name, and their names are rendered in different ways in different contexts. For example, the name of Richard Wong Yue-chim, a professor of political economy at the University of Hong Kong, is sometimes rendered that way. But it also appears just as Richard Wong or as Yue Chim Richard Wong. For purposes of documentation, in cases like this I use the form used in the original source. Finally, "Hong Kong," "Chiang Kai-shek," and "Sun Yat-sen" are rendered in their conventional way even though that is inconsistent with the Romanization systems based on standard Chinese.

Unless otherwise indicated, currency values are given in U.S. dollars. Since October 1983, the Hong Kong Monetary Authority, the equivalent of the central bank, has pegged the value of the Hong Kong dollar to that of the U.S. dollar at the rate of US$1.00 to HK$7.76.

HONG KONG IN THE SHADOW OF CHINA

ONE

The Hong Kong Hybrid

Hong Kong was not expecting the mass protests that erupted in late September 2014. A dispute that had started out as an argument among politicians and intellectuals over the details of the electoral system, an argument that had lasted for over two decades, suddenly morphed into a mass occupation of major urban thoroughfares by average citizens. The struggle began with high drama and pictures of the Hong Kong Police firing tear gas into the crowds—pictures that were quickly texted and retweeted around the world. A peaceful standoff ensued for some two months and ended not with a bang but with a whimper. The only certainty was that nothing in Hong Kong politics would be the same.

Prior to the protests, local observers knew that *some* kind of trouble was looming. The Chinese government in Beijing, which has had sovereign authority over Hong Kong since 1997, had signaled back in December 2007 that the 2017 election for Hong Kong's chief executive would be on the basis of universal suffrage for the first time. Many in the city therefore believed that full democracy was around the corner. Yet like morning mists, those hopes quickly dissipated. It started with a disagreement over whether the term "universal suffrage" would be defined narrowly or broadly. China made progressively clear that although it was now willing to have eligible voters themselves choose the next chief executive, it wished to have a say over which candidates would be on the ballot. A nominating committee, composed mainly of local supporters of the Beijing government, would set the list of candidates. The system, it seemed, would remain rigged after all. Preparations thus began for mass protests, which had become the main way for the Hong Kong public to participate in politics.

People thought they knew how that protest would unfold. Pro-democracy professors and activists, drawing on the ideas of deliberative democracy and civil disobedience, had devised the Occupy Central movement, Central being the principal business and financial center on Hong Kong Island. A stated purpose of the movement was to alert all parties concerned that Hong Kong would go off a "political reform cliff" if electoral change did not occur.[1] To sound that alert, Occupy organizers promised that if the Chinese and Hong Kong governments did not back down from their restrictive nominating committee approach and accept the idea of nominations from the public, they would mobilize several tens of thousands of protesters to take over key streets in Central. The assumption was that the Occupy protesters would follow the norms of civil disobedience and submit to arrest. That was the scenario for which the Hong Kong Police planned. Hong Kong companies whose offices were in Central made arrangements to continue operations even if the area was inaccessible for a couple of days. Individual citizens made their own preparations, but those who did not work in Central believed they would be unaffected by the protest. The Chinese government stated repeatedly that electoral arrangements had to accord with its legal parameters, that it would not be intimidated, and that Occupy Central was illegal. It was a classic game of chicken, where everyone thought they knew the rules. But then, the game changed.

Enter Hong Kong's high school and university students. They joined with their elders in the democratic camp in opposing the screening of candidates by a nominating committee biased toward Beijing and in giving the public the broadest possible role in the nomination process. But once Beijing ruled that the nominating committee and it alone would decide whom to consider, the students decided not to follow the preordained Occupy Central script and chose instead to preempt their elders. Full of idealism, they decided themselves—and for everyone else—the timing, locales, and scope of the protest movement.[2] If they followed any script, it was the one that had been written in Taiwan six months before. There, a student activist group angry about a trade in services agreement that the government had negotiated with Beijing undertook a lightning occupation of the island's legislature that lasted for twenty-three days. Even though the specific issues in Hong Kong were very different, the political tactics gave evidence of a diffusion effect from Taiwan.[3]

After students boycotted classes during the week of September 22, some of them moved on the evening of September 26 to take over a small area within the government complex at Tamar, in the Admiralty district. Over the next two days, through both arrests and the use of pepper spray, the police tried to disperse the crowds, which were still modest. Then, on Sunday, September 28, the police used tear gas, which was reported on both television and social media. Instead of dispersing, the crowd grew to tens of thousands, more than the police could handle. The crowds took over the main thoroughfares that ran through Admiralty parallel to Hong Kong harbor. Protesters also took over two other sites: Causeway Bay, a shopping area on Hong Kong Island frequented by tourists from the mainland of China, and Mong Kok, a district in the middle of Kowloon Peninsula, across the harbor. And Central was never occupied. Umbrellas used to protect against tear gas, pepper spray, and sudden thunderstorms provided a symbol and a name for what became known as the Umbrella Movement.

An uneasy standoff ensued. Both police and protesters generally exercised restraint. Attempts to encroach on the protesters' tent villages were effectively resisted. The most violence occurred in Mong Kok, which is a socially mixed area with a significant presence of Triad gangsters. Some of those groups launched serious attacks on the local occupiers. In student-dominated Causeway Bay and Admiralty, peaceful coexistence prevailed as long as the police did not try to change the status quo, which they had discovered would only trigger a surge in the number of protesters. Gradually the number of "permanent" demonstrators in these three areas declined. Numbers swelled in the evenings and on weekends, when most people didn't have to go to work or to class, but the potential for rapid mobilization remained.

Beijing responded with a hard line. It cast itself as the defender of the rule of law and the protestors as lawbreakers. If universal suffrage was to happen, it would be within the parameters that the government had laid down. Beijing had spurned proposals that would produce a genuinely competitive election within Chinese parameters.[4] Beijing also sought to divert blame away from its own recalcitrance and onto alleged "foreign forces" that it asserted were instigating the disorder.[5]

More ominously, there was a lurking fear that sooner or later Beijing would carry out a violent crackdown, as it had done across China in the spring of

1989. Deng Xiaoping had contemplated precisely this contingency when he said, in 1987, "After 1997 we shall still allow people in Hong Kong to attack the Chinese Communist Party and China verbally, but what if they should turn their words into action, trying to convert Hong Kong into a base of opposition to the mainland under the pretext of 'democracy'? Then we would have no choice but to intervene. First the administrative bodies in Hong Kong should intervene; mainland troops stationed there would not necessarily be used. They would be used only if there were disturbances, serious disturbances. Anyway, intervention of some sort would be necessary."[6] As unhappy as Beijing was about the ongoing occupation in the fall of 2014, it was prepared to follow Deng's dictum and have the Hong Kong government take the lead. The apparent strategy was to let the movement peter out as the inconvenience it caused wore on affected citizens.

How long this patience would have lasted is anybody's guess, because in the end, Chinese intervention was not necessary. There was an effort to end the occupation by negotiation, but it fizzled. On the evening of October 21, senior officials of the Hong Kong Special Administrative Region (Hong Kong SAR) government conducted a televised dialogue with the leaders of the Hong Kong Federation of Students, one of the leading protest groups, but there was no movement on the key issues because neither side had much flexibility: The Hong Kong government's hands were tied by Beijing's uncompromising attitude toward election arrangements. The Hong Kong Federation of Students was handicapped by the loose and leaderless character of the movement. Consequently, the first dialogue session was the last one.

In the end, it was Hong Kong's much respected judiciary that paved the way for the end of the protests. Beginning in the latter part of October, groups of taxi drivers and minibus companies and others who believed the occupation had deprived them of their livelihood filed suits in local courts, seeking clearance of the protest areas. The plaintiffs won their cases and the Hong Kong Police were authorized to assist court bailiffs in carrying out the injunction. The first action occurred during the week of November 17 in the Mong Kok area, but not without violent clashes between police and the protesters there. Student leaders responded with improvisation, first trying to travel to Beijing to speak with Chinese leaders (they were not allowed to leave Hong Kong) and then participating in a brief hunger strike. More radical elements attempted to break into the Legislative Council Building on November 18 and stormed the government administration offices at the end of the month (the Legislative Council is the unicameral legislature of the Hong Kong

SAR). But enforcement of the court order continued, and Admiralty was eventually cleared on December 10 and Causeway Bay shortly thereafter. After seventy-five days, the most dramatic event in Hong Kong's political history had come to an end.

The Umbrella Movement may have surprised residents, the Hong Kong government, and the People's Republic of China (PRC) government in how it occurred, but it was only the latest and most contentious episode in a three-decade struggle by proponents of a more democratic system. Moreover, the movement also manifested a number of widening cleavages in Hong Kong society: between the PRC and Hong Kong governments, and the Pan-Democratic movement; between the local, wealthy business elite and the middle class; between the young and their elders; between those who give priority to political order and economic growth and those who value open participation; between those who wish to limit the competition for political power and those who wish to remove those limits; and between those who fear populist politics and those who embrace them. This book explores these cleavages and what they mean for both Hong Kong's future prosperity and its governance.

Becoming Hong Kong

For anyone whose impressions of Hong Kong were formed before 1989, the events of fall 2014 would come as a great shock. In the decades after World War II, the prevailing wisdom was that Hong Kong's people had a single-minded focus—or obsession: making money and securing a decent standard of living.[7] In the days of rapid economic growth, the general idea of popular elections for the territory's leaders was probably far from most people's minds—and the details even further. Even today, some Chinese officials would like to believe that the Umbrella Movement did not reflect mainstream sentiments and concerns, and that Hong Kong should go back to being an "economic city" with a solely economic reason for existing. One of the purposes of this book is to explain the transition from a focus on the economy to one on politics, and therefore a brief review of Hong Kong's history is necessary to set the broad context.

BEFORE 1945

The name Hong Kong is an approximate phonetic rendering of the pronunciation in Cantonese or Hakka dialects of *xianggang*, meaning "incense (or fragrant) harbor" (represented by the characters 香港).[8] Before 1842, the name referred to a small inlet between Aberdeen Island and the south side of the bird-shaped island now known as Hong Kong Island, and to the village of the same name, *xianggangcun* (香港村). At one time the village was a key export point for incense; later it was one of the first points of contact between British sailors and local fishermen.[9]

In the early nineteenth century, this speck of an island on the south coast of China at the mouth of the Pearl River was a backwater of no significance. It was a place for farming, fishing, and smuggling as early as the Song Dynasty (960–1279 AD), but it paled in significance to Guangzhou (Canton), the major metropolis up the Pearl River to the northwest.[10] Guangzhou was the administrative capital for two provinces, the core of the regional economic system, and the only place designated for Western traders to trade with Chinese merchants. The ascent of Hong Kong was a consequence of the critical intersection of two trajectories. One was the projection of British power into East Asia in the first half of the nineteenth century in order to open the Chinese economy to trade with Western nations on Britain's terms. And Britain had a reason to try: it seemed a promising market for British exports. China's GDP in 1820, as estimated by Angus Madisson in 1990 dollars, was over US$228 billion, more than double that of India and more than the combined GDP of the world's eight next largest economies.[11] The other trajectory was imperial China's stubborn insistence that it would define the rules of trade, particularly since imports of opium from India were causing a destabilizing outflow of silver, China's currency of exchange. China was prepared to use coercion to preserve relative autarchy; Britain was just as prepared to use force to get its way and to expose China to what we now call globalization. The Opium War of 1840–42 was the result, and the quick British victory signaled the rise of the West and the decline of China. In the process, Britain got Hong Kong as a spoil of war.

Actually, what Britain annexed from China in 1842 was only one part of today's Hong Kong. In the first of three transfers, Britain acquired Hong Kong Island, whose northern shore looks out over one of the world's magnificent deep harbors. The new colonial government called the island Victoria, after the reigning British monarch. The second transfer occurred in 1860, after Britain's victory over China in the Arrow or Second Opium War, when it secured the lower Kowloon Peninsula, which was across the harbor from Victoria, and some associated islands. Hong Kong remained the name of the original Victoria Island, but also became the name of the colony as a whole. The third transfer came in 1898, after the "scramble for concessions" by various imperialist powers. Britain got both a northern extension from the Kowloon Peninsula and a number of additional islands. These new acquisitions became known as the New Territories. The first two acquisitions were secured in perpetuity (or so the British thought), but the New Territories were transferred pursuant to a ninety-nine-year lease—the lease that would trigger the process that culminated in the return of all of Hong Kong to China in 1997.

Since the 1840s, Hong Kong has been an interface between China and the international economy. In some periods it was the primary meeting point between the two. But the character of that interface has changed dramatically in the seven decades since the end of World War II. Until World War II, its duty-free trade regime and British legal system made Hong Kong an attractive business center for British and Cantonese businessmen alike.[12] Opium remained a leading commodity throughout the nineteenth century. The gradually urbanizing, commercial areas of Hong Kong Island and Kowloon experienced significant modernization, while most of the New Territories retained the agricultural and socially traditional character of rural China.[13] The British colonial administration was staffed with competent people who had a limited mission of maintaining public health and safety and looking after British residents. There was no thought of an ambitious civilizing mission or even of much intervention in the economy. Most British residents, whatever their occupation, viewed the colony's Chinese residents, a majority of the population, with intense racial prejudice. Consequently, the only way in which Chinese business and community leaders participated in government was through community functions such as sanitation. As such, they became a significant link between state and society.[14] Yet the colonial government never gave much thought to building on that connection by allowing some degree of popular representation. Ethnocentric prejudice concerning the Chinese was too strong. The Western members of the community were too few to aspire to democratic government: granting democratic privileges solely to them would make the denial of the same privileges to the Chinese all the more obvious.[15]

With the weakening of the Chinese imperial system in the nineteenth century, Hong Kong also became a haven for revolutionaries on the run, and some of its Chinese inhabitants provided financial support to those same revolutionaries. Both before and after the end of the imperial system in 1911, turmoil in China spread occasionally and temporarily to Hong Kong, but by and large it was an island of stability, not least because judicial and law enforcement institutions were much superior to those in China. In late 1941 Japan extended its military occupation of East China to Hong Kong in a violent takeover, and the four-year occupation that followed brought hardship to all and brutal treatment to some. The fact that Britain had been defeated by an Asian power was not lost on long-time Hong Kong residents, and the Japanese actively sought to humiliate Britain in the eyes of the local Chinese.[16]

FROM 1945 TO 1979

With the end of the war and the British recovery of their colony, there was some belief in Hong Kong that a new era was about to begin. That optimism waned quickly as the colony witnessed the advent of civil war in mainland China between Chiang Kai-shek's Nationalists and Mao Zedong's Communists. By late 1949 the Chinese Communists controlled the mainland, and the units of the People's Liberation Army marched right up to Hong Kong's border and then stopped. Not stopping, however, were millions of refugees who streamed into Hong Kong both before and after the Communist victory. From then on, the Hong Kong administration focused on ensuring economic survival and social stability.

In this "borrowed time" environment, in which no one knew when PRC restraint might end, Hong Kong began to transform into the society we know today, driven by three converging forces. First, the refugees from southern China who were able to sneak into the colony swelled the population to around 3 million people by 1960, four times the population at the end of the war. Their welfare needs were manifold, but they constituted a pool of low-wage labor for anyone who could provide jobs. Second, in 1949–50 the newly declared People's Republic of China closed its border with Hong Kong, and Western countries led by the United States imposed an economic embargo on both exports to and imports from the PRC. That meant that Hong Kong could no longer serve as an entrepôt for China's trade, as it had for a century. Third, multinational companies searching for platforms on which they could outsource production of goods that would meet their quality control standards discovered Hong Kong.

Hong Kong therefore saw its opportunity for growth, and the colonial government, whose intervention in the economy and society had hitherto been minimal, concluded that it would have to expand its role to ensure that the opportunity was seized and the basic human needs of the refugee population were met. For its part, the business community urged the government to follow the industrial-policy course set by Japan, Korea, and Taiwan, and resisted proposals to provide social services because it feared it would have to pay higher taxes to fund new programs.[17] The government took neither suggestion. It provided public health and education (free primary education became available for all by 1970). It moved refugees from unsafe and unhealthy shanty towns into basic, low-rent public housing. It worked out arrangements with Beijing to ensure supplies of water and food for the colony.[18] The government built transportation infrastructure, both to get workers to their jobs and the goods they produced onto the ships headed for global markets. The Hong Kong Police fostered a relatively safe social environment and the courts protected property rights. This social management was accomplished by a competent civil service through which talented Chinese officials rose to higher and higher positions of responsibility.

Postwar colonial policy was quite successful. Economic growth was rapid, and Hong Kong became a generally stable middle-class society with only occasional major disruptions. Real GDP per capita increased by 46.4 percent from 1961 to 1966, 23 percent from 1966 to 1971, 13.3 percent from 1971 to 1976, and 11.9 percent from 1976 to 1981.[19] Ethnic Chinese firms grew up alongside the British ones and were happy to be co-opted by the colonial administration. With the border with China closed, the colony's Chinese population became far less transient than it had been before the war. Hong Kong became truly their home. The refugees and their children came to acquire a separate Hong Kong identity that complemented their sense of being Chinese. But there was a downside to the government's assumption of responsibility for delivering social services: Chinese community leaders who had provided social services in the past lost their previously significant position as the link between the government and the people.[20]

As for the "New China" whose policies had driven them from their native places, Hong Kong's refugee population was happy to have nothing to do with it. At the same time, China's leaders were willing to tolerate Hong Kong's separation from the mainland from 1949 to the late 1970s. The differences between Maoist China and capitalist, colonial Hong Kong were too great to bridge, and the success of the latter probably posed something of an ideological challenge to Beijing. Furthermore, Hong Kong was useful to the Communists. It was a conduit for remittances from people outside of China to their relatives in the People's Republic, and a place for intermittent contact with representatives of the Republic of China on Taiwan. The Chinese Communist Party sustained an underground presence in the colony that had begun in the 1920s.[21] The only disruption of this limited coexistence occurred in 1967 during Mao's "Great Proletarian Cultural Revolution," which energized leftist activists in Hong Kong to mobilize protests and engage in terrorist acts.[22]

The Hong Kong government took a firm stand, and Beijing soon brought its minions under control.

Mao Zedong died in 1976, and his radical supporters were purged; at this point Hong Kong became more valuable to the PRC. Deng Xiaoping's new policy of economic reform and opening up, first announced in late 1978, was a tremendous boon for Hong Kong. Deng recognized that if the Chinese Communist Party (CCP) was to regain some of the legitimacy it had lost after three decades of Maoist policies, it would need to stimulate economic growth and improve the livelihood of the Chinese people. But growth could only happen with the capital, technology, and management skills that external governments and companies could provide. From the beginning of reform, Deng regarded Hong Kong companies as a critical resource, and the fact that many of those companies were owned and managed by ethnic Chinese was an important advantage. For their part, Hong Kong industrialists were eager to move production and assembly into southern China and convert their Hong Kong operations into service centers, thus enhancing their firms' place in global supply chains. This complementarity not only helped power China's rapid economic growth and poverty reduction, but also buoyed Hong Kong's prosperity at a time when the costs of local labor were rising.[23] After declining to modest rates of increase in the 1970s, real GDP per capita soared by 26.0 percent between 1981 and 1986, and 32.7 percent from 1986 to 1991.[24]

BRITAIN DEFERS DEMOCRACY

Hong Kong was one of Great Britain's most unusual colonies. John Darwin, a specialist on British colonial history, trenchantly sums up the situation: "Hong Kong's political history makes nonsense of the decolonizing process as it is usually imagined.... It underwent no significant constitutional change. It [would] never travel the colonial *cursus honorum* from crown colony rule to representative and then responsible government."[25] Beijing and some in Hong Kong have long complained of a double standard here. Since the British were unwilling to bestow popular rule on Hong Kong during the century and a half it possessed the territory, Chinese often ask, why should China be required to do so now?[26] Animating the question is not only a not-so-latent nationalism and a resentment that the West is now asking Beijing to practice what London has only recently begun to preach. There is also fear that Britain and the United States will use democratic processes as a political tool to exercise remote control over the territory.

After World War II there was a fleeting but genuine possibility of opening the *cursus honorum* to Hong Kong.[27] Britain's prestige as the colonial ruler had declined with Japan's rapid seizure of the colony in late 1941. Once London resumed control after the war, articulate members of the Chinese population formed a coalition for a "1946 outlook." They called for a variety of reforms, particularly a constitutional system with political participation. At least some British officials were responsive. The most prominent of these was Mark Young, the prewar governor who had suffered through four years of Japanese internment in Hong Kong but resumed his position in 1946. He proposed that London apply a "traditional Colonial Office policy . . . of introducing representative government" to Hong Kong.[28] He sought to foster a city-state with its own identity and a stronger political attachment to Britain and recommended creation of an elected municipal council. But Young remained in office for only a year. His successor, Alexander Grantham, did favor modest reform. Specifically, he proposed to change the membership of the Legislative Council, which up until then had been composed of officials and individuals appointed from the British community. Grantham's idea was that some of these "unofficial members" would be elected rather than appointed, but that did not happen because the incumbent unofficial members evinced little interest. More generally, Grantham resisted the general impulse of the Labor governments in London to institute self-government in Britain's remaining colonies and used delaying tactics to block significant change.[29]

Three factors in particular delayed any broader reform. The first was social instability that the flood of refugees had brought to the Hong Kong community. They came both during the Chinese civil war and as the CCP imposed harsh policies after victory in 1949, such as land reform, political campaigns, collectivization, and the Great Leap Forward. The rapid increase in population imposed significant demands on the colonial government, which responded in stages to the unprecedented situation. Although it worked actively to promote economic development and provide jobs for the burgeoning population, it did not always keep up with the public's demand for social services. Disgruntled residents found ways periodically to register dissatisfaction, even in the absence of a democratic system, through demonstrations, riots, and so on. Eventually the government got the message and provided more generous benefits in housing and education, and redesigned the government to make it less bureaucratic and remote, and more responsive to the people.[30] Yet there were few "demand signals" for democracy from most of the colony's new Chinese

residents. Their sole priority was survival, not self-government, and they es-
chewed politics, since politics was what had led most of them to seek a safe
haven in Hong Kong in the first place.[31]

Second, Britain feared Communist movements in its remaining Asian
colonies. Labor movements in Malaya and Singapore destabilized towns and
cities, and a rural insurgency in Malaya tested the capacity of colonial governments to keep order (they prevailed in the end).[32] With the Communist victory on the Chinese mainland, the Colonial Office in London feared that
Hong Kong would be targeted next and that Hong Kong's security forces
were not prepared for the challenge.[33] So on security and other issues, it applied the policy model developed in Britain's other Asian colonies to Hong
Kong.[34] The local garrison was strengthened to back up the police.[35] Through
the Societies Ordinance, the government prohibited foreign political parties
(both the Chinese Communist Party and Chiang Kai-shek's Kuomintang
[KMT], or Nationalist, Party) from having branches in Hong Kong. Clashes
between CCP and KMT partisans in the colony actually broke out into riots in
1956, and those two groups would likely have had an advantage if elections had
been permitted.[36] The government also had authority to ban political strikes,
restrict the media, deport unwanted aliens, and close Communist educational
institutions.[37] Despite these prohibitions, the CCP continued to have an underground presence in the colony and sought to manipulate social tensions to
place the British government on the defensive.[38] Alexander Grantham's policies in Hong Kong may not have been as draconian as those adopted in Malaya and Singapore, but they were still robust, and from time to time the drag-
net also picked up moderate, middle-class people and groups who advocated
for democratic political reform. Thus, Hong Kong's British rulers used both
the refugee crisis and the perceived danger of Communist movements to preserve Hong Kong as the exception to the rule in British policy of fostering a
transition to a representative government. Efforts to control dissent continued
late into the 1970s.[39]

There was a third way in which Hong Kong was distinctive. It was one of
only a few colonies that had been acquired from a state that still existed after
World War II, in this case, China.[40] This colored the views of British officials
with Foreign Office backgrounds, such as Governor Grantham, who believed
that "Hong Kong from beginning to end should always have been viewed as
part of China, and thus relations with China were always paramount, not issues of the legislative or municipal councils."[41] Over the years, Beijing sent

several signals that it considered Hong Kong to have special importance to China:

- In October 1955, when Grantham met with PRC premier Zhou Enlai during a private visit to Beijing, Zhou told Grantham that the British presence in Hong Kong would be tolerated, provided that the colony was not used as an anti-Communist base, that the government allowed no activity that undermined the PRC, and that it protected the Chinese government's representatives and organizations there.[42]
- In 1958, Zhou conveyed a "personal" message to Prime Minister Harold Macmillan claiming a plot was being hatched with American support to "make Hong Kong a self-governing dominion like Singapore," a move that Beijing would see as "a very unfriendly act."[43]
- In 1971, Zhou told a retired Colonial Office official that China would recover the entire territory of Hong Kong when the New Territories lease expired in 1997.[44]
- The same year, China requested that the United Nations remove Hong Kong and Portuguese Macau from its list of non-self-governing territories, thus ruling out their political independence (Britain raised no objection regarding Hong Kong).[45]

London's decision not to treat Hong Kong as it had other crown colonies does raise a counterfactual question: If Britain had granted that option, would Hong Kong residents have chosen political independence? Would they have sought to create a city-state in the British Commonwealth, à la Singapore? Or would they have opted for something similar to the Cypriot Greeks' unification (called *enosis*) with mainland Greece, but with Chinese characteristics?[46] The question is impossible to answer, of course, but a voluntary vote to rejoin China seems unlikely, since most of the older residents were refugees from communism, and their children were gradually taking on a Hong Kong identity. On the other hand, Hong Kong people were not foolish. An independent Hong Kong that lacked either the capacity for self-defense against the People's Liberation Army or an ally willing to defend it could only survive on PRC sufferance, and Beijing had already made clear that it opposed decolonization of the territory. Hong Kong qua part of China trumped Hong Kong qua colony deserving democratization and independence.

As a result of Britain's failure to set Hong Kong on the independence track, in 1980 a process of engagement began between Great Britain and the

People's Republic of China, which claimed the territory and insisted on re-suming sovereignty. The trigger for this process was the practical matter of land leases: some of the leases that the Hong Kong government issued to pri-vate entities had a fifteen-year term, which meant that any lease negotiated after 1982 might be under a legal cloud after 1997. After tortured negotiations, in which London was usually on the defensive and Beijing the *demandeur,* in October 1984 the two countries signed a Joint Declaration that announced Britain's intention to transfer sovereignty over Hong Kong to China and laid out the parameters of Beijing's "one country, two systems" model for the terri-tory after reversion. Beijing, as the prospective sovereign, then initiated the drafting of a Basic Law for Hong Kong, which translated the general princi-ples of the Joint Declaration into greater detail and was enacted by China's National People's Congress in April 1990. Both before and after that event, the British and Hong Kong governments sought to prepare Hong Kong po-litically for its new life as part of China, but did not always do so in ways that the new sovereign approved of nor fast enough for residents who desired a more open political system. Some in the British and Hong Kong governments tried, and usually failed, to expand the scope of democracy, both in the nego-tiations of the Joint Declaration and in post-1984 governance of the territory. A growing cohort of pro-democracy professionals (lawyers, educators, social workers, and so on) tried, and usually failed, to use the negotiations over the Basic Law to ensure political freedoms and broaden the role of elections. Local Chinese businesses decided that the best way to protect their interests was to align themselves with the Chinese government, not the British authorities or professional and social groups seeking democracy.[47] This split in the broader colonial Chinese elite between business executives and professionals would dominate the political debate and persist into the post-reversion era. (See chapter 2 for a detailed discussion of the decisions that were made regarding Hong Kong's political system and the struggle to augment or minimize the degree of democratic government.)

Those negotiating on behalf of Hong Kong, particularly for a more open and competitive system, worked under two severe constraints. The first was the calendar. Every year that passed was a year closer to the expiration of the New Territories lease. Many Hong Kong residents, too, were aware that the clock was ticking, partly because of the lease issue and also because it became clear that China sought the return of both the leased New Territories and the parts of the colony that Britain thought it owned in perpetuity. The pressures for post-1997 certainty began to build at just the point when Hong Kong companies began to seize opportunities of doing business in China. The second constraint was the CCP's crackdown on demonstrations in Beijing and other cities in June 1989. The crackdowns heightened the fears of Hong Kong residents that Beijing might employ similar violent tactics against them. But it also raised fears in the Chinese regime, which inferred from the sympathy felt by many in Hong Kong for the plight of the demonstrators and the assistance that some protest leaders received from the territory, that Hong Kong's political system might be used as a platform to subvert the Communist regime.

AFTER REVERSION

Reversion occurred on July 1, 1997. The Hong Kong SAR government's first fifteen years after this date were star-crossed. The Asian financial crisis began the day after reversion, on July 2, 1997, and created serious economic stress in Hong Kong. Stock prices plunged by as much as 60 percent, some property lost more than half its value, per capita GDP declined by 7.8 percent in 1998, and the number of unemployed workers more than quadrupled from 1997 to 2002. The administration of Tung Chee-hwa, Hong Kong's first chief executive, struggled to respond as it faced hard choices. It had to abandon its original, worthwhile goal of expanding the number of housing units to benefit the lower and middle classes when that program only depressed housing prices even more. The Hong Kong government imposed an austerity regime at a time when it had planned to prime the pump, and probably should have.[48]

Then, in early 2003, Hong Kong faced the sudden acute respiratory syndrome epidemic. The authorities responded slowly because they did not wish to cause China embarrassment by publicly admitting that the disease had originated in China. Neither did they privately seek Beijing's assistance in coping with the outbreak. The crisis caused a damaging credibility blow to the Hong Kong government. Public opinion polls indicated that residents' satisfaction with their life in Hong Kong, which had peaked at 90 percent in early 1997, dropped to as low as 51 percent in late 2003. Similarly, the percentage expressing satisfaction with the performance of the Hong Kong government plunged from 73 percent in February 1997 to 16 percent in December 2003.[49]

China soon came to the rescue with a package of measures that stimulated the Hong Kong economy, which helped the territory reach an average annual growth in GDP of 7 percent from 2004 to 2007.[50] But Beijing also pressed for the adoption of anti-subversion legislation. That demand alarmed the Hong Kong public, half a million of whom turned out on the sixth anniversary of reversion to protest this perceived threat to their freedoms.[51] The administration withdrew the legislation, and the unpopular Tung was encouraged to resign before his term ended. His successors, Donald Tsang and now Leung Chun-ying (C. Y. Leung), have had to face new demands from the Pan-Democrats movement that the government move toward electoral democracy. By and large these demands were rejected, and the political system in 2013 was essentially the same as it had been in 1997, with one major exception: political activists had learned how to mobilize protests on all manner of issues to compensate for their lack of access to government institutions.

Hong Kong as a Hybrid

Hong Kong's reversion to China in 1997 only reinforced its uniquely hybrid character. Of all the places in China that had a prolonged foreign presence before the Communist takeover in 1949, Hong Kong is the most interesting. Macau, the first European outpost, was a full-fledged Portuguese colony, but it dozed through most of its history, particularly the postwar decades, when Hong Kong experienced its most explosive growth. The treaty ports that were established during the Qing dynasty, such as Shanghai, Tianjin, and Hankou, had a colonial flavor similar to Hong Kong's, but they remained Chinese territory and were governed by members of local expatriate communities, not by agents of Western governments. Hong Kong, in contrast, was a British crown colony that ultimately became a vibrant, middle-class society that is a unique mix of China and the West.

Socially, Hong Kong is a very Chinese city: attachment to family is strong and materialism reigns. The style, accents, older buildings, and some folkways reflect the Cantonese origin of most of the population. Yet Hong Kong also has strong vestiges of the British colony that it was until July 1, 1997. Street signs evoke memories of nineteenth-century governors, judges still wear wigs, English with British orthography is common in many public settings, and vehicles drive on the left side of the road. Hong Kong was the first Chinese society where people queued up for buses, trams, bank tellers, government clerks, and so on in the English fashion; Taipei in the mid-1970s was not so orderly. And on February 14 each year, many young men can be seen on streets and subways carrying bouquets of roses for their sweethearts, actual or potential.

Economically, too, Hong Kong is a hybrid: it has performed different functions in the international economy and vis-à-vis China at different times. Cut off from the Chinese economy after the victory of the Communist forces in 1949, it survived and thrived as a platform for production or assembly of manufactured goods for multinational corporations and became known as one of the four East Asian export "tigers," along with Korea, Taiwan, and Singapore. But once China opened up to foreign investment in 1979, Hong Kong companies moved their production into South China. Still, many of these firms maintained their place in global supply chains, with Western markets as the final destination for exports. The economy as a whole made the transition into the service sector: financial services, global logistics, and so on. Yet doubts remain about Hong Kong's status as a "global city"—that is, a city with a significant role in the international economy.

Constitutionally, Hong Kong is also a hybrid. Although it has the feel of places such as Singapore and Taipei, or even parts of Vancouver and San Francisco, it is still the Hong Kong Special Administrative Region of the PRC. China's national flag, crimson with five yellow stars, flies over all official Hong Kong buildings. Most Hong Kong residents carry a PRC passport. The Central People's Government in Beijing, as the Hong Kong government now refers to the authorities in Beijing, appoints the territory's senior political leaders and has a Liaison Office in the Hong Kong SAR to monitor leaders' performance and measure broader social, economic, and political trends. China's People's Liberation Army has a garrison in the Hong Kong SAR as well. Three local newspapers—*Ta Kung Pao, Wen Wei Po,* and an edition of the English-language *China Daily*—take their editorial direction from the Propaganda Department of the Chinese Communist Party. In some ways, therefore, Hong Kong is a Chinese city, not just ethnically but also administratively. Nevertheless, although the PRC presence may not actually be the "high degree of autonomy" that Hong Kong's residents originally expected, here the CCP does not exercise the sort of dominance that it does in Shanghai, Chongqing, Xi'an, and Guangzhou.

Socially, Hong Kong is a hybrid, and its residents understand clearly that their society is very different from that of the Chinese mainland. The great majority of the members of both societies are ethnic Chinese, but the social norms that each group follows can be very different. The contrast starts with different life experiences. According to recent censuses, about 60 percent of the Hong Kong population were born in Hong Kong, and 32 to 33 percent were born on the mainland, Taiwan, or Macau.[52] A significant share of the mainland-born refugees from the 1950s and 1960s have lived in Hong Kong for several decades. Although this group experienced some of the convulsions of the Mao period, they shared in the social and economic modernization that began in Hong Kong in the 1950s. On the mainland, economic reforms did not start until the 1980s, and then evolved incrementally.

China's opening up created a complementary interdependence that both fueled China's rapid economic growth and boosted prosperity for Hong Kong's maturing middle-class society. Since 2003, however, the dependence has gone the other way, with the central government in Beijing taking a number of policy steps to sustain local Hong Kong growth. Some of those steps brought mainland people and Hong Kong people into direct contact, daily reminders that the mainland may no longer be Maoist but it is still very different socially. The movement of mainland Chinese into Hong Kong for shopping, schooling, jobs, housing, and social services has created competition that did not exist before. Pregnant mainland women (43,000 in 2011) coming to Hong Kong to deliver their babies and so secure local residence permits for their children have been a point of controversy.[53] Mainland tourists began coming to Hong Kong in 2003 and the more wealthy among them boosted profits for the hospitality and high-end retail sectors, even as local people look down on them as nouveaux riches. But it was the less well-off mainland visitors who really rankled local residents, either because their behavior in public places did not meet Hong Kong standards or because they bought up daily supplies and necessities for their own use or to resell them back home for a profit. Generally, the visitors made a congested city even more crowded.

Finally, Hong Kong is a political hybrid (discussed in detail in chapters 3 and 4). Suffice it to say at this point that Hong Kong has the rule of law and civil and political rights common in most democracies, but it is only partially an electoral democracy. The procedures for selecting both the chief executive and the Legislative Council provide special clout to some sectors, particularly the business community, so the results do not necessarily reflect popular sentiment. Moreover, Beijing has ways to influence local politics behind the scenes and below the surface.

In sum, the Hong Kong that took shape during the decades after World War II is both Chinese and cosmopolitan; an economic success story that must always assume failure is looming on the competitive horizon; a society that is different from the one across the border to the north and views itself differently; and a constitutional and political idiosyncrasy that possesses liberal norms and the rule of law but denies citizens the power to pick their senior leaders in free and fair elections. If Hong Kong was born as the trajectories of Western and Chinese power crossed in the first half of the nineteenth century—the former ascending and the latter descending—it must now endeavor to survive in the early twenty-first century when Chinese power is growing and Western power is in relative decline. If historically Hong Kong rode the wave of the West's ascent, it must now navigate the sometimes smooth and sometimes treacherous tide of China's revival.

Plan of the Book

Looking forward, Hong Kong's hybrid character is up for grabs. The Basic Law dictates that its status as a special administrative region under one country, two systems—Hong Kong being the "second system"—will last for fifty years after the reversion of sovereignty in 1997. If the provision is followed, Hong Kong's "second system" will disappear and it will become part of Beijing's administrative structure, perhaps as a special municipality like Shanghai. Of course, the option exists to extend that time period if there is reason to do so. But some in Hong Kong have already begun to worry about the Basic Law's looming deadline. Just as holders of land leases in the early 1980s wondered about the status of their leases, today companies considering long-term investments are starting to ask whether Hong Kong's common law system or the PRC's Party-controlled one will govern their contracts beyond 2047.

As China and Hong Kong approach the twentieth anniversary of reversion, in 2017, when there will be thirty years left until 2047, there are likely to be pressures to end or alter the Hong Kong SAR's hybrid character, at least concerning economic and political affairs. Hong Kong's ability to remain a global business city will only be more challenged as China's economy grows more robust. What must Hong Kong do to preserve global competitiveness and avoid marginalization? Politically, will China be content to sustain a system that is ordered, liberal, and led by individuals who defer to its wishes? Or will protests such as the Umbrella Movement lead it to either accommodate a liberal democracy or change the system so it is neither democratic nor liberal? And, in the grand scheme of things, does Hong Kong really matter?

To bring these issues into sharper relief, I adopt three different perspectives. First, I tell the story of the contest over how to select Hong Kong's future senior leaders, a story that ends, rather tragically, with no electoral reform and a reversion to existing undemocratic mechanisms. In the process, I explore the likely and mutually reinforcing reasons for the eruption of the Umbrella Movement in fall 2014. The first of those reasons is the cumulative impact of a struggle between the city's democratic camp and its establishment camp (generally allied with Beijing) over just how much democracy to create (chapter 2). The second reason is unintended consequences of Hong Kong's political hybrid system, which advocates political freedoms and rule of law but lacks competitive elections for higher offices (chapter 3). A third reason is the overlapping concentration of economic and political power in the Hong Kong elite, which has led to growing social and economic inequality (chapter 4). The fourth reason is the way the process of interaction among democrats, members of the elite, the Hong Kong SAR government, and Beijing—a process sadly marked by mistrust and missed opportunities—generated an ultimate outcome that was acceptable to none (chapters 5 and 6).

The second perspective is to step back and address a series of "so what" questions, questions about the significance of the debate over electoral reform and the protest movement for other features of Hong Kong's system and for actors outside Hong Kong. The first question is: How would democratic procedures contribute to and ensure good governance? In Hong Kong, for example, would the selection of senior leaders by voters necessarily ensure that those leaders will adopt and implement policies that are in the best interests of the public? Small-d democrats either assume that full democracy will ipso facto ensure good government, or that it is at least a necessary condition for good policy. Democratic skeptics argue that there is no connection between how leaders are picked and how they perform, and in the current era they have plenty of examples to point to—including the United States. In chapter 7 I probe the relationship between democracy and governance. In chapter 8 I examine the area of government performance that has always been highly relevant to Hong Kong residents: the competitiveness of the economy.

These two perspectives are related and interact with each other. Economic performance, current and future, has significant domestic political sources and consequences. Prolonged political instability can retard growth and reduce competitiveness with other economies. On the other hand, Hong Kong's particular growth path over the last decade has widened income inequality to the point that income distribution is more skewed than in most other developed economies and so has created grievances against the government among those who feel left behind. The public perception that the political system benefits the business elite raises questions about whether "executive-led government" can actually serve the interests of the entire public. In the minds of many in Hong Kong, full and genuine democracy became a means to restore a just balance of power and wider prosperity.[54] Chapters 9 and 10 inventory suggestions on what, as a practical matter, the Hong Kong and Chinese governments might each do to ensure better governance and competitiveness.

How well Hong Kong does in preserving prosperity and promoting good governance can produce a variety of outcomes. Success on both dimensions spells a future of prosperity, political stability, and government legitimacy. To preserve competitiveness and its attendant prosperity but defer full democracy is a suboptimal result because political instability is likely to persist. If, in contrast, Hong Kong falls behind economically but institutes democracy, that, too, is suboptimal. The economic pie will shrink; even though a democratic government might be able to divide up that pie more fairly and so be seen as more legitimate than the current government, that outcome is far from guaranteed. A failure in both competitiveness and governance spells greater class conflict, political instability, and weak governance. The blame for such a disaster is likely to fall on China.

The third perspective is to pose "so what" questions relevant to issues outside of the Hong Kong SAR. Hong Kong is a very small place: 7.25 million people in an area of 426 square miles. The economic and political development of China and how Beijing chooses to use its growing power externally is objectively far more consequential for East Asia and the world than whether political reform succeeds or fails in Hong Kong. Despite its diminutive size, however, Hong Kong's fate is far from trivial. In the first place, it is one of several peripheral territories that the People's Republic incorporates within its sovereign territory, or would like to incorporate.[55]

These peripheral territories come in two types, special autonomous regions and special administrative regions, and the latter have a lot more autonomy than the former. There are five special autonomous regions in China's west: Guangxi, Inner Mongolia, Ningxia, Tibet, and Xinjiang, and a relatively large share of their populations are ethnic minorities. Politically, they are subject to tight government control and hence are autonomous in name only. Tibet and Xinjiang are the most prominent examples of this: Each has experienced tight coercive control from the central government and a significant influx of ethnic Han Chinese. Yet ethnic Tibetans in Tibet and the Uighur Muslims in Xinjiang have not all submitted quietly to CCP controls and to demographic disruption, and the two territories have suffered chronic instability in the last decade. Less well known but not insignificant are the special autonomous regions Guangxi (Zhuangs), Ningxia (Muslims), and Inner Mongolia (Mongols), none of which has been totally quiescent.

The former colonies of Hong Kong and Macau were incorporated as sovereign parts of the PRC in 1997 and 1999, respectively, as special administrative regions under the one country, two systems approach. They have much greater latitude to conduct their own affairs than special autonomous regions. Constitutionally, Beijing retains jurisdiction over their defense and foreign affairs, even as it works to control some local affairs through institutional measures and behind-the-scenes manipulation.

Finally, there is the case of Taiwan, to which Beijing would still like to apply the one country, two systems approach, even though it has never been able to convince Taiwan leaders or citizens of the virtue of that proposal.

For different reasons and in different ways, Beijing has been unable to fashion a satisfactory political design for each of these three types of peripheral territories. Social, geographic, and historical distance have all worked to frustrate its application of either direct or indirect rule. The difficulties that the PRC government has experienced in incorporating Hong Kong have a particular relevance for unincorporated Taiwan, since the use of one country, two systems in the former was supposed to provide a positive demonstration effect for the latter, and so speed the day that Taiwan would voluntarily give up its separate status and character. Chapter 11 details the failure of this demonstration effect, particularly during Hong Kong's struggle over electoral reform. Interestingly, Taiwan politicians and the media emphasized Hong Kong's significance for the island's future much more than the public at large, which believed that the two cases were fundamentally different.

The "so what" question is also relevant for U.S. policy (discussed in chapter 12). Superficially, Hong Kong would seem to be a symbolic asset for the United States. Indeed, it was regarded rhetorically as an outpost of anti-Communist freedom up until the beginning of the Washington and Beijing rapprochement in the early 1970s. As democracy promotion became a goal of American foreign policy in the 1980s, the city seemed to be an ideal candidate for Washington's focus. The reality was something different. From 1950 to the early 1970s, the U.S. economic embargo against China placed limits on Hong Kong's economic growth. The efforts in the U.S. Congress to impose economic sanctions on China in retaliation for its suppression of the protests in 1989 also had a direct impact on the Hong Kong economy. By the 1990s, promoting democracy in Hong Kong had to be balanced against more pressing issues within U.S.-China relations. Finally, there is the issue of effectiveness. During the events between 2013 and 2015, the Obama administration acted on the (probably correct) premise that too-public and too-intrusive U.S. support for the city's democratic camp would set back the goal of meaningful electoral reform rather than advance it. The U.S. position, therefore, was to keep its distance from a particular camp or political party, and instead take a general stance supporting universal suffrage according to the Basic Law.

The "so what" question is also relevant for the political development of China itself and its role in the world (covered in chapter 13). Might Hong Kong have a demonstration effect for the character, pace, and sequencing of political reform that might occur in China, which in turn is tied to the much broader global debate over governance for the twenty-first century? Of course, China's Leninist leaders may never give consideration to the idea that the CCP's own interests might be served by exposing their regime to institutional restraints and public accountability mechanisms. If they did, borrowing and adapting some of Hong Kong's institutions would be an obvious place to start. Its rule of law and independent judiciary create a check on the arbitrary exercise of state power. The city's institutions for deterring, detecting, and enforcing anti-corruption norms offer a corrective to one of the most debilitating features of the Chinese system. If adopted in China, genuine rule-of-law and corruption-control institutions could improve the country's governance without its having to simultaneously tackle the much tougher task of a democratic transition. When it comes to democracy, if Chinese leaders so chose, they could use Hong Kong as a test bed for experimenting with a more pluralistic and competitive political system in Chinese cities. In all these areas, the CCP must decide for itself that political reform is in its interests, but a well-governed and democratic Hong Kong would inform that choice. Finally, there is the biggest question of all: Does China's treatment of Hong Kong tell us anything about what kind of great power China will become?

TWO

Negotiating Hong Kong's Political System

H ong Kong began its unique transition from crown colony of the United
Kingdom to special administrative region of the People's Republic of
China (PRC) once Deng Xiaoping's reforms made China attractive to global
business interests. The British felt the need to reduce the legal uncertainty that
would accompany any fifteen-year land leases concluded after the early 1980s,
and so they put the issue of Hong Kong's future on Deng's agenda, probably
earlier than he wanted it there. A key question soon emerged: What degree of
popular government would be established to ensure a role for the public in the
administration of the new special administrative region?

How Much Democracy: Five Questions

Hong Kong's political transition occurred in three stages: Britain's negotiations with China on reversion (1979–84); China's drafting of the Hong Kong
Basic Law (1985–90); and the run-up to reversion (1991–97). Others have
told the chronological story, and often in gripping detail, so there is no need to
repeat it here.[1] Instead, I address five specific questions regarding Hong Kong's
political system in the transition period. The answers to these questions set
the context for what happened after reversion, for the Umbrella Movement,
and for the future.

1. Were the people of Hong Kong able to formally register their views on the negotiations that culminated in the Joint Declaration in 1984 of the United Kingdom and China?
2. To what extent did that agreement call for a democratic form of government after reversion?
3. How much popular rule did the 1991 Basic Law permit?
4. In what ways did Britain seek to expand the scope of democracy before reversion, and to what effect?
5. How did members of the democratic camp seek to expand that scope after 1997?

The implication of this retrospective analysis is that the desire and demand for democracy is not something that has surfaced just in recent years. The aspiration for more democratic governance in Hong Kong is at least three decades old, as are the disappointments that these objectives never became reality. This long-prevailing gap between hopes and the reality helped produce the Occupy Movement and was widened because of it.

WOULD HONG KONG HAVE A FORMAL SAY IN NEGOTIATIONS?
The Britain-China negotiations over Hong Kong were protracted and contentious. The basic story line is one of incremental British accommodation to Beijing's refusal to give in to Britain's demands:

- That the United Kingdom would retain sovereignty over the parts of Hong Kong that had been ceded in perpetuity (no)
- That Britain would continue its administration over the territory after the return of sovereignty (no)
- That China would accept the preservation of institutions and policies such as rule of law and civil and political rights (on balance, yes)
- That China would accept a measure of representative government in the territory, which could serve as a check against poor government performance or the arbitrary exercise of state power (on balance, no)

In 1983 Britain decided to concede to China on the first (in March) and second (in October) demands. The third and fourth demands were answered during the negotiations over the text of the Joint Declaration, which were most intense in the summer of 1984. London's working assumption was that if it demanded too much, Beijing would carry out its repeated threat to unilaterally impose its own plan for Hong Kong's political system. Moreover,

Britain also had to balance its goals for Hong Kong against its other interests concerning China.

During the negotiations both Britain and China played a public and private game. Publicly, British officials inflated Hong Kong's expectations at various points. For example, Prime Minister Margaret Thatcher openly stated in Hong Kong that Britain had a "responsibility" and "moral duty" to the colony's people. Beijing publicly refuted Thatcher's statement of British responsibility for Hong Kong, stating: "It is only the government of the People's Republic of China which has the right to say that, as a sovereign state, it has responsibility for the Chinese residents of Hong Kong."[2] Additionally, London made implicit promises on the issues of sovereignty, administration, and democratization, but China effectively used propaganda and economic leverage to deflate Hong Kong's hopes. The British ultimately had to back down. Although the negotiations were supposed to remain confidential, China repeatedly revealed its bottom line in order to undermine Britain's position and Hong Kong's confidence in it. Beijing assumed that Hong Kong residents were strongly pro-China and anti-Britain, and appealed to those sentiments to advance its own goals. In the fall of 1983, as London held out for continuing British administration after relinquishing sovereignty, Beijing publicly signaled that the talks were going badly. That caused the Hong Kong equity and foreign exchange markets to plummet, and British decisionmakers saw no choice but to concede on the issue of post-reversion administration.

The situation was equally complex on the specific question of whether Hong Kong itself should have a role in these negotiations (question 1). Some on the British side, particularly Prime Minister Thatcher, believed that the views of Hong Kong residents should be heard. In a September 1982 meeting with Premier Zhao Ziyang in Beijing, Thatcher made clear that "if suitable arrangements for the administration and control of Hong Kong could be worked out, and if they commanded confidence and were acceptable to the people of Hong Kong and to the British Parliament, she would consider the question of sovereignty."[3] In March 1983, in internal discussions on how to end the impasse over whether China or Britain would have sovereignty over Hong Kong in the future, Thatcher suggested a UN-supervised referendum in Hong Kong to let the people choose which country they wanted to be ruled by, but her advisers talked her out of it. Instead, she was persuaded to change her conditionality formula: the British government would not just "consider" the merits of a Chinese proposal but "would be prepared to recommend [it] to Parliament." Beijing chose to interpret this shift as the answer to the question of sovereignty.[4]

If acceptability among Hong Kong residents was one standard by which London would judge an agreement with China, the question still remained of how to register those sentiments in the absence of democratic mechanisms. Officials in the colonial government quietly measured the pulse of elite sentiment, but the default solution was to rely on the views of the "unofficial" members of the Hong Kong Executive Council. This body was the governor's cabinet and its membership was a mix of officials and prominent individuals outside the government (hence, the "unofficials").[5] The six unofficial members were the elite of the elite, at the core of the Hong Kong business establishment, and were very wealthy. Although they took seriously their responsibilities to represent the interests of the whole colony, and at some stages urged London to maintain a tough negotiating position, they were ultimately handicapped by their elevated social position and their obligation to preserve secrecy over the negotiations as the price for being consulted. Also undermining their standing was that Beijing took the position that it would deal only with Britain because it was sovereign over Hong Kong and that it knew what was best for the territory. In a meeting with three Executive Council members in June 1984, Deng Xiaoping told them that Chinese policies "coincide with the interests of Hong Kong's five million people. We've heard many different opinions, but we don't recognize that they represent the interests of the people of Hong Kong."[6] In the end, the Executive Council members endorsed the Joint Declaration. By mid-October, the Legislative Council (LegCo), whose members at that time were appointed by the colonial governor, held two days of debate, and then "formally commended the agreement to the people of Hong Kong."[7]

The only British step toward actually measuring the people's will came in July 1984 with the announcement that the Hong Kong government would establish an office to assess public views. This would not be a formal referendum, a mechanism that China strongly opposed, and those who chose to express their views had only two choices: accept or reject the Britain-China deal. In the end, a majority of respondents supported the agreement, but, as the assessors noted, with "very qualified enthusiasm."[8]

In short, Hong Kong's public was merely a spectator at the British-Chinese deliberation over the new political order, and only to the limited extent that officials chose to reveal the content of the negotiations. By and large, Hong Kong residents rode a roller coaster of expectations, usually with Britain raising hopes and the Chinese deflating them. To the extent that Hong Kong interests were represented at all, it was by senior officials of the Hong Kong government, such as Governor Edward Youde, and the unofficial members of the Executive Council, who had a paternalistic sense of responsibility for the people. For example, it was the unofficial Executive Council members who urged British negotiators to hold out on the continued British administration issue in the latter part of 1983. But they were hardly representative of the public at large, and had little way of confirming that the public agreed with their views, because, as stated earlier, they were not permitted to reveal the content of the talks.

WOULD THE HONG KONG SAR POLITICAL SYSTEM BE DEMOCRATIC?

The character of Hong Kong's post-reversion political system—the second of the five questions—was not addressed until late in the negotiations. It was only in May 1983 that China allowed any post-1997 arrangements on the negotiation agenda.[9] British negotiators were not exactly in agreement on proposing democratic mechanisms, since their government had itself been slow to institute such measures. But they might have argued that democratic mechanisms were less necessary under Britain's benign colonial rule than they would be in light of the CCP's long record of harsh and arbitrary rule of the mainland. Additional causes for concern were Beijing's arrogant assumption that it knew what the Chinese people of Hong Kong wanted and its suspicion that Britain sought democracy in order to rule the territory from behind the scenes.[10]

Early on, all China did was enunciate the principles that Hong Kong's people would rule Hong Kong and that the new special administrative region would have a high degree of autonomy. When the negotiations began in earnest in the late spring of 1984, British negotiators initially focused on ensuring that the institutional pillars of the current Hong Kong system were preserved. Their position was based not on the virtues of representative government but rather on the claim that existing institutions were necessary to ensure continued prosperity and stability, a line of argument appropriate for China's definition of the "two systems" in economic terms. During the summer of 1984 the British first made a push for an elected governor and legislature, but ultimately it was to no avail, and the issue was deferred.[11]

The British were more successful, however, on the question of civil and political rights, and they skillfully convinced their Chinese counterparts that those rights were essential for the operation of a capitalist economy (again, China's second "system"). In order to ground Hong Kong's political system in international law, in late July Britain secured Beijing's concession that the International Covenant on Civil, Political Rights, and the International Covenant on Economic, Social, and Cultural Rights, which the United Nations adopted in 1966 and that came into force in 1976, would remain in force "according to law" and "as currently applied" in Hong Kong. (The latter phrase was an indirect reference to the reservation that Britain had made when acceding to the covenant of civil and political rights that the clauses on representative government and self-determination did not apply to Hong Kong.) Although China wanted a Hong Kong government that was "executive-led," it agreed that the territory's "independent judicial power" would also continue to hold the power of final adjudication.[12] The clauses in the International Covenant on Civil and Political Rights pertaining to due process of law were particularly important in this regard. The final issue, which was not decided until mid-September and required the intervention of Geoffrey Howe, the U.K. foreign secretary, was how to select the chief executive and members of the legislature. The Chinese proposed that both "consultations" and elections should be used. At Howe's urging, Beijing agreed that the legislature would be "constituted by elections" only, but the Chinese were unwilling to remove the word "consultations" when it came to the chief executive. Moreover, no one was sure what the Chinese meant by the word "elections."[13]

In sum, the Joint Declaration preserved civil and political rights, and held some promise for representative government. But it was far from certain whether and when that promise would be realized. After all, China's various people's congresses are "constituted by elections," but the process is hardly democratic or competitive. And nothing in the Joint Declaration prevented Beijing from working covertly to shape the political landscape to its advantage. The devil for Hong Kong would be in the details of the Basic Law, which became the territory's mini-constitution.

POPULAR RULE AND DRAFTING THE BASIC LAW
During the drafting process of the Basic Law the three governments in London, Beijing, and Hong Kong consistently went back and forth on how much popular rule the mini-constitution would provide. In drafting Hong Kong's mini-constitution, the Chinese government created the impression that the territory's people were participating while it simultaneously ensured that it actually controlled the process and outcome. It did this by establishing the Basic Law Drafting Committee (BLDC), 60 percent of whose members were from the PRC and 40 percent from Hong Kong. Moreover, Beijing packed the territory's delegation with individuals who it thought shared its views on the desired political system.[14] At the same time, Beijing facilitated the formation of

the Basic Law Consultative Committee in order to create the impression that it was drawing on local opinion in writing the Basic Law. The committee was composed of Hong Kong residents who were not BLDC members but who supported China's approach to Hong Kong. The only Hong Kong members of the BLDC who argued for preserving the rule of law and expanding popular rule were Martin Lee, a prominent barrister, and Szeto Wah, the head of the teachers union. The dynamic within the BLDC was an uneven contest between a majority coalition of members from the PRC and Hong Kong's economic establishment on the one hand, and a minority representation of pro-democracy advocates on the other.

When it came to representative government, the key argument was over the mechanisms that would be used to select the chief executive and the Legislative Council. The pro-democracy forces in Hong Kong, embodied by Szeto Wah and Martin Lee, aimed to achieve majority rule. But early on, in an April 1987 meeting with the BLDC, Deng Xiaoping made his preferences clear. He ruled out the British parliamentary system, the U.S. congressional system, or any other kind of separation-of-powers arrangement, noting that a legislature was useful only if it maintained "the right policies and direction." He insisted that those who ruled Hong Kong had to "love the motherland and love Hong Kong," and questioned whether "universal suffrage" could produce such people. Even if there were "general elections" someday, it would have to come after a period of transition. He was prepared to "allow people in Hong Kong to attack the Chinese Communist Party and China verbally, but what if they should turn their words into action, trying to convert Hong Kong into a base of opposition to the mainland under the pretext of 'democracy'? Then we would have no choice but to intervene."[15]

The pro-democracy members of the BLDC sought a leadership-selection mechanism that would reflect the views of the population as a whole via majority rule. Beijing pushed for arrangements that would ensure that a pro-democracy leader like Martin Lee could never even get nominated for chief executive, much less elected. And Beijing worked to guarantee that political parties it regarded as anti-China, such as Lee's Democratic Party, would never control the Legislative Council. In the end, Beijing insisted that an election committee, not the public, would elect the chief executive and that a controlling share of LegCo seats would be selected from "functional constituencies." The functional constituencies, and the LegCo members that they selected, would represent socioeconomic sectors that tended to be aligned with China: for example, banking, real estate, commerce, and so on. The election committee replicated this pro-Beijing sectoral approach, and the members of each sector picked could be counted upon to pick a chief executive with whom China was comfortable (for details, see chapter 4).

There was only one instance when the pro-democracy group had a serious chance to achieve its majority-rule objective. That was after the CCP regime's violent suppression of the popular Tiananmen Square uprising in Beijing in spring 1989. In Hong Kong there was deep sympathy for the demonstrators. Two weeks before the crackdown, 1 million people—the largest crowd in Hong Kong history—marched in support of the Tiananmen demonstrations. After the People's Liberation Army Hong Kong Garrison suppressed the rallies, some Hong Kong BLDC members quit the committee in protest. Hong Kong became the final station on an underground railway for Tiananmen leaders fleeing China, and pro-democracy groups formed the Hong Kong Alliance in Support of the Patriotic Democratic Movement of China. These actions only fostered more suspicions in Beijing of subversion in Hong Kong, and Martin Lee and Szeto Wah were later expelled from the BLDC for their association with the Alliance.

Looking forward, the use of violence shattered the illusions of Hong Kong residents that the CCP was a humane regime, and called into question the widespread assumption that Beijing would take a benign approach to Hong Kong after reversion. The crackdown led a growing number of people to emigrate to the West and strengthened arguments for democratic checks to deter such an arbitrary exercise of state power in Hong Kong and to encourage political restraint from executive and legislative leaders.[16] Even BLDC members who were from the Hong Kong establishment were rattled and joined the pro-democracy members in a coalition that proposed to expand the degree of post-reversion representative government. The Hong Kong members proposed what came to be called the "4-4-2 approach" to the composition of the Legislative Council after 1997: 40 percent of the membership chosen by universal suffrage, 40 percent by functional constituencies, and 20 percent by an electoral college. The Hong Kong coalition made its proposal in December 1989; although Britain initially encouraged Beijing to accept it, Beijing refused to even discuss the idea, which irritated even conservative Hong Kong members in the BLDC.[17] To make matters worse Beijing used its majority in the BLDC to push through a requirement in Article 23 for Hong Kong anti-subversion laws, which included a prohibition on foreign political organizations' engaging in activities in the territory or having links with local Hong Kong organizations.[18] London then reversed course, much to the consternation of both establishment and pro-democracy Hong Kong members of the BLDC. Percy Craddock, Thatcher's foreign policy adviser, opposed proposals that Beijing would likely reject on the grounds that Beijing would simply reverse them once it took over in 1997. Thatcher agreed with Craddock.[19]

The BLDC approved the final text of the Basic Law in February 1990 and the National People's Congress enacted it two months later. It prescribed that the election committee for the chief executive would have 800 members (later increased to 1,200), from four main groups: 200 members from industrial, commercial, and financial subsectors; 200 from the professional sectors; 200 from labor, social services, and other community groups; and 200 members from the Legislative Council, representatives of district organizations, and the Hong Kong members of the National People's Congress and representatives to the Chinese People's Political Consultative Conference (which provided token representation to a variety of social, cultural, and economic groups). Of the four groups, pro-establishment people were certain to dominate all but the labor and social services group, and even that was mixed. A LegCo-passed electoral ordinance required that a prospective chief executive candidate receive support from at least 100 members of the committee to be nominated and over 400 for victory.[20]

The Basic Law stated that the Legislative Council picked in 1998 would have twenty members selected through "direct elections" in geographic constituencies, thirty chosen from among functional constituencies, and ten chosen by an election committee (actually, the same committee that picked the chief executive). The total number of electors picking legislators from the functional constituencies would be less than 200,000. In the 2000 elections, the number of directly elected seats would increase by four, taken from the set picked by the election committee. And then by 2004, LegCo would have thirty directly elected members and thirty from functional constituencies.

Articles 45 and 68 of the Basic Law contained a promise that the antimajoritarian character of leadership selection would be a transitional phenomenon. The method for choosing both the chief executive and LegCo would be formulated "in light of the actual situation in the Hong Kong SAR and in accordance with the principle of gradual and orderly progress," and the "ultimate aim" was elections by universal suffrage for "all the members of LegCo" and the chief executive. The only condition was that candidates for chief executive would be chosen "upon nomination by a broadly representative nominating committee in accordance with democratic procedures."[21] Just how representative that nominating committee would be and whether its procedures would be truly democratic became the central issue in the Hong Kong debates on electoral reform between 2013 and 2015.

The Basic Law's provisions on the rule of law and protection of political rights (along with representative government the other two pillars of a democratic system) were better than those regarding representative government, but they were not perfect. Article 39 prescribed that the provisions of the International Covenants on Civil and Political Rights and on Economic, Social and Cultural Rights[22]—"as applied to Hong Kong" would remain in force and would be implemented through domestic legislation.[23] The main bone of contention concerning the judiciary was the right of final adjudication, that is, whether the Basic Law would be interpreted by Hong Kong courts only or in Beijing as well. The Joint Declaration had vested that power in Hong Kong, but PRC officials subsequently said that the Standing Committee of the National People's Congress (convened between plenary sessions of the National People's Congress) could be the final adjudicator. Over a period of months, Martin Lee fought to keep final adjudication in Hong Kong, in part to preserve the integrity of Hong Kong's common law system, which was to continue after reversion, and in part to prevent litigants from appealing the rulings of Hong Kong judges to the National People's Congress Standing Committee (NPC-SC). Mainland officials, however, felt they needed some power to correct "wrong decisions."[24] Lee was in a minority on the BLDC, and his arguments were merely a rearguard action. In the end, Article 19 of the Basic Law dictated that Hong Kong courts would have no jurisdiction over "acts of state such as defence and foreign affairs"; aside from those two areas, which were explicitly outside of Hong Kong's autonomy anyway, there was no definition provided for "acts of state."[25]

EXPANDING DEMOCRACY BEFORE REVERSION

Meanwhile, there were moves in Hong Kong toward advancing democracy after the conclusion of the Joint Declaration, and both before and after drafting the Basic Law. After 1979, British officials recognized that they would have to move quickly to leave some measure of popular rule in Hong Kong. Yet the steps they took to give the populace a say in picking the territory's leaders were modest and halting. The first step, in 1982, was to make the selection of local district boards elective rather than appointive. This change came as Hong Kong was becoming a more middle-class and urban society, even in the New Territories, and provided an outlet for citizens to express their concerns about social services and local programs. This meant that the individuals who had previously led the boards and often reflected more traditional local elites had to adapt to politicking among the populace or retire to the sidelines.[26] By October 1983, when London decided to give up not only sovereignty but also administration, the Hong Kong government considered new democratization steps. For instance, Philip Haddon-Cave, the colony's chief secretary and the governor's number two, began exploring ways to make government more representative through the Legislative and Executive Councils. There was also talk of erecting institutional "roadblocks" that could keep Beijing from interfering in Hong Kong's internal affairs too much. In April 1984, Geoffrey Howe, the U.K. foreign secretary, made a public commitment to foster democratic government before reversion.[27]

Haddon-Cave was the official most committed to turning that promise into reality. He had come out of the Colonial Service, which administered most of Britain's overseas possessions, and believed that "if the colonial system were not replaced, the [existing] system of 'benign patronage' . . . would be replaced by something very much less benign."[28] Yet even his proposal, first made public in July 1984, was incremental in scope: Beginning in 1985, Legislative Council members, hitherto all appointed and all from functional-constituency groups, would gradually become elected. The district boards and other representative bodies would also elect their own representatives to LegCo. And then in 1988, LegCo would pick four of its members to serve on the Executive Council.[29] This was still indirect democracy, not dissimilar in form to how the people's congresses in the PRC were constituted. Still, the Hong Kong government forged ahead, issuing a formal public proposal on political reform in November 1984 and holding the first elections the following year.[30]

Publicly, Beijing tolerated both the Hong Kong government's initiative and the 1985 elections. Privately, however, it believed it had been tricked and that Britain intended to use a democratic system to preserve its influence in the territory. Even as Thatcher and Deng signed the Joint Declaration, lower-level Chinese officials charged that the Hong Kong political reform plan violated the agreement. Beijing was aided in its opposition by members of the Hong Kong elite who feared the effects of greater popular rule on their ability to pursue their interests unfettered. Thus, in the Executive Council's discussions on the political reform plan, unofficial members got Haddon-Cave to withdraw the proposal to begin direct elections to LegCo in 1985 (they were delayed until 1988).[31] In the end, Beijing successfully pressured the Hong Kong government to pledge that it would make no "major constitutional change" before the Basic Law was enacted in 1990. Britain covered its tracks by stressing the need for "convergence" between Britain's pre-1997 political reforms and China's post-1997 political order. However, a dispute later ensued over whether the direct elections in 1988 constituted a "major constitutional change," and Lu Ping, the Chinese official in charge of Hong Kong affairs, issued a threat that in 1997, Beijing would overturn any British change that it did not like.[32] This was a threat that Percy Craddock, who controlled Hong Kong policy in London, respected and used to stave off initiatives that he regarded as too radical.[33]

As noted earlier, the Tiananmen protests altered the Hong Kong government's and public's views on whether the arrangements in the Basic Law would protect the territory against similar repression by Beijing. The crackdown stimulated emigration from Hong Kong at much higher levels than normal as people sought to find safe havens overseas. The Hong Kong governor, David Wilson, reportedly believed that "on a deeper level, people's view of China had changed, and therefore, their perception of their future under Chinese rule would be dramatically altered. The British government had to take steps before reversion to repair the damage." In late 1989, Wilson proposed three such steps: accelerating democratization, enacting a bill of rights, and granting some Hong Kong residents a means of escape.

While the coalition of democracy advocates and conservative members of the Basic Law Drafting Committee worked to craft and then promote the 4-4-2 plan on the post-reversion political structure (see previous section), members of the Executive and Legislative Councils in Hong Kong supported Wilson's idea of creating a new pre-reversion status quo. Wilson suggested expanding pre-1997 enfranchisement, and formulated a consensus proposal to elect twenty LegCo members by universal suffrage in 1991 and no less than half of the body in 1995. Beijing regarded both proposals as another British plot to preserve its influence. Creating an electoral status quo before reversion would magnify the pressure on Beijing to expand direct elections thereafter. Despite British and Hong Kong Chinese entreaties, PRC officials rejected both proposals. As previously noted, for the 1998 elections the Basic Law mandated that twice as many seats would be selected from functional constituencies and the election committee as the seats from the geographic constituencies, which were selected through universal suffrage. This became the point of departure for any discussion on pre-reversion formulae.[34]

As with drafting the Basic Law, the Hong Kong government had more success on the issue of political and civil rights than with the electoral system.

In July 1990 the Legislative Council passed the Hong Kong Human Rights Ordinance, which incorporated, in its section 8, the provisions of the International Covenant on Civil and Political Rights. This section outlined that political rights of expression, assembly, and association could only be restricted by law to protect "national security, public order, public health or morals." On the one hand, article 21 of section 8 said that Hong Kong residents had the right "to vote and to be elected at genuine periodic elections which shall be by universal and equal suffrage and shall be held by secret ballot." On the other, section 13 stated that: "Article 21 does not require the establishment of an elected Executive or Legislative Council in Hong Kong."[35] (In 2013–15, democracy advocates in Hong Kong would place their emphasis on the International Covenant and on article 21 of section 8 of the Hong Kong Human Rights Ordinance; Beijing and the Hong Kong government would rely on section 13 of the ordinance. The issue remains contested.)[36]

In the 1991 elections, the Pan-Democrats—democracy advocates in an array of parties and groupings—won 71 percent of the popular vote and 89 percent of the LegCo seats for the geographic constituencies. Then, Christopher Patten, who in the summer of 1992 became Hong Kong's next and last governor, energized the acceleration cause and inflated the expectations of Hong Kong people in the process. Patten was a product of neither the Colonial Office nor the Foreign Office but knew democracy first-hand as an elected politician. He had the strong support of John Major, Margaret Thatcher's successor as prime minister, who saw no policy reason to conciliate China but did see a political advantage in crossing it.

In October, Patten proposed to make the LegCo selection process in 1995 more representative of the population as a whole. He did this by exploiting loopholes in the Basic Law: He accepted the reality of thirty seats being elected from functional constituencies, but proposed to greatly expand the number of people who were eligible to vote in the election for the LegCo representative for their functional constituency. The original presumption was that the entities that made up the functional constituency would decide who had the right to vote: the companies themselves; all the members of the boards of directors; all individuals who were managers and above; or all full-time employees. Thus, the financial services functional constituency had decided that only the constituent companies would vote. Under Patten's plan, all full-time employees of banks, insurance companies, securities firms, and so on could cast a ballot. Ultimately, the member corporations of that sector would later decide that only the companies could vote. He also proposed to make all district board members elected and co-opt them as members of the electoral college.[37] When Chinese officials accused him of violating the Basic Law, he asked them to point to the provision he had violated, knowing full well they could not. When the same Chinese officials changed tack and said he had violated "the spirit of the Basic Law," he asked them to define that spirit. Their response was that they, and only they, would define the Basic Law's spirit and determine whether he had transgressed it.[38]

Beijing did more than remonstrate privately with Patten. Through official statements and commentaries in the Chinese and Hong Kong press, it mounted a series of rhetorical political attacks that mercilessly demonized Patten and played on anti-British nationalism (Premier Li Peng accused him of "perfidy and unilateralism").[39] It engaged in economic warfare as well, stating in November 1992 that China would deem any Hong Kong government contract, lease, or agreement invalid if it had not received Beijing's prior approval. That called major infrastructure projects into question and sent the Hong Kong stock exchange into a tailspin. Beijing also publicly declared its intention to establish and appoint its own provisional government to take over in July 1997.

When Patten and London declared a willingness to negotiate on his proposals, Beijing played hard to get, knowing that time was on its side. In the end, it carried out its threat to reverse any British or Hong Kong initiative it did not like. Patten did win a short-term victory: a version of his reforms for the 1995 LegCo elections was enacted, and the Pan-Democrats won 42.3 percent of the vote and 60 percent of the seats. But the LegCo members elected in 1995 served less than two years and were replaced by a substitute legislature created by Beijing. Patten may have won a battle over interpretation of the Basic Law, but Beijing won the war.[40] Its electoral arrangements became the rules of the game. The single-minded way China crafted and implemented the Basic Law permits only one conclusion: that it wished to control the selection of the territory's leaders and to ensure that only certain, *trusted* Hong Kong people would govern the Hong Kong SAR.

The Legislative Council was not the only elective body that Beijing diluted. Before reversion, the Hong Kong government changed membership selection for municipal councils and district boards from appointive to directly elective. The municipal councils had executive powers over public hygiene, leisure, and recreation services; the district boards advised the government on local matters. The most important function of both was to serve as a training ground for future elected representatives; parties would groom their activists by running them in local elections. In 1999, however, the new Hong Kong

SAR government secured legislation that abolished the municipal councils and added appointed members to the district boards—which it renamed district councils—to balance the elected members.[41]

By way of evaluation, and whatever one thinks about the value of democracy, the PRC regime's ability to get its way concerning Hong Kong's political system was quite impressive. No doubt, Beijing was misguided in its reasons for denying democracy: for example, its belief that it knew what Hong Kong's people wanted simply because they were Chinese. But its tough tactical moves in opposing British negotiators and Hong Kong democrats were usually successful.[42] China exploited the July 1, 1997, deadline and played on the divisions within the British–Hong Kong side: between the Foreign and Colonial Offices; between the London and Hong Kong governments; and between Hong Kong residents who liked the political status quo and those who feared Beijing would exploit loopholes in the Joint Declaration and the Basic Law to arbitrarily exercise its power. The British hurt themselves by regularly raising Hong Kong expectations and then having to back down. China offered its own rhetorical assurances but was prepared to put the territory's economy at risk in order to ensure its political objectives.

Still, Beijing made some concessions. It was unwilling to give Hong Kong voters free rein to select key officials, which would have given them an electoral power to hold incumbent leaders accountable for their performance. But it allowed other types of checks on the Hong Kong SAR government. The Joint Declaration and the Basic Law guaranteed that the pillars of a liberal order would remain in Hong Kong, notably, civil and political rights and the rule of law. This was a decision Beijing likely came to regret, because after reversion, the city's residents regularly took advantage of the political opportunities that the system provided. Implementation of this liberal order, however, has not been perfect; chapter 3 inventories the ways that critics believe rights and freedoms have been undermined. Hong Kong's post-1997 political system may not have been a fully competitive system, but it was, at the very least, still a liberal system.

POST-REVERSION DEMANDS TO EXPAND ELECTORAL DEMOCRACY

The final question to examine is how members of Hong Kong's democratic camp (the Pan-Democrats) sought to expand democracy after 1997. With its move in 2002 and 2003 to secure passage of anti-subversion legislation pursuant to article 23 of the Basic Law, Beijing revealed a growing unhappiness with the consequences of Hong Kong's liberal order. But this demand for more explicit limitations on the exercise of political freedoms was both heavy-handed and counterproductive. The proposal invigorated the members of the Pan-Democrats, who mounted mass protests of unprecedented size, created splits in the establishment camp that forced the withdrawal of the bill, and helped the democrats do exceptionally well in the fall 2003 district council elections. To make matters worse for the PRC, the Pan-Democrats sought to extend their victory by reopening the issue of the electoral system. They mounted a campaign to get Beijing to honor its promise of "ultimate" universal suffrage in time for the 2007 chief executive and 2008 LegCo elections. The Central People's Government countered with allegations that those who sought electoral changes were "unpatriotic" and it altered the rules on how such procedural changes would occur.[43]

In April 2004, the NPC-SC enunciated a five-step process whereby the Basic Law provisions on the selection of the chief executive and LegCo members would be changed:

- The Hong Kong SAR government submits a report to the NPC-SC on the need for change.
- The NPC-SC concurs that change is needed.
- The Hong Kong SAR government sends a proposal to the Legislative Council, which must pass it by a two-thirds majority.
- The chief executive signs the enacted proposal.
- The Hong Kong SAR government submits the proposal to the NPC-SC for final approval.[44]

Later that same month, the NPC-SC issued another ruling stating that although there could be changes in the procedures for the 2007 and 2008 elections, those changes could not institute universal suffrage for the chief executive election and the ratio of Legislative Council members selected from functional constituencies had to remain at 50 percent.[45]

Professor Ma Ngok, in the Department of Government and Public Administration at Chinese University of Hong Kong, has observed that NPC-SC's early April decision imposed procedures that were not even implied in the Basic Law and had the effect of depriving the Legislative Council of any authority to initiate a reform process, which did seem to be an option under the Basic Law. It reserved the right of the Beijing government to specify the range of political reform available to Hong Kong.[46] The Hong Kong SAR government did propose reforms for the 2008 LegCo elections that would have slightly altered the composition of legislative membership but without changing the balance of political power between directly elected and functional-constituency seats. The Pan-Democrats opposed the proposal, which left the government short of the two-thirds support needed for passage.

The scenario for the 2012 elections for chief executive and the Legislative Council began in a similar manner but had a different outcome. In response to a report from the Hong Kong SAR government, the NPC-SC had set the terms of discussion in 2007, almost five years before the elections. It had dictated that there would be no shift to universal suffrage for choosing the chief executive in 2012 and the share of functional-constituency Legislative Council seats would stay at 50 percent. This time, however, the National People's Congress SC did say that the chief executive "may" be chosen by universal suffrage in 2017 and that LegCo members "may" be selected on the same basis after it has been used for the chief executive (meaning that the first possible LegCo election by universal suffrage could be in 2020). In late 2009, the Hong Kong SAR government proposed that the LegCo selected in 2012 have ten new seats, five to be elected from geographic constituencies and five in a new functional constituency, called District Council (Second) because district council members already had one functional constituency that selected one LegCo member. In this new constituency, district council members, some of whom were popularly elected, would pick individuals to fill five seats.

What made this round different, however, was a growing split within the democratic camp, between the moderate legislators of the Democratic Party and more radical groups like the League of Social Democrats and the Civic Party. The radicals rejected the government's proposal outright, and, supported by civil society activists who were not affiliated with a political party but promoted an array of causes in street protests, advocated a public, symbolic action that would demonstrate the greater community's support for universal suffrage and opposition to the government. In January 2010, five popularly elected LegCo members, one from each of Hong Kong's five geographic districts, resigned, thus forcing by-elections in May. The Basic Law has no provision for a referendum, but the radicals claimed that the aggregated votes from each district would constitute a de facto referendum on the Hong Kong SAR's political order on how leaders were selected. Beijing strongly opposed the tactic, alleging that it was moving one step toward de jure independence for Hong Kong. The Democratic Party regarded the move as irresponsible, while the establishment camp organized an effective boycott of the by-elections. In response, "Young activists became even more militant in their attempts to sabotage the government's public relations campaign."[47]

The moderate democrats, on the other hand, saw reason to negotiate. Surprisingly, the Central People's Government, through its Liaison Office in Hong Kong, was willing to negotiate with the Democratic Party members. In the end, Beijing accepted their proposal that the members of the District Council (Second) functional constituency be picked not by the members of the district councils themselves but by the over 3 million voters who were not electors in any other functional constituency. With Beijing's agreement on this point, which was the first time that the Chinese Communist Party made a concession to another political party in the PRC, the Democratic Party members of the Legislative Council were prepared to vote for the revised reform proposal, which gave the government the two-thirds majority it needed. (The democrats failed in their effort during the negotiations to get a more detailed commitment from Beijing on the 2017 and 2020 elections.)

With this compromise, forty out of seventy seats in the Legislative Council were now in effect popularly elected: thirty-five from geographic constituencies and five from the new District Council functional constituency. But this modest gain came at a serious cost. Chinese University's Ma Ngok concludes that the radical League of Social Democrats "and other civil society groups saw the DP's compromise as a 'betrayal' of the democracy movement, and blasted the DP's secret dealings with Beijing."[48] And voters agreed with the radicals. In the 2012 elections, the number of LegCo seats the Democratic Party won in geographic districts declined from seven in 2008 to four, and its share of the total vote fell from 20.6 to 13.6 percent.[49] In the elections for the new District Council functional constituency, the outcome reflected the basic 60–40 balance of public sentiment in favor of the opposition: three Pan-Democrats and two pro-government candidates won seats.[50] But the split between radicals and moderates within the democratic camp would persist into 2014 and 2015 and limit the prospects for compromise on future electoral reform.

Indeed, it is remarkable how long the same people have been engaged in political combat over the same issues. C. Y. Leung, who became chief executive in 2012, got his start in politics in 1985 as a member of the Basic Law Consultative Committee. In 1988, he became the committee's secretary-general. Hong Kong's first chief executive, C. H. Tung, named Leung to his cabinet (called the Executive Council) in 1998 and then as convener of that body in 1999. Leung held that position until 2011, at which point he began to prepare his own campaign for chief executive.

On the pro-democracy side, a number of young professionals came together in the late 1970s and early 1980s in support of democracy. The core group consisted of members from the Meeting Point, a monitoring organization, and the United Democrats of Hong Kong, which ultimately became the Democratic Party. By 2015, some prominent people associated with these two organizations had died, a few had fled Hong Kong, and others had either made peace with the establishment or left politics completely to pursue teaching and other careers. A few early democratic activists sought to make an impact from within the system: Anthony Cheung Bin-leung and Christine Loh were senior officials in government departments in the C. Y. Leung administration, and Anna Woo was an unofficial member of the Executive Council at the same time. Nonetheless, a number of early democrats are still at the rhetorical barricades. Martin Lee is their éminence grise. Emily Lau is head of the Democratic Party. Albert Ho was the Democratic Party's candidate for chief executive in 2012. Andrew To, Raymond Wong, and Albert Chan gave up on the Democratic Party and formed radical splinter groups—the League of Social Democrats and People's Power.[51] Anson Chan, a career civil servant who served as the government's chief secretary under Chris Patten and C. H. Tung, quit when Tung changed the basic structure of the civil service. She soon joined the pro-democracy cause and became one of its leaders. For many on both sides of the political divide in Hong Kong, political activism evolved into permanent occupations.

Conclusion

The 2010 Democratic Party and CCP "compromise" episode had two related negative consequences. The first was the crystallization of what Professor Ma Ngok calls "transition fatigue" among Hong Kong's democrats. After holding on to some hope that either London or Beijing would be willing to make the reforms they thought were necessary, Ma writes, "The lack of progress toward democracy left Hong Kong's democrats dispirited and frustrated."[52] As discussions of universal suffrage began in 2013, past disappointments made these democrats averse to putting their faith in Chinese intentions and to considering even the possibility of compromise. Ultimately, this "deep-down frustration" would intensify the Occupy Movement.[53]

The second consequence of the 2010 "compromise" was a fragmentation among Hong Kong's political parties. Party building had begun in the early 1990s. On the pro-democracy side, the United Democrats of Hong Kong, predecessor to the Democratic Party, was founded in 1990, and was the only party for more than a decade. On the pro-establishment side, the pro-Beijing

Democratic Alliance for the Betterment and Progress (DAB) was formed in 1992, and was followed by the pro-business Liberal Party in 1993. Additionally, the pro-establishment Federation of Trade Unions, which had existed since 1948, began to participate in electoral politics in the 1990s. This party structure persisted until the early 2000s, when the democratic camp splintered, creating a proliferation of new parties. The moderate Civic Party, composed mainly of professionals, and the radical League of Social Democrats, were both formed in 2006. Then in 2010 and 2011, there were more splinters: the New People's Party, was supported by civil servants. People's Power split off from the League of Social Democrats. The Neo-Democrats splintered off from the Democratic Party, and an independent Labor Party formed.

The establishment camp was equally prone to division, as the dynamic nature of the 2012 election for chief executive created a split as well. Henry Tang was the candidate preferred by the corporate sector and a majority of the election committee established in the Basic Law to pick the chief executive and composed mainly of members aligned with Beijing. Tang, who came from the business community and had served in government, was opposed not only by Albert Ho from the Democratic Party but also by another pro-Beijing candidate, C. Y. Leung (both men had gotten the necessary one-eighth support from members of the election committee that was needed to compete). Still, Tang appeared to have a significant majority. But then, he became the victim of mounting media criticism over the expansion of his luxury dwelling, which violated building codes. Beijing took note of Tang's declining public approval and switched its support to Leung, its second choice, and reportedly pressured Tang's supporters on the election committee to abandon him.[54] The 2012 campaign season illustrated how Hong Kong was taking on a characteristic of authoritarian systems facing pressures for liberalization: the existence of moderate-hardliner splits in both the reform and anti-reform camps. Whether democratization took place was a function of the strength of the two moderate factions vis-à-vis the two radical ones—whether they could come together to conclude a reform pact.[55]

The results of the 2012 LegCo elections within geographic districts, where public sentiment dominated, demonstrated the extent of this fragmentation. Overall, the pro-establishment camp won 42.66 percent of the total vote and the Pan-Democrats won 57.26. Within the establishment camp, the Democratic Alliance for the Betterment and Progress and the Federation of Trade Unions (the most pro-Beijing parties) won 27.28 percent of the total vote while the other parties won 15.38 percent. In the Pan-Democratic camp, the Civic

Party and the Democratic Party (the more moderate groups) won 27.73 percent of the total vote, while seven other parties and some independents captured the rest. When it came to LegCo seats, the Democratic Alliance for the Betterment and Progress won nine of the seventeen seats that the pro-government coalition obtained, while all but one of the rest of the seats were won by four different parties. The Civic and Democratic Parties won half of the democratic camp's eighteen seats (five and four seats, respectively), and four parties secured all but one of the rest. Compared with the 2008 election, the dispersion of support was greater on the democratic side. Then, the Civic Party and Democratic Party share of the Pan-Democratic total vote had been much higher (34.29 percent), while the Democratic Alliance for the Betterment and Progress and the Federation of Trade Unions' share of its camp's votes was marginally greater (28.62 percent).

There were many reasons for this proliferation of parties, one of them being the use of proportional representation in geographic electoral districts. But the key cause was Beijing's rejection of efforts by long-time leaders of the democratic camp to secure, even gradually, progress toward genuine democracy.[56] Party fragmentation would complicate any effort to reach consensus on goals and tactics within each camp. If one element of the democratic camp chose to negotiate independently with either the Hong Kong government or Beijing, as some Democratic Party legislators did in 2010, they would open themselves up to punishment from more radical parties and voters. In the universal-suffrage debate, therefore, moderate democratic leaders felt compelled to fortify their flanks by pledging that they would maintain a strong united front.[57] This pressure for unity in the democratic camp moved the point of consensus in a radical direction and would make a reasonable compromise over the electoral system nearly impossible.

THREE

Hong Kong's Liberal Oligarchy

CIVIL AND POLITICAL RIGHTS

I t is appropriate to pause at this point and examine the political system that was implemented in Hong Kong after July 1, 1997, and was in place at the time of the fall 2014 protests. A detailed understanding of the boundaries of political participation in the territory and of who holds what kinds of economic and political power yields a greater appreciation of the character and intensity of the Occupy Movement.

A Political Hybrid

In chapter 1 I referred to the Hong Kong Special Administrative Region (Hong Kong SAR) as a political hybrid. Its political system is what political scientists call a hybrid regime—neither a full, liberal democracy nor a closed authoritarian system. But Hong Kong is different from most hybrid regimes, such as the "illiberal democracies" that typically conduct elections for leading officials but skew the results by suppressing political freedoms.[1] Russia, for example, has nominally competitive elections but constrains political freedoms and emasculates judicial independence to the point that the elections are not objectively free and fair. Similarly, Singapore holds elections but has traditionally restricted the exercise of political rights, restrictions that have only recently begun to weaken.[2] Illiberal democracies' elections do not necessarily produce meaningless results: a decline in electoral support for the ruling party may induce it to respond to this demand signal by changing the policies that created dissatisfaction, as the Singapore government did after the 2011 elections.

The Hong Kong style of hybrid might be called a liberal oligarchy. In this chapter I examine how Hong Kong's liberal institutions have fared since reversion and discuss evidence of possible atrophy. In the next chapter I explore the oligarchic aspects of this hybrid.

Hong Kong has a liberal system in which human rights and freedoms are generally protected, with rule of law and an independent judiciary as the ultimate bulwark. But the system is oligarchic in the sense that both economic and political powers are concentrated in the hands of a relatively small elite. What deprives Hong Kong the full label of liberal democracy is the limited role for free and fair elections in picking all the territory's principal leaders, which could provide a check on the concentration of economic power. The scope of the electoral system has been the focus of political debate for decades and was the triggering issue for the Umbrella Movement. Competitive elections are held for a share of the seats on district councils and for around half the members of the Legislative Council (often shortened to LegCo). For selection of the chief executive, the maximum number of electors before the debate over electoral reform began in 2013 was 1,200, a majority of whom supported the economic and political status quo. The average electorate for a geographic seat in the LegCo is 232,677 voters, and the average number of voters for each of the thirty functional constituency seats is 2,256. This means that each vote for a functional-constituency representative has an impact 103 times that of a geographic-constituency vote. Even though the Pan-Democratic camp usually gets around 60 percent of the vote in the geographic races, structurally it has been blocked from forming a majority in the LegCo.[3] Thus, the Hong Kong hybrid system limits the degree to which voters can use elections to replace unwanted leaders and thereby to influence government performance.

This situation is reflected in the annual assessment of civil and political rights by Freedom House, a Washington-based organization dedicated to promoting human rights and democracy worldwide. From 2003 to 2015, it labeled Hong Kong only "partly free" because the assessment rates civil liberties higher than political rights. Civil rights, which in Freedom House's definition addresses the liberal side of Hong Kong's liberal oligarchy and includes freedom of expression and belief, associational and organizational rights, rule of law, and personal autonomy and individual rights, received the relatively positive score of 2 on a scale of 1 to 7 (1 is best and 7 is poorest). Political rights, which focus more on the oligarchic side and include the subcategories of electoral process, political pluralism and participation, and functioning of government, consistently gets a lower score of 5.[4]

For advocates of formal democratic institutions, the optimal outcome for Hong Kong would be electoral reform that allows the residents to pick their leaders and legislative representatives through genuinely competitive elections. Those who care about effective governance might acknowledge that democratic institutions do not necessarily guarantee good government, but they would also argue that well-designed institutions can be a good check on poor performance and abuse of power by government (a subject to which I return in chapters 7 and 9). Yet each of these groups would insist on preserving the liberal side of the Hong Kong hybrid, even as the debate over the parameters of the electoral system proceeds. Neither group wants to see restrictions on the Hong Kong SAR's existing political and civil rights and rule of law.

In my discussion of Hong Kong's liberal institutions I rely considerably on the annual human rights report for Hong Kong of the U.S. Department of State because it follows an established methodology. Prepared by the U.S. consulate general in Hong Kong, the report provides the consulate's own judgments on specific issues, which can be compared from year to year, and documents complaints by people and groups in Hong Kong regarding violations of human rights.

Rule of Law

Hong Kong's common law system and independent judiciary have profound importance not only for governance but also for the economy. With its guarantees of property rights and its ability to authoritatively resolve contract and other disputes, the judicial infrastructure has been vital to the territory's development. Chinese firms considering an initial public offering often prefer Hong Kong because they respect and trust its legal system. Even the government of the People's Republic of China (PRC) and its agents in Hong Kong are not averse to appealing to Hong Kong law when it suits their political purpose.[5]

The World Justice Project, an NGO based in Washington, D.C., publishes an annual Rule of Law Index based on eight categories: constraints on government powers, absence of corruption, open government, fundamental rights, order and security, regulatory enforcement, and civil and criminal justice. For

2013, Hong Kong ranked sixteenth in the world (the PRC ranked seventy-sixth; the United States was in nineteenth place). Singapore, Japan, and South Korea were the Asian systems judged higher than Hong Kong.[6]

The U.S. State Department's annual human rights report for China (including Hong Kong) notes that the Hong Kong Basic Law mandates an independent judiciary. The government, it said, "generally respected judicial independence" and "the judiciary provided citizens with a fair and efficient judicial process." On the specifics of due process of law (standards for arrest, trial, and so forth) the report found that although the Hong Kong government is not perfect in this respect (no government is), it still meets a high standard for the protection of civil rights.[7] One guarantee of judicial independence in Hong Kong is autonomy in the selection of judges, who are picked by the judiciary itself, and thus their selection is immune from external pressure or control.[8]

A fundamental principle of the rule of law is that no one is above the law. Thus, a test of any political system and its judiciary is their capacity to combat corruption. Corruption involves not only officials' using their position to benefit themselves, but also collusive behavior in the private sector. The Hong Kong SAR ranked seventeenth among 175 societies on Transparency International's global Corruption Perceptions Index for 2014, with a score of 74. China had a score of 36 and was ranked one hundredth.[9] This is not because Hong Kong's residents are innately more virtuous than their cousins on the mainland. Rather, it is because in the early 1970s the colonial government recognized that it had a serious corruption problem, as police and economic regulators enriched themselves at the public's expense. Before 1970, the colonial government lacked the capacity and the will to tackle the rampant abuse. By 1974, however, Governor David Trench created an entity with the necessary legal capacity: the Independent Commission Against Corruption (ICAC).[10]

The immediate focus of the ICAC, which reported to the governor before 1997 and has reported to the chief executive thereafter, was the entrenched system of kickbacks and payoffs to Hong Kong Police officers. Once that was accomplished, the commission turned its attention to other parts of the government and the private sector, and has since adopted a comprehensive approach to reducing corruption by pinching it in the bud. It has framed and pushed the passage of detailed laws that define the limits of acceptable behavior. It has instituted a training program for government employees and an education apparatus to ensure that all public employees understand those limits.

It created a set of mechanisms through which members of the public can report corrupt activity without exposing themselves to retribution. It developed its investigation and prosecution capacity. By the 1980s, "The ICAC ha[d] managed to instill in the local population the value that corruption has no place in Hong Kong society."[11] Ian Scott, a professor at the University of Hong Kong specializing in Hong Kong's civil service and other governing institutions, concludes—despite the administrative difficulty and cost involved—that "Hong Kong is fortunate that its civil servants at the departmental level do not question the importance of corruption prevention and that they give high priority to attempt to ensure that their departments are not infected by it."[12] The foundation for this ethics superstructure is a complex set of rules that reduce officials' discretion and highlight the moral values on which those rules are based.[13] The State Department's 2014 human rights report judged that "the ICAC generally operated effectively and independently, actively collaborated with civil society, and had sufficient resources."[14]

Political Freedoms

From the perspective of Hong Kong's residents, the rule of law guarantees that their government will not subject them to the arbitrary and extralegal abuses. It is in effect a defensive mechanism. Political freedoms are more of an offensive instrument, in that they allow citizens to question the government's performance and try to hold it accountable. (If the government tries to limit the exercise of those rights, the courts are then called on to block or reverse the government's action.)

FREEDOM OF EXPRESSION

The State Department's 2014 human rights report states that in Hong Kong, "the law provides for freedom of speech and press" and that "the government generally respected these rights. An independent press, an effective judiciary, and a generally supportive government combined to promote freedom of speech and of the press."[15] Hong Kong has a number of print newspapers, in both Chinese and English. Even though *Ta Kung Pao, Wen Wei Po*, and *China Daily* primarily disseminate the PRC government's perspective and policy views, Hong Kong residents (unlike people in the mainland) have a lot of other choices.[16] Outlets that are motivated by profits focus more on scandals and the sensational news, while other sources act as a public conscience. On every conceivable issue where there are contested views, the media display the thrust and parry of public debate. Commentary critical of the Beijing and Hong Kong SAR governments appears regularly in the *South China Morning Post* and *Ming Pao*, the leading English-language and Chinese-language papers, respectively. On a daily basis, government critics heap verbal and written attacks on officials, from the chief executive to local council representatives.[17] In 2014, the Democratic Party even raised funds by selling toilet paper and facial tissues with the picture of Chief Executive C. Y. Leung on each sheet as a means to criticize him and his policies.[18]

One morning in April 2014 I bought a selection of Hong Kong newspapers to compare the stories in their sections on China and Chinese news: this is the subject where journalists and editors would be most likely to exercise self-censorship.[19] Some Hong Kong papers had coverage of sensitive issues in China while others avoided them. The coverage in *Wen Wei Po* was what one might expect in a Communist Party paper: exhortation of the People's Liberation Army to study Xi Jinping's discourses; a long, favorable story about a Beijing automotive company that was expanding its international reach; and articles critical of Japan, U.S.-Japan relations, and American arms sales to Taiwan. In the other papers' China sections were covered cases of crime and abuse of power, a fire in the old city of Lijiang, and efforts in Taiwan to end a student occupation of the legislature (relevant to Hong Kong discussions about Occupy Central). *Sing Tao Daily* reported on a demonstration in Dongguan, while *Ming Pao* devoted a whole page to opposition to a chemical plant in Maoming City, both cities in Guangdong Province. *South China Morning Post* and *Apple Daily* both reported on corruption in the People's Liberation Army, and the *Apple Daily* had an article on corruption within the Communist Party. *Ming Pao* had two items relating to human rights. Even *Wen Wei Po* had articles on a failure to properly compensate citizens who were losing their homes because of a construction project in Zhejiang, and on the "unnatural death" of students in Hebei. Subjects that got covered in China were fair game in Hong Kong. Readers no doubt knew where to go for the different types of and perspectives on China coverage.

Freedom of expression covers more than newspapers. Hong Kong is also a center of publishing, and that includes books in both English and Chinese that are critical and often accurate accounts of CCP rule. Whether they are accounts of the horrors of the Great Leap Forward, the Cultural Revolution, or the rise and fall of past PRC leaders or exposés of current ones, all are available in Hong Kong bookstores. Such books would never pass the Chinese Communist Party's censors for publication in the PRC, but the material they contain often circulates because tourists from the mainland buy the books and bring them back home.[20] One of the publishers whom Beijing tolerates most of the time is Bao Pu, the son of Bao Tong, a key adviser to Zhao Ziyang, who was the CCP's general secretary from 1987 to 1989 and the most senior official purged after the Tiananmen protesters. Publishers such as Bao Pu still have to calculate what material the mainland authorities will tolerate, particularly when border checks are occasionally tightened up. Sometimes mainland officials advise these publishers to stay away from publishing certain sensitive manuscripts, and publishers gauge their compliance according to how strenuously they are pressured.[21] The relative freedom to print books critical of the mainland came under serious challenge in late 2015 (discussed in more detail in chapter 6).[22]

FREEDOM OF ASSOCIATION

The State Department 2014 human rights report offers this assessment: "The law provides for freedom of association, and the government generally respected it."[23] Quantitative measures of civil society bear this out. In 1997, 8,695 private, non-commercial organizations were registered under Hong Kong's Societies Ordinance, the best indicator of the breadth of civil society and freedom of association. The number increased steadily thereafter and by 2012 had reached a total of 30,531, an average increase of 1,456 per year.[24]

One significant area of political association is the creation of trade unions and the limits under which they may act. According to the human rights report, "The law, including related regulations and statutory instruments, provides for the right of workers to form and join independent unions without previous authorization or excessive requirements and to conduct legal strikes, but it does not protect the right to collective bargaining or obligate employers to bargain."[25]

There is one exception to the report's generally positive judgment: the treatment of household workers from Southeast Asia employed by Hong Kong families. The report states: "There also were reports that some employers illegally forbade domestic workers from leaving the residence of work for non-work-related reasons, effectively preventing them from reporting exploitation to authorities. Hong Kong SAR authorities claimed they encouraged aggrieved workers to lodge complaints and make use of government conciliation services, as well as actively pursued reports of any labor violations."[26] A 2013 Amnesty International report charged that about two-thirds of household workers endured physical or psychological abuse, and described their conditions as "slave-like."[27] In one high-profile case, a local court sentenced an employer to six years in prison for beating and threatening her Indonesian maid.[28] The underlying issue in many of these cases is racism regarding non-Chinese in Hong Kong. One survey found that 27 percent of respondents did not want to have a neighbor of a different race.[29]

Religious organizations and the beliefs and practices of their members and members' freedom to practice their religions unhindered are a second important aspect of freedom of association. The Basic Law as well as specific legislation protects religious freedom in Hong Kong, and the 2013 State Department report on international religious freedom states, "In practice the government generally respected religious freedom."[30] Various Chinese religions and an array of Christian denominations are active, and also sponsor and support educational and social welfare institutions. The Catholic archbishop of Hong Kong even takes positions on local political issues.

The exception to the rule for religious organizations in Hong Kong is Falun Gong, a movement that combines breathing exercises, exotic ideology, and a charismatic, dominant leader, Li Hongzhi. It was fairly widespread in China until April 1999, when Falun Gong followers held a large demonstration outside the party and state leadership compound in central Beijing, calling for legal recognition and freedom to practice their religion. Thereafter, the regime labeled Falun Gong an "evil cult" and has directed the full power of the state against it.[31] Falun Gong has a branch in Hong Kong, and its members engage in a variety of public activities, including worship and demonstrations. They have far more freedom in Hong Kong than in other PRC jurisdictions, but Central People's Government representatives in the territory still exert pressure on the Hong Kong SAR government to restrict the movement's activities. Overseas members of Falun Gong have found it difficult to enter Hong Kong, and members who are residents in the Hong Kong SAR claim they cannot get permission to use public buildings for events, as other private groups are allowed to do.[32] In its 2013 report, the State Department stated that Falun Gong members "reported a significant increase in harassment from a pro-Beijing group called the Hong Kong Youth Care Association (HKYCA) beginning immediately before the July 2012 inauguration of Hong Kong Chief Executive C.Y. Leung."

FREEDOM OF ASSEMBLY

In Hong Kong, demonstrations against the policies and actions of both the Hong Kong SAR and PRC governments are frequent and peaceful. The State Department's human rights report declares that "the government generally respected" the legal right of freedom of assembly.[33] In 2013 there was an average of approximately seventeen demonstrations a day.[34] Rallies are usually well prepared and coordinated with the authorities—in fact, the Hong Kong government website even alerts motorists in advance of which streets will be affected.[35]

Demonstrations vary widely in the number of participants and the reason for protesting. Many are political but some are not. Some are designed in such a way to stay within existing law and so take account of the rights and freedoms of others. But others constitute civil disobedience—breaking the law to advance a political objective—and some civil disobedience actions are disruptive and violate others' rights. Some demonstrations are one-off and others are planned to be repeated. Of the latter, the longest running is the annual early June procession to commemorate the massive demonstrations that occurred all over China in the spring of 1989. The Hong Kong government's permission for these annual demonstrations contrasts sharply with the Chinese government's thorough effort to stamp out any memory or knowledge of the events and to tighten restrictions on political activity at the time of the anniversary.[36]

The most contentious question regarding freedom of assembly in Hong Kong has been whether Falun Gong members can peacefully gather in Hong Kong's parks and march in its streets to publicly protest the Beijing government and its crackdown on the group. For example, in March 2002, the police arrested sixteen Falun Gong members demonstrating outside the Liaison Office of the Central People's Government and charged them with obstructing a public place and assaulting a police officer. The territory's pro-PRC media loudly echoed Beijing's charge that the movement poses a threat to social stability. Yet in the end, Hong Kong's judicial system upheld Falun Gong's right of peaceful assembly.[37] The Court of Final Appeal in Hong Kong dismissed the obstruction charge.[38] (By 2013, when I visited Hong Kong for the first time after a long absence, Falun Gong had a small but permanent presence just outside the entrance to the LegCo Building. They slept overnight in a tent and posted a guard to prevent their removal by the Hong Kong Police.)

Ultimately, the one area of political and civil rights the State Department faulted Hong Kong was the ability for residents to change their government. The report says, "The Basic Law limits the ability of residents to change their government through the right to vote in free and fair elections."[39] Without saying so, the human rights report confirms the classification of Hong Kong as a liberal oligarchy.

Fears of Attrition

When it comes to the various elements of liberal political order, the promises provided in the Joint Declaration and the Basic Law have generally been met. This is surprising because the PRC government, which has sovereignty over Hong Kong, does not protect political freedoms or the rule of law within any other area under its jurisdiction. And yet, most of these phenomena are common in the Hong Kong SAR, so the liberal part of the Hong Kong hybrid persists. For at least some of the people of Hong Kong, however, the fact that the territory's political freedoms are much greater than those of the mainland is less important than the perceived danger that these rights are being eroded, or that they could be. Whatever one's views about free and fair elections, observers and activists plan to defend Hong Kong's liberal foundation at all costs. The perceived threats to that foundation are both overt initiatives and subtle gambits used by the Central People's Government.

One type of explicit initiative involves the authority for final adjudication and interpretation of the laws governing Hong Kong, as briefly discussed in chapter 2. The Joint Declaration said that the Hong Kong Court of Final Appeal would have the "power of final judgment." But the Basic Law stated that although the Court of Final Appeal had the authority for laws pertaining to Hong Kong's autonomy, the Standing Committee of the National People's Congress, which acts on behalf of the NPC when it was not in session, would have the power to interpret the Basic Law and any legislation concerning "affairs which are the responsibility of the Central People's Government, or concerning the relationship between the Central Authorities and the Region."[40] The Basic Law also authorized appeals of Court of Final Appeal decisions to be sent to the Standing Committee. This created disagreement as to which concrete issues were covered by the outlined exception and whether the Standing Committee could use different or more political criteria. The first test case emerged two years after reversion; it concerned Hong Kong residency rights for children born in the territory to mainlander women who were not Hong Kong permanent residents. In January 1999 the Court of Final Appeal ruled that these children did have the right of residence in Hong Kong. The Hong Kong SAR government appealed the decision, arguing that it had the right to appeal and that the Basic Law had vested the Standing Committee with powers to interpret it. Moreover, if the appellate court's ruling was allowed to stand, it would grant the right to abode to 1.67 million mainland Chinese, and thus, place an undue burden on Hong Kong.[41] The Standing Committee reversed the Court of Final Appeal's decision.

Over time, a pattern of mutual accommodation appears to have emerged. In recent years, the Court and Standing Committee have tended to avoid zero-sum conflicts over specific cases that raise constitutional uncertainty.[42] Nevertheless, as a former Hong Kong justice has stated, the local legal system had to recognize that "the gravest danger to the rule of law in Hong Kong is in allocating to the 'one country' component [of one country, two systems] what truly belongs to the 'two systems' component."[43] More recently, some opponents of the Umbrella Movement have criticized Hong Kong judges for being too lenient on protesters arrested for unauthorized assembly or for obstructing police.[44]

The threats to the legal system may be as much operational as substantive, according to Dennis Kwok, a member of the anti-administration Civic Party who holds the functional-constituency LegCo seat for the legal profession. But the effect of restricting judicial effectiveness can be the same as actual attempts to do so. In September 2013, Kwok called public attention to several points of institutional weakness in the judiciary: inadequate resources and support; judicial vacancies aggravated by looming retirements; and longer waiting times for cases to be heard and decided. Kwok stated that "the heavy workload has . . . partially contributed to difficulties in the retention and recruitment of judges from the private sector. . . . Overworked judges and a backload of cases have a direct impact on the quality of justice."[45]

Beijing's most overt initiative to restrict political freedoms came in late 2002, not long after Hong Kong courts decided in favor of Falun Gong, as discussed earlier. Beijing began pushing the Hong Kong SAR government to pass a national security, anti-subversion law, and had reason to expect that it would do so, since article 23 of Hong Kong's Basic Law states that the Hong Kong government "shall enact laws on its own to prohibit any act of treason, secession, sedition, [or] subversion against the Central People's Government." The Hong Kong SAR government tried to carry out Beijing's wishes and was able to place a bill before the LegCo. Opposition parties and the middle class, fearing their freedoms would be revoked, mobilized and pressured the government and LegCo to back down. On July 1, 2003, half a million people—about 13 percent of the territory's total population—marched to protest passage of the legislation. It didn't take long for the Liberal Party, which initially had supported the government, to withdraw its backing, which quickly killed the bill.[46] This successful act of defiance served to encourage the use of demonstrations to influence policy on other issues.

Another threat to Hong Kong's liberal foundation comes from gradual and covert actions to restrict political freedoms, yet it is unclear how great the actual danger is, and whether the threats are real or imagined. Concerns are repeatedly expressed about incursions on the freedom of the press and expression in Hong Kong. For example, the State Department's 2013 report stated, "Throughout the year there were complaints lodged by free media groups about what they viewed as increasing challenges in this area."[47] Local journalist groups have warned of growing dangers to media freedom.[48] Reporters Without Borders, a Paris-based monitoring group that evaluates press freedom in 180 countries and regions, ranked Hong Kong 54th in 2012, 58th in 2013, and 61st in 2014. An irregular poll conducted by the Chinese University of Hong Kong found that the aggregate credibility of the city's media organizations had dropped over time.[49] Francis Moriarty, the head of the Foreign Correspondents' Club, Hong Kong, has warned against the chilling effect of attacks by masked men on local Chinese journalists.[50]

However, not everyone agrees with these negative assessments. A January 2015 report by the PEN America Center examined both recent events and longer-term trends in Hong Kong media freedom, and the title, "Threatened Harbor," telegraphed its growing concerns.[51] But writing in the *New York Times,* Chris Buckley and Michael Forsythe offered a more balanced evaluation. They noted that during the Occupy Movement, despite some altercations between reporters and police, "The protests in Hong Kong were intensely covered by the local news media, including by freelance journalists on a proliferation of blogs and websites."[52] A columnist for the *South China Morning Post* asserted that "Hong Kong has one of the bitchiest, liveliest media environments I have seen anywhere in the world," and took issue with the standards by which Hong Kong was judged by outsiders.[53] On the conservative side of the issue, a scholar at Hong Kong's Lingnan University suggested in 2014 that limits should be placed on press freedoms in order to reduce the increasing frequency of hate speech, false and sloppy media reporting, violations of privacy, and cyber-harassment, and advocated stricter limits on expression. He did say that, of course, these limits "must be set by the community at large and with community participation under standards and procedures acceptable to it."[54]

The Internet exacerbates commercial pressures on print media. Conflicts between reporters and editors within a newspaper or other medium over the right degree of criticism of both China and the Hong Kong government can be as much generational as ideological.[55] One scholarly study discussed a constant struggle between reporters and their bosses. Journalists believed they themselves were politically "liberal" in their outlook, more so than their employers, but self-censorship was still widespread. For members of the Hong Kong media, it seems that "both professional norms and journalists' largely liberal political outlook are important forces counteracting the pressure to conform to the power center."[56]

Trends in the ownership of media organizations may trigger public anxiety about press freedom. Changes in the pattern of media buyouts by other businesses are often examined for evidence of PRC political pressure.[57] Whenever a new media organization is formed or an old one gets sold, suspicions arise that the new owners are sympathetic to Beijing and will use their outlet to inject China-friendly coverage of issues and events. In January 2014, *Ming Pao*, the well-respected Chinese-language paper that had carried stories about dissidents in China and the wealth of Chinese leaders, was sold. The new owners soon replaced the chief editor, Kevin Lau Chun-to, which was bad enough for those anxious about press freedom. Then, in late February, Lau was attacked and almost died from his injuries, provoking a new round of worries about the newspaper that was more independent than any of its Chinese-language competitors. In late 2015 questions were raised about the independence of the *South China Morning Post* after it was purchased by the mainland e-commerce company Alibaba Group, discussed in detail in chapter 6.

A further constraint on freedom of the press in Hong Kong is geography. Existing norms may block Beijing from punishing Hong Kong residents whom it believes to be working to support dissidents in China or to have published information critical of Chinese leaders—but only as long as they remain in the Hong Kong SAR. If they dare to go to the mainland, they are often detained, arrested, and jailed. In early 2014, the Duihua Foundation, in San Francisco, estimated that some of the approximately 2,000 Hong Kong residents in PRC prisons and detention centers were incarcerated for political reasons.[58] For example, in October 2013, Yiu Mantin, who was writing a book critical of the Chinese leader Xi Jinping, was arrested during a routine trip to the mainland and seven months later was convicted of smuggling in a mainland court and sentenced to ten years in prison.[59] Even if such arrests occur only in China, the chilling effect in Hong Kong is palpable. Since 2012, Beijing has imposed tighter controls on the materials that travelers from Hong Kong can bring to the mainland, confiscating books that the regime deems provocative or embarrassing. The Hong Kong publishers of most of these items have noticed a drop in sales.[60]

Finally, concerns have grown in recent years over a decline in the effectiveness of the anti-corruption fight. At least one Hong Kong scholar worried in 2006 that adherence to the social norms against graft had not only declined after reversion, but that corruption in fact had accelerated as a result of the "wheel-greasing" practices of the many PRC firms that had relocated to Hong Kong.[61] The number of complaints to the ICAC declined between 2011 and 2014, and reports that the head of the ICAC had engaged in lavish spending were released in 2013, embarrassing the agency and weakening its credibility.[62] Some observers theorized that changes introduced with reversion that eliminated government pensions for civil servants recruited after 2000 would increase the incentive for them to engage in corrupt activity, and that modest salaries for junior corruption investigators would reduce the ICAC's capacity.[63] Moreover, recent ICAC reports suggest that the corruption problem today is more concentrated in the private sector, particularly in construction and building management. Finally, some believe that the underlying political economy of Hong Kong is fundamentally corrupt, because the wealthy business elite has preferential access to government institutions. The poster child for this theory was the case of Raphael Hui, who was the chief secretary (the number two after the chief executive) in the Hong Kong government from 2005 to 2007, and then continued as a member of the Executive Council thereafter. In late 2014 he was convicted of taking massive bribes from real estate executives who wished to use him as their "eyes and ears" in government.[64] As the well-respected columnist Philip Bowring wrote after the trial, "The public is rightly suspicious of the ethical standards prevailing at the top."[65]

Conclusion

A number of episodes have, at the very least, raised concerns about the integrity of the liberal foundation of Hong Kong's political order and, gray areas notwithstanding, give evidence of a change in the status quo toward a less-free society. A strong case can be made that owners of certain mass media organizations have taken steps to shift political coverage in a more China-friendly direction. It is difficult to determine whether political loyalties of the owners, political pressure, or commercial imperatives not only in Hong Kong but also in the mainland market have stimulated this evolution. Despite justified worries, on balance, no significant change in the degree of freedom that Hong Kong citizens enjoy seems to have occurred as of September 2014. The principal reason has been that citizens have been vigilant, even hyper-vigilant—as indeed they should—in guarding against efforts to constrain their exercise of their rights, and the judicial system has been steadfast in sustaining the liberal order when called to do so, which it should. In the State Department's 2014 human rights report, the key assessments were essentially no different from those of 2009, indicating no atrophy of liberal freedoms during what was a rather convulsive period.[66]

The Occupy protests would pose a new and serious challenge to Hong Kong's liberal order. Would China possibly conclude that some in Hong Kong had abused their freedoms to the point that more than attrition at the edges was required? I return to that question in chapter 6, with particular emphasis on freedom of the press and freedom of expression.

FOUR

Hong Kong's Liberal Oligarchy

ECONOMIC AND POLITICAL INEQUALITY

As noted in the previous chapter, the Hong Kong political system that opened for business on July 1, 1997, is a hybrid regime, what I call a liberal oligarchy. The Hong Kong Special Administrative Region (Hong Kong SAR) has rule of law, an independent judiciary, and the political freedoms found in most democracies around the world. But it also manifests a concentration of economic and political power generally uncommon in democratic systems. A relatively small number of large firms dominate the economy, and income and wealth are highly concentrated among a select few. Access to housing, education, and employment are also skewed in their favor. In the Legislative Council (LegCo), functional constituencies with limited franchises favor the economic and social elite, as do the subsectors of the election committee, which picks the territory's chief executive. These mechanisms give elites preferential access to political power, which in turn may be used to shape government policies. In effect, the elites constitute an oligarchy. The broader public may use political freedoms to criticize those policies, but they lack the option to replace government leaders through competitive and representative elections. The problem for the oligarchy is that some parts of the public have grown increasingly unhappy with the hybrid nature of the regime and have taken advantage of the freedoms afforded by the liberal order to engage in mass protest.

This chapter examines the oligarchy side of Hong Kong's hybrid regime. First I review Hong Kong's growing social and economic inequality—in income, wealth, and access to housing and employment—to the detriment of the lower and middle classes. Second, I examine the configuration of the political system and how it privileges the economic elite and Beijing supporters. In the third section I review polling data on political attitudes in Hong Kong toward these concentrations of power. The final section outlines a consequence of this concentration of power: the emergence of a culture conducive to protest by a significant segment of the Hong Kong public.

Economic Inequality

Inequality of some sort is inevitable in all societies and certainly those with advanced economies. The starting point is the innate difference in skills, which rapid technology change and the advantages that one generation leaves to another through inheritance only exacerbates. Efforts to compensate for those differences through policy measures can stifle initiative and creativity. A political failure to redress excessive inequality can have other negative consequences. This section looks at inequality in Hong Kong when it comes to income, wealth, education, employment, and housing.

INCOME AND WEALTH

Quantitative data tell a clear story of Hong Kong's growing economic inequality:

- Nominal median monthly employment earnings were basically stagnant from 2005 to 2010, rising from $1,289 to $1,418, and only inching up to $1,727 in 2014.[1]
- In 2011, the lowest five deciles of economically active households accounted for 20.3 percent of monthly household income, the sixth and seventh deciles had 19.9 percent, the ninth decile had 15.3 percent, and the highest decile had 38.8 percent.[2]
- Real per capita income has shown only modest growth since reversion in 1997: in 1997 it was $24,513; in 1992, $25,045; in 2007, $33,477; and in 2013, $37,520—an average annual rate of increase of 0.15 percent.[3] Wages remained stagnant over a sustained period. The real wage index of wage workers, compiled by the Hong Kong Council of Social Science, was 99.8 in 1991, rose to 102.8 in 1996, jumped to 120.3 in 2001, fell to 116.1 in 2006, and stood at 115.8 in 2014.[4]

- According to government statistics, in 2014, 61.8 percent of households had monthly salaries of under $3,866, and 15.5 percent had salaries over $7,732.[5]
- The top 10 percent of Hong Kong's households possessed 65.6 percent of the territory's wealth in 2000, 69.3 percent in 2007, and 77.5 percent in 2014.[6]
- The number of high net worth individuals in Hong Kong increased by 63 percent from 2009 to 2013.[7]
- For 2011, Hong Kong's Gini coefficient, which measures the degree of inequality in the distribution of family income in a country, was 0.537, the twelfth highest in the world (the more inequality, the higher the coefficient).[8] In 1971 it was 0.430. If household income is adjusted to take account of transfer payments and subsidies, the 2011 figure goes down to 0.475, but that is still high—the decline from the recalculation will be small comfort for those who are the victims of inequality.
- According to the Forbes rankings, in 2014 Hong Kong had 55 billionaires, about half of China's 109. In contrast, Japan had only 25, Taiwan had 33, and Singapore, which is similar to Hong Kong in size and GDP, had only 19.[9]

Despite the overall growth of the economy, poverty remains a serious problem. According to a government report, the average gross household income of the poorest 10 percent of the population fell 16 percent from 2001 to 2011, a decade when income for the richest 10 percent jumped by 12 percent, to $17,716 a month.[10] The Hong Kong government set the poverty line at 50 percent of the median household income (adjusted for household size) before any policy interventions, such as taxation or cash transfers. Working from this basic definition, the Census and Statistics Department of the Hong Kong SAR government found that the poverty rate was 19.6 percent with 1.31 million people affected. After recurrent cash welfare payments the percentage dropped to 15.2 percent. Including payments made on an ad hoc, annual basis, it dropped to 12.0 percent. And if the benefit of public rental housing is added as a recurrent cash payment, the rate fell to 10.1 percent. That is still a high rate for an affluent society.

Several factors contributed to this degree of poverty. The larger the size of the household, the larger its income, whereas a lot of underage, unemployed, economically inactive, and elderly members tended to pull down the household income average.[11] Critics noted that in addition to level of income, poverty could also be measured by access to housing, health care, and education. Leo

Goodstadt, a retired government official, had this blunt assessment: "Today's poverty is due to misuse of the city's prosperity and policies which favour businesses and the rich but are terrible for the poor."[12]

Inequality is experienced not just as the imbalanced distribution of wealth and income but also in terms of consumption; that is, what households spend with their money. A 2010 survey found that 32.8 percent of the expenditures spent by an average Hong Kong family of four went to housing, 27.1 percent on food, 8.3 percent on transportation, and the rest on everything else. This means that over two-thirds of expenditures were spent on necessities.[13] As of 1980, the expenditure shares for housing and food were essentially reversed. Based on the total for household expenditures in 1991 and 2010, the monthly amount spent on housing increased from just under $387 to just over $1,031.[14] Low-income households (defined as those whose household income is less than half the median) spent around 60 percent of their income on housing and food.[15] That leaves few resources for all other consumption categories.

The income level for the working population must be slightly discounted because almost half—41 percent of those surveyed in 2013—contribute to their parents' income. Breaking down the contribution levels, the survey found that 23 percent gave less than 20 percent, 13 percent gave between 20 and 40 percent, and 5 percent gave between 40 and 60 percent. Half of respondents under thirty contributed (perhaps because they still lived at home) and 45 percent of those between thirty and fifty-nine. Some transfers to older parents likely take place because of a quirk in the retirement system, which stipulates that even though the retirement age is sixty, retirees cannot draw from the government's provident fund until they are sixty-five.[16]

EDUCATION AND EMPLOYMENT

Data on income and wealth, both objectively measured and subjectively felt, are important indicators for understanding inequality in Hong Kong, but they are just the first steps. Access to education and employment are two other indicators of Hong Kong's progressively unequal society.

The territory of Hong Kong has a well-established, multifaceted educational system that receives strong government support. Free education is available through the twelfth grade in government-run schools, and there are also private schools. In September 2014, public primary and secondary schools had over 266,000 and 302,000 students, respectively. There are nineteen degree-granting universities, eight of which are supported by the University Grants Committee, a government advisory committee. In September 2014, those eight institutions had 87,600 full-time and 3,900 part-time students.[17] According to the 2011 census, 16.7 percent of the population fifteen years of age and older had attended primary education; 49 percent had at least some secondary education; and 27.7 had attended a postsecondary institution.[18] According to UNESCO 2013 data, 66.8 percent of those qualified for post-secondary education were attending an institution that provides it, giving Hong Kong a world rank of 30.[19]

In terms of employment opportunities, services strongly dominate the Hong Kong economy, accounting for 93 percent of GDP in 2013 (the industrial sector accounted for 6.9 percent).[20] Within the service sector there is significant segmentation by subsector and education. A household survey in the fourth quarter of 2014 showed that 26.5 percent of the workforce worked in public administration and social and personal services (including education); 19.3 percent in finance, insurance, real estate, and professional and business services; 16.8 percent in retail, accommodation, and food services; 12.3 percent in transportation, information, and communications; 8.2 percent in construction; and 3.3 percent in manufacturing.[21] The same survey found that 29.6 percent of the workforce had secured a postsecondary degree; 14.7 percent had some tertiary education but no degree; 36.1 percent completed upper secondary school; 15.6 percent completed lower secondary school; and 9.6 percent went no further than primary school.[22]

There is a fairly strong correlation among education level, sector or type of employment, and income:

- Lower levels of education are more common in fields like construction, transportation, accommodation and food services, and administrative and support services. Higher educational attainment is found in financial services, real estate, information and communication, scientific and technical professions, education, health care, and social services. In fields such as trading, the skill levels are more evenly distributed.[23]

- Regarding income and type of work, the median monthly wage in mid-2013 was $1,211 for those in "elementary occupations" (low-skill positions); $1,379 for service workers and retail workers; $1,495 for clerks; $1,997 for craft and factory workers; and $2,964 for managers, administrators, professionals and associates. Thus, the latter group's average salary was more than two and a half times those in elementary occupations.[24]

- Concerning education and income, in late spring 2013, the median monthly wage for people was $1,211 for those who only completed primary school, $1,405 for those who completed lower secondary school, $1,753 for those who completed senior secondary school, and $2,925 for those who completed tertiary education. Thus, the median income of the highest category was over three times that of the lowest category.[25]

Yet despite the relative advantage of a university degree, the immediate benefits for new graduates have declined over time. A study based on Hong Kong government statistics found that the median monthly income of new university graduates declined by 17 percent between 1993 and 2013. A study by researchers at the Chinese University of Hong Kong reveals the cause of this decrease: in 2011, only 73.4 percent of university graduates were able to land positions as managers, administrators, professionals, and associate professionals (in the category "middle class jobs"), down from 82.5 percent in 2001.[26]

Patterns of unemployment also manifest Hong Kong's high degree of inequality. In the fourth quarter of 2014, the overall jobless rate was 3.1 percent, but lower (1.5 percent) for positions in public administration, insurance, real estate, professional and business services, and financial services, transportation, and information and communications. The rate was above average (4.6 percent) for manufacturing, trade, retail, accommodation and food services, and construction.[27] When it came to age, each of the ten-year cohorts of people between thirty and sixty had unemployment rates below the overall 3.1 percent average in 2013. But the rate for those twenty to twenty-nine was 5.6 percent and for the fifteen-to-nineteen cohort it was 14.5 percent.[28] Furthermore, 25.5 percent of the youngest cohort, not controlling for employment, came from low-income households.[29]

Competition for both university places and well-paying jobs is fairly intense. Only one in eleven applicants to the top-ranked University of Hong Kong matriculated in 2012, and, as noted, the number of well-paying sectors is quite low.[30] The competition is not just within the Hong Kong community, as local people have always faced some degree of competition from outsiders. In 2011, 7.4 percent of the population was born outside Hong Kong, and universities have a number of nonlocal students (around a third of Hong Kong University's applications in 2012 were from outside of the territory).[31]

It is the students and young job seekers from the mainland who are most likely to cause resentment from their Hong Kong–born peers. Yet compared to the population as a whole, there are not that many recent arrivals from the mainland. The 2011 census found that 60.5 percent of the total population was born in Hong Kong and 32.1 percent was born on the mainland or in

Macau or Taiwan. But of this 32.1 percent, 39.4 percent were born before 1952 (that is, mostly before the major refugee waves), 44.5 percent were born between 1951 and 1980 (the refugee generation), and the remaining 16.1 percent were born after 1980. Some of the mainland people who came to Hong Kong beginning in the 1980s did so under a program that allowed them to get a one-way exit permit for Hong Kong from their local public security bureau if they already had family there. The maximum number of permits the PRC granted rose from 75 a day before 1994 to 150 a day after 1998. From 1992 to 2013, just over 1 million people took advantage of this program, and the number has dropped each year from an annual average of 51,676 in the years from 1994 to 2003 to 45,709 from 2004 to 2013.[32] At the time of the 2011 census, the number of migrants who had been in Hong Kong for less than seven years was 171,322, which was 74 percent of the previous decade's number.[33] The downside for those who received permits is that they had to give up their mainland household registration and the benefits associated with it.[34] The downside for the Hong Kong government was that it had no say over which mainland residents received permits.

Then there are mainland young people who come to Hong Kong for post-secondary education.[35] The Hong Kong SAR government has established a 20 percent limit on the number of undergraduates from outside Hong Kong who can enroll in the territory's universities. Nonlocal applicants to undergraduate programs must fulfill the same language and academic requirements as other applicants, and for mainland students that is measured by their performance in China's own national exam and a standardized test for English-language ability.[36] Mainland applicants to graduate schools must first get a minimum score on a test of English-language proficiency, and then survive a qualification test or an interview or both, depending on the procedures of the school in question. In addition, there are rumors that mainland students receive school placements through "faking transcripts or pulling *guanxi*"—family connections. How well Hong Kong universities are able to spot and screen out such applicants is unclear.

This program raises two issues. First, do mainland students take admissions spots away from local students? Although mainland undergraduates make up 80 percent of the nonlocal students admitted, there is still a 20 percent cap, so if the mainlanders take spots away from anyone, it is applicants from other places. The issue is whether the cap is set at a fair level. At the graduate level, more than 70 percent of the nonlocal postgraduates in local universities are from the mainland. From the schools' point of view, they see value in recruiting talented students from China who are generally ambitious and dedicated, and thus raise the institutions' reputations. They also bring in additional revenue—not unlike the situation with mainland Chinese in American universities.

The second question is whether mainland graduates of Hong Kong universities out-compete their local classmates for jobs. Hong Kong's immigration law permits them to stay to work, and when their combined education and work time in Hong Kong reaches seven years, they may become permanent residents of the territory. About half of mainland students who receive undergraduate degrees and around 30 percent of those who receive postgraduate degrees end up working in Hong Kong. As one mainland student in Hong Kong commented, "No doubt [the mainland graduates] add to the cutthroat competition of Hong Kong's job market, but employers naturally want the best and brightest."[37] To the extent that these young people increase the economy's competitiveness, they also may expand the size of the job market.

HOUSING

The area where the effects of inequality in Hong Kong are starkest is probably the property and housing sector. As too many families try to squeeze into too few housing units while prices remain high, households and home life are affected. Furthermore, because land is a factor of production for commerce and industry, small and medium-sized industries have found it increasingly difficult to compete for space. As rents and leases soar, the mom-and-pop stores that were once a pillar of the Hong Kong economy are driven out of business.[38] There is a sense among long-time residents that the commercial shopping areas they used to frequent are now effectively off-limits to them because most shops carry luxury goods that they do not need. Tourists, particularly those from the mainland, who account for 75 percent of visitors entering Hong Kong, have replaced them as the target consumers.

Some of the reasons for the tight property market are not unique to Hong Kong. Globalization has fostered rapid economic growth and an increase in personal wealth in all advanced economies. Real estate is usually the first place that newly rich families and investors use as a store of value. Hong Kong is no exception. Also, in many countries, local groups and civil society organizations place a high priority on preserving open spaces, heritage sights, and the environment. For them, the principal enemies of preservation are property developers.[39] Again, Hong Kong is no exception, with district councils and activist groups leading that opposition. This limits the number of housing units built. Moreover, higher frequency of divorce in most advanced societies increases overall demand for housing.

In addition to these general worldwide trends, the Hong Kong property market has its own special characteristics. There is the simple fact that Hong Kong has no hinterland where new development can occur. It would be comparable to Manhattan without the surrounding suburban areas. Purchasing property across the border in Guangdong Province is not really an option for Hong Kong citizens: they would be giving up valued elements of the Hong Kong system, among them more secure property rights. The 1983 decision to peg the Hong Kong dollar to the U.S. dollar effectively links Hong Kong's monetary policy to that of the U.S. Federal Reserve Board. Low American interest rates automatically translate into low interest rates in Hong Kong, which incentivize investors in both Hong Kong and China to buy property.

The most significant Hong Kong–specific factors for housing inequality have to do with government policy and the political economy. Here, it helps to distinguish between public and private housing. According to the 2014 Hong Kong Housing Authority report, 53.7 percent of the total population of 7.235 million lived in private permanent housing; 29.3 percent in public rental housing; and 16.5 percent participated in the home ownership scheme (HOS), subsidized by the Hong Kong SAR government, whereby some residents in public housing are enabled to purchase their units.[40]

In *Hong Kong Land for Hong Kong People*, Yue Chim Richard Wong delivers a pointed indictment of the government's policy on public housing. As with similar systems in other societies, current occupants of public housing often do not benefit from the rising home values that private homeowners enjoy and aren't as able to increase their children's chances for upward mobility.[41] In a rising property market, private residences climb in value faster than the wages of public housing clients, which limits their chances of buying a private dwelling. Intergenerational mobility within the public housing sector is limited, because there is no real market for rental units and occupants quickly become tied to their apartments, often far from good schools, good jobs, and family members.[42] The share of households in public housing who were in the group with the lowest 20 percent by income nearly doubled from 1976 to 2011, from 25.5 percent to 48.4 percent.[43]

Since the 1970s, the government has sought to make it possible for some public housing renters to buy their residences, as is done in Singapore.[44] The first Hong Kong SAR chief executive, C. H. Tung, undertook the latest iteration of this option, now known as the home ownership scheme, right after reversion. That initiative was quickly abandoned when housing values dropped sharply during and after the Asian financial crisis. The terms of the HOS were then revised to the disadvantage of occupants. All land is owned by the government and the government charges a premium when a plot of land is transferred. HOS participants who wished to purchase their units from the government had to pay the land premium at the price assessed at the time of transaction, not at the time when they first became occupants. But since land prices increase faster than the rate of inflation and are difficult to estimate, the occupant-purchaser is often priced out of the market. "Thus, HOS occupants also become nailed to their units in the same way as [public rental housing] tenants did," Wong notes.[45] The overall impact of Hong Kong's public housing policy is to create a wall between the public and private sectors.

Government policy also has an impact on price levels and inequality in the private housing sector, such as regulations that impose "transaction costs" on developers. These include adherence to planning rules and building codes, extra time needed for public consultations, and the delays created by the existing owners of property slated for redevelopment by private firms. For example, when developers wish to renovate older apartment buildings, a substantial percentage of current owners must agree to sell before the developers can get government approval for a compulsory sale of the entire property. Some current owners can no longer be contacted, which increases the share of owners among those who can be contacted who must agree to sell, which makes the task harder for developers. Because of these kinds of transaction costs, a number of development companies have gone under.[46]

But a separate and independent cause of inequality is the oligopolistic nature of Hong Kong's property markets.[47] The core of this structure is the Hong Kong government, which technically owns all the land in the territory and has done so since the colonial era. The government makes land available to private parties on long-term leases either through public auction or applications. The policies that regulate how land is released for the market help set the level of competition and prices. The second part of the oligopolistic structure is the small number of large property firms that own—that is, have long-term leases on—a substantial share of Hong Kong's land, both old housing that can be developed and agricultural land that can be converted for other purposes. They dominate the market such that they can both control the pace at which property is placed on the market (usually when demand is strong, which affects price levels), and use these resources in times of recession to preserve their market share and expand it by buying up available property at lower prices.

These large firms are also in a better position to hire the expertise needed to surmount regulatory barriers.[48] For almost half of Hong Kong's billionaires, real estate was the principal domain of business activity in 2015.

To make matters worse, the dominant real estate firms have not confined themselves exclusively to ownership of property. They have also acquired public utilities, transportation companies, grocery chains, and telecom companies. Thus, the key products and services consumed by the great majority of the population are subject to oligopolistic markets. Furthermore, several independent authorities, such as the Mass Transport Railway Corporation, also make property available for real estate development, and these properties also often end up in the hands of the market dominators. For example, the MTR sells space over and around new subway stations for residential and commercial purposes. A study released in early 2015 by Land Watch, a housing policy think tank, revealed that between 2001 and 2014, the three biggest property developers were able to buy 80 percent of the residential sites released by the MTR, amounting to more than 43,000 apartments.[49]

Given all the factors that together limit the supply of housing, it is no surprise that the number of units available has declined over time. The supply of new public housing apartments fell from an annual average of 38,900 units between 1997 and 2002 to an annual average of 14,600 units from 2007 to 2012, a total drop of 62.5 percent. During these two periods, a decade apart, the average number of new private units made available per year was essentially halved, from 21,900 to 9,900.[50] In early 2015, when the Housing Authority put 2,160 apartments up for discounted sale under the HOS, they received 130,000 applications—more than the number of HOS dwellings that the government planned to build over the next decade.[51] According to Hong Kong government studies, between 2013 and early 2015, the price index for all owned housing went from 242.4 to 291.1 (a 20.1 percent increase), and the index for all rental property went from 154.5 to 167.8 (an 8.6 percent increase).[52] At the same time, the share of average household expenditures spent on housing increased, from around 20 percent in the early 1980s to around 25 percent in the early 1990s, before stabilizing at just under 33 percent in the first decade of the twenty-first century.[53] By late 2014, property developers began marketing tiny apartments that were smaller than 196 square feet for around $206,000.[54] A survey conducted in March 2015 found that 34 percent of respondents wanted to buy an apartment, but 77 percent could not afford one, and half of young adults wanted to buy, but 88 percent were shut out of the market.[55] Richard Wong states that "most local purchases of new [private] flats in Hong Kong in recent years have been made by households that have property of their own to begin with." His conclusion applies more broadly: "Housing wealth is increasingly becoming concentrated among the haves. The have-nots are increasingly left out, and they certainly feel this."[56]

The real estate sector has formal and less formal ways of advancing its interests in government. Through the functional-constituency (FC) system, the sector has its own member of the Legislative Council and its own subsector in the chief executive election committee. Other FC members, too, are prominent and have personal stakes in the property sector. The most telling example of "less formal" influence was the bribery case of Raphael Hui, the former chief secretary in the Hong Kong government. He was bribed by members of the Kwok family, owners of Sun Hung Kai, the second largest property firm. The exposés detailing the favors Hui received were topic number two in the local media in 2014, just behind Occupy Central. This clear case of improper exercise of influence by senior civil service staff confirmed in the public mind "what is long believed—that there was collusion between property tycoons and officials."[57] A respected newspaper columnist, Philip Bowring, described the property sector and its partners in the financial services industry as "a business cabal that speaks with one voice to protect its interests and exercises enormous influence over the Hong Kong government and has the ear of its masters in Beijing."[58]

Analysts have disagreed and will continue to do so about the various factors that increase both housing costs and inequality of access: global and social factors, government policy, or collusive behavior by property developers? Richard Wong emphasizes government policy, whereas Alice Poon, who worked in the real estate industry for twenty years, stresses oligopolistic behavior by private property firms. But all of these factors have contributed to the quantitative and qualitative housing shortage, and any solution will have to tackle the various causes simultaneously. Politically, the objective facts are less important than what citizens believe, because that will determine public attitudes toward the Hong Kong SAR government and the firms that dominate the market. In Hong Kong, the mainstream view is that the market is rigged against average citizens.

SOCIAL MOBILITY

More politically significant than the degree of inequality at any single point in time are both the trend over time and the strength of belief of those who have less now that they have both the opportunity and the skills to move up the social and economic ladder later.[59] A January 2015 research brief prepared for LegCo detailed the impact of these inequality trends on social mobility.[60] Cumulative median monthly employment earnings increased by 139 percent from the mid-1970s to 1996 but by only 14 percent between 1997 and 2013. In 2008, 62.9 percent of the workforce was in the same income quintile they had been in five years before, and 47.2 percent were in the same quintile as ten years before. For workers in the lowest quintile, 54.1 percent were in the same place they had been a decade earlier. Another measure of wealth mobility is the ratio of owner-occupiers in private residential apartments, which increased from 40.6 percent to 67.1 percent between 1981 and 1996, but stayed at 67 percent in 2013. Although the share of young people with postsecondary education increased from 13.7 percent in 1991 to 39.3 percent in 2011, most of the growth from 2001 to 2011 was in two-year programs, not full-time degree programs. Finally, although parents generally hope that their children will enjoy a better life than they do, in Hong Kong today the income, educational, and occupational achievements of young people are often basically the same as that of their parents. The overall conclusion: "Recent statistics and research studies have revealed limited opportunities for upward earnings, educational and occupational mobility. There is also a statistically significant correlation between the socio-economic status of parents and their children, suggesting low inter-generational social mobility."[61]

Hong Kong is certainly not unique in the skewed distribution of the benefits from economic performance. Most advanced economies are in the same boat. Globalization—particularly the cross-border mobility of capital and labor, the geographic dispersion of manufacturing, and inclusion of China after its economic reform began in 1979, which meant that workers in other places were effectively competing with China's low-wage workforce—has made it harder for companies in all advanced economies to preserve global competitiveness and market share, and has reduced governments' capacity to shape economic performance. Rapid technological change can easily leave all but the most talented employees behind. Whether it is Hong Kong, Taiwan, Korea, Israel, Western Europe, or the United States, these trends put their middle classes at risk, create winners and losers, and foster greater inequality and uncertainty about the future. In addition, Hong Kong faces unique challenges: its domestic economy is small and cannot thrive by relying on domestic demand alone; aging populations and smaller household size exacerbate inequality; and governing institutions, which successfully fostered growth with equity during Hong Kong's take-off period, have not done as well more recently to distribute wealth equitably. It should be no surprise that the same type of populist movement that has surfaced in most advanced economies has emerged in Hong Kong as well.

Political Oligarchy

Yet this growing confluence of wealth, income, and opportunity only reinforces the political concentration of power that occurred much earlier, when Hong Kong was poor and in the early stages of economic growth. In the absence of electoral democracy, the British colonial government co-opted the leaders of major, predominantly British-controlled firms, appointing them to positions on the Executive Council, the Legislative Council, and, in much larger numbers, to various advisory bodies that brought together officials and corporate executives on a sector-by-sector basis to discuss the details of government policy. This government-business partnership continued even as control of major firms shifted from Britons to ethnic Chinese and as ethnic Chinese rose to the higher levels of the civil service.[62] Research by Synergynet, a local think tank, found that "the current membership make-up of various advisory bodies is biased toward the industrial, commercial, and professional sectors, and does not match the development of an increasingly pluralized civil society" (author's translation).[63]

When the advisory groups worked well, they were platforms for private-sector members to convey their specialized expertise and consult with officials on policy. However, Leo Goodstadt concluded that this input from the business community did not improve the administration.[64] Politically, the message was that the government cared about the views of only part of the public and that private interests had too influential a voice concerning government policy.[65]

During the colonial period, the Chinese Communist Party initiated its own co-optation strategy in order to secure local backing for PRC interests and to prepare for a formal takeover. The Federation of Trade Unions (FTU), established in 1948, was leftist in ideology and loyal to Beijing. In addition, China enlisted "patriotic" individuals in the business, education, media, publishing, and culture sectors and gave them, along with some FTU leaders, seats in the National People's Congress and Chinese People's Political Consultative Conference. Formally, they were part of the Guangdong Province delegation. Once the transition toward reversion was under way, Beijing created its own advisory bodies in Hong Kong, such as the

Basic Law Consultative Committee, and used them to expand its influence. Overall, business executives continued to dominate these committees, while the relative number of professionals declined. Leaders of larger corporations, who were previously not deemed to be patriotic, became members of the National People's Congress and Chinese People's Political Consultative Conference.[66] Gradually, cross-memberships grew among the boards of corporations, government organizations, and universities, creating a type of interlocking directorate.[67]

By the 1980s the colonial government was undermining its closed-door, consultative approach to government by initiating democratization of the political system. Elected politicians became an independent force that challenged the way things had always been done. As Anthony Cheung writes, "Legislators now operated mostly as critics and watchdogs over the government while advisory committee appointees were expected to remain partners of the administration, if not loyal advisers as they had [been] previously."[68] On the other hand, functional constituencies, which had been established under the British and entrenched in the Basic Law, provided a greater elite check on the new prominence of elected politicians and restored some unity of purpose between the new Hong Kong SAR government, the business elite, and other Beijing support groups. Depending on one's point of view, advisory committees either became one of several venues for grooming establishment individuals for higher office, or a way to dole out patronage.[69]

Functional constituencies allowed the economic elite to redress some of the balance between themselves and politicians, but politics after reversion remained very complicated. FC members were more active vis-à-vis the government than advisory committee members had been. Cheung writes: "In the process of political bargaining, these dominant elites are not reluctant to defy government wishes nor to use the threat of withdrawn support to bargain for policy concessions and political benefits."[70] The civil service, which had coexisted synergistically with the business and professional communities during the colonial period, now had to adjust. It could no longer serve as the "imperial arbiter" in cases of conflict of interests between major economic players, but was now "dragged into rivalry among these [business] groups whenever it sought to intervene in the economic sphere."[71] Business did not always get what it wanted, either, because government regulators hung tough in some cases, such as those regarding companies heavily invested in transport and energy infrastructure, or because of populist opposition from certain LegCo members.[72] Unlike in the colonial period, however, business executives who had trouble getting what they wanted from the Hong Kong SAR government used their access in Beijing to circumvent local opposition.[73]

China did not rely solely on elite co-optation to maintain a degree of control over Hong Kong. The strategy the Chinese Communist Party usually used when confronted with a situation over which it could not dominate, whether it was urban centers such as Shanghai after the Communist victory in 1949 or Hong Kong after reversion, was to build a "United Front." Having accepted in the Joint Declaration of 1984 the obligation to permit indirect rule over the Hong Kong SAR, Beijing created mechanisms to mitigate the unpredictability its pledge entailed. In Hong Kong, this strategy certainly included, first, reliance on the Federation of Trade Unions and, later, cultivation of the business community. It also co-opted existing social and local organizations to join the pro-Beijing coalition and facilitated the rise of new ones. These organizations then became accessible and available tools for mobilization to counter protests from the democratic camp.[74] Mao Zedong had stated that the United Front "isolates the enemy by winning the vast majority to the side of the revolution; then, through struggle, the isolated and now vulnerable enemy is destroyed."[75] The key method for "isolating the enemy" was stigmatization and demonization. Suzanne Pepper, an independent scholar specializing in Chinese politics, writes, "The pattern is always the same. There are targets, exemplary villains, political sins, and paths to redemption."[76]

The Central People's Government also recognized the need to compete with the democratic parties on their main turf: LegCo geographic constituency elections and local councils. It stimulated the formation of a new political party, the Democratic Alliance for the Betterment and Progress of Hong Kong (DAB), which supports the Hong Kong SAR government and Beijing on constitutional issues but seeks lower- and middle-class support in elections. To improve the DAB's chances to win seats for the Legislative Council in geographic districts, proportional representation replaced the single-member-district, first-past-the-post voting system elections that had been instituted during the late colonial period. The results may have been less than Beijing hoped but were not trivial. The DAB won 20 percent of the vote in the 2012 LegCo elections, much more than any other party but still much less than the Pan-Democratic parties combined (57 percent). It won thirteen LegCo seats, nine in geographic districts and four from functional constituencies. As such, it was the largest single party in LegCo; one of its leaders, Jasper Tsang Yok-sing, was named president of the body.

The DAB has done even better in elections for the eighteen district councils, which are the training ground for future political leaders. At this level, the party's mobilization machinery and constituency service generally outpace those of the democratic parties. DAB candidates receive additional organizational support from pro-Beijing groups such as the Federation of Trade Unions. Supervising the campaigns behind the scenes is the Central People's Government's Liaison Office in Hong Kong, which some local scholars have termed the "babysitter" or "hidden but crucial chess player."[77] In the 2011 elections, the DAB won 136 of the 412 contested seats, with 24 percent of the vote and 55.4 percent of the seats.[78] For the 2015 district council elections—the first ones since the Umbrella Movement—pro-establishment candidates won 191 seats, an increase from 160 in 2011, while Pan-Democratic candidates captured 94 seats, up from 83 in 2011. The bigger stories were the success of the "umbrella soldiers," candidates associated with the Occupy Movement, and the fall of two veteran Pan-Democratic leaders. Of the fifty umbrella soldier candidates who ran, seven won seats, with several defeating veteran incumbents. The Democratic Party chairman, Albert Ho Chun-yan, and Frederick Fun Kin-lee of the Association for Democracy and People's Livelihood, both lost to pro-establishment candidates after facing competitive Pan-Democratic third-party contenders.[79]

THE STRUCTURE OF POLITICAL POWER

Although the interests of the various groups and individuals in the pro-Beijing United Front did not have the same interests on all issues, they still proved an effective instrument for Beijing to manage risk in a complex transitional environment that was relatively unfamiliar to the CCP. In the 1984 Joint Declaration, the PRC government had promised that Hong Kong would have home rule and had agreed to general principles about how leaders would be selected: the chief executive through "selection or election" and LegCo through elections. To ensure that selection processes would produce results to CCP's liking and guarantee a central role for its loyalists, it drafted the Basic Law to properly engineer the electoral system to give extraordinary power to its loyalists. For the selection of the chief executive, the key institution was the election committee and for LegCo, it was functional constituencies, or FCs.

As outlined earlier, each FC and election committee subsector represents a specific business, professional, social, or political group. But, each FC is also an election committee subsector. Each FC elects a specified number of members for the chief executive election committee as well as one or more members for LegCo.[80] There are a few social and political groups that are election committee subsectors but not a separate FC; for example, the religious and Chinese medicine election committee subsectors are not a separate FC. In 2012, the District Council (Second) FC was created, whose five LegCo members were drawn from the district councils, but who were elected by voters unable to vote in any other FC.

From 1997 through the election in 2012, the number of FC seats in the LegCo has always been half of the total, so they have evenly balanced the directly elected seats.[81] In addition, the Basic Law dictated that individual members were not permitted to offer bills that related to "public expenditure or political structure or the operation of the government" (those were introduced by the government). Bills that concerned government policies could only be introduced by individual members with the written consent of the chief executive. Moreover, whereas government bills only required a majority vote for passage, individual bills, to pass, needed a separate majority from both directly elected and FC members.[82]

The average number of votes cast for each LegCo member elected in geographic districts is many times the average number of votes cast for each FC member (see table 4-1). This means, inversely, that the political impact of FC electors is much greater than that of those in geographic districts. In some FCs, election committee and LegCo members are selected by a vote of corporations, not individuals. The lowest voter-to-seat ratio is 124 per seat, in the finance FC (it uses corporate voting), whereas the education FC has the highest ratio, 89,704 per seat, which is approximately double the total number of people employed in the education sector.[83] The total number of voters in FC elections for the 2012 LegCo was 232,677, so the average for each of the thirty seats was 2,256 voters. A total of 3,507,786 people cast ballots in geographic-constituency races to fill thirty-five seats, so the average number of voters per seat was 116,926. The total number of voters for the new District Council (Second) FC was 3,251,275, so each of the five seats represented, on average, 650,255 voters.

A comprehensive study of FCs published in 2006 confirmed that they are a latter-day manifestation of the mutually beneficial government-business alliance created in the nineteenth century, with small electorates compared to those of the geographic constituencies. The government has ceded much power to the FCs to craft their structure themselves and function in a non-transparent way. Within the LegCo, FC members first and foremost protect and promote the interests of their sector. On issues where those interests are

TABLE 4-1. Election Committee (EC) and Functional-Constituency (FC) Subsectors

Subsector	Elector type	Number of EC seats	Number of EC electors	EC elector weight	Number of LegCo seats	Number of FC electors	FC elector weight	2012 LegCo election	2011 EC elections
Heung Yee Kuk	Individuals	26	146	6	1	146	146	Uncontested	—
Agriculture and fisheries	Corporate body	60	158	3	1	158	158	...	Uncontested
Insurance	Corporate body	18	127	7	1	129	129	Uncontested	...
Transport	Corporate body	18	200	11	1	200	200	Uncontested	...
Education	Individuals	30	81,831	2,728	1	89,704	89,704	...	...
Legal	Individuals	30	6,436	215	1	6,440	6,440	...	...
Accountancy	Individuals	30	25,085	836	1	25,092	25,092	...	...
Medical	Individuals	30	10,762	359	1	10,764	10,764	...	...
Health services	Individuals	30	36,971	1,232	1	37,007	37,007	...	...
Engineering	Individuals	30	9,077	303	1	9,078	9,078	...	...
Architectural, surveying and planning	Individuals	30	6,803	227	1	6,804	6,804	...	...
Labor	Corporate body	60	644	11	3	644	215	2 uncontested seats	...
Social welfare	Individuals	60	13,986	233	1	13,709	13,709	...	...
Real estate and construction	Mixed	18	708	39	1	717	717	Uncontested	Uncontested
Tourism	Corporate body	18	1,195	66	1	1,313	1,313	...	...
Commercial (first)	Corporate body	18	842	47	1	884	884	Uncontested	Uncontested
Commercial (second)	Mixed	18	1,580	88	1	1,611	1,611	Uncontested	...
Industrial (first)	Mixed	18	543	30	1	545	545	Uncontested	Uncontested

(continued)

TABLE 4-1. (*continued*)

Subsector	Elector type	Number of EC seats	Number of EC electors	EC elector weight	Number of LegCo seats	Number of FC electors	FC elector weight	2012 LegCo election	2011 EC elections
Industrial (second)	Corporate body	18	769	43	1	774	774	Uncontested	Uncontested
Finance	Corporate body	18	121	7	1	124	124	Uncontested	Uncontested
Financial services	Corporate body	18	573	32	1	573	573	...	...
Sports, performing arts, culture, and publishing	Mixed	60	2,545	42	1	2,554	2,554	...	Uncontested
Import and export	Mixed	18	1,355	75	1	1,377	1,377	Uncontested	Uncontested
Textiles and garment	Mixed	18	2,827	157	1	2,829	2,829	...	Uncontested
Wholesale and retail	Mixed	18	6,957	387	1	6,978	6,978	Uncontested	...
Information technology	Mixed	30	5,816	194	1	5,821	5,821	...	...
Catering	Mixed	17	6,280	369	1	6,291	6,291	Uncontested	...
District Council (First)	Individuals	...	...	...	1	411	411	Uncontested	...
District Council (Second)	Individuals	...	...	...	5	3,251,274	650,255	...	...
District Council—HK and Kowloon	Individuals	57	200	4	...	...	...	...	...
District Council—New Territories	Individuals	60	211	4	...	...	...	...	...
Hotel	Corporate body	17	110	6	...	...	...	...	...
Higher education	Individuals	30	7,824	261	...	...	...	...	...

Employers' Federation of Hong Kong[a]	Corporate body	16	105	7	...	...	...	Uncontested
Hong Kong Chinese Enterprises Association[a]	Mixed	16	298	19	...	...	...	Uncontested
Chinese medicine[a]	Individuals	30	5,912	197	...	...	...	No election
Chinese People's Political Consultative Conference[a]	Individuals	51	92	2	...	...	...	No election
Religious[b]	Individuals	60	...	...	...	...	...	No election
National People's Congress[b]	Individuals	36	...	...	...	...	...	No election
Legislative Council[b]	Individuals	70	...	...	...	...	...	No election
Geographical Constituency								
Hong Kong Island	Individuals	...	...	...	602,122	86,017	7	...
Kowloon West	Individuals	...	...	...	447,006	89,401	5	...
Kowloon East	Individuals	...	...	...	566,277	113,255	5	...
New Territories West	Individuals	...	...	...	1,001,652	111,295	9	...
New Territories East	Individuals	...	...	...	890,729	98,970	9	...

Sources: Author's compilation, based on "Composition of the Legislative Council" (www.legco.gov.hk/english/education/files/Teachkit/LegoInPic/note1.pdf); "Sectors and Subsectors of the Election Committee" (www.eac.gov.hk/pdf/ecse/en/2011ecse/guidelines/2011ecse_Appendix_b.pdf); "Relationship of the 28 Functional Constituencies and 38 Election Committee Subsectors" (www.eac.gov.hk/pdf/ecse/en/2011ecse/guidelines/2011ecse_Appendix_f.pdf); "Voter Registration Statistics: govt.hk/en/statistic20141.html#2"; "Voter Registration Statistics: Functional Constituency" (www.voterregisstration.gov.hk/eng/statistic20143.html).

a. Election Committee subsectors without a corresponding functional constituency (optional subsectors).

b. Subsectors that do not require an election. The religious subsector is to return its election committee members by nomination. The Hong Kong deputies to the National People's Congress and the members of the Legislative Council are ex-officio members of the election committee.

not in play, representatives who are members of a political party follow the party's lead or support the government. Rather than fortifying capitalism at large, FCs tend to facilitate self-interested corporate welfare.[84]

WHO ARE THE EC AND FC MEMBERS?

A detailed study of the election committee by Simon N. M. Young and Richard Cullen of Hong Kong University concluded that it favored some social interests over others: it is based in part on the FCs, which are "deliberately tilted in their representation of certain viewpoints (e.g., pro-business, pro-government views)." It also "performs poorly" in giving any role to "women, young adults, retired senior citizens, ethnic and religious minorities, and persons from disadvantaged groups." To make matters worse, the EC's fourth sector includes Hong Kong members of the National People's Congress and the Chinese People's Political Consultative Conference, who are, almost by definition, supportive of Beijing.[85] The same study provided the professional titles listed for members of the election committee subsectors for the 1998, 2000, and 2006 committees. In 2006, all the members of the first sector, the one drawn from the business community, had high-ranking titles such as "merchant," "managing director," "CEO," and "chairman." But so did almost all of those from the sports and performing arts subsectors, and the one that represented the rural village councils, called Heung Yee Kuk *(xiangyihui)*.[86] A different study revealed that 300 election committee members, most of whom were Beijing loyalists, had been members in all four elections for which the committee voted.[87]

The picture is similar for FCs in the LegCo, many of which overlap with the election committee subsectors. Table 4-2 shows the distribution of those LegCo members who included a current profession on their biographical information for the institution's website, according to the professions mentioned and the type of constituency they are from: geographic, functional, and District Council (Second) seats first filled in 2012 (these are elected by voters who are not part of an FC).

The bias of the functional constituencies toward the economic elite creates a class cleavage within LegCo. Table 4-3 shows the number of company directorships and properties that LegCo members own, controlling for the orientation of their political party they provide (nonpartisan, Pan-Democratic, pro-government).

Table 4-3 suggests that although Pan-Democratic legislators are by no means poor, they are not in the same wealth category as their establishment

TABLE 4-2. Professions of LegCo Members, by Type of Constituency

Profession	Geographic	Functional	District Council (Second)[a]
Law	3	2	2
Corporate	2	13	0
Medical	0	3	0
Journalism	1	0	0
Information technology	1	0	0
Miscellaneous	1	3	1
Labor	2	3	1
Social work	0	3	0
Teacher	3	0	0
District council member	6	0	0

Source: Legislative Council website, Members Biographies (as of 2015) (www.legco.gov.hk/general /english/members/yr12-16/biographies.htm). Not all members provided a profession.
a. New in 2012 election.

TABLE 4-3. LegCo Members' Directorships and Properties Owned, by Party Grouping

Directorships	Number	Percent of Total Directorships
Nonpartisan	2	6.7
Pan-Democratic	6	23
Establishment	25	61

	No property	Percent	One property	Percent	Multiple properties	Percent	Total
Nonpartisan	2	67	0	0	1	33	3
Pan-Democratic	7	27	9	35	10	38	26
Establishment	3	7	12	29	26	63	41

Source: Website of Hong Kong SAR government, Legislative Council, "Register of Members' Interests: Fifth Legislative Council (2012–16)" (www.legco.gov.hk/general/english/cmi/yr12-16/reg _1216.htm).

colleagues. Moreover, there are cases where the wealth profile of an FC LegCo member is not entirely consistent with the apparent interests of the corresponding membership. Tommy Cheung Yu-yan, the catering FC member, is the chairman or a director of ten different companies, including oil, marketing, and technology systems companies.[88] Steven Ho Chun-yin, the FC member for agriculture and fisheries, has a degree in communications and computer system engineering from the University of Birmingham.[89]

But the most obvious case of concentrated representation and thus power is the Heung Yee Kuk FC. This functional constituency represents village assemblies and residents in the New Territories whose families were there at the start of the British lease in 1898. Its franchise is one of the smaller ones (146 electors) and its LegCo member up until 2015 was Lau Wong-fat, who is no simple farmer, but rather a major residential and commercial property holder.[90] More than that, Lau was able to use his influence with Beijing and in the LegCo to entrench the right of each constituent to own a small house despite a general housing shortage, which became known as the "small house policy." One cynical commentator writes, "The kuk is often described as the rural body that represents the interests of the indigenous population in the New Territories. A better way to look at it is as a property organization whose foundation is built on the so-called small house policy of the government. This enables the indigenous male line to claim a house in their villages without a time limit."[91] To add insult to injury, Lau passed the leadership of Heung Yee Kuk to his son when he retired in June 2015.[92]

ON REPRESENTATION

Clearly, economic sectors receive exceptional representation in both the election committee and the FCs and, presumably, could be expected to echo the interests of the pro-establishment and business community on issues important to Beijing (see table 4-1). The apparent logic operating here was that stability in Hong Kong was a function of continued economic growth and that the business community had delivered on those expectations for decades. The business community was perfectly happy to be co-opted and thus preserve its preferential position in policymaking.[93] Too much power for the democratic camp, it feared, would only lead to an expansion of costly social welfare programs.

To be fair, the idea that certain elite sectors should be over-represented is not a Chinese invention. Political philosophers going back to Aristotle have stressed the value of a mixed system that combined monarchy, aristocracy or oligarchy, and democracy. In the United Kingdom, the House of Commons had its pocket boroughs and rotten boroughs until 1832. The House of Lords, composed of unelected individuals from the social and economic elite, had the institutional power to check the Commons until the House of Lords' powers were gradually whittled away. America's Founding Fathers shared their British cousins' preference for a mixed government. In the 1780s, a time when popularly elected state legislatures were unable to govern effectively, conservative reformers undertook to set property qualifications for electors in the upper houses of state legislatures in order to introduce greater balance in state governments.[94] The preference for some degree of elite representation was also manifest in the 1787 Constitution, which established the U.S. Senate and Electoral College. In Hong Kong, the colonial government instituted the equivalent of functional constituencies in the late nineteenth century.[95]

It is unlikely that Beijing cared about the Western precedents for the approach to political representation that it adopted for the election committees and FCs. What is critical to understand, notes Simon Young, a law professor at Hong Kong University, is that the Basic Law facilitates the representation of interests, not people.[96] China's goal was to use these bodies to give preferential access and political power to the local interests that it believed could best assure *its* interests in the Hong Kong SAR—namely, stability and ultimate control. The Hong Kong people as a whole had representation through elections of LegCo members from geographic constituencies and through certain FCs and election committee subsectors. Beijing's emphasis of interests over people ultimately played out in the debates over the "representativeness" of the chief executive nominating committee that was a central element of electoral reform proposals in 2014 and 2015.

Also worth noting is that not all members of the election committee and LegCo functional constituencies support the establishment and Beijing. The democratic camp usually wins the seats in the social welfare, education, and legal FCs.[97] The FTU is anti-business but not anti-Beijing, while the Confederation of Trade Unions is pro-democracy. In the election committee, the Pan-Democratic camp held enough seats in 2012 to muster the 150 votes needed to nominate Albert Ho, a leader of the Democratic Party, for chief executive, but lacked enough votes to secure his victory.

Nor do the parties of each camp vote as a bloc on all issues. There is a limit to the level of unanimity among the pro-business members, because different economic sectors have conflicting interests.[98] A study by the *South China Morning Post* found some cross-cutting cleavages in LegCo voting. The Civic Party and Democratic Party sometimes collaborated with pro-establishment parties, whereas the Liberal Party, a moderate, pro-establishment party, voted with the Pan-Democrats 40 percent of the time. The pro-government Democratic Alliance for the Betterment and Progress of Hong Kong, which seeks to appeal to the middle class, was sometimes at odds with the leftist Federation of Trade Unions, an integral part of the establishment coalition. This reflects a larger identity crisis for the FTU. It was the first organization in the United Front, and Beijing expects its loyalty and support. Yet it is criticized for "betraying the workers" and creating an opening for the pro-democracy Confederation of Trade Unions.[99] The study concludes that ultimately it's the nature of the issue under debate that dictates whether the establishment and democratic caucuses in the LegCo vote together. Crossing the aisle is more common on issues of social and economic policy, whereas constitutional issues, such as the scope and pace of democratization, are the main fault line that divides the two camps. For those, the establishment camp is usually united.

So, although Beijing cannot depend on total support from all of the LegCo's FCs all of the time, it can count on most of those members, and particularly when it really matters. The net effect is that election competition in geographic districts might be quite free and competitive, but it is not necessarily fair because of the number of LegCo FC members whose policy views are inconsistent with the community at large. Hong Kong has a government that is more responsive and effective than many, but it lacks one that is fully representative.

Public Attitudes

In general terms, Hong Kong residents are satisfied with life in the territory. In a January 2013 poll by the Hong Kong Transition Project, a nonprofit public-opinion survey organization based at Hong Kong Baptist University, 71 percent of respondents said they were satisfied or very satisfied with life, while only 27 percent felt the opposite. But this satisfaction did not carry over to the performance of the Hong Kong government: 54 percent were dissatisfied or very dissatisfied, and 42 percent expressed some degree of satisfaction. Looking at the history of the Transition Project's surveys, the division of opinion was in the middle range. The level of dissatisfaction had been as high as 79 percent in the aftermath of the Article 23 protests in 2003, and as low as 27 percent in June 2008, after a period of economic recovery and right before the Summer Olympics in Beijing. In 2013, attitudes toward Chief Executive C. Y. Leung were almost exactly the same as those for the government: 53 percent were dissatisfied to some degree and 41 percent were satisfied.[100]

When asked an open-ended question about the most urgent issue in Hong Kong that political candidates should address, 56 percent identified housing, 34 percent highlighted poverty (including the wealth gap), and 10 percent mentioned reform of the political system.[101]

A couple of questions in the poll elicited views from which one could infer that they reflect opinions on the distribution of power. When respondents were asked whether they supported the abolition of FCs in the LegCo, 24 percent of those who expressed an opinion were strongly in favor, 49 percent were in favor, and 27 percent were opposed. That is, almost three-quarters of respondents supported abolition. This included even the recently established seats for the District Council (Second) FC, whose members were arguably elected on a popular basis. A similarly high proportion supported ending the requirement in the LegCo that a majority from both generally elected members and functional-constituency members was needed to amend a government bill or pass a measure introduced by a member, a rule that advantages FC members. Seventy percent of respondents believed that the government makes policies unfairly and favors certain interests over others. These feelings are strong for both those most concerned about housing and those worried about poverty and the wealth gap. Interestingly, the group that felt most strongly that government policy was made unfairly was civil servants, the people who carry out such policies.[102]

People under thirty, who have spent all or most of their adult life under the Hong Kong SAR government, felt most negatively about Hong Kong's economy and political system. They score highest for concerns about unfair government policymaking, dissatisfaction with the Hong Kong and central governments, and doubts of Chief Executive C. Y. Leung's ability to both protect the territory's interest vis-à-vis China and handle relations with the poor and the public at large. They are most skeptical about economic opportunities, quality of life, and political and civil freedoms in the future. Those who identify with a political party tend to support one in the democratic camp. Michael DeGolyer, the coordinator of the survey, stated, "This younger generation [those under thirty] is clearly reinterpreting what it means to be Chinese or Hong Kong Chinese, and . . . for the vast majority of this rising generation this does not mean unwavering, unquestioning support of Beijing."[103]

In surveys conducted between 2010 and 2013, Asian Barometer, a project of the Center for East Asia Democratic Studies at National Taiwan University, revealed important findings about the attitudes of Hong Kong "millennials," those under thirty in 2012. The Hong Kong millennials had one of the highest rates of Internet usage in East Asia (98 percent), were less likely to vote than their elders (58 percent voted, versus 74 percent for those thirty to fifty-five and 82 percent for those over fifty-five), and were more dissatisfied with "the way democracy works in our country" (one-third were dissatisfied, versus one-quarter and one-fifth for the other two age groups, respectively). In their conception of democracy, they gave more or less equal weight to good governance, social equality, norms and procedures, and freedom and liberty.[104]

Qualitative commentary by informed and thoughtful individuals is consistent with these polling results.

- Yue Chim Richard Wong, economics professor at the University of Hong Kong: "In the past 30 years, Hong Kong's economy has prospered, but growing numbers in the low- and middle-income classes, have been left behind.... Under-provision of education opportunities means the income gap has failed to narrow as economic and technological advances increasingly reward those with more human capital.... Society is now divided into 'haves' and 'have-nots' based on property ownership."[105]
- Janet Pau, an executive at the Asian Business Council: "The first generation in Hong Kong whose future living standard may be worse than that of their parents is coming of age. Although these young people have already lowered their expectations about owning a home or starting a business, they feel hopelessness about securing a productive future for themselves and sharing the elusive sounding 'prosperity' that politicians and business say Hong Kong possesses."[106]
- Perry Lam, a journalist and cultural critic: "Protests are really about young people raging against a system that has made them serfs.... What came as a revelation [from the Occupy Movement] isn't how much the protesters love democracy, but how much they hate the status quo."[107]
- Siegfried Sin, a law student at Chinese University of Hong Kong: "We feel frustrated and angry about the future of Hong Kong. Politically, we are offered a 'fake democracy,' with Beijing giving the final 'blessing' on chief executive candidates, and a crippled Legislative Council. Socially, welfare is minimal and housing is starting to become an impossible dream for young people. Economically, [Hong Kong] now clings on to finance and trade with mainland China."[108]
- Bernard Chan, a well-to-do member of the Executive Council: "We cannot expect people—of any age or group—to welcome changes to our economic structure if the rising prosperity passes them by. If big trends leave them worse off, we can only expect them to be unhappy, and ultimately to protest. A growing economy needs to benefit all or most of the people—not just a relatively small group of them."[109]

Culture of Protest

On a Sunday afternoon in October 2013, I walked into my first Hong Kong demonstration, organized by the Civic Party and People's Power. Civic Party is divided over its basic political stance; People's Power is on the radical wing of Hong Kong's opposition spectrum. Through social media they had mobilized a large middle-class crowd to protest the government's recent rejection of the application for a television license of Ricky Wong, a telecommunications entrepreneur, because they believed that Beijing had worked behind the scenes to limit diversity in broadcast media. The demonstrators, who filled the neighborhood near my hotel in Causeway Bay, wore black T-shirts, the local protest uniform. The Chinese characters for "black box" *(heixiang)*—referring to closed-door government decisionmaking—were printed boldly on shirts and signs. Fueling the complaints about lack of transparency was the suspicion that Hong Kong authorities made this decision not on its merits, but because the central government in Beijing wished to limit freedom of the press. The rally was noisy yet orderly. A lot of police were on duty but the crowd complied with the crowd-control arrangements that had been put into place. Clearly there had been some advance coordination between the organizers and the police to balance the rights of protesters with the needs of vehicles and shoppers going about their business. (A Hong Kong official later told me that protest leaders were not always reliable when it comes to controlling their people.)[110] Toward the end of the afternoon, the crowd, which was estimated at over 30,000 people, marched to the government complex in the Central neighborhood of Hong Kong. Order was maintained, nobody was hurt, and the protest was covered well by the mass media. Perhaps the most important observers that afternoon were Chinese tourists shopping in Causeway Bay. For me, at least, it was impossible to know whether they were impressed by the freedom of demonstrators to express their views or annoyed by the noise and crowds.

This was but one "day in the life" of Hong Kong's culture of protest. Demonstrations were not new, of course. The seminal event was a large demonstration in June 1989 to show solidarity with the protesters in Beijing's Tiananmen Square and other cities in China. Politics and democracy in Hong Kong remained the focus for the next decade, most notably at the July 1, 2003, protest against national security legislation.[111] But economic and social issues came to the fore in the recession that followed the Asian financial crisis of 1999. On just one day in June 2000, there were different demonstrations by doctors,

TABLE 4-4. Trends in Hong Kong Protests, 2004–13

Year	Number of legal processions	Events with prosecutions	Percentage of events with prosecutions	Number of illegal processions
2004	1,974	1	0.05	52
2005	1,990	2	0.11	65
2006	2,228	4	0.18	83
2007	3,824	4	0.10	55
2008	4,278	4	0.09	89
2009	4,222	3	0.07	45
2010	5,656	10	0.18	93
2011	6,878	15	0.22	30
2012	7,529	22	0.29	131
2013	6,166	31	0.50	123

Source: Edmund W. Cheng, "How Feedback Matters: The Diffusion of Vigorous Activism in Postcolonial Hong Kong," paper presented at Contemporary China Studies Workshop, "The Boundaries of Democracy: New Developments in Hong Kong and Taiwan's Relations with China Mainland," Hong Kong, October 10, 2014 (author's collection), p. 6.

social-welfare workers, small-scale property owners, opponents of urban re-newal, and residents from the mainland protesting over their legal status in Hong Kong.[112]

As the issues proliferated, so did the number of protests. Table 4-4 docu-ments the number of "legal processions" that had a minimum of thirty par-ticipants; they were "legal" because organizers and the police had reached an understanding about the route and assembly areas in accordance with the Public Order Ordinance. These increased dramatically, from 1,974 in 2004 to 7,529 in 2012—approximately 20 protests a day. The number and percentage of legal processions when the prior understanding with the police was violated ("events with prosecutions") also increased, but was still at a low level. More significant, the number of "illegal processions," which were characterized by a degree of civil disobedience, more than doubled over the decade.[113]

Edward Cheng of the Open University of Hong Kong identifies a shift in the character of protests with 2006 as an approximate inflection point. Prior to that, protests predominantly took the form of demonstrations (*youxing*) and rallies (*jihui*) that were organized by union members and politicians, and through which "a small group of organized elites articulated and expressed public interests through contentious yet controlled means" to the point that their actions took on a routine and ritualized nature. Most of them were small, but some could be very large, and were primarily focused on political issues, particularly democratization, with an intended outcome to reaffirm existing values. The participants were inclined toward the Pan-Democratic camp, but supporters of Beijing and Hong Kong government policies sometimes mounted their own events.[114]

Gradually, the character of these protests changed. The average number of participants increased and the decision to join became more spontaneous. The organization time declined from months to weeks or days, and the time between major events became equally short, ranging from several weeks to one day or even a few hours. The "organizers" were not linked to political parties or conventional NGOs. As with activist groups elsewhere, they were increasingly mobilized for political action through personal networks and information evoked in the media rather than by leadership direction.[115] Social media now permit rapid mobilization for rallies and demonstrations, leading to "a more lively, spontaneous, and creative style of protest, and the state finds this elusive organizational form even harder to suppress."[116] Sometimes participants were young activists who appeared out of nowhere. Instead of marches or rallies, these leaders tended to undertake "nonviolent but provoking actions, such as . . . sit-ins, hunger strikes, occupation or siege."[117] The focus was not always explicitly political but encompassed a wider array of causes, such as preservation of historic buildings, traditional neighborhoods, natural wildlife habitats, and colonial-era postboxes with their royal symbolism.[118] Professor Ma Ngok of the Chinese University of Hong Kong described these new movements as "civil society in self-defense."[119]

Radicalization also became more common in certain parties within the Pan-Democratic coalition, stimulated in part by the adoption after 1997 of a proportional representation system for LegCo elections in geographic constituencies.[120] Having concluded that moderation would never yield genuine change, the spin-offs from the Democratic Party became radical not only in terms of ideology and their views of Beijing, but in their political tactics as well. One Democratic Party member–turned-radical told me, "Without struggle, there will be no change."[121] The League of Social Democrats is the most obvious case in point. It has acted as the grassroots champion of underprivileged groups, and its leader, Leung "Long Hair" Kwok-hung, uses his personal appearance to distinguish himself from the clean-cut, tailored establishment. He often wears a Che Guevara T-shirt and allows his hair to grow to the middle of his back. A member of the LegCo, Leung has regularly disrupted proceedings with publicity-grabbing stunts: chanting slogans in the middle of one of the chief executive's annual policy addresses or throwing an effigy of Pinocchio (complete with a long nose) in another to imply that C. Y. Leung did not tell the truth.[122]

Whether the activists came from political parties or civil society, they were propelled by a belief that "direct democracy," as expressed through the more radical form of protests, was a more effective way to achieve their goals than by working through the established political system based on indirect and limited representative democracy. And they could point to various victories that demonstrations and protests had scored. The massive turnout in the 2003 protest against the anti-subversion legislation forced the withdrawal of the proposed bill. Then, in 2012, just after he became chief executive, C. Y. Leung proposed that public schools should give more emphasis to "moral and national education." The likely assumption of this initiative was a belief that young people did not sufficiently appreciate that Hong Kong and its residents were part of "one country." But the proposal backfired after an activist group of secondary school students calling themselves Scholarism (*Xuemin Sichao*, literally "student thought tide") emerged out of nowhere and mounted vigorous opposition to the plan. By September 2012, Leung capitulated and canceled the 2015 deadline for mandatory implementation.[123]

Needless to say, the establishment camp regarded these developments with great concern. Ho Lok-Sang, a conservative Lingnan University scholar, warned in the *China Daily,* a pro-PRC newspaper, political polarization casts a "dark shadow" over constitutional reform. The "anti-Beijing camp . . . directly challenges the Basic Law." The pro-Beijing camp has "panicked" and is "tightening up the rules. . . . These are signs of a vicious cycle which could certainly bring about the demise of universal suffrage," because mutual antagonism would negate any possibility of securing a two-thirds majority in the LegCo.[124] Furthermore, the growing number of protests have made anachronistic the principle in the Basic Law concerning the pace and scope of political reform: that it should occur "in light of the actual situation in the Hong Kong SAR and in accordance with the principle of gradual and orderly progress." More civil disobedience meant that if political change was gradual, it would not be orderly. Conversely, preserving order would require more rapid reform.

The evolution of Hong Kong protests sowed the seeds for the 2014 Umbrella Movement, which possessed many of the more recent demonstrations' characteristics: spontaneity, diffused leadership, mobilization through both traditional and social media, confrontation with the sources of order, and, most of all, civil disobedience through occupation of public spaces. In contrast to most post-2006 protests, however, this demonstration was about fundamental constitutional issues, which had been the stock and trade of the Pan-Democratic leaders who had organized and led pre-2006 rallies. But these traditional leaders were effectively sidelined in the fall of 2014, when student leaders and their radical supporters set overly ambitious goals and remained resolute.

The focus of the Occupy protests was not inequality; rather, it was the future of the political system and whether voters could pick their senior leaders. But the concentration of economic and political power that disenfranchised the middle class fueled a much larger confrontation than otherwise might have been the case. In a letter sent to the PRC's Premier Li Keqiang during the protests, the Hong Kong Federation of Students complained about the "extreme inequality of opportunity" and the dominance of a "few elites" over the "political and economic lifeline." The letter continued, "Under an undemocratic system, political and business elites collude to manipulate society, the government ignores public opinion, the government doesn't have the heart nor the ability to promote any just reform, and the public grievances get bigger and bigger."[125]

Conclusion

Hong Kong's protest culture is not an idiosyncratic phenomenon. Throughout East Asia, the "millennial" generation is emerging as a distinct political force. Surveys by the Asian Barometer indicate that millennials in the region are well educated and follow politics closely, which has given them a sense of their own power. Compared to their parents' and grandparents' generations, they are not apathetic about politics and are strongly committed to democracy. However, they have high expectations that government will perform well and ensure equity for all. Moreover, they "eschew traditional forms of political participation such as voting, campaigning, and joining political parties." They rely more on mobilization through networks and social media and have less confidence in the "normal channels of vertical accountability"—elections, representative government, and so on—and more on direct action.[126]

If Karl Marx and Frederick Engels were living today, they might even conclude that the oligarchic character of Hong Kong's system met their definition of "the executive of the modern [capitalist] state"; the state in a capitalist system had little or no autonomy of its own but was no more and no less than "a committee for managing the common affairs of the whole bourgeoisie."[127] They would also likely note the irony that this system, created by the British imperial government, has been sustained and institutionalized by the Chinese *Communist* Party, which still purports to be a Marxist-Leninist party.[128] Nor would Marx and Engels be surprised that a liberal oligarchy has produced popular alienation and social conflict. For many in Hong Kong, the absence of electoral democracy became a potent explanation for decline of social and economic opportunity. Achieving democracy came to be valued not just for its own sake but also as a means to promote equity. Excluded from both boardrooms and government chambers, many citizens believed that their only option was to take to the streets in mass protests. The Occupy and Umbrella Movements of 2014 may have focused on reforming the electoral system to correct the concentration of political power, but they were fueled by frustrations over the concentration of power.

FIVE

Debating Universal Suffrage Before Occupy

ROUND I

In the decision it made on electoral reform in Hong Kong in December 2007, the Standing Committee of the National People's Congress of the PRC (NPC-SC) sent an ambiguous message regarding democracy and universal suffrage in Hong Kong. It declared that the election of Hong Kong's chief executive in 2017 "may be implemented by the method of universal suffrage," thus increasing hope that the general promise in the Basic Law would be fulfilled.[1] Furthermore, once such an election for chief executive took place, universal suffrage "may" then be used to elect "all" the members of the Legislative Council (LegCo) in 2020. For the election of the chief executive, however, the NPC-SC set the condition that "in accordance with the Hong Kong Basic Law and this Decision," a "broadly representative" nominating committee using "democratic procedures" would pick "a certain number of candidates." To optimists, the decision seemed to promise that voters in Hong Kong would decide who would be their chief executive and who would serve in the LegCo. To pessimists, the stipulation regarding the nominating committee suggested that Beijing would still seek to control who was elected chief executive. For better or for worse, the NPC-SC decision was the designated way to break the logjam over Hong Kong's political system.

Yet the NPC-SC decision was only a point of departure. Its words were subject to competing interpretations and thus were an invitation for political struggle. Start with the term "universal suffrage": it became clear that for the election of the chief executive (CE), what Beijing meant by this term was that all qualified local voters would choose among a list of candidates and the winner would become CE, subject to Beijing's formal appointment. That is, the entire electorate of the Hong Kong Special Administrative Region (Hong Kong SAR) would replace the very narrow franchise of the 1,200-member election committee. The Pan-Democrats agreed that the franchise for the CE election included all voters, but they interpreted "universal suffrage" also to mean an end to any procedural control over the electoral outcome. For that broad interpretation, they appealed to the "international standard" of article 21 of the Hong Kong Bill of Rights Ordinance, which was copied from the International Covenant on Civil and Political Rights, which states that "every permanent resident shall have the right and the opportunity . . . without unreasonable restrictions . . . to vote *and to be elected* at genuine periodic elections which shall be by universal and equal suffrage" (emphasis added). For its narrower interpretation of universal suffrage, Beijing and the Hong Kong government asserted that, on the basis of the exclusive authority of the Basic Law itself and article 13 of the relevant Hong Kong ordinance, "article 21 does not require the establishment of an elected Executive or Legislative Council in Hong Kong."[2]

Just because the PRC government had opened the door to more popular government did not mean that all the parties concerned would find a way to walk across the threshold together. The implication discussed in chapter 2 is that the two political camps began the debate over electoral reform with a serious deficit of mutual trust, and the implication of chapter 4 is that other socioeconomic grievances also fueled the demands of the democratic camp. Even if a compromise was possible in the abstract, whether the contending forces could actually come to a point of consensus, and with enough broad support to secure a two-thirds margin in the LegCo, was another question. As a practical matter, because establishment members already had a simple LegCo majority, the government would only have to secure the support of four Pan-Democratic LegCo members to create that majority. But getting those votes was not a certainty. In the event, and as intimated in chapter 3, both camps engaged in tactics that only deepened the other's suspicions about its intentions, such as street demonstrations by radical democrats and "the authorities know best" dictates from Beijing. And finally, there were splits within each camp. The disagreement within the establishment over who should be its candidate in the 2012 CE election still festered, while moderate and radical democrats struggled over more portentous, and emotionally raw, tensions.

The Umbrella Movement in the fall of 2014 was the dénouement of a drama in three acts. The first act, a period of positioning on both sides, unfolded throughout 2013. The critical event was the emergence of Occupy Central as the key instrument of opposition to Beijing's approach. The second act began in December 2013 with the Hong Kong SAR government's issuance of the first public consultation document on electoral reform, which began to clarify the NPC-SC's 2007 decision. The third act was a period of maneuvering: the Hong Kong SAR government formally sought Beijing's guidance on parameters for the CE election; the NPC-SC responded with a new decision on August 31, 2014; and then the opposition mobilized in earnest, but in a way very different from the Occupy Central plan.

The drama's major characters remained constant throughout all three acts: the central government in Beijing; the Hong Kong SAR government, which acted as Beijing's agent but also sought to preserve its autonomy; Hong Kong's political parties; several "eminent persons" such as Anson Chan, a former chief secretary, and local political scientists; media organizations across the political spectrum; the business community, which generally supported the Hong Kong SAR government; civil society organizations, which backed the Pan-Democrats, particularly the radical wing; ad hoc groups such as the Alliance for True Democracy, which brought together pro-democracy members of the LegCo; and finally, like a Greek chorus, the citizens of Hong Kong.[3]

In every scene of this drama, the various actors played their assigned roles and spoke their appropriate lines. Still, the debate was continuous and lively. There was a degree of improvisation, with new ideas emerging almost daily, and criticisms and counter-ideas following the very next day. Each side sought to frame discussions in ways that would shape outcomes in a direction favorable to its own agenda. The Beijing and Hong Kong governments stressed the parameters defined by the Basic Law and NPC-SC decisions, whereas the democrats argued for "genuine universal suffrage based on 'international norms,'" a reference to the International Covenant on Civil and Political Rights. The Communist and conservative newspapers supported the government, whereas *Apple Daily* championed the democrats. In the middle, the *South China Morning Post* and the Chinese-language *Ming Pao* consistently called on the two camps to find a compromise. Although neither silent nor inactive, student groups mostly waited in the wings until the last scene of the third act, at which point they made their dramatic entrance.

As for plot, there were four ways the story could end. The first was that the threat of mass civil disobedience would lead Beijing and the Hong Kong SAR government to back down from their proposal and offer an alternative plan acceptable to the democrats. The second was that Beijing would persist and hold to a hard line: ruling out any compromise and reinstating CE selection by the 1,200-member election committee for the 2017 elections if the democrats did not capitulate. The third was that the two camps would reach a mutually acceptable compromise that incorporated elements of their respective proposals. The fourth was that the two sides would not agree because of the deep fog of mistrust between them, even though a "good enough" compromise was objectively available. That would be a genuine tragedy.

China Focuses More on National Security

The fragmentation and polarization of the Hong Kong political system and the deepening inequality in Hong Kong society discussed in earlier chapters shaped the contest over electoral reform. But there was one other factor that has also had an impact: the Chinese leadership's increasingly dire assessment of the national security of the People's Republic. To understand the consequences, a basic understanding of the PRC policy-formulation and implementation process is needed.

The PRC regime is divided into three principal hierarchies: the Communist Party, the government, and the military. Each hierarchy has a leadership component: in the Party, the Political Bureau (Politburo) and its Standing Committee (PBSC); in the government, the State Council or cabinet; and in the military, the Central Military Commission. Below the leadership level, each hierarchy has policy and operational units (e.g., the organization department in the Party and the ministry of foreign affairs in the government hierarchy).

Although separate and distinct on an organization chart, in reality the three hierarchies overlap considerably. In an effort to enhance coherence in formulating, executing, and monitoring policy on major issues, the regime's leaders employ a task-force system. The authority to create task forces, which are termed either commissions or leading groups, is in the hands of the Politburo and PBSC. Task forces are led by a member of the Politburo. A senior official at the level of a government state councilor or minister assists the head of each task force and is responsible for its operation. There are also select "primary leading groups," which are headed directly by PBSC members.[4] Their purpose is to coordinate policy among the various agencies that have some stake in the issue concerned. Each agency has its own views of what each policy should be and believes its own views are most important.

In August 1978, when institutions were being created or recreated during the early post-Mao period, the Hong Kong and Macau Affairs Leading Group (HKMALG) was established under the aegis of the Party. Presumably it was this body that played the central role in guiding the policy that Deng Xiaoping set concerning negotiations with the British, the drafting of the Basic Law, and the management of Hong Kong policy after reversion. From 2008 to early 2013, the head of the HKMALG was Xi Jinping, who was then a member of the Politburo Standing Committee and vice president of China. After Xi became general secretary of the Party and the president of the government, Zhang Dejiang became head of the HKMALG.[5] Zhang was ranked number four in the PBSC and served as chairman of the National People's Congress, China's legislature. It made sense that the NPC chairman would be in charge of Hong Kong affairs, since the Basic Law is so central to policy toward the Hong Kong SAR. In addition, Zhang had served as the Party's first secretary in Guangdong Province, which borders both Hong Kong and Macau. Zhang's deputy was Wang Guangya, a career diplomat with minister rank. He headed the Hong Kong and Macau Affairs Office of the State Council, which provides staff support to the leading group.

The Beijing government does not announce the members of the HKMALG, but a Hong Kong media report in May 2016 revealed some of them: the director of the Hong Kong and Macau Affairs Office, the ministries of public security, state security, and commerce, and the People's Bank of China. Other members, I would speculate, likely included the minister of foreign affairs, the director of the Party's United Front Work Department, and a vice chairman of the Chinese People's Political Consultative Conference responsible for Hong Kong.[6]

Some of these entities have field offices in Hong Kong, such as the commissioner for foreign affairs, the garrison of the People's Liberation Army, and the Liaison Office of the Central People's Government, which serves under the Hong Kong and Macau Affairs Office of the State Council. Agencies that do not have their own dedicated field offices in Hong Kong most likely send officers to serve in the Liaison Office. The party's Propaganda Department conveys daily messages through *Ta Kung Pao, Wen Wei Po, China Daily,* and other media outlets, while the United Front Work Department cultivates ties with a variety of pro-Beijing groups. Liaison Office personnel support the electoral activities of the Democratic Alliance for the Betterment and Progress of Hong Kong and the Federation of Trade Unions, and the security agencies liaise with their Hong Kong SAR counterparts.

These field operations, representing different bureaucratic interests, are also the central government's eyes and ears on Hong Kong developments. Their respective analyses inform senior decisionmakers' deliberations for better or for worse, and probably distort Hong Kong reality to some extent. The analysis from Hong Kong that evokes the most resonance among senior leaders in Beijing can empower some agencies over others.

The Xi Jinping leadership took the reins of governing China in late 2012 and early 2013 with a heightened sense of the internal and external dangers facing China and a need to respond with more vigilance. This affected how Beijing perceived the tension between those in Hong Kong who sought democracy quickly and those who preferred it gradually or not at all, and this in turn affected how Beijing set the parameters for universal suffrage.

Feeling vulnerable was not a new phenomenon for the Chinese Communist regime, and it has not lacked institutions and capabilities to respond. Even before the arrival of the Communist regime, Chinese statecraft had been shaped by something of a siege mentality. It may not have been as intense as during the Cold War or right after the Tiananmen protests of 1989. Yet there remains a "tight linkage between external and internal security in Chinese thinking." That is, "internal chaos" *(neiluan)* is an invitation to "trouble from outside" *(neiluan waihuan)*. "Many Chinese are predisposed to think that the weapon of choice for the outside world (not least the United States) to defeat China is first to attack the periphery and diminish internal social and political cohesion."[7] Fears of separatist activity in Taiwan, Tibet, and Xinjiang Province were long-standing, and the Falun Gong cult spooked President Jiang Zemin in 1999, which led to a root-and-branch suppression of the organization. Over the next decade, the number of "mass incidents"—protests—on the mainland grew, usually the product of corrupt deals between local officials and businessmen at the expense of common people. The regime, which had been relatively tolerant of the presence of foreign NGOs in China despite its long-standing fear of independent organizations, came to see them in a more paranoid light after 2005, when Russian President Vladimir Putin alerted Hu Jintao, Xi's predecessor as president, that foreign NGOs engaged in subversive activities. In light of these long-standing threat perceptions, Beijing created a complex web of institutions and capabilities on which the regime relied to respond.[8] This blending of internal and external concerns was captured in the formulation, in a 2011 official statement, of China's "core interests," the issues that Beijing would defend at all costs: "state sovereignty, national security, territorial integrity and national reunification, China's political system established by the Constitution and overall social stability, and the basic safeguards for ensuring sustainable economic and social development."[9]

Once Xi Jinping became China's paramount leader, he placed even greater priority on the protection of national security and on enhancing the regime's institutional capacity to respond. This became a problem for Hong Kong because the implementation of Xi's new policy emphasis took place at precisely the time when political conflict intensified in the Hong Kong SAR.

The first sign that the new leadership was taking a new tack came in December 2012 when Xi made a speech that revived an early 1990s discussion among Chinese policy circles on the reasons for the fall of the Soviet Union. Although the text of Xi's address was not published, he reportedly attributed the collapse to wavering "ideals and convictions" of Soviet Communist leaders. During the 1990s discussion, Mikhail Gorbachev's decisions to democratize the Soviet system had come under heavy Chinese criticism.[10] In 2013, the Chinese Communist Party (CCP) elaborated on Xi's theme of the danger of following a Soviet path by disseminating a four-part video on the decline and fall of the USSR.[11]

The next signal came in spring 2013, when the CCP issued the major policy statement Document Number 9; it conveyed the leadership's views and instructions on what it regarded as pressing issues in political and ideological spheres. It inveighed against seven ideas that were circulating in China and that, the Party asserted, represented a challenge to its rule. The first six were dangers posed in some way by the West: constitutionalism, universal values, civil society, economic neoliberalism, independent mass media, and the historical "nihilism" of criticizing the Party's record. Document Number 9 warned that "failure in the ideological sphere can result in major disorders" and called on leaders at all levels to face the threat posed by Western political ideas.[12] The irony of Document Number 9 was that at least some of these "threatening" ideas were entrenched realities in the Hong Kong SAR.

More consequential than Document Number 9 was the November 2013 decision by the Party's Central Committee to establish the National Security Commission. The CCP already had a number of organizations in charge of protecting the regime and China from threats. But none of its arrangements provided the level of coordination among different bureaucracies that the leadership sought, or adequately managed to address both internal and external threats. The National Security Leading Group, established in 1999, was the most recent example of institutional engineering, but it had apparently not met expectations. The creation of a commission, which administratively is at a higher level in the Communist system than a leading group, reflected both the leadership's dissatisfaction with prior experiments and its commitment to find a viable solution: the commission would be better able to integrate the handling of internal and external threats.[13]

Over the next year the Party leadership initiated a series of steps to realize Xi's objective to strengthen the PRC's national security:

- The commission was formally established in January 2014. Xi Jinping was named chairman and Premier Li Keqiang and President Zhang Dejiang of the National People's Congress were named vice-chairmen.[14]
- The National Security Commission's first session was held in April and was chaired by Xi. Soon after, national security was declared the topic of a Politburo study session, a signal that this was an issue of high salience. Xi spoke and called for "a resolute strike on secession, infiltration and sabotage by hostile forces within and outside China."[15]
- In May 2014, the PRC released its first National Security Blue Book (a Blue Book is one way that the regime presents its policies to the general public). Reportedly, the publication warned that China was threatened by the "export of Western democracy." A *People's Daily* article published the same day described the NSC's four functions, one of which was to coordinate the response to specific threats involving international actors. Hong Kong was apparently mentioned.[16]
- In December 2014, a draft National Security Law was submitted to the National People's Congress (of which Zhang Dejiang was chairman).
- In January 2015, the Politburo approved a blueprint of national security policies. In its decision, it said that "social conflicts are frequent and overlapping, and security risks and challenges, both foreseeable and hard to anticipate, are unprecedented."
- In late May 2015, the government released a document on the country's military strategy that, among other things, cited the growing complexity of internal and external security and the need to "uphold a holistic view of national security and to balance the two."[17]

What did all of this have to do with Hong Kong? The most authoritative signal came in June 2014 when the PRC State Council Information Office issued a white paper on Hong Kong, just as debate over electoral reform in the Hong Kong SAR was becoming more intense. The document by and large was an explicit restatement of Chinese policy concerning Hong Kong, and a catalogue of all the ways that Beijing thought the territory should be grateful to be a part of China. But it also included not-so-subtle hints that officials in the capital viewed developments in Hong Kong through a more focused lens of national security. It noted the three core interests—sovereignty, security, and development interests—and stressed the need for "patriotic" Hong Kong SAR officials to protect them. And it reminded readers of the dangers of collusion between external and internal adversaries, stating: "Meanwhile, it is necessary to stay alert to the attempt of outside forces to use Hong Kong to interfere in China's domestic affairs, and [to] prevent and repel the attempt made by a very small number of people who act in collusion with outside forces to interfere with the implementation of 'one country, two systems' in Hong Kong."[18]

The National Security Law, which the NPC passed on July 1, 2015, had its own signals for Hong Kong. Article 11 stated, "China's sovereignty and territorial integrity brook no division. Safeguarding national sovereignty, unity, and territorial integrity is the common obligation of all the Chinese people, *including the compatriots in Hong Kong, Macau, and Taiwan*" (emphasis added). According to article 40, "Hong Kong Special Administrative Region and Macau Special Administrative Region shall exercise their responsibilities for safeguarding national security."[19] (Was this perhaps a reference to the unfulfilled requirement in article 23 of the Basic Law that the Hong Kong SAR enact anti-subversion legislation?)

David Zweig, a professor of social science at Hong Kong University of Science and Technology, writing in September 2014 right before the beginning of the Occupy Movement, presciently and convincingly argued that Beijing increasingly viewed the Hong Kong issue through national security terms. Radicalism within the Hong Kong SAR and the growing misperception that "foreign forces" were creating the trouble gave the Chinese leadership reasons to take a hard line. Zweig concluded that for the PRC, "Allowing a system that could even possibly allow for the election of a chief executive with close ties to the US or Britain was simply too scary." The irony is that mandating a system that either would be rejected in the LegCo or would lead to the selection of a CE without public legitimacy would arguably promote more instability than a genuinely competitive process.[20] Alex Lo, writing in the *South China Morning Post,* noted that Beijing and the democrats were each acting on the basis of their fears, which would foster an outcome that neither wanted. He held out the hope that each side might go halfway in addressing the fears of the other: "The two sides should negotiate a quid pro quo. If Beijing has a security guarantee in Hong Kong, it may be more open to a system of free elections in future."[21] Yet the increased scope of China's national security fears suggests that isolating the Hong Kong issue as a subject for creative diplomacy would not be so easy.

Proposing Occupy Central

Given Hong Kong's emerging protest culture, it was almost inevitable that some sort of movement would become part of the universal suffrage contest. Occupy Central was formulated by Benny Tai Yiu-ting, a professor in the Faculty of Law at the University of Hong Kong; Chan Kin-man, a sociologist at the Chinese University of Hong Kong; and the Reverend Chu Yiu-ming, a Baptist minister. Although Hong Kong, like other major cities around the world, had its own anti-capitalist "Occupy" movement in 2011, the version that Tai, Chan, and Chu unveiled in March 2013 was unique. It had deeper intellectual grounding and its civil disobedience component came at the end of the process rather than constituting the entire initiative. The plan had four proposed stages:

1. Participants take an oath, to be cast as a legal document, recognizing the nonviolent character of the movement but leaving it up to each individual whether to actually break the law.
2. Occupy Central holds "deliberation days," modeled on the concept of public consultation developed by the American political scientists Bruce Ackerman and James Fishkin.[22] The concept is for participants to be assigned to small focus groups to discuss political-reform proposals. "The key point of the movement is about developing a democratic culture of rational discussion and consensus building by the people themselves," Tai said. "It is like an open-source [computer] program, with any opinions welcomed."
3. The movement holds some type of voting on the main proposals that emerge from the deliberation days. One means would be a civil referendum, which would create the "authorization" of citizens. An alternative would be a by-election triggered by the resignation of a lawmaker to take place by April or May 2014 to, again, obtain citizens' "authorization."
4. The final stage is a blockade of the roads in the Central District on Hong Kong Island. But Tai regarded this as "the last resort." Deployment of this plan would depend on whether Beijing fulfilled "the expectation of Hong Kongers for genuine universal suffrage that meets international standards." According to the norms of civil disobedience, anyone engaged in disrupting traffic would submit to police arrest and whatever punishment a court imposed.

Not surprisingly, representatives of the PRC government and pro-establishment figures in the Hong Kong SAR criticized the confrontational character of Occupy Central. Focusing on the civil-disobedience part of the campaign, a former Hong Kong member of the National People's Congress predicted that it would "paralyze Hong Kong."[23]

Parallel to the effort of Tai, Chan, and Chu to develop and "sell" the Occupy Central plan, politicians looked for ways to improve the nominating committee created to "suggest" candidates. Most ideas would make that body more representative of the Hong Kong public and so reduce the relative clout of the pro-Beijing members, who dominated the election committee that the nominating committee was to replace. One option offered an alternative route to nomination: getting the signatures of 2 percent of registered voters (about 80,000 signatures).[24] It happened that the civic or popular nomination idea—a variation on the direct-democracy theme—had been proposed before, in 2009, by a radical legislator. At that time the main parties in the democratic camp had rejected it.[25] Not so this time. Predictably, radical democrats supported it; moderates did not oppose it but sought to pair it with other mechanisms; and, Beijing, of course, rejected it.

The First Public Consultation

The issuance of consultation papers is the Hong Kong SAR government's established means for soliciting public views on any major issue requiring significant policy and legislative change. A consultation paper is a type of document that was used by the British government and the British Commonwealth (and is used now in the European Community). The colonial government employed them in Hong Kong before reversion in 1997. In British and colonial practice there were two types of consultation documents: green papers issued early in the policymaking process, and white papers, which set out specific policy ideas and sought additional, more detailed feedback before a bill for legislation was drafted.[26] The post-reversion Hong Kong government dropped the color scheme but preserved the iterative process. Specialists in Hong Kong differ on the value of the mechanism for governance: some believe its actual purpose is to build support rather than elicit contrary views; others think it is effective in securing public input on concrete matters of policy but less so than on questions that are more "constitutional" in character.[27]

The consultation document on universal suffrage—prepared by a government task force composed of Chief Secretary Carrie Lam, the number two person in the government and head of the civil service; Justice Secretary Rimsky Yuen, and Secretary for Constitutional and Mainland Affairs Raymond Tam—was made public on December 4, 2013. It focused on the 2017 chief executive election and the formation of the Legislative Council in 2016 (deciding on how the 2020 LegCo would be elected was deferred to a later time). The paper sought public comment on issues relevant to universal suffrage. In theory, those views would shape the report that Chief Executive C. Y. Leung would make to the Central People's Government, the first step in the five-step process that the NPC-SC had specified in April 2004 for changes in electoral arrangements (see chapter 2). The document was supported by a broad publicity campaign. To provide an initial framing, Li Fei, the chairman of the Basic Law Committee of the PRC National People's Congress, made a highly publicized visit to Hong Kong in mid-November. His principal message was, in effect, that there would be a screening of CE candidates: "The chief executive is accountable to the central government as well as the Hong Kong SAR; this means that the post must be taken up by a person who loves the country as well as Hong Kong—anyone opposed to the central government cannot [take up the top job]." The local Communist press amplified that the Basic Law and NPC-SC statements were the framework for the outlined process. Meanwhile, critics responded that a screening system was actually inconsistent with their reading of the Basic Law.[28]

The paper was quite descriptive, with no overt bias in favor of one approach or the other. On a number of specific issues, it presented (albeit, in footnotes) many of the proposals that were already under public discussion. A reader who was willing to take the time could get some sense of the array of those opinions. Despite its projection of apparent neutrality, however, the document was constructed according to the rigid and sacrosanct blueprint of the Basic Law and NPC-SC pronouncements. The implication was that neither could be amended nor superseded even if it might make policy sense to do so. The document made clear that the nominating committee was the only mechanism available for the selection of CE candidates (hence, no civic nomination), and that it was to be as "broadly representative" as the election committee, which had selected previous CEs—in other words, selectively representative).

Critics responded quickly. Anson Chan, who as the government's chief secretary during the 1990s had been responsible for many consultation papers, said that "no self-respecting administrative officer" would have presented the current document. Frank Ching, a columnist for the *South China Morning*

Post, pointed to several places where the consultation document had prejudged the outcome of the exercise, writing that it was "intended to show that the government listens to the people, but [it was] clearly designed to make the people listen to the government."[29] *Ming Pao* editorialized on a scenario in which the nominating committee, operating under the government's constraints, might not select a candidate from the democratic camp, even though in the LegCo geographical district elections, the Pan-Democrats typically garnered almost 60 percent of the total vote. *Ming Pao*'s conclusion: "If society is denied the democratization it has craved for three decades, public resentment will erupt like a volcano."[30]

What were the public's views at this point? During the final fortnight of 2013, the Hong Kong Transition Project conducted a survey on political attitudes, and the results were released in April 2014. The survey found that:

- An all-time high of 89 percent of respondents favored direct election of the CE.
- Eighty-five percent supported direct election of LegCo.
- Sixty-four percent opposed converting the CE election committee into the nominating committee required by the Basic Law.
- Within these results, support among young people for the more democratic option exceeded that of the population as a whole.
- As for Hong Kong's political parties, 17 percent of respondents said that the pro-government parties best represented them, 7 percent picked the pro-business parties, 22 percent sided with the moderate democratic parties, 10 percent favored the radical democratic parties, and 43 percent didn't know or had no opinion.[31]

Having set rather strict general parameters for elections by "universal suffrage," which the opposition could not be expected to accept, Hong Kong SAR government officials now called on the democrats (or a few of them) to be pragmatic and find a path to consensus. Xi Jinping reaffirmed the regime's commitment to bringing about universal suffrage, but "urged different sections of Hong Kong society to work together to reach a consensus on constitutional reform based on the Basic Law and decisions by the National People's Congress Standing Committee." NPC Chairman Zhang Dejiang echoed Xi but also said that universal suffrage "shall not undermine national sovereignty, security, developmental interests of the relationship between the central government and the Hong Kong Special Administrative Region." He also implied that the idea of civic nomination was a nonstarter because it was contrary to the Basic Law.[32] Wang Guangya emphasized the need for pragmatism: "To be pragmatic is not to stick to your own thoughts and [to] try to alter [others']. [It is] only by mutual respect that we can reach for a consensus." He still opposed public nomination.[33]

The establishment and Pan-Democratic coalition engaged in thrust and parry on these terms throughout the spring of 2014, but the principal lines of argument did not change. The establishment and Beijing insisted on adherence to past documents and on the right to define what they meant, even as they called for pragmatism and compromise. The opposition emphasized what it regarded as the blatantly anti-democratic character of a system that allowed all Hong Kong voters to cast ballots for the new CE but restricted who could run. Each side questioned the sincerity of the other while newspapers published regular editorials on the specific issue of the day, with conclusions that were usually predictable.[34] Some key figures persevered in trying to find a formula that would bridge the gap between the establishment and democratic camps. Some sought to change the composition of the nominating committee and make it more representative than the Beijing-friendly election committee. Others advocated for setting a lower threshold of the share of committee members required to select a candidate to be considered by the nominating committee.[35] Jasper Tsang Yok-sing, president of the LegCo and no flak for Beijing, offered his view that there were democrats who were patriotic and therefore eligible for nomination.[36] Joseph Cheng, a prominent scholar working with Pan-Democratic legislators, pleaded with moderates and radicals to come up with a single proposal: "If we split, we will be letting our supporters down, and it will greatly weaken our power in struggling for universal suffrage."[37] But divisions within the Pan-Democratic camp made compromise difficult. For instance, Ronny Tong Ka-wah, a Civic Party legislator, was criticized harshly by his own party rank and file for proposing an approach to universal suffrage that excluded popular nomination (or civil nomination, that is, selection of candidates by public petition).

These divisions were on display when I visited Hong Kong in early April 2014. Each person I spoke to favored universal suffrage but differed on the terms and conditions. Each understood that a one person, one vote system for electing the chief executive and LegCo members would not in itself ensure an effective governance system, but they differed on how important electoral reform was to good governance. Moderates at least understood that there might be a solution that would meet each side's minimum demands, but were not willing to make these concessions for fear of appearing weak to both adversaries and allies. Meanwhile, the radical and conservative ends of the spectrum chose to delay any initiative. Beijing and the Hong Kong SAR government were reluctant to table or announce a plan until it became clear what the democrats and Occupy Central would do.

For their part the leaders of Occupy Central were waiting for the government's proposal before deciding whether to go forward with a civil disobedience campaign, but they warned that they might not be able to control their young supporters in the interim. Each side's mistrust of the other's intentions ran deep. Democrats justified their pessimism by pointing to the CCP's growing preference to use repression against internal dissent. Moderate democratic legislators, the ones most likely to support a government proposal, believed that at a minimum the reform package had to ensure a competitive contest in which one of their own could run. Otherwise, they would likely face anger from their radical colleagues and challenges from the left if and when they ran for reelection to the LegCo in 2016.

Also, in mid-April, Beijing made a token effort to advance the discussion by inviting all members of the LegCo to meet PRC officials in Shanghai. Not all democratic members attended, and some who did used the occasion to make symbolic appeals to their core supporters, not to promote compromise.[38] The meeting turned out to be unproductive. The officials' presentation was anything but encouraging to the Pan-Democratic participants. Wang Guangya made the main presentation and only reiterated the centrality of the Basic Law, the requirement that the electoral system must produce a CE who "loved the country and loved Hong Kong," and the need for legislators to "set aside personal opinions, seek common ground, and reserve differences."[39] Li Fei, director of the PRC's Basic Law Committee, was more specific, saying that Beijing opposed nomination by civic petition, political parties, or legislators. Relying on the nominating committee would reduce the risks of "political confrontation, constitutional crisis, and populism."[40]

The five-month period for the public to offer views on the consultation document ended on May 3, 2014. At that point, the government had received approximately 130,000 submissions, 40,000 of which were form letters, suggesting organized and directed efforts to "stuff" the government's mailbox (this was confirmed by a later study: over 90 percent of comments did reflect coordinated efforts).[41] There were eighteen specific proposals from groups running the gamut from Scholarism and the Federation of Students on the left to several moderate proposals in the middle to the DAB and Progress in Hong Kong on the right. Secretary for Constitutional and Mainland Affairs

Raymond Tam announced that the government would take about two months to prepare a consultation report to submit to the CE. He would in turn prepare his own report to submit to the NPC-SC (the first step in the five-step process).[42] One observer remarked that although the consultation process was "less than honest" because, he believed, it introduced requirements that had no legal basis, he did concede that the process "did achieve its main purpose, which was to draw out all the major strands of public thinking."[43]

Moving to the Brink

On May 6, 2014, the Occupy Central movement held its third deliberation day at several venues around Hong Kong. The result was counterproductive and confirmed views that Occupy Central was not a force for compromise. Radical groups dominated the sessions and secured the selection of three proposals, all of which included public nomination, which Beijing had already rejected and which moderate democrats did not deem mandatory. *Ming Pao* editorialized, "Those who took part in the deliberation day discussion are not representative of society"; the two radical ends of the political spectrum were feeding off each other's rigidity. Hong Kong 2020, a political group led by Anson Chan, declared that the outcome had "disenfranchised a large section of the community." One LegCo member insightfully noted that the radicals had created a "small circle" power monopoly similar to Beijing's nominating committee. Even the organizers admitted that the handling of the event was "undesirable."[44] Meanwhile, Regina Ip, head of the pro-Beijing New People's Party, declared that Occupy Central lacked sufficient "moral justifications" to rationalize civil disobedience and was naive about its ability to coerce Beijing on civic nomination.[45]

Then, just as the radicals had marginalized themselves from the community dialogue on universal suffrage, Beijing gave them new relevance. On June 14, when all eyes looked toward the public referendum phase of Occupy Central and the annual July 1 protest, the Information Office of the PRC's State Council issued a white paper on the implementation of its "one country, two systems" policy in the Hong Kong SAR.[46] An already tense situation became even more strained. Beijing believed that too many people in Hong Kong, particularly young people, neither fully understood the "one country, two systems" design nor fully appreciated all that the mainland had done to boost and sustain the Hong Kong SAR's prosperity. For people well versed in minutia of the Basic Law and the catalogue of statements by PRC officials over a long time, this was nothing new.[47] Concerning some issues, such as linking Hong Kong to core security interests, the white paper only made explicit what was already implicit in Chinese policy.[48] Hong Kong's lawyers argued over the implications of the document for the judiciary's independence and the rule of law.[49] What was indisputable was that in stressing the importance of "one country," Beijing had seriously misjudged how its citizens in the "second system" would react to the tone and timing of its persuasion effort. It likely increased turnout for both the referendum and the July 1 demonstrations.[50] And Chief Secretary Carrie Lam was frank to admit that it made the Hong Kong SAR government's job of convincing enough Pan-Democratic LegCo members to support a future reform package more difficult, and it would therefore have to wage a battle for public opinion.[51]

The mid-June Occupy Central public referendum was probably more successful than its organizers expected, even amid intense cyberattacks from opponents.[52] Almost 800,000 people "turned out," either online or in person, and the result was a bit of a surprise. Of the three proposals available, the one made by the less radical ad hoc group Alliance for True Democracy, which did not require civic nomination, got the most votes: 42.1 percent. The two proposals put forward by the Federation of Students and Scholarism and People's Power, which did require civic nomination, got almost 49 percent combined.[53] Finally, 88 percent of the self-selected participants called on the LegCo to reject any proposal that did not meet the standards set forth in the International Covenant on Civil and Political Rights. The government acknowledged that the vote was "one of the ways for Hong Kong citizens to express their opinions."[54] But the most consequential effect of Occupy Central's plan of deliberation and voting was the decision by six Democratic Party members of the Alliance for True Democracy, all moderates, to depart the ad hoc group due to frustration with the lack of compromise. By pushing too hard for their own preferences, the radicals had alienated the moderates and destroyed opposition unity.[55]

The turnout for the July 1 march was also large, so large that it was impossible to estimate accurately how many people participated. But it appeared to approach or equal the size of the 2003 protest, which had swelled owing to opposition to a proposed National Security Law.[56] This time the mostly young crowd was likely motivated by their desire for a public-nomination option in a reform package, but was divided on whether they would actually participate in Occupy Central.[57] After the march ended, several hundred protesters remained and occupied a key thoroughfare in the Central District, apparently to practice techniques of civil disobedience. The police arrived in large numbers after 1:30 A.M. and removed the young people. They avoided using physical force overtly by separating the demonstrators into smaller groups and reduced resistance by incapacitating individual protesters by applying physical pressure to specific nerve points.[58] A former Hong Kong SAR government official soon predicted that Beijing was unlikely to be moved by the protest.[59] A State Department spokesperson provided the U.S. perspective on recent events, stating, "We are not taking positions about what particular [electoral] formula is right for [Hong Kong]. But we certainly believe that an approach that is judged credible by the people of Hong Kong will extend credibility to the person who is ultimately selected as the chief executive and contribute to the long-term stability and prosperity of Hong Kong."[60]

On July 15, Chief Secretary Carrie Lam presented to the LegCo the results of the consultation process that had begun the previous December: government officials had engaged the public on 226 occasions and had received almost 123,000 submissions during the consultation period. The views expressed, plus the results of opinion polls, were compiled in forty-five volumes that were uploaded to the government website. Lam reported "general" agreement on the need to implement universal suffrage for the 2017 CE election based on the Basic Law and NPC-SC decisions, and stated that such a reform would benefit Hong Kong. She also indicated that contending views had been submitted on all the specific aspects of the reform package: composition of the nominating committee; maximum number of candidates; procedures for nomination; and the threshold for nomination. Lam did not provide a clear or detailed breakdown on which of these issues commanded majority support and which did not. On the process for forming LegCo in 2016, she advocated no change from the status quo.

Simultaneously, Chief Executive C. Y. Leung delivered his report on universal suffrage to the NPC-SC, the first step in any constitutional reform process. Regarding the most divisive issue, public nomination, C. Y. Leung told a press conference that the mainstream opposed the idea.[61] There ensued an intense public discussion about the report and its findings. Carrie Lam amplified her stance with essays in major newspapers, but LegCo members challenged her interpretations, and scholars and lawyers disputed the scientific basis of the conclusions.[62] Emily Lau, the head of the Democratic Party—the most moderate among the parties in the Pan-Democratic camp—called on Beijing to "listen to and trust the Hong Kong people," while five chambers of commerce warned of social instability and dire economic consequences if

Occupy Central went forward.[63] Despite—or because of—the continuing polarization of views, there were even louder calls for a reasonable compromise, with the *South China Morning Post* and *Ming Pao* leading the way. *Ming Pao* urged moderates on both sides to assert themselves and to limit the influence of "extremism."[64] Meanwhile, the leaders of Occupy Central reaffirmed their intention to go forward with their protests if the NPC-SC did not accept civic nomination.[65] The position of the government-establishment side was essentially that Pan-Democrats should have to concede, be willing to accept modest change, and have confidence that reform would continue in future years.[66] The most specific olive branch came from Zhang Dejiang, who reportedly said that not all Pan-Democrats should be deemed "unpatriotic," which suggested that some of them might be acceptable candidates in the election for CE. Zhang also appears to have clarified two of Beijing's criteria for candidates: whether the individual allowed foreign interference in Hong Kong's affairs, and whether he or she questioned CCP rule on the mainland.[67]

In the month of August there were restatements of established positions, warnings of consequences if the other side did not back down, calls for moderation and compromise, continuing disagreements within the Pan-Democratic camp, and dueling polls that did little to clarify what the public at large really thought. On August 19, a meeting took place between Pan-Democratic members of the LegCo and Zhang Xiaoming, the head of the Liaison Office of the Central People's Government in Hong Kong, but the frank interchange made no progress in bridging gaps.[68] There were bewildering moments, as on August 28, when a PRC scholar told an audience at the Foreign Correspondents' Club that preserving functional constituencies was necessary to protect the interests of the capitalist class, or when, on the same day, armored vehicles of the People's Liberation Army drove through at least two Hong Kong neighborhoods.[69]

Then, on August 31, the Standing Committee of the National People's Congress announced its formal decision. It reaffirmed its desire that the 2017 election for chief executive be conducted on a one person, one vote basis, but it also confirmed the pessimistic predictions on how candidates would be nominated: solely by the nominating committee, which would be modeled on the old election committee. Over half of the members of the nominating committee would have to approve each candidate in order for him or her to run in the general election.[70] Reactions were consistent with past positions. People aligned with the establishment supported the decision, and those inclined toward the Pan-Democrats opposed it. The general initial assessment (including my own) was that this formula made a competitive election impossible, approval of the decision by the LegCo was highly unlikely, and continued instability was certain.[71]

The fight began over what should happen next. Individuals supportive of the decision hinted that there were still a number of details to be worked out regarding the makeup of the nominating committee, that there were ways to make it more representative, and that not all Pan-Democrats would be screened out.[72] A few scholars offered suggestions to make a competitive election by tinkering with the nominating committee within the parameters that the NPC-SC had laid down.[73] C. H. Tung, a former chief executive, emphasized the importance of having all Hong Kong voters choose the next CE rather than the 1,200-person nominating committee.[74] A local Communist paper, *Wen Wei Po*, was more heavy-handed, indicating that now that Beijing had spoken, it was up to LegCo members in the moderate opposition to ensure that universal suffrage happened.[75] Neither inducements nor warnings had any effect. All twenty-seven Pan-Democratic members of the LegCo vowed to veto Beijing's plan—enough to kill it, given the two-thirds requirement for passage of legislation—and the organizers of Occupy Central vowed that civil disobedience would begin soon.[76]

Evaluation

Before the formal decision of the Standing Committee of the National People's Congress on August 31, it is likely that a sensible compromise could have been found that facilitated the nomination of a Pan-Democratic politician without requiring mechanisms such as civic nomination. This would have required making the nominating committee more representative of Hong Kong society and more flexible in the way it nominated candidates. But the two sides of the debate were unwilling to engage on that basis. This chapter has outlined how the interaction between the two camps in 2013 and 2014 made it much less likely—if not impossible—to reach a mutually acceptable deal.

In late August 2014, Michael DeGolyer, then a professor of government and international studies at Hong Kong Baptist University, compiled the most exhaustive inventory of statements each side had made in this suboptimal interaction.[77] In his view, the establishment side erred in the following ways: it used a policy consultation mechanism to consider constitutional issues; its methods for measuring public sentiment were defective; since C. Y. Leung could run for reelection in 2017, he had a vested interest in the substance of the reform proposal; establishment tactics empowered radical democrats and so undermined the position of moderate centrists; the establishment failed to understand the depth of the governance problems created by functional constituencies and their analogues in the nominating committee; it ignored the alienating effects of housing and pension policies on the sentiments of lower- and middle-class people; and it underestimated the negative public reaction to mainland tourists.[78]

On the pro-democratic side, DeGolyer outlined these strategic errors: ignoring how the new Xi Jinping government would "read" a civil disobedience campaign; attacking democratic moderates for making the compromise they did in 2010 on composition of the LegCo; Occupy Central's adopting only radical proposals in its final consultation deliberation; continuing to ally with or tolerate local groups that sought the overthrow of the CCP; persisting with Occupy Central in the name of democracy when opinion polls demonstrated that a majority of the public was opposed to Occupy Central; undercutting the rule of law through civil disobedience; and rejecting approaches that would improve the nominating committee within Beijing's parameters. Throughout the interaction process, DeGolyer concludes, "Trust building gestures have largely been lacking from both the Pan-Democrats and the Pro-Beijing forces."[79]

However one evaluates the motives and actions of government officials, politicians from both camps, and university professors, it ultimately was high school and university students who translated the general opposition to the NPC-SC's August 31 decision into action. On September 22, three weeks after the NPC-SC decision, they began a week-long boycott of classes. At the end of that week they mounted public protests in the public spaces of the government office complex. Negating both their elders' design for Occupy Central and the plans of Hong Kong Police for a political protest that never happened, they jump-started the Umbrella Movement.

SIX

Electoral Reform After Occupy

ROUND 2

I n the end, the Umbrella Movement changed some things but not others. And the changes were not necessarily for the better.

Postmortem

What the movement did not change was the deep, mistrust-driven conflict over electoral reform. Beijing and its agents and allies in Hong Kong did not bow to the demands of the protesters or become more overtly accommodating toward electoral reform. Far from it; Xi Jinping's authoritative view was to "stay on Beijing's designated path." Hong Kong's people should "take the country's fundamental interests and the overall welfare of Hong Kong as their key consideration, protect social stability, promote economic development, recognize the rule of law and ensure that the region moves steadily along the path of 'one country, two systems' and the Basic Law."[1]

Other Beijing officials weighed in during and after the protest clearance operations that occurred after Hong Kong courts ordered the occupations end. Zhang Rongshun, vice-chairman of the Legislative Affairs Commission of the Standing Committee of the National People's Congress (NPC-SC), said on December 13 that Hong Kong needed "re-enlightenment" toward the one country, two systems principle, because some people there lacked the feeling of belonging to one nation. He also admitted that the opposition had won the battle in Hong Kong society over what the principle meant, and so a better explanation of the principle by the authorities to the people was required.[2] On December 12, immediately after the protests ended, Chen Zou'er, former deputy director of the State Council's Hong Kong and Macau Affairs Office, called for a "comprehensive treatment" of the city's problems, not "small fixes and patches." He called for a "rational and pragmatic discussion" on political development, and to build a consensus with the parameters laid out by the central government.[3]

PRC media amplified Xi's prescriptions. One essay called on Hong Kong residents to abandon their bias for civic nomination and against Beijing's approach to universal suffrage, as if those were the only two options.[4] Another essay counseled the protesters to learn the key lesson: that "treating Beijing as an enemy, instead of a friend, will only lead Beijing to treat them as enemies. And Beijing will not allow its enemies to rule Hong Kong. Confrontational, antagonistic tactics will fail."[5] *Wen Wei Po,* one of Hong Kong's Communist newspapers, argued that moderate democrats had been the biggest losers from the protest movement and should support Beijing's reform package to regain the support of neutral voters.[6]

The Hong Kong SAR government expressed different views at different times. As clearance of the protest sites wrapped up in mid-December, Chief Secretary Carrie Lam said it would be "naive" to assume that clearing occupied areas would end the protest movement, and that the government had a lot of work to do in addressing the political and social problems that the protests had exposed.[7] In his annual policy address, Chief Executive C. Y. Leung provided a blunt and selective message on electoral political reform.[8] He quoted relevant sections of the Basic Law and past NPC-SC decisions to make the point that "the substantive power to decide on constitutional development rests with the Central Authorities," and called for wariness regarding proposals that were inconsistent with the Basic Law. The fact that 5 million voters would be able to select the chief executive in 2017 was in itself a "big step forward." Leung said that conflicts over universal suffrage reflected misunderstandings about the Hong Kong SAR's status under one country, two systems and asserted that the Hong Kong public had resorted to "means of expression that deny others of their rights, and [he would] not condone any unlawful acts." Through all of this, Leung offered no ideas on how the nominating committee might be "perfected" to facilitate a competitive election or explain why that was not possible. The closest he got in his policy address to acknowledging the sources of middle-class alienation were his proposals for tackling the housing issue (but this was presented as a "livelihood" issue, not a political one).

Going forward, the range of views among Hong Kong's political parties on election reform was predictable. Democrats remained unalterably opposed to "screening" and became even more pessimistic that compromise was possible. Regina Ip, chair of the conservative New People's Party, offered the most alarmist retrospective view from the establishment side on the goals of the Umbrella Movement. The rhetoric may have been about democracy, but "right from the start, the quest for self-rule was evident from slogans ... writ large on the backdrop of the stage when students kicked off their sit-in."[9] Ip and other conservatives were no doubt sincere in their belief, and some in the protest movement certainly had goals more radical than a genuinely democratic electoral system. Yet for conservatives to start with the unproven belief that the movement as a whole was essentially seditious did not bode well for a compromise on electoral arrangements.

In editorials, the two most independent newspapers cautioned the government against interpreting the end of the protests as the end of its problems. *Ming Pao* worried that a second consultation process based on Beijing's August 31 decision would "again lead to citizens' dissatisfaction and spark confrontations." The *South China Morning Post* reminded the government that however inappropriate the students' goals and tactics were, "Their grievances embrace widespread dissatisfaction with Hong Kong's governance that goes beyond its current chief executive or political reform." Yet the editorial stated there was an opportunity with "sharpened focus and new urgency to engage the whole community in finding a way forward on political reform, and more effective ways to deal with long-standing issues."[10] A pro-Beijing commentator blamed Hong Kong's problems on "spoiled and immature young people," whereas those sympathetic to the students commended them for their restraint.[11] Writing in the *South China Morning Post*, the veteran columnist Philip Bowring acknowledged that the students had lacked a strategy and Mike Rowse criticized the Pan-Democrats for bringing the work of LegCo to a halt and fostering political paralysis. But Bowring also questioned "whether the government itself and its core in the business and bureaucratic elite have learned any lessons about the links between economic discontent and political representation."[12] Yue Chim Richard Wong, a *South China Morning Post* columnist and Hong Kong University professor, concurred on the deep causes of the city's discontent and the need for a political system that accommodated both majority wishes and minority interests. But he said, "This is not the time for political brinksmanship."[13] Meanwhile, across the border, the PRC regime relaxed its usual restrictions on mainland netizens writing on affairs in Hong Kong, allowing criticism of the protests.[14]

Finally, at a conference in Beijing in March 2015, mainland officials, former officials, and scholars with access to the government held their own postmortem and "self-criticism" reflection. The consensus seemed to be that Beijing had been too "lenient" with Hong Kong. It had not pushed hard enough on initiatives such as national security legislation (article 23 of the Basic Law) and national education. It had emphasized "one country" too little, which allowed certain elements in Hong Kong to stress "two systems" too much.[15] The same month, Yu Zhengsheng, the member of the Politburo Standing Committee responsible for United Front work, called for greater communication and exchanges with Hong Kong's "youngsters."[16] The high-level focus on shaping the thinking of young people would be a continuing theme, as if Beijing's only problem was with the younger members of the population.

The quantifiable economic consequences of the Umbrella Movement were mixed. The Hang Seng Index, the best measure of short-term business sentiment in the territory, rose throughout the spring and summer, reaching a peak of 25,317.95 on September 3, 2014. It then began to slide, going to under 23,000 on September 30, the first trading day after the Umbrella Movement began, and then again on October 16. By November it briefly rebounded, reaching 24,411.98 on November 26, before sliding again, to 22,585.84 on December 17, just when protest sites were being dismantled. A bull market then emerged and the daily index was safely over 24,000 for most of January and February 2015.[17] The Hang Seng's December 2014 decline preceded that of the S&P 500 by a few weeks, and its January rebound may have been a bit stronger than that of the S&P. So, if there is any correlation between the Hong Kong stock market and the political instability caused by the Umbrella Movement, it is modest.[18]

The provisional figure for Hong Kong's GDP during the fourth quarter of 2014 (more or less the duration of the protests) was $78.8 billion, which was almost 5 percent more than the figure for the fourth quarter of 2013, and 2 percent more than the third quarter of 2014.[19] Retail sales declined marginally from the year before, and foot traffic in Pacific Place, a shopping mall in the Admiralty neighborhood, dropped by 6 percent. Naturally, retailers blamed the protests for these declines.[20] In February 2015, Financial Secretary John Tsang warned that "prolonged political bickering" might affect investor confidence.

A poll conducted in late 2014 by the Institute of Asia-Pacific Studies of the Chinese University of Hong Kong found a partial shift in public attitudes. While respondents did not really change the political camp they supported, there was growing opposition, even within Pan-Democratic supporters, to the "radical behavior" of anti-government forces. The inference was made that the democratic camp was losing support from middle-of-the-road citizens.[21] A mid-January poll commissioned by the *South China Morning Post,* however, found that 48 percent of respondents wanted legislators to vote down any electoral reform proposal drafted according to Beijing's stated parameters, and almost 42 percent supported approval—a balance of opinion that had barely changed from right after the NPC-SC decision.[22]

The opposition stood its ground, or at least sought to create an impression of unity and resolve. All twenty-seven Pan-Democratic LegCo members vowed to vote against Beijing's reform proposal, thus killing any prospect for the government to reach the two-thirds threshold for passage. One LegCo member from the Democratic Party asserted, "C.Y. can give up his hope of splitting the pan-democrats."[23] The groups that had occupied the three public places acknowledged that they had not retained the "hearts and minds" of the people, and promised a continued effort to spread their views to the public. But they also vowed to pursue their goals through other means, for example, through a "non-cooperation movement" that urged citizens to delay paying their rent and only pay taxes bit by bit. Benny Tai, a founder of Occupy Central, warned that "more radical actions" could occur in the future if the government did not institute "genuine" universal suffrage.[24]

Beneath the surface, however, divisions remained between moderates and radicals, and between young people and their elders. The Hong Kong Federation of Students (HKFS) began to collapse from within as university student unions launched a movement to leave the federation due to unhappiness over HKFS leaders' lack of transparency and consultation during the protests.[25] Meanwhile, new radical groups, such as Student Front and ChildeaHK, emerged and further reduced the possibility of unity in the future.[26] Joshua Wong, the head of Scholarism and one of the self-appointed leaders of the Umbrella Movement, said that its main achievement was to increase political awareness and make civil disobedience more acceptable as a political instrument. "Of course, this time we gained nothing by way of political reform . . . but we didn't lose the war, because we'll start the next round stronger than we did this one."[27] Some participants focused mainly on their motivations for joining and ways the protests had raised their political consciousness. One said, "We didn't successfully fight for what we wanted, but more and more teenagers will think more about the government and society, and one day we will have some success."[28] One activist did comment on the results of the movement vis-à-vis the larger goal of democratization: "In terms of legacy, I still don't know. It's not necessarily good. Differences and divides have grown."[29]

This realistic assessment might also have included the judgment that the Umbrella Movement failed in its primary stated objective of pressuring Beijing and the Hong Kong SAR government to change their starting point for discussing universal suffrage. Whether it happened before or after the protests, the deepening "differences and divides" probably decreased the likelihood of salvaging a competitive election within Beijing's procedural parameters.

Shifts in Sentiment

Even if the Umbrella Movement failed to achieve its objectives, and even though the democratic opposition was in a weaker position after the protests than before, Beijing and its allies faced a broader and more disturbing reality: growing localist or nativist sentiment. Since 1997, the Public Opinion Programme at Hong Kong University has asked residents whether they see themselves as a "Hongkonger," "Hongkonger in China," "Chinese in Hong Kong," or "Chinese." Between late 2001 and mid-2009, the share who regarded themselves as "Hongkongers" was about 30 percent. Thereafter, it was generally at 40 percent. There was a similar rise in the share of respondents who saw themselves as Hongkongers in China.[30] The Hong Kong Transition Project found in a late 2012 poll that, significantly, young people identified with Hong Kong much more than their elders. Only 4 percent of those eighteen to twenty-nine years old regarded themselves as Chinese, as opposed to 48 percent of those thirty to fifty-nine. Sixty-five percent of the younger cohort regarded themselves as Hong Kong Chinese and 17 percent of the older cohort did so.[31] Some scholars believe that China's own policies and behavior had caused this shift.[32]

In the Hong Kong Transition Project poll, changes in identity translated into clear preferences on what those surveyed wished to promote and protect in Hong Kong. "Chinese historical and cultural identity" was selected by 33 percent of respondents, and "Hong Kong's identity as pluralistic and international" was chosen by 52 percent, a balance of opinion that was fairly constant across generational groups.[33] For at least a few people, these preferences translated into actions. Groups emerged to protect historical sites, for example, an iconic train station and ferry piers, and ancient villages set for destruction to make way for a high-speed, cross-border rail line. Mainlanders who exploited Hong Kong's resources (hospital beds, milk powder, and so on) or flooded the territory to buy luxury goods became easy targets for Hong Kong residents' frustration.

There were other sprouts of localism. In 2011, a Lingnan University professor published a book called *Hong Kong as a City-State*, while some localists began to shun the annual commemoration of the June 4, 1989, Tiananmen incident, on the rationale that "building a democratic China should not be the responsibility of Hongkongers." In the 2012 LegCo elections, two Pan-Democrats ran on a localist platform, and students created the activist group Scholarism to oppose national and moral education.[34] Localism sometimes mixed with radicalism, such as when radicals forced the departure of a mainland-born twelve-year-old who had been kept in hiding in Hong Kong for nine years by relatives.[35] Very few people took the next step: advocating for political independence, or seeking a so-called "second country," but a sentiment of alienation from the existing "one country" and identification with Hong Kong as separate from China was clearly on the rise. By mid-2015, the localist logic was, "For the city to self-govern . . . it must fight off a mainland 'incursion' that threatens the city's language, culture, and traditions that are distinct—and superior, [localism advocates argue]—from those of the People's Republic."[36]

Even though the link between subversion and changing sentiment on localism and identity was weak, this did not stop Beijing from perceiving—or misperceiving—a serious threat to its sovereignty over Hong Kong in the form of an independence movement. Certainly, a few university students favored the idea, but since Hong Kong is a pluralistic society, it would be surprising if no one held that view. True, a small group calling itself the Hong Kong Independence Party registered itself in London in April.[37] True, too, that activists from Taiwan had come to Hong Kong during the protests to provide help on creating an online communication platform—fueling a continuous stream of articles in the Hong Kong Communist press claiming an external hand in all of these actions.[38] A Hong Kong barrister went so far as to propose amending the Basic Law to criminalize actions in support of "splitting the country, promoting full autonomy, and opposing, undermining, and resisting the central government's overall jurisdiction."[39] Yet there was no evidence of any degree of widespread support for a separatist campaign. The LegCo president, Jasper Tsang Yok-sing (Jasper Tsang for short), sought to defuse the issue: "Independence theories have circulated in society for some time already . . . but I don't see there is a market for them. As far as I know, Beijing has no intention to make an anti-independence law."[40]

Chinese and Hong Kong authorities acknowledged a more serious challenge: how to cope with the large mass of student activists. In his 2015 policy address, C. Y. Leung somewhat paternalistically acknowledged the students' political aspirations and the need for society to "commend them for their merits and correct their mistakes." But, he said, "They should be guided towards a full understanding of the constitutional relationship between our country [meaning China] and Hong Kong so that the discussion on constitutional development would not be fruitless." Leung directed particular criticism to a couple of Hong Kong University student publications that advocated "self-reliance and self-determination."[41] Chen Zou'er, the former deputy director of the State Council's Hong Kong and Macau Affairs Office, asserted that "a considerable portion of [Hong Kong] young people had been lacking national and civic awareness" and blamed a lack of patriotism for Occupy Central. His remarks, clearly intended to resuscitate the 2012 national education initiative that protesters had blocked, stimulated quick responses regarding the factual basis for Chen's charge (actually, Chinese history education is available for 88 percent of junior secondary school students) and the inappropriateness of his interference in what was considered a local matter.[42] Beijing supporters' belief that an educational effort would prevent future protests only demonstrated their own disconnect from Hong Kong's fundamental problems. The students on the front lines of the Umbrella Movement could not have achieved what they did without the support of the middle class. The sense of alienation among students and their elders had less to do with not taking enough patriotism classes in school or their disloyalty to the "one country" than with their perception that the political and economic cards in the "second system" were stacked against them.

The Second Public Consultation

On January 7, 2015, the Hong Kong government issued the second consultation document on universal suffrage. It focused on how to turn the objective into a reality in light of the August 31 decision by the NPC-SC.[43] Had the Occupy Movement not occurred, the document would have been issued in October 2014, but delay wasn't the only result of the protests. More consequential was the exacerbation of the deep substantive differences and mistrust. The preface to the consultation document acknowledged the growing polarization between two irreconcilable approaches and the need for "mutual understanding and acceptance."[44]

Right after the NPC-SC issued its decision on August 31, 2014, observers drew the quick conclusion that giving the nominating committee sole power to select candidates ruled out a genuinely competitive election, since the balance of power in the committee would favor members of the establishment. That was certainly my initial conclusion. Larry Diamond, a leading democracy scholar at Stanford University, expressed this negative viewpoint most graphically in an email interview with the *South China Morning Post,* stating, "It is difficult to see how, under this Iranian-style rigged system, pro-democracy forces will have any chance of nominating a candidate of their own."[45]

The reference was to Iran's Council of Guardians, which screens all the individuals who apply to run for the presidency. For the 2013 elections, the council had ruled Hashemi Rafsanjani, a founder of the regime and a former president, ineligible to run. The analogy to the nominating committee proposed for Hong Kong was obvious. Or was it? In a narrow sense it was. The "Guardians" of the Iranian regime would be the last ones to nominate anyone who might mount a challenge to the theocracy and the senior ayatollahs, who as the ultimate guardians of the regime still retained a veto over the policies of whoever was ultimately elected president. But within those significant limits, could a competitive election be possible? Iran's 2013 elections provided a positive answer. Hashemi Rafsanjani may have been sidelined, but that opened the way for the dark-horse reformer Hassan Rouhani, prompting Suzanne Maloney, a Middle East policy analyst, to write: "A funny thing happened on the way to the conservative cakewalk in Iran: a supposed sleeper of a presidential campaign got interesting. Rouhani himself had much to do with sending the anticipated narrative off the rails. This was a surprise. By virtue of his long-standing association with the regime, he was expected to toe the official line. Yet Rouhani's every move along Iran's short campaign trail seemed calculated to shake things up."[46] Once elected, President Rouhani has still been held on a leash by the Supreme Leader, Ali Khamenei. Indeed, he's in the no-win situation of any reformer, in that he brings change faster than the old guard finds comfortable and slower than the increasingly impatient public desires. Still, as a cleric who supported Ayatollah Khomeini in carrying out the Iranian Revolution of 1979, Rouhani is certainly no radical, but his revolutionary pedigree gives him more rein to experiment—for example, on a nuclear agreement—than would otherwise have been the case.

So the concrete question for Hong Kong might have been whether the electoral system created by the August 31 decision would be competitive enough to yield a Rouhani-like reform candidate. People on the establishment side believed the proposal would provide sufficiently competitive elections. As Holden Chen, a vice-chairman of the DAB, put it, "In a universal suffrage election you have . . . to court support from some in the middle. You even have to court support from some Pan-Democratic supporters to win." The Pan-Democrats rejected that view, but it triggered an even more specific question: Could the nomination process be designed in such a way that a candidate of the democratic camp could be nominated within the NPC-SC parameters? An affirmative answer creates a two-part problem: Beijing would have to signal whether a democratic candidate was sufficiently "patriotic," and the democrats would have to put forward someone who would not only be tolerated by Beijing but also command broad public support in the election. Moreover, any democrat who was nominated and actually elected would not have free rein to pursue radical policies, if only because the establishment would still have significant legislative power. But those limits would never be tested if a genuinely competitive election were not possible in the first place.

The consultation document set forth two ways of "perfecting" the system outlined in the NPC-SC's August decision. Regarding the composition of the nominating committee, it offered essentially two options. One was to model its membership on the current election committee (which most objective Hong Kong observers believe over-represents certain economic and social sectors) and to maintain the electoral base of each subsector. The other option was to broaden the electoral base of the subsectors to make the committee more representative: "Provided that there is sufficient support, introduce new subsectors in the NC to increase the representativeness of those groups which are not sufficiently represented in the existing 38 subsectors."[47]

The document also presented two options for the procedures for selecting nominees. The first would have simply adapted the restrictive selection method of the election committee to the nominating committee, which would have limited the prospect of nominating a democrat. The other option proposed a preliminary "member recommendation" stage:

- The committee would initially consider more "potential candidates" than the two or three allowed for the final nomination.

- A modest number of members (at least 150 members, so less than a 50 percent majority) could nominate a potential candidate.
- The recommended candidates would have an opportunity to transparently present their policy platforms to the nominating committee and the public.[48]

The question was whether Beijing, members of the local establishment, and a sufficient number of democratic LegCo members would approve these fixes, and so facilitate their incorporation of a plan that could pass the LegCo with a two-thirds margin. Beijing certainly had given its go-ahead already; otherwise the proposal would not have seen the light of day. The members of the establishment camp who subsequently expressed their views supported the "member recommendation" idea. A few Pan-Democratic leaders did counsel moderation, and mainstream newspapers expressed their hope for a compromise.[49] Even though a leading establishment figure called for mutual tolerance, the prospects for a mutually acceptable bargain remained dim.[50] Pan-Democratic legislators vowed to boycott the consultation process and vote against the plan, and Joshua Wong, leader of Scholarism, remarked that trying to improve the plan was "useless."[51] The public remained divided as well. In a Lingnan University poll in late January, 49.5 percent of respondents said the reform plan should be passed, but 38 percent said that it should be rejected. Significantly, half of the latter group said they would shift to support the proposal if improvements were made.[52]

The substantive differences between the two sides were not trivial, but the key obstacle to a convergence was a lack of mutual trust at various levels. There was a split within the Pan-Democratic camp over whether to seek a compromise with the government, insist on Beijing's withdrawal of the August 31 decision, and then restart the five-step process. The hard-line position was sustained for the time being, and its advocates threatened potential "defectors" with disciplinary action.[53]

In addition, there was the toxic relationship between the democrats and Beijing, which was on display in the first half of March. Li Fei, the chairman of the National People's Congress's Hong Kong Basic Law Committee, had planned to visit Hong Kong with an expectation that he might meet with democratic legislators. On March 9, however, all twenty-seven democratic LegCo members announced that they would veto any plan that was based on the August 31 decision, declaring it "unreasonable and unconstitutional."

Li Fei then canceled his trip, reportedly because he regarded the allegation as an unacceptable challenge to Beijing's authority.[54] Ronny Tong, a moderate democratic legislator and founder of the Civic Party, opined, "Instead of trying to find a way out of this morass, [the Hong Kong government and democrats are] both doing their utmost to swing popular opinion, blaming the other side for this likely political failure. How pathetic."[55] More fundamentally, at least one commentator detected a generational difference within the opposition on why democracy was necessary in the first place: "Democracy camp old guards . . . see so-called genuine democracy as, firstly, a shield against our communist rulers, and eventually as a way to democratize China. . . . Students and young people . . . see democracy more as a way to revive hope for their disillusioned generation. Only a small fringe group wants independence. Most just want the upward mobility their parents and grandparents enjoyed."[56]

One pro-democracy advocacy group took the ideas of the consultation document seriously and provided concrete recommendations. That was Hong Kong 2020, headed by the former chief secretary Anson Chan Fang On-sang (Anson Chan, for short). Hong Kong 2020 advocated two steps to democratize the nominating committee. The first was to terminate corporate voting, whereby the members of some subsectors connected with the business community were elected by constituent companies and not by a larger constituency such as the employees of those companies. The second was to compose one of the nominating committee's four sectors with members popularly elected by citizens who did not have a vote in another sector—similar to the District Council (Second) FC in the LegCo. The Hong Kong 2020 plan also suggested that there be two types of candidates: the formal nominees who received support of over 50 percent of the members of the nominating committee; and "recommended candidates" who received over 10 but less than 50 percent. In the general election, 50 percent of the total vote would be required for victory, to ensure that the elected chief executive was legitimate.[57]

Final Proposal

On April 22, 2015, Chief Secretary Carrie Lam presented a detailed final proposal to the Legislative Council.[58] The plan was clearly consistent with the parameters that Beijing had laid out in 2014 regarding the central role of the nominating committee. Not surprisingly, it received Beijing's strong public endorsement.[59] That meant that whom the nominating committee considered before making its final nominations would be the critical issue at hand. The

Hong Kong SAR government recommended a procedural mechanism in line with the second option in the consultation document: any individual who got recommendations from one-tenth to one-fifth of the nominating committee would be a "potential candidate" and have the opportunity to articulate his or her policy views to the committee and the public in a transparent way.[60]

In effect, this meant that the nominating committee would likely consider five to ten individuals for final nomination. Because Pan-Democrats would have at the very least a minority of the nominating committee membership, as they had in the election committee, they could be able to recommend at least one of their members as a potential candidate. That in turn created the possibility that a democrat could become a final nominee and compete to become chief executive. In that case, voters who had supported the democratic camp and believed current economic policies were flawed would have a candidate who shared their general outlook. Nonetheless, the Pan-Democrats were quick to reject the proposal. They opposed anything based on the NPC-SC August 31 decision because, they asserted, it allowed candidate screening by mainland China.

In three respects, the Hong Kong SAR government missed opportunities to make meaningful reforms (much to the regret of the Pan-Democrats), all of them concerning the subsectors that would make up the nominating committee. The question was whether to change the makeup of the subsectors so that under-represented groups received more nominating committee seats. As noted earlier, the government had floated the democratizing idea in the December 2014 consultation document, but on one condition: "provided that there is sufficient support." In the end, Carrie Lam deemed there wasn't enough backing and recommended no change, stating that there was no social consensus to make this change and that doing so would only create more political controversy. Of course the subsectors that stood to lose the most relative power would not be willing to have their oxen gored, so the idea died. The second issue was corporate voting, and here again, no change was suggested. Opportunities to win the confidence of the public were missed. Finally, the Pan-Democrats sought a promise from Beijing that this stage was not the end of the reform process when it came to the election for chief executive. Anson Chan even suggested embodying such a pledge in legislation, but all Beijing officials were willing to offer was that further reform could occur if Hong Kong's conditions required it and only after the initially proposed system was tested.[61]

Having vowed to vote against the Hong Kong SAR government's proposal, the Pan-Democratic bloc in the LegCo now had to maintain unity in its camp. Beijing and the Hong Kong SAR government needed to peel off four opposition legislators to secure the necessary majority, and they hoped there might be enough moderate politicians who would be convinced that the reform package was "good enough" compared to the alternative—reversion to the 1,200-member election committee. The danger for these moderates in voting for the proposal was that they would be excoriated by their colleagues for defecting and betraying principles, to the point of facing a challenge from within their camp in the next legislative election. By early May, it appeared that moderate democrats were sticking with their less moderate colleagues and dissenters would face party discipline.[62]

As legislative action neared, the competing scripts were consistent. Civil society and the other subsectors that had opposed the August 31 template continued to oppose the government's proposal, while the Hong Kong government, business leaders, chambers of commerce, and editorials from the centrist papers all urged passage.[63] Regina Ip, head of the pro-establishment New People's Party, asserted, "The package is arguably more liberal than expected, and offers a much greater chance for a Pan-Democratic candidate to be nominated."[64] Both the *South China Morning Post* and *Ming Pao* called on the LegCo to pass the reforms. A veteran journalist, Frank Ching, whose sympathies had long been with the democrats, was a bellwether voice of pragmatism. He argued that as unsatisfactory as the government package was, vetoing it would not lead Beijing to concede to the democrats but instead Hong Kong would have to "wait five, 10 years or even longer before reintroducing reform."[65]

The establishment side was not averse to exercising a bit of muscle. At a May 31 meeting in Shenzhen, ostensibly convened to give compromise one last try, PRC officials reportedly took some democratic LegCo members to task for all manner of political sins and warned them that their vote on electoral reform would be a litmus test of whether they supported "one country, two systems."[66] There was also talk of restarting legislative action on the package after the September 2016 LegCo elections, when, it was assumed, voters would punish democrats for blocking universal suffrage and place the establishment in a dominant position to go through with electoral reform.[67] But there were doubts in other quarters whether the establishment could be certain of winning a two-thirds majority. (In fact, results of the district council elections in November 2015 indicated little change in the balance of public support for the establishment and democratic camps, which showed that winning a super-majority was far from a sure thing.)[68] Even if pro-government parties won a two-thirds LegCo majority in 2016, it was doubtful from a procedural point of view that there would be enough time to ram through the package before the 2017 election.[69] And even if the new LegCo could pass the reform quickly, that might only magnify public animosity. Beijing may well prefer to keep the old system for 2017 and 2020 and restart the reform process at a later time. Meanwhile, members of the establishment were reportedly in a dilemma. Generally they benefitted from the existing system, but they had a specific dislike of C. Y. Leung, whom Beijing had imposed on them in 2012. Passage of the government package would reduce his chances of reelection as chief executive because the public disliked him even more than the tycoons did.[70]

Obviously, establishment members of the nominating committee could go through the motions of considering a Pan-Democrat and then not give that person the majority needed for nomination. The procedure and their numerical majority would give them the power to do so, but bait-and-switch tactics might be counterproductive. Beijing had already signaled that at least some democrats were "patriotic," and would have a decent chance of winning more than 50 percent of the votes in the general election. If the Pan-Democrats acted strategically and set a goal to elect one of their own as chief executive, that would mean backing a relative moderate, who was not automatically anathema to Beijing. If that candidate presented reasonable policy proposals and enjoyed broad support as measured by public opinion surveys, the pro-government forces would face a tough choice. To reject such a person as a candidate would only confirm that the process was a sham and that screening was designed to deny voters a meaningful choice. This likely result would render the elected chief executive illegitimate from day one and could ignite even more political polarization, obstructionism, and protests. But even if establishment members of the legislature were strategically prepared to nominate a moderate democrat and saw the downside of rejecting one, no outcome could be guaranteed in practice once the tactical games began.[71]

I visited Hong Kong in late May 2015 to update myself on the state of play. The interlocutors whom I consider to be objective and well-informed agreed with me that, in the abstract, the April 22 plan created a narrow path for the Pan-Democrats. One or two held out the optimistic hope that a two-thirds majority in the LegCo would appear at the final moment. But most were pessimistic. Mutual mistrust, born from the decades-long struggle over whether Hong Kong should have a genuinely democratic system, was just too deep. This was probably why the substance of the Hong Kong SAR government's proposal got only limited public discussion. Surveys showed that the share of the public that opposed the plan was gaining supporters.[72] Some polls suggested that the support rate would increase if the government made just modest improvements to conciliate the democrats.[73]

Yet last-minute concessions were not part of Beijing's endgame. On June 10, a "staff commentator" at *People's Daily* restated the case for why Beijing's policies and the Hong Kong SAR government's plan were just fine: "The universal suffrage bill has provided a legal guarantee for ensuring that persons who love the country and love Hong Kong will become the chief executive. To ensure the election of a chief executive whom the central government trusts and the people of Hong Kong support is a necessary condition for the HKSAR government to maintain good relations with the central government and carry out good governance. It is conducive to *safeguarding national sovereignty, security, and development* interests, and is also conducive to maintaining long-term prosperity and stability in Hong Kong" (emphasis added).[74] The coded reference to national security concerns was not accidental. As one Hong Kong political scientist said, "Beijing believes that the struggle is no longer over democracy at all but about who has control in Hong Kong. Maintaining control is Beijing's top priority. . . . If [the plan] passes, fine. But maintaining control is more important."[75] A poll taken in early June with a large sample of more than 5,000 people found that 48 percent of respondents approved the government's proposal and 51 percent favored LegCo approval; but 38 percent disapproved of the plan and favored rejection.[76]

As widely predicted, the LegCo rejected the government's plan. For many this outcome was a tragedy. Yet at the final moment, there was also an element of farce. As the vote neared, word spread that Lau Wong-fat, the LegCo member for the Heung Yee Kuk functional constituency, was on his way from his sickbed to the legislative complex but needed more time to arrive. (Recall that Lau was a prime example of the skewed character of functional constituencies: formally he represented rural residents but he was a prominent property tycoon.) To accommodate his late arrival, some pro-establishment legislators decided to exit the chamber to deny a quorum. But not enough of their colleagues received word of the plan in time, so a quorum still existed and the vote went forward. Ultimately, twenty-seven democratic members and one pro-establishment legislator voted against the plan and only eight establishment members voted in favor. It was a disappointment for Beijing, which had expected a simple majority to favor the plan.[77] It was not the first surprise in a protracted and unpredictable process.

Threats to the Liberal Order?

The tumultuous and inconclusive struggle during 2014 and 2015 raised a larger question: Would Beijing, which had bet some degree of prestige on passage of the universal suffrage package, continue to tolerate the liberal provisions of the Hong Kong SAR political system that had contributed to the unwelcome outcome? The likely logic was as follows: if some in Hong Kong had used the territory's political freedoms to challenge central authority, undermine national security, and threaten to turn the territory into a base for subversion, then the Hong Kong political hybrid should be revised and political freedoms restricted.[78]

METHODS OF CONSTRAINT

As discussed in chapter 5, the Hong Kong protests occurred during a period when the Chinese regime became increasingly alarmed about internal and external security and took steps to tighten political restrictions on the mainland.[79]

Steve Vickers, an officer in the pre-1997 Hong Kong Police, judged that the protests had weakened the role of the Hong Kong SAR government vis-à-vis the Central People's Government and its local representatives. He warned of several steps that Beijing might try to take (specific possible measures are my suggestions):[80]

- Strengthen its security presence in Hong Kong (beef up the presence of its own personnel in Hong Kong agencies)
- Constrain citizen activism (restrict the presence of foreign NGOs in the territory)
- Bring the education and media sectors under greater control (impose more national education and encourage takeover of the more independent media outlets)[81]

Vickers concluded: "Hong Kong's existing freedoms are now under greater pressure than before, because an enlarged PRC intelligence and security presence has been justified to the wider local population."

These concerns were most common in the weeks after the end of the protests, as rumors and isolated violent incidents seemed to confirm Vickers' warning. A Reuters report detailed a PRC domestic security operation, presumably conducted by personnel of the PRC Ministry of Public Security and Ministry of State Security, to monitor the activities of pro-democracy members of the

LegCo, professors, activists, and Catholic clergy.[82] The Communist *Ta Kung Pao* reported that Beijing wanted the Hong Kong SAR government to prosecute organizations that supported the protest movement (because they had aided an "illegal assembly"), instruct the mass media to end the pro-Occupy bias in their coverage, force schools to punish students who skip class to protest, and desensitize the public's opposition to police violence.[83] Masked attackers even tried to firebomb the residence and office headquarters of Jimmy Lai, a pro-democracy publisher and Occupy backer.[84]

Predictably, there was talk among Beijing supporters about trying to enact the national security legislation that had been introduced and withdrawn in 2003. Others countered that Hong Kong already had effective security laws, and after government officials denied any plans for such legislation, the idea soon died a quick death.[85] Some in the pro-Beijing camp criticized judges for being too lenient in its rulings on cases involving Umbrella protesters, but this brought a sharp rebuke from the legal community. A veteran prosecutor said, "The suggestion that the police arrest but the courts release is very unfair to judges, because they rule only on the evidence."[86] The police did take steps to more strictly enforce public order laws to ensure that public gatherings did not turn into unauthorized protests, but this was essentially a return to the status quo ante. In any event, objective commentary concluded that, overall, the police had done a good job of balancing political rights and securing order.[87]

SHRINKING FREEDOM OF SPEECH AND THE PRESS

One potentially unsettling development was the announcement in December 2015 that Alibaba, the Chinese Internet giant, would purchase the *South China Morning Post*. The paper had generally maintained a reputation for balanced and objective reporting; indeed it was one of the specific institutions that justified the conclusion that Hong Kong's liberal order persisted under one country, two systems. And Joseph Tsai, the Alibaba Group's executive vice chairman, pledged that it would remain so: "At the core of a news property, we have to have the readers' trust. That will depend on reporting that is objective, balanced and fair. If we don't have that trust, we cannot build up our readership. Even though we are the corporate owner, we will let the editors decide the editorial policy and direction of coverage for any story." But Tsai also contended that Western media were biased against China and that one goal of the *South China Morning Post* under Alibaba's ownership would be to "help people around the world to understand China better."[88] So did the new owners believe that the *South China Morning Post*'s coverage of events in Hong Kong also had an anti-Beijing bias? Was the paper's reputation as an objective source of news and opinion in jeopardy? That independence was brought into question when the senior editor, Keung Kwok-yeun, was summarily sacked by the publisher after the paper had printed a story regarding the offshore holdings of members of the CCP elite.[89]

On March 28, some of the young activists who led the Umbrella Movement founded the Hong Kong National Party, with independence for the territory as a key goal. That set off a new round of debate over the terms of political participation. Wang Zhenmin, an official of Beijing's liaison office in Hong Kong, asserted that public advocacy of independence constituted treason, and some members of the establishment agreed. Many in the legal profession disagreed, saying that without overt action to achieve its goals, what the new party had done thus far constituted speech only and was protected under the Basic Law. There was suspicion that Beijing and its allies in Hong Kong were using the episode as a pretext to create pressure for passage of long-sought national security legislation pursuant to Article 23 of the Basic Law.[90]

THE LEE BO CASE

Up until the end of 2015, it seemed that most of the post-Umbrella actions reflected at most a nibbling around the edges of the liberal order, a view that was confirmed by polls.[91] But early in 2016, news surfaced regarding an episode that raised unprecedented questions about the Central People's Government's respect for and confidence in Hong Kong's legal system.

On December 30, 2015, Lee Bo (also known as Lee Po), a major shareholder in Causeway Bay Books, was reported missing. The store was owned by the Mighty Current publishing company, which specializes in books about political infighting among CCP leaders and critical, even salacious, information about their private lives. It was rumored that Mighty Current was working on a book about a former mistress of Xi Jinping and had come under pressure to halt the project. The night Lee disappeared, Lee called his wife from a number in Shenzhen, which borders Hong Kong, and told her that he was assisting mainland authorities on a case.[92] On January 2, it was revealed that Lee was not the first person associated with the bookstore who had gone missing over the preceding three months. At least three of his colleagues in the bookstore had been detained while traveling in the mainland and another colleague had been detained in Thailand.[93] The British government took an interest in this case because Lee Bo held a British passport, and in mid-February it issued a report to Parliament that confirmed what many in Hong Kong feared. It stated that "the full facts of the case remain unclear, but our current information indicates that Mr Lee was involuntarily removed to the mainland without any due process under Hong Kong SAR (Special Administrative Region) law."[94] A Chinese Foreign Ministry spokesman retorted that London should stop meddling in "Hong Kong affairs."[95] The U.S. State Department's annual human rights report for 2015, in commenting on the five cases, stated that "credible reports gave rise to widespread suspicions that PRC security officials were involved in their disappearances."[96]

The Lee case set off widespread public alarm: if an individual associated with a minor publishing company could be kidnapped by agents of the Central People's Government, then all Hong Kong residents were potentially vulnerable to the same abuse.[97] *Ming Pao* editorialized: "For Hong Kongers, what is of paramount importance at present is the assurance that their personal safety and freedom and their right to freedom from fear remain unthreatened and unimpaired. Many are feeling anxious."[98] Even if the controversial content of Mighty Current's list was a problem that needed to be addressed, resorting to abduction was not the way to do so. Hong Kong's law enforcement agencies sought information in the PRC about the fate of those who had disappeared, using an established mechanism whereby the Hong Kong Police can query the mainland authorities whether Hong Kong residents have been detained on the mainland.

Meanwhile, Chief Executive C. Y. Leung reaffirmed the centrality of the autonomy of the Hong Kong legal system. "It would be unacceptable if mainland law enforcement agents enforce laws in Hong Kong because this violates the Basic Law."[99] Yet Leung could have gone further and noted the specific ways in which action in Hong Kong by mainland agencies would violate the Basic Law:

- Article 22 of the Basic Law forbids any PRC government agency or department from interfering in the affairs administered by the Hong Kong SAR.
- Article 28 states that "No Hong Kong resident shall be subjected to arbitrary or unlawful arrest, detention or imprisonment."
- Article 35 provides that Hong Kong residents must have access to legal services, including "confidential legal advice, access to the courts, choice of lawyers for timely protection of their lawful rights and interests."[100]

To put it differently, abduction of Lee Bo violated the Basic Law's guarantee of civil rights and due process of law, one element of Hong Kong's liberal order.

As of early 2016 China had not responded to the request for information from law enforcement agencies nor to Leung's statement on Hong Kong's legal system. On February 29, Lee, still across the border, met with Hong Kong Police officials and told them that he had not been abducted and had left Hong Kong on his own. The police commissioner said afterward that "he suspected that Lee Po was hiding something." Most Hong Kong residents were likely even more suspicious than the commissioner.[101] The Lee Bo case was by far the clearest and most serious Chinese challenge to the Hong Kong SAR's liberal order since reversion. Beijing's total lack of transparency only exacerbated the sense of fear in Hong Kong and put the Hong Kong SAR government in an extremely awkward position.

Controlling from behind the Screen

Beijing had other ways besides weakening the liberal order to manage Hong Kong's unpredictable politics without violating the Basic Law. The key was the United Front, specifically, identifying and weakening "enemies" and strengthening the hand of "friends."

In January 2015, a mainland scholar expressed concern about the "radicalization in the thinking behind Hong Kong's social movements." In May, the *South China Morning Post* fired Frank Ching and Philip Bowring, two respected senior columnists who were known for their sometimes biting commentary on Hong Kong's political development.[102] This was seen by some as a sign of tightening the boundaries of media freedom, but the circumstances of the action did not permit a clear-cut judgment.[103] In August, *People's Daily,* the official newspaper of the CCP and therefore the PRC regime, asserted that students at Hong Kong University were "brainwashed radicals." *Wen Wei Po* called on the police to crack down on and eradicate radical forces. In June, *Ta Kung Pao,* in good United Front fashion, called on democrats to clearly differentiate themselves from "pro-independence" forces.[104] Hackers stepped up their penetration of the computer networks of Hong Kong activists; the sophistication of the tactics used suggested to computer experts that the hackers were directed by Beijing.[105]

The process of clarifying who were enemies and who were friends allowed for some score settling. The universities became a major battleground. Some professors centrally involved in opposing Beijing's approach to electoral reform found themselves in difficult situations. The Education Bureau of the Hong Kong SAR government pressed the Hong Kong University's Council, its governing body, to investigate how Benny Tai, one of the three leaders of Occupy Central, had handled donations he had received for the university and that, it was alleged, he had used for activities related to the protest movement. Democratic legislators warned about the effect on the university's autonomy, but the Education Bureau spokesman said that the government's financial support of the university gave it standing to ensure that funds were handled appropriately.[106] Joseph Cheng Yu-shek, a respected scholar at City University of Hong Kong who had advised Pan-Democratic legislators on electoral reform and had at one point pleaded for unity between radicals and moderates, was demoted from professor holding an endowed chair to regular professor.[107] In February 2016, Lingnan University did not renew the contract of Horace Chin Wan-kan, the author of *Hong Kong as a City-State*.[108]

Johannes Chan, a professor of law at Hong Kong University, became the key target. He became linked to the investigation of Benny Tai's donation to the university because he was Tai's dean before and during the protests. He was also part of Hong Kong 2020, Anson Chan's effort to find a mutually acceptable compromise on electoral reform. When Chan's nomination as vice-chancellor at Hong Kong University stalled in spring 2015, there were accusations that C. Y. Leung, as the university chancellor, was exerting inappropriate political pressure concerning the selection process.[109] The dispute continued until late September, when the Council voted to reject the search committee's recommendation of Chan.[110] The decision clearly reflected one dimension of the United Front's m.o.: embedding individuals likely to be loyal to Beijing in the decisionmaking bodies of major local institutions. Of twenty-one members of the Council, thirteen were "external members who are established figures in business, political or educational fields," and six were appointed by the chief executive. In this case, seven of the external members were either deputies to the National People's Congress or the Chinese People's Political Consultative Conference—Beijing loyalists by definition.[111] Radical university students would continue to disrupt Council proceedings into 2016, leading Vice-Chancellor Peter Mathieson to condemn the actions as "mob rule."[112]

Meanwhile, in late July, out of the blue, C. Y. Leung removed Tsang Tak-sing, secretary for home affairs, and Paul Tang Kwok-wai, secretary for the civil service. It was rumored that Tsang had done a poor job of rallying the Hong Kong SAR's young people to the establishment's cause, that Tang had not managed civil servants properly, and that Beijing was behind Leung's decision. The fact that Tsang Tak-sing was the brother of the LegCo president, Jasper Tsang, who had maintained the neutrality of his position during the universal suffrage debates and had not advocated the government's proposal, gave the dismissal a special political significance. All the same, the Communist publication *Ta Kung Pao,* which Tsang Tak-sing had edited at one time, published an editorial supporting him.[113]

When it came to consolidating its core support, Beijing focused on the Democratic Alliance for the Betterment and Progress of Hong Kong (DAB). A delegation of DAB party leaders went to Beijing in late July, and Zhang Dejiang, the Politburo Standing Committee member in charge of Hong Kong policy, gave them a series of instructions to convey to DAB members: have a "clear-cut stand on loving the country and Hong Kong"; broaden political support in the city; back C. Y. Leung; and win two-thirds of the LegCo seats in the 2016 elections (which would neutralize the Pan-Democrats' veto on major issues).[114] In addition, the establishment strengthened its control over the LegCo by taking the positions of chair and vice chair of the most important committees instead of following the past custom of sharing the posts with democratic members.[115] Incentives were offered to bolster the pro-government coalition, including initiatives to broaden economic integration, which were announced in late 2014. One measure was connecting the Shanghai–Hong Kong stock markets, which removed some obstacles facing investors in both cities from trading stocks of the other economy.[116] The other was an agreement between the Central People's Government and Hong Kong SAR government, signed in December 2014, that liberalized the access of firms to Guangdong Province's service sector, hitherto closed to Hong Kong companies.[117] In late May, the two governments agreed on an arrangement whereby mutual funds in each jurisdiction could be traded across the border.[118] And after the government's electoral reform proposal was defeated in June 2015, C. Y. Leung announced a series of initiatives to "improve people's livelihood and propel economic growth."[119]

Along with identifying and bolstering natural allies, the United Front aimed to win over independent actors and groups who were not dedicated opponents. Two important groups were young people and members of the Democratic Party. In July, Yu Zhengsheng, the fifth-ranking member in the CCP Politburo's Standing Committee, urged delegations to Beijing by young people from Hong Kong and Macau to increase their identification with the nation. "Younger generations in Hong Kong and Macao are fresh forces to carry forward the cause of 'one country, two systems,' and they should be courageous in assuming their mission for the times," Yu Zhengsheng reportedly exhorted the youths.[120] Later that month, C. Y. Leung told a group of summer-camp participants in Hong Kong, "Hong Kong society values individuality more than unity, rights more than obligations, and what to fight for more than what to give. [But you] should also fulfill your duty to sacrifice for the community . . . [and] acquire the spirit of serving society and contribute to our mother country."[121] The Democratic Party was targeted by the United Front as the most moderate party in the Pan-Democratic camp. In late August Feng Wei, the deputy director of the PRC State Council's Hong Kong and Macau Affairs Office, met with a delegation of Democratic Party members with the likely aim of probing their willingness to desert their Pan-Democratic colleagues.[122] But Beijing had missed several opportunities before the June 2015 LegCo vote to bring those moderates to its side, and now the September pleas for their support going forward rang a bit hollow.[123]

These various steps to "isolate the enemy and win over the vast majority" did not exactly work out as planned. Some Democratic Party members who had not been part of the delegation that met with Feng Wei criticized those who had. Platitudes about the need for patriotism among the youth fell on deaf ears except for those already committed. DAB leaders wondered whether they would be able to navigate "that fine line between being supportive of the Hong Kong government but also staying close to and being a voice for the people."[124] Perhaps most serious, in late August, the LegCo's president, Jasper Tsang, was unusually critical of the government; it was reported that he called for "an urgent review of Beijing's implementation of the 'one country, two systems' policy for Hong Kong, at the same time warning of its demise if the central government interferes more frequently in the running of the city."[125] (Tsang did not challenge one country, two systems per se but criticized Beijing's implementation of the formula.) A United Front strategy may have made sense in a less complex society lacking widespread opportunities for political expression and weak barriers against the CCP's latent coercive power. But in Hong Kong in 2015, the strategy wasn't working so well.

Conclusion

Although the pro-government camp blundered on the final vote for electoral reform and so deflected blame away from the democrats, the most important and enduring question was whether a better outcome might have been possible.

Neither side had achieved its real objective: for government supporters, passage of the plan; for the democrats, a system without screening of candidates. Each camp gained merely a second-best alternative, if that: democrats rejected what they didn't like and the establishment won the blame game. One thoughtful observer concluded: "All parties involved contributed to the death of the universal suffrage babe in arms before it could leave the crib, let alone grow into a sturdy teenager."[126]

There were probably some turning points and lost opportunities that made the ultimate outcome more inevitable. In retrospect, the first was at the time of reversion or, at the latest, in the early 2000s, after the collapse of the housing market. From then on, the Hong Kong SAR government, with enlightened support from establishment leaders, should have done more to mitigate growing inequality. That is certainly easier said than done, but some issues were under Hong Kong's control. For example, the government should have continued the programs proposed soon after reversion to permit residents of public housing and participants in the Housing Ownership Scheme to purchase their dwellings on favorable terms. The new owners would then have benefitted from wealth appreciation over the next decade or more.[127] Instead, the government revoked the programs in order to stop the slide in housing prices. More generally, although public dissatisfaction with the concentration of economic and political power was not the only or primary reason for opposition to the electoral reform proposals, it certainly was an intensifying reason. Government action to slow the growing inequality and accelerate the implementation of universal suffrage might have mitigated the effect of the concentration of economic and political power.

The second turning point was around 2007, when Beijing signaled that Hong Kong would have to wait another decade before it would have any chance of electing the chief executive by universal suffrage. That year is significant because the radicalization of Hong Kong politics had only just started to emerge. If Beijing had announced in 2007 that genuine universal suffrage for the chief executive election would occur in 2012 and for the LegCo in the election after that, it would likely have empowered moderate democrats and made some kind of compromise possible. As it was, the mid-to-late 2000s was the last time that electoral reform could occur in both a "gradual and orderly" way, as the Basic Law requires. With radicalization, each new incremental step would be countered with disorder. At this point, it seems that only a sudden transformative initiative from Beijing to address the grievances of the majority of the public could ensure stability.

Third, in 2010 it was unfortunate that members of the Democratic Party chose to negotiate with Beijing over changes to the 2012 LegCo elections. It is true, as the political scientist Michael De Golyer observes, that this was "the only time on Chinese soil that any party has negotiated with the Communist Party and got them to compromise and accept [its] proposal."[128] But even though the 2010 compromise did increase the number of popularly elected LegCo seats, it really did not change the balance of power in the legislature, but instead provoked charges of betrayal from radical democrats toward their moderate colleagues. The price paid for a very modest gain was a deepening division within the democratic camp and a new push from radicals to be sure to keep moderates in line in the future. In June 2015, despite problems moderates had with the government proposal, some of them might have wanted to vote for it. Yet they feared the retribution that radicals would inflict on them. The radicals may have had a selfish reason for blocking moderates from agreeing to the government's proposal. They did not want a process in which a moderate democrat could win, but one in which a radical would have a chance—something Beijing would not countenance.

A fourth turning point was when the democratic camp changed its position on civic nomination. It had rejected the idea in 2009, but then accepted it in 2014.[129] Worse than that, this mechanism for producing nominees for chief executive became the only option that the democrats seriously considered, which both scared Beijing and limited the democrats' room to maneuver and negotiate.

Fifth, as the public debate on electoral reform began, Beijing and at least some establishment leaders should have thought twice about their allegation that the United States was the "black hand" behind the democratic and the public opposition. Even if American or private groups had sought to influence the struggle over electoral reform, the issue was how much impact that intervention had on the outcome compared with the impact of local factors like Pan-Democrats' mistrust of Beijing or the middle class's anger over inequality. In fact, the U.S. government was extremely careful not to create any basis for the allegation. Private American organizations had little or no impact on events. Those in Beijing and Hong Kong who emphasized the American role avoided focusing on significant local reasons for opposition.

The less transparent decisionmaking in Beijing becomes, the harder it is to know why it made the tactical moves it did from late 2013 to the summer of 2015. Blaming foreign forces and fear of a subversion platform in Hong Kong are probably two drivers. Bad advice from its allies in the Hong Kong SAR was probably another. Growing intolerance toward the perceived desire of some in Hong Kong for special treatment may be another. In the end, the Central People's Government may have believed that it had set a generous bottom line and that it should ride out whatever storm that leniency created. Giving any more leeway fostered too many risks.[130] Yet it is difficult to avoid the conclusion that if Beijing had played its tactical hand better in the spring and early summer of 2014—engaging moderate democrats on constructive changes to the nominating committee and eschewing heavy-handed hectoring with the white paper—it might have gotten a much more favorable outcome.

Two Hong Kong commentators observed that the dynamic in Hong Kong regarding electoral reform was similar to a security dilemma in international relations. Objectively, there was a substantive outcome that was acceptable to the two contending camps, but each side so mistrusted the other that it believed any offer it made wouldn't lead to good will or a reciprocal offer from the other side, but instead would lead to further demands. The only way to defend one's interest was to take a hard line. In hindsight, the suboptimal outcome was not inevitable.[131]

SEVEN

Democracy and Good Governance

Thus far I have examined in fine detail the political system of the Hong Kong Special Administrative Region (Hong Kong SAR) and the ways it dealt with the issue of electoral reform from 2013 to 2015, or failed to do so. In this chapter I zoom out to examine Hong Kong in a broader context. In a sense, the remaining chapters of this book ask the "so what?" question, that is, what is the significance of recent events in Hong Kong for larger issues of governance, economic competitiveness, and so on.

The Value of Democracy

An unspoken question lurks in any discussion of Hong Kong politics and the struggle over universal suffrage: What, after all, is the value of a liberal electoral democracy? The Pan-Democratic forces sought to establish such a system as strenuously as conservative forces and Beijing worked to retain some degree of screening for candidates to the post of chief executive. But is such a fully democratic system the best one at all times and under all conditions? In many parts of the world—Western Europe, North America, and parts of Asia and Latin America—the reflexive answer to that question is "Yes, of course." That judgment has a substantial degree of truth when the points of reference are

China's authoritarian system, with its abuse of power and denial of civil and political rights, or the obvious sham of Russia's "illiberal democracy."

But for those who advocate both liberal freedoms and fully competitive elections, Hong Kong constitutes more of an intellectual challenge. After all, the "liberal" part of the Hong Kong SAR's hybrid system does provide checks against abuse of power and bad policy, even if those checks show signs of atrophy. The representatives of the "oligarchy" who serve in government do reflect some social interests (but certainly not all). At least some of Hong Kong's leaders are chosen by popular elections (slightly over half the members of the Legislative Council). Even if universal suffrage were enacted and the nominating committee only picked two establishment candidates, there would still be some degree of choice. What would be the real value-added of using genuinely democratic elections for picking all members of the LegCo and the chief executive, particularly when it comes to the quality of government in Hong Kong? To what extent is the presence of the institutions we associate with democracy a sufficient condition for good governance? Is it a necessary condition? Or is it neither?

These may seem to be odd questions, given the privileged place that full democracy, with its free elections and political freedoms, has in any discussion of political systems. Democracy has been the focus of Western political thought since Aristotle and is now the presumptive standard to which all countries are expected to aspire. The essential rationale is that democratic institutions render leaders accountable for their actions and policies—"approving good performance and punishing poor performance"—and better ensure achievement of prosperity, welfare, and peace.[1] Abraham Lincoln's cogent formula in his Gettysburg Address—"government of the people, by the people, and for the people"—captures democracy's essence: it is through mechanisms that are of and by the people that government for the people is assured and the arbitrary exercise of state power is deterred.

Even China recognizes that it is useful to have the appearance of a democratic system. Liberal freedoms are written into the constitution of the People's Republic of China (PRC) and the rule of law is upheld in state propaganda. Elections take place at all levels of the system, and those at the local level even permit some measure of competition. China has legislatures—people's congresses—at higher levels that provide some opportunities for limited consultation and dissent. But in China, law is used to proscribe freedoms. Selection of candidates for elections above the lowest level of the system is done on an indirect basis and is controlled by the Organization Department of the Chinese

Communist Party. The method for selecting legislators and the powers allocated to them limit their ability to truly check the executive branch of government and the ruling Communist Party.

In very general terms, there is a consensus in Hong Kong that democracy is a good thing. Lam Woon-kwong, a former civil servant and since July 2012 the convener of the government's Executive Council, or cabinet, says that "liberal democracy is the only sustainable form of government with relative stability."[2] George Cautherly, vice-chairman of the Hong Kong Democratic Foundation, asserts, "As power only listens to power, and when unchecked, tends to corrupt, democracy as the form of government that empowers the people to keep power in check is the best hope we have."[3]

Yet some in Hong Kong believe democracy should fulfill other purposes. They echo early twentieth-century Chinese intellectuals, such as Liang Qichao, who favored democracy because it could serve the long-standing Confucian goal of fostering unity and harmony among contending viewpoints and interests.[4] Ho Lok-sang, a scholar at Hong Kong's Lingnan University, writes: "According to Western culture, adversarial democracy is the only way democracy should work. But from the point of view of Chinese culture, democracy should not work this way. Democracy is not putting different interest groups at loggerheads against one another. Democracy is laying down one's own interests in pursuit of the common good. Democracy should not imply promising favors to constituents in order to win votes. Democracy should involve everyone working hard to promote the common good."[5] In another essay, Ho argues that Hong Kong lacks a democratic culture, which, he says, is the foundation of a good democratic system. Yet among the elements of his democratic culture are a "readiness to avoid conflicts of interest," "an understanding of what constitutes the public interest," and a commitment to that public interest as opposed to the interests of one's party.[6] In contrast, the typical Western view (as reflected, for example, in *The Federalist Papers*) is that social conflict is unavoidable but that a democratic system can provide institutionalized mechanisms for regulating and mitigating conflict and formulating policies that reflect the broader public interest. On this, the Hong Kong political consultant Alice Wu agrees: "What democracy is supposed to do is enable opponents, even enemies, to co-exist in a shared future. What a democratic culture fosters is an environment where differences can be worked out without destroying communities."[7]

Hong Kong and Democracy in a Comparative Perspective

Whatever the doubts of people like Ho Lok-sang, scholars who have studied democratic systems around the world would argue that absent Hong Kong's unique political context, the odds are very strong that it would make a successful transition to full democracy. It shares all the attributes of other places that have made that transition and consolidated a liberal and competitive order. That is, democracy has not only a normative advantage but also a measure of historical determinism.[8] The basic idea is that authoritarian governments that attempt to strengthen their countries by modernizing their societies become the victims of their own development success, in four ways.

First of all, economic and social change creates sociological and attitudinal conditions that undermine authoritarian rule and foster more pluralistic and competitive systems. Larry Diamond of Stanford University summarizes, "The higher the levels of education, income, mass media exposure, and occupational status, the more democratic the people's attitudes, values and behavior."[9]

Second, modernization fosters the emergence of civil society, which mounts campaigns for a variety of objectives, including political change. A variety of social groups exert pressures for democracy, which increasingly taxes the regime's capacity for repression and threatens the ruling order. Diamond states, "While some regimes dissolve because they never intended to remain in power, most authoritarian rulers only abandon power because society will not let them hold it indefinitely without costs the elite do not wish to pay."[10] In many cases, the opposition's key demand is that elections be held, which, if granted, accelerates the process of democratization. (But note that a civil society campaign will only succeed if its constituent groups can unite to form a broad, anti-government coalition. Division often leads to failure.)

Third, external influences have an impact. Pro-democracy groups in one country can borrow the approaches from their counterparts in another, a phenomenon that was evident in the 2011 Arab Spring as protests echoed across the greater Middle East region. Governments in countries with established democratic systems sometimes exert pressure on authoritarian regimes facing a popular campaign for political liberalization, as the United States did with the democratic transitions in Korea and Taiwan in the late 1980s.

Fourth, as an authoritarian regime tries to respond to demands for democratic change, it often develops splits over strategy and tactics. Stand-pat conservative officials think that continuing repression is the best and only way to preserve the regime's existence. Reformers believe that opening up the political system is necessary to preserve social stability, economic growth, and the regime itself.

Just because these factors are present in a political system does not mean that it will undergo a democratic transition. Indeed, democracy scholars disagree on whether economic and social development actually bring about liberal democracy or are simply associated with its emergence.[11] But there is stronger agreement that once a transition takes place, higher levels of social and economic development will sustain democracy.[12]

Even if such a transition occurs, how it occurs is not preordained. Much depends on the contingent interaction between the regime and the public that seeks to change it: the relative strength of each side, the degree of unity within each camp, and the decisions of each side's leaders on how to proceed at each point in the struggle. In a number of cases, the transition occurs and is defined by a "pact" between the regime and its political opposition, inducing a more incremental process of change.[13] When the struggle for power results in the collapse of the regime, change is more sudden and volatile.

Clearly, these factors have been present in Hong Kong. First of all, Hong Kong is a society that has already traveled the social and economic development road. The best measure of this is the United Nations Development Program's Human Development Index (HDI), which also happens to correlate strongly with the existence of democracy.[14] Of the forty-eight countries that had a very high HDI index in 2014, only eight are not democracies and their rich endowment in natural resources, such as oil, can be associated with their authoritarian politics.[15] Singapore is the only independent Asian country in that category, with an index of .912 and world ranking of eleven. In the same year, Hong Kong was twelfth with an index of .910 and a rank of thirteen.[16]

Second, as expected, social and generational change promoted a broad change in the values of Hong Kong's residents away from their previous accommodation to the status quo and toward skepticism of authority and a belief in the value of political participation.[17] A 2005 study of political attitudes in Taiwan, Hong Kong, and the mainland found a strong correlation between the level of education and political views. Traditional Confucian values are stronger among people with less education, and democratic ones are more common in people with a higher level of schooling. Modernization and the education that comes with it are more powerful than the legacy of traditional culture in defining value sets in contemporary societies.[18]

The Asian Barometer Survey has sought to measure the degree to which people in several Asian political systems have made the transition from subjects

to citizens and from a Confucian deference to authority to a democratic assertion of authority. The survey has developed a battery of questions to rigorously
test the degree of attitude shift. For Hong Kong in 2011:

- 56 percent of those surveyed disagreed that "government leaders are like
  the head of a family; we should all follow their decisions" (23 percent
  agreed).
- 68 percent disagreed that "the government should have the right to prevent the media from publishing ideas that might be destabilizing"
  (14 percent agreed).
- 49 percent disagreed that "the government should decide whether certain
  ideas should be allowed to be discussed in society" (38 percent agreed).
- 46 percent disagreed that "when judges decide important cases, they
  should accept the view of the executive branch" (42 agreed).
- 51 percent disagreed that "if the government is constantly checked by
  the legislature, it cannot possibly accomplish great things" (34 percent
  agreed).
- 54 percent disagreed that "if we have political leaders who are morally
  upright, we can let them decide everything" (37 percent agreed).
- 55 percent disagreed that "when the 'country' is facing a difficult situation, it's OK for the government to disregard the law in order to deal
  with the situation" (30 percent agreed).[19]

Third, Hong Kong has seen a steady growth in its civil society. Community organizations were formed as early as the nineteenth century, mainly to
mediate between Chinese society and the British colonial government. Business, religious, and labor organizations followed, and social service and char-
ity organizations played an important role in coping with the surge of refugees
from the mainland after 1949. In the 1970s and 1980s, a new network of social movements and grassroots groups focused on the consequences of the government's policies of rapid economic growth. Political parties formed in the
early 1990s to participate in the first popular elections and joined the activist
network in the quest for a more democratic system. Thus, a dualistic civil society emerged in Hong Kong: On one side are organizations that are willing to
be co-opted by the government, both pre- and post-reversion, and support its
policies. On the other are groups that remain outside the ambit of the administration and criticize its policies. In Hong Kong's "demonstration a day" culture, more recently facilitated by social media mobilization, the latter groups
exert pressure toward different types of change, including democratization.[20]

Fourth, external factors affect the prospects for democracy in Hong Kong, but in a unique way. Although the Chinese government regards itself as Hong Kong's sovereign and not as an "external" actor, in fact it is an outside actor—the most significant external influence. Overtly through the Basic Law and covertly through its United Front, Beijing sets the boundaries for political contestation in Hong Kong and shifts and redefines those parameters when it deems necessary. The Hong Kong SAR government does not have the absolute right to rule in the territory under its jurisdiction, and who rules in Hong Kong is not determined solely in Hong Kong.[21] Of course, there are other outside influences beyond the PRC. Beijing claims that the United States, the United Kingdom, and Taiwan independence forces are making trouble from behind the scenes. Even if Beijing's claims have an element of truth, these outside forces have a minor, even trivial, impact when compared to the effects of modernization, attitude change, civil society, and Beijing's own policy on political and other aspects of the evolution of Hong Kong.

Finally, there is the issue of whether the establishment and opposition are united or divided. To be sure, there are disagreements within and among the Hong Kong powers that be: the Chinese government, the Hong Kong SAR government, and the business community. The splits over the 2003 National Security Law and questions surrounding the 2012 election for chief executive are the best examples. But by and large, the establishment has held firm, and this relative unity is the strongest reason for the persistence of a political status quo that changes only incrementally, if at all. In contrast, the divisions within the democratic camp have weakened its effectiveness. Even if the authorities were willing to negotiate a pact of some kind to facilitate democratic reform, the opposition might not be sufficiently united to come to the table.[22]

In sum, the policies that the colonial government adopted after World War II to reduce the misery of the refugee population and foster some measure of social stability became the seeds of Hong Kong's democratic momentum. Even if one remains skeptical that economic and social development automatically cause democratization, Hong Kong's modernization certainly makes a transition to democracy more plausible and indicates that Hong Kong should be able to sustain a free, open, and competitive political system once it exists.

Hong Kong's incomplete transition to full democracy was not because its social and economic development was too low, but rather, because the resistance to political change by united power holders, whether British or Chinese, was too high. In effect, the post-reversion system Beijing designed was a poison pill. Ironically, had Chinese officials understood the political consequences of colonial economic and social policies, they might not have maintained the liberal oligarchy version of a hybrid system. But at that time, they likely assumed that Hong Kong residents would continue to worry only about material well-being and did not appreciate the material and attitudinal transition that was already under way.[23] The PRC regime made the commitment in the Joint Declaration to guarantee political rights, but it was spooked by Hong Kong's support for the Tiananmen protests. The only way Beijing thought it could preserve a degree of control in the territory was to tilt the playing field when it came to picking the Hong Kong SAR leaders. In retrospect, Hong Kong's contentious post-reversion politics were almost preordained.

Democratic Dysfunction

In question is not democracy's value in theory or in a comparative perspective but its performance in practice. In the second decade of the twenty-first century, some of the world's democratic systems have been dysfunctional. This point was brought home to me during a visit to Hong Kong in October 2013 to talk with people there about universal suffrage. When I boarded my Hong Kong–bound flight in San Francisco, Washington was enduring another episode of brinksmanship concerning the budget. The federal government had already closed for lack of congressional appropriations, and House Republicans were threatening to block a routine extension of the federal debt ceiling if they didn't get their preferences on taxes and spending. It was not certain that the President, Senate, and House of Representatives would agree on a way to reopen the government and avoid an embarrassing and unprecedented U.S. default. Fourteen hours later, by the time I arrived in Hong Kong, an agreement had been reached and enacted. The debt limit was extended, federal workers returned to their jobs, and financial markets heaved a sigh of relief. Still, it was not the first shutdown, and Hong Kong friends couldn't resist asking what the recurring pattern of brinksmanship said about the quality of American democracy. Why should anyone, they asked, copy a system that allowed a small faction of House members to single-mindedly and recklessly put U.S. national interests at risk? Not bad questions.[24]

The United States is not the only system that elicits such skepticism. Democracy scholars, who both intellectually and normatively believe that democracy is the best political system, have questioned the robustness of worldwide democracy since the mid-2000s. Larry Diamond identified four salient trends:

1. A growing number of democratic breakdowns (coups and the under-mining of electoral freedom and fairness).
2. Weakening rule of law and democratic freedoms as a result of bad governance (corruption, abuse of power).
3. A resurgence of authoritarian regimes.
4. The "decline of democratic efficacy, energy, and self-confidence," including in the West.[25]

There may be disagreements on how severe these trends are, but their existence is without dispute.[26] Russia and Venezuela are obvious examples of leaders' subverting the democratic order; in Greece and Thailand democratic institutions were never firmly consolidated; Taiwan is a case of great, initial promise followed by decay and dysfunction in some areas.[27]

In the eyes of democracy skeptics, a principal cause of democratic dysfunction is "populism," which the democracy scholar Marc F. Plattner defines as a tendency for leaders to press what they assert to be the will of the majority without much regard to "liberalism's emphasis on procedural niceties and protection of individual rights."[28] Those in Hong Kong who prefer gradual political reform or none at all emphasize this danger and the ways radical democrats and civil disobedience actions such as the Occupy Movement are already disrupting politics. Some local political scientists worry that populist forces are and would be independent from existing political formations, such as political parties, which would threaten political stability. They observe that these forces have emerged not just in the Pan-Democratic camp but also on the establishment side. The chances of clashes between protest groups and the authorities are growing, which tests the tolerance of the Hong Kong Police and the Central People's Government in Beijing, which would regard a higher level of social mobilization as a threat to the PRC's national security.[29]

Many members of the business community have the particular fear that an electoral system that empowers the public as a whole and restricts or eliminates their own privileged position will stimulate irresponsible and irresistible demands to expand government-funded social welfare programs. Satisfying those demands will mean imposing heavier tax burdens on them or threaten the fiscal position of the government, and in doing so, undercut economic competitiveness. Ultimately, they argue, choices will have to be made between growth and democracy—and choosing growth has long served Hong Kong well. In October 2014, in the middle of the Occupy Movement, Chief Executive C. Y. Leung famously argued that it was necessary to structure the electoral system to protect the interests of all social sectors. If group representation on the chief executive nominating committee was proportionate to the size of different economic groups in the population, "then obviously you would be talking to half of the people in Hong Kong who earn less than $1,800 a month. Then you would end up with [a populist] kind of politics and policies."[30]

In fact, the economists Robert Barro and Xavier Sala-i-Martin found a suggestive correlation between democracy and growth: in authoritarian countries democratization may foster growth, but in countries that are already substantially democratic it retards growth (Barro and Sala-i-Martin do not examine whether democracy causes variations in growth).[31] The experiences of Asian political systems that expanded civic participation in the 1980s lend credence to the hypothesis that democratization leads to increased welfare spending. Stephan Haggard and Robert Kauffman found that "parties and politicians scrambled to position themselves with respect to pressing social policy issues," and that a high-growth economy enabled further expansion of services. Taiwan and Korea were the most prominent examples of this trend. By implication, in a more democratic Hong Kong the middle class would make the strongest demands and popularly elected politicians would respond. Interestingly, however, the shifts in Korea and Taiwan happened not because lower-class parties demanded more benefits, but because conservative parties preemptively promoted programs such as health care and pensions, which appealed to the middle class, instead of programs that would be attractive to workers.[32] Haggard and Kauffman also found that a reduction of military expenditures changed budget shares in the direction of welfare.

More general viewpoints about democracy are likely in play as well. Yue Chim Richard Wong, of Hong Kong University, is no hidebound conservative. He favors liberal democracy because its elections, rule of law, and political freedoms work together to deter abuse of power by the government. But Wong distinguishes such a "liberal democracy" from "populist democracy," and defines the latter as operating on the premise that every citizen shares a common view of the good and right thing to do. In a populist system, political institutions exist to determine this "general will" and then to enact the desires of the majority. Checks on the popular will are, by definition, unacceptable.[33]

An analysis of the 2007 Asian Barometer Survey data by Chu Yun-han and Huang Min-hua, two democracy scholars in Taiwan, found even more complex distinctions than Wong's when they asked respondents about their underlying attitudes to democracy. Respondents fell into four groups: On one end of the spectrum were "consistent democrats," whose support for democracy was strong and explicit. On the other end were "non-democrats," who had major doubts about democracy and believed in authoritarianism, and "superficial democrats," who only paid lip-service to democracy, but held many contrary attitudes. In the middle were "critical democrats," who believed in liberal democratic principles but also "harbor[ed] some reservation about democracy's preferability, desirability, suitability, efficacy, or priority in a specific historical context." In Hong Kong in 2007, 39.3 percent of respondents were critical democrats, only 26.4 percent were consistent democrats; 19.5 percent were non-democrats, and 14.8 percent were superficial democrats.[34]

For both normative reasons and self-interest, Hong Kong's democracy advocates and democracy skeptics will continue to wage their debate in spite of the public's ambivalence. Perhaps the two sides will never reach common ground; perhaps they will find a path toward a mutually acceptable compromise. The focus for over twenty years has been on elections, and this will likely continue. Yet the fact that some political leaders and some segments of the public have doubts about democracy as a whole highlights the need to probe more deeply into the circumstances under which democracy works well and when it does not.

Widening the Analytic Lens

One way to reconcile the differences between democracy advocates and democracy skeptics is to widen the lens of analysis. This broader view exposes four interrelated distinctions:

1. Between democracy and governance.
2. Between the formal institutions of democracy and the concept of feedback.
3. Between legitimacy based on political process and legitimacy based on performance.
4. Between political development and decay.

THE DISTINCTION BETWEEN DEMOCRACY AND GOVERNANCE

The World Bank defines governance as consisting of "the traditions and institutions by which authority in a country is exercised. This includes the process by which governments are selected, monitored and replaced; the capacity of the government to effectively formulate and implement sound policies; and the respect of citizens and the state for the institutions that govern economic and social interactions among them."[35] Thus, the institutions we associate with democracy—elections, political freedoms—may be a means to the end of good governance but do not guarantee it. Governance also includes the dimensions of state capacity and respect for governing institutions by citizens and the state alike.

This definition places emphasis on the capacity of the state to devise and execute policies in an effective way.[36] This is not a new approach. It stretches back to at least the work of Max Weber and his stress on the necessity of a strong and effective civil service in the management of complex, modern societies. Samuel Huntington elaborated on this Weberian perspective in *Political Order in Changing Societies*. For him, political development and responsible government require the creation of capable, autonomous, and clean institutions before the expansion of political participation (for example, through democratic institutions).[37]

More recently, Francis Fukuyama has comprehensively updated Huntington's work in a major, two-volume study.[38] Fukuyama argues that a well-developed political system must do three basic things: build and maintain an effective state, institute the rule of law, and create methods for accountability. A strong state provides the public goods that society requires for development, and the rule of law and accountability serve to check potential excesses and mistakes of the state. A political system that has all three elements can overcome the most common and problematic characteristic of premodern and modern systems, called by him patrimonialism: when social forces such as families, clans, and economic elites corrupt and subvert both the autonomy and effectiveness of the state and its mechanisms of accountability.

In effect, Fukuyama proposes what Pippa Norris terms a "unified theory" of governance. This approach avoids a "false dichotomy" between democracy and state capacity and instead combines them. In Norris's view, "Development is most often achieved and sustained in societies where the formal institutions of both liberal democracy and bureaucratic governance are simultaneously strengthened in parallel."[39] She evaluates a large number of political systems according to these two variables, using information from the Quality of Government Dataset created by the Quality of Government Institute at the University of Gothenburg.[40] Her analysis resulted in four types of regimes: bureaucratic democracy, where each variable is high; patronage democracy, where state capacity is low and democracy is high; patronage autocracies, where both variables are low; and, bureaucratic autocracies, where state capacity is high and democracy is low.[41] Unfortunately, Hong Kong is not included in the dataset from which Norris draws her analysis, but it would most likely measure high on state capacity and medium-to-low on democracy (Singapore is Norris's poster child for bureaucratic autocracy).[42]

The idea that good governance requires more than one element, as Norris and Fukuyama suggest, raises the issue of sequencing. Norris argues that state capacity and democracy should be developed in parallel. Fukuyama says political development will occur in stages and that outcomes vary according to the sequence in which the building blocks of a developed system are implemented. For instance, England first created a rule of law, then built a strong state, and finally fostered democratic accountability. Germany emphasized a strong state first, with rule of law and democracy coming later (a process interrupted by two devastating wars). The United States did democracy first, beginning in the early nineteenth century and only built a strong state and autonomous rule of law in the twentieth century. For Fukuyama, the best sequence is one in which state building is preceded or accompanied by creation of rule of law to check the state, and then democracy third.[43]

DISTINCTION BETWEEN THE FORMAL INSTITUTIONS
OF DEMOCRACY AND THE CONCEPT OF FEEDBACK

Feedback is a concept used in a variety of fields, including biology, mechanical and electronic engineering, and cybernetics, to name a few. It refers to the process by which the outputs of a system generate signals that feed back into the inputs of that same system and affect its future outputs. David Easton applied systems theory to the study of politics, and feedback is a key element in his theory.[44] Normatively neutral, the use of the concept of feedback has the merit of not placing an ideologically derived value on some forms of feedback over others. Feedback occurs in all political systems—democratic, authoritarian, totalitarian, and others.

Feedback can take many forms, including the institutions and practices that we associate with democracy: elections, legislators' representation of constituents, activities of civil society organizations, the content of a free media, public expressions of political views (rallies and demonstrations), court cases, public opinion polls, lobbying, and so on. Thus, the liberal and electoral dimensions of a liberal democracy institutionalize certain kinds of feedback. In addition, many governments, including the United States, create advisory bodies to explain policies and elicit the opinions of affected interest groups. In systems with a British heritage, the government invites comment on consultation documents on important issues before initiating the legislative process. But feedback can take other, less obvious, forms as well. Some government agencies have an information-gathering function, and others establish reporting systems and mechanisms to monitor their performance. In certain arenas, rumors may drive decisions. Some individuals or groups may bribe officials to secure policies or decisions that favor their interests—this bribery is a form of feedback. Others may mount violent protests because they believe that is the only way to get the government to listen.

In terms of governance, the concept of feedback provokes several questions. Are the signals that officials receive from the public accurate? Reporting to and through government agencies can create a bias in favor of established policy. The findings of public opinion polls can reflect sampling bias or be influenced by the wording of questions. The quality of media information depends on the professionalism of journalists and whether it is respected by media owners. Elections purportedly produce leaders who reflect and support the policy choices of at least a majority of their constituency, but other factors, such as campaign funding, media advertising, and mobilization capacity, are often more important in shaping election outcomes than voters' policy preferences.

Second, which forms of feedback are most reliable as a basis for policy-making? On the one hand, the quantity and quality of information available to government agencies would seem to be more reliable than that available to the media and the public. On the other hand, even though the media, legislators, and the public rely on the information they have, what nongovernmental actors believe to be reality may be more relevant to political action and policy decisions than what officials actually know. On some issues, imperfect, less-informed feedback is the only way to force a government to abandon a policy disaster.

The question of reliability is even more germane to any system of representative government constituted by elections. Elections can be fairly blunt instruments in revealing the balance of public sentiments because factors that have nothing to do with policy preferences often affect voting choices. Sometimes the issues that should be on the policy agenda get ignored or are distorted beyond recognition. Legislators are often torn between supporting the narrow interests of their constituents and donors, and what they themselves understand to be in the best interests of society as a whole.

Third, which types of feedback are most authoritative and legitimate? Here the answer takes a different direction. For all the defects of elections, representative government, and the contemporary media as sources of reliable feedback, and despite clear examples of democratic failure and dysfunction, the formal institutions of democracy are still regarded by most political scientists and many governments as the best way to pick and evaluate leaders, and to formulate policies. Illiberal democracies can maintain the pretense that their leaders have public validation through elections, even though these contests don't permit genuine competition. An authoritarian system like China's may claim that it is a meritocracy, but factors unrelated to talent—such as corruption—may have more impact than merit on personnel choices.

DISTINCTION BETWEEN LEGITIMACY BASED ON POLITICAL PROCESS
AND LEGITIMACY BASED ON PERFORMANCE

Legitimacy is usually defined as the rulers' right to rule and the citizens' obligation to obey. Sources of legitimacy may vary: Max Weber distinguished between tradition, charisma, and a rational-legal order as sources of obedience. An issue of long scholarly debate has been whether it is possible to objectively establish the basis of the right to rule.[45] Some contemporary political scientists usefully distinguish between legitimacy derived from process, such as elections, and legitimacy derived from substantive performance. These are sometimes termed input and output legitimacy.[46]

Representatives of nondemocratic governments such as China's argue that their government derives performance legitimacy from its effectiveness in dealing with the array of problems facing society. They might also argue that process legitimacy is sufficient when the people accept the basis on which leaders are picked and decisions are made in the absence of elections. Singapore's rationale for its system is that citizens accept being governed by officials who are talented and virtuous and are selected through a rigorous and objective selection process. Citizens therefore willingly accept the decisions made by officials based on the officials' expert knowledge and experience. Daniel Bell, a political theorist at Beijing's Tsinghua University, writes, "The basic idea of political meritocracy is that everybody should have an equal opportunity to be educated and to contribute to politics, but not everybody will emerge from this process with an equal capacity to make morally informed political judgments. Hence, the task of politics is to identify those with above average ability and to make them serve the political community. If the leaders perform well, the people will basically go along."[47]

THE DISTINCTION BETWEEN POLITICAL DEVELOPMENT
AND POLITICAL DECAY

One value of Fukuyama's perspective, like that of Huntington before him, is its rejection of the assumption that political systems will necessarily succeed in creating state capacity, rule of law, and accountability once they embark on the road of development. They may accomplish some but not all: imperial

China established state capacity early on and had a semblance of a legal system, but never created mechanisms for popular accountability.

Fukuyama also rejects the idea that a developed political system is immune from political decay. In fact, this can occur in at least two ways. The first is a resurgence of patrimonialism or other dynamics that can corrode a developed system. Social forces capture and corrupt the state and then undermine effective and autonomous governance, the rule of law, and democratic accountability. The second is a power imbalance among the three pillars of a developed state. Fukuyama argues, "A well-functioning and legitimate regime needs to achieve balance between government power and institutions that constrain the state. Things can become unbalanced in either direction, with insufficient checks on state power on the one hand, or excessive veto power by different social groups on the other that prevent any sort of collective action."[48] In the second volume of *Political Order and Political Decay* Fukuyama reserves special criticism for the "political decay" that has beset the United States over recent decades: the declining autonomy of executive branch agencies, a revival of the nineteenth-century dominance of courts and parties, the growing role of money in politics, particularly in Congress, and the power of small minorities to block the will of the majority ("vetocracy").[49]

Assessing the Quality of Hong Kong's Governance

The World Bank, which has been in the vanguard of promoting stronger state capacity and good governance, developed six indicators to assess political systems around the world: voice (the freedoms of expression, assembly, association, and so on) and accountability, political stability and absence of violence, government effectiveness, regulatory quality, rule of law, and control of corruption. It then generated indices for each of these by combining the results of several existing indicators.[50] The results for Hong Kong are mixed (see table 7-1). When it comes to the work of government per se, Hong Kong is a world leader. The indicators on the rule of law and control of corruption are not quite as high, but are still very strong. For political stability, and voice and accountability (the indicator most relevant to democracy), however, Hong Kong is only around the seventieth percentile.

POLITICAL DEVELOPMENT

Pippa Norris and Frank Fukuyama basically share the World Bank's view on the components of a well-governed political system, so it is interesting to speculate on how they would evaluate Hong Kong's political development. Norris

TABLE 7-1. World Bank Governance Indicators for Hong Kong, 1998–2013

Global percentile ranks

Indicator	1998	2006	2013
Government effectiveness	86.8	97.1	95.7
Regulatory quality	98.5	100	99.5
Rule of law	80.4	90.9	91
Control of corruption	91.7	93.7	92.3
Political stability/absence of violence	64.4	87.5	74.4
Voice and accountability	45.7	62.5	69.2

Source: World Bank, "Country Data Report for Hong Kong, SAR, China, 1996–2013" (http://info.worldbank.org/governance/wgi/index.aspx#countryReports, for link to Hong Kong SAR report).

would probably give high marks to Hong Kong for its relatively strong bureaucratic institutions, but fault both the British and Chinese governments for allowing liberal democracy to lag behind state building. Fukuyama would likely agree that the territory was ready a while ago for better mechanisms of accountability, but he would have approved the British sequence. The rule of law came first, in the early days of colonial rule, followed by the creation of strong state capacity after World War II, to facilitate economic development and human welfare as well as defend against the dangers of leftist destabilization. Finally, the initial foundation for democratic accountability was established. He would likely regret that neither the colonial government nor the Chinese sovereign has seen fit to finish that job, even if he might understand the Hong Kong–specific reasons at play. Moreover, Fukuyama would be alert to signs of political decay: some decline in the autonomy of the civil service; cases of corruption involving senior officials; and the proliferation of "vetocracy," where small groups of politicians or civil society groups are able to block government initiatives by legislative tactics or through public protests. In short, he would say Hong Kong's political development is marked both by incomplete progress and some signs of political decay.

GOVERNANCE AND DEMOCRACY

There is a temporal correlation between the purported decline in the Hong Kong government's effectiveness and its partial democratization. Up until the early 1990s, the system was meritocratic with a highly effective civil service, for which officials were recruited and then promoted on the basis of their ability.[51] The system adopted "an elitist and even authoritarian approach to policymaking, in which career and non-elected bureaucrats, as an elite group and an intellectual class, serve as the guardian of the public interest."[52] To be effective, the civil service required sound direction from the political leadership and public compliance, but four factors ensured its autonomy and capacity:

1. Ultimate political authority was outside Hong Kong.
2. The civil service acted as an arbiter among various social interests above and for the good of society as a whole.
3. The legislature followed the executive's lead.
4. The colony's population was politically quiescent.

Complications began to arise in the early 1990s—the reason why is a matter of some dispute. Regina Ip, a pro-establishment politician and member of the LegCo who came out of the civil service tradition, has argued that governance has suffered since direct elections began in 1991. She has criticized the quality and motives of some of her fellow LegCo members and called for a political system that "would actually work, in a way that will increase our overall happiness and wealth."[53] Scholars removed from politics offer similar yet more analytical explanations, stating that during the 1990s the previously effective integration of the British political leadership (the civil service, LegCo, and political parties) and social interests eroded.

But a correlation does not necessarily reflect a causal relationship. A lot was happening in Hong Kong in the early 1990s and in its relationship with the mainland. Whereas the territory's public had had no say in whom London appointed as the colonial governor nor what his policies would be, Beijing had mandated that Hong Kong residents would govern Hong Kong. Naturally, who those people were, how they were chosen, and what policies they would pursue became the subject of local political struggle. More broadly, democracy was regarded not as inherently desirable but as a means to check how Hong Kong's new sovereign, an authoritarian China, would exercise its power. Elections alone did not lead to a decline in governance.

Hong Kong scholars have come up with different explanations of why the quality of governance declined. Zhang Baohui, a professor of political science at Lingnan University, believes that dysfunction is the result of poor institutional design—more precisely, an institutional design based on an anachronistic assumption: that executive-led government would continue, but with Chinese rather than British characteristics. The Basic Law and local ordinances promoted a version of executive-led government by restricting the powers of the

Legislative Council and by mandating that the chief executive should be above partisan politics and not a member of any political party. But the post-reversion system did not work as intended. At least half of the LegCo members were democratically elected and those members soon discovered procedural ways to hold the chief executive and his subordinates accountable in spite of the Basic Law's restrictions on the LegCo's powers. When it came time to vote on draft laws, the chief executive could not count on support from even the legislators whose policy orientation was similar to his own, because he lacked the leverage that being head of the majority party or a coalition of parties might provide. Adoption of a proportional representation system for democratically elected LegCo seats only fostered more political fragmentation.[54]

Scholars have offered different terms to characterize the system that resulted. Anthony B. L. Cheung, C. Y. Leung's secretary of transportation and housing and a former president of the Hong Kong Institute of Education, once described the Hong Kong system under the Basic Law as one of "disabled governance."[55] Synergynet, a Hong Kong think tank whose members' views tend to align with those of the Pan-Democratic camp, states: "In the process of governance it is not possible to coordinate among different stakeholders (principal officers, political parties, political groups, civil groups). In the end, this creates an administrative problem of 'multiple disconnection of the governance system.'"[56] Ian Scott of Hong Kong University speaks of a "disarticulated system," in the sense of becoming unhinged.

Scott's analysis is important because he looks in detail at the decline in the effectiveness of the civil service after reversion.[57] As of 2016, the institution is composed of thirteen policy bureaus that are the permanent agencies for formulating and implementing the government's policies. In effect, they constitute the core of the executive branch. The head of the civil service is the chief secretary for administration, who oversees nine policy bureaus: civil service, constitutional and mainland affairs, education, environment, food and health, home affairs, labor and welfare, security, and transportation and housing. Under the finance secretary are four policy bureaus: commerce and development, development, financial services and treasury, and innovation and technology. If Hong Kong were a country, the policy bureaus would be the government ministries. (The judicial branch of the government is headed by the secretary of justice, who supervises the department of justice.)

In the colonial period, the civil service was a highly autonomous institution, staffed by highly trained and disciplined individuals who regarded public service as a vocation. It was the policy instrument of London-appointed governors—not a perfect tool, but still highly effective. After 1997, the integrity of the bureaucratic instrument came under pressure from two directions. On the one hand, the new Hong Kong SAR leadership sought to impose a different form of political control, which was not surprising, because broad policy direction would no longer be coming from colonial governors. The second source of pressure came from the PRC. Beijing's appointing Hong Kong people to govern Hong Kong meant that these people needed to find their own means of establishing authority.

The first chief executive, C. H. Tung, used two ways to create political dominance over a civil service accustomed to autonomy. The first was the principal officer accountability system, whereby the government's "principal officers"— the chief secretaries for administration, finance, and justice and the heads of the policy bureaus—would be political appointees chosen by the chief executive, formally appointed by Beijing, and reporting directly to the chief executive. The expectation was that these officers would, unlike before, come from outside the civil service and therefore be more loyal and responsive to the chief executive. But that was not what happened. Because talented people were not always willing and available to be public servants, the chief executive often had to rely on senior civil servants to become principal officers. This presented the senior civil servants who had been picked with a choice between political loyalty to the chief executive and adherence to norms of the administration. Ultimately, those who agreed to serve did not form a coherent group in terms of political philosophy and background as Tung had originally expected.[58]

Tung's second measure was to institute management reforms that placed emphasis on responsiveness to the political leadership rather than on the norms of public service. The reforms set terms of employment on a contractual basis and privatized some functions that previously had been performed by the government. These shifts had the (unintended) effect of reducing both the size of the civil service cadre and the sense of public service as a vocation. If these pressures from Hong Kong's new political masters were not stressful enough, legislators, political parties, and civil society leveled criticisms of government policy. Civil servants were no longer the arbiters of social interests but became one of several contestants in the struggle over policy. Disarticulation was the result.

Brian Fong of the Hong Kong Institute of Education attributes the problems of the post-1997 system less to its design per se and more to the weakening of its ties to the community at large. From the nineteenth century on, local Chinese businessmen provided those links and facilitated certain social services. Gradually, representatives of the local elite were appointed to advisory boards and as unofficial members of LegCo, but economic modernization and the government's assumption of responsibility to provide social services weakened the business community's ties to society. These new trends also took away the nondemocratic but still representative function that local elites played. Once reversion occurred, the Hong Kong SAR leadership could not govern because it lacked broad social support and could only rely on the more wealthy elements of the business elite, who had already been co-opted by Beijing and only represented their own sectors.[59]

FEEDBACK IN HONG KONG

Hong Kong displays many of the feedback mechanisms associated with effective political systems. Civil service departments have routines for assessing and reporting their performance and that of their employees. They commission public opinion polls to measure levels of approval and disapproval, and conduct studies on specific issues. The consultation process invites public views on policy proposals and the government uses an array of advisory committees and bodies to tap into expert and stakeholder opinion. The Independent Commission Against Corruption system facilitates the exposure, investigation, and punishment of official abuses great and small. Local scholars produce assessments of government policy and some newspapers provide critiques on a daily basis.[60] Orderly demonstrations, conducted in coordination with the police, have become a daily occurrence, and political parties and civil society groups organize to lobby for their programs and causes. At least some seats in the LegCo are filled by popular elections (the rest in functional constituencies). LegCo members use weekly question time and their power over the purse to shape government policy and get information into the public domain. The Central People's Government in Beijing periodically comments on government performance.

In the last decade, other forms of feedback have appeared:

- Democratic legislators who oppose government policies engage in LegCo filibusters to throw sand in the gears of the legislative process. For example, in early 2015 they blocked passage of funding for a new information and technology bureau.
- Citizens who are unhappy with government initiatives, particularly those that affect local communities, mount noisy opposition, both directly and through members of district councils. The list of issues where proposals have been set aside because of citizen opposition is

long: land reclamation, importing labor, health care, pension reform, garbage treatment, tax reform, and improving tunnel traffic under Hong Kong harbor.[61]

- Opponents of policies that do get enacted have the option of seeking judicial review with the Court of Final Appeal, which assesses whether laws are consistent with the Basic Law. From 2004 to 2013, there were 1,451 applications for review, an average of 145 per year. Although the court sided with the government in 76.7 percent of the cases, fighting them still consumed time and resources.[62] Andrew Li, the court's first chief justice, argued that the increase in these cases was a "reflection of the unsatisfactory functioning of the political process [which was] entirely outside the judiciary's responsibility."[63] However, he felt it was still possible for the court to properly accept or reject such cases on procedural grounds.

- Although traditionally the Independent Commission Against Corruption process begins with confidential citizen complaints, some individuals make complaints quite publicly. One observer asked, "Why do the complainants—all active in political affairs—do this [make public complaints]? Because it is an easy way to generate good publicity for themselves and smear their opponents, or those associated with them. They are, in short, using the ICAC as a political weapon."[64]

- The Umbrella Movement rhetorically promoted democratic objectives but relied on civil disobedience methods (see chapter 4).

Thus, Hong Kong's pro-government camp would likely argue that their radically inclined opponents are subverting legitimate and perfectly effective forms of feedback, and are doing so not to improve governance but just to engage in a political struggle. It would say that any movement toward the type of accountability that full electoral democracy might provide should occur gradually. The democratic camp might agree that some current feedback techniques are excessive, but that the effectiveness of government will be undermined unless and until voters can use elections to express their preferences. In their view, unorthodox feedback mechanisms have surged because formal mechanisms are deficient.

LEGITIMACY

Hong Kong observers clearly understand the distinction between performance legitimacy and process legitimacy. In the wake of the Umbrella Movement, the veteran journalist Michael Chugani vented his frustration that "politicians and government officials are so locked in clashes over [democracy] that they have neglected other things that actually make a difference in people's everyday lives. . . . It would be nice to know democracy would fix all the things that are broken, but we know it's not a magic wand."[65] The *South China Morning Post* rejected the "false dichotomy" that individuals in the establishment camp had posed. "Enhancing economic competitiveness and advocating democratic reform are not two incompatible goals. Indeed, many have argued that the one needs the other."[66] Meanwhile, Benny Tai (in Chinese, Dai Yaoyan), the lead organizer of the original Occupy Central, sought to identify a middle ground by stating precisely the distinction between performance and process legitimacy: the first was based on results and the second, on compliance with "principles." Tai urged Beijing to seek a better balance between the two.[67]

In a sense, the views of contending Hong Kong political forces on the two types of legitimacy are just a matter of different emphasis. Pan-Democrats argue that improving process legitimacy by instituting "genuine" universal suffrage is the precondition for restoring some measure of performance legitimacy. Conservatives would say that what the democrats seek will only undermine performance legitimacy and destabilize a perfectly effective political process. In reality, the two kinds of legitimacy must work together.

Conclusion

Obviously, there is both overlap and tension between different elements of governance. Process legitimacy is more associated with democratic institutions (accountability) and certain kinds of feedback. Performance legitimacy is more associated with state capacity and other types of feedback. If governments were omniscient, clean, and staffed by individuals who were both talented and humble, there might be no reason for external feedback and accountability mechanisms. But governments never reach that ideal standard. Officials lack complete knowledge of the effects of their policies and can be tempted to use their public power for private gain. They do not always tell their superiors the unvarnished truth. So external checks are necessary. If voters, civic activists, and interest groups were both self-interested and all-knowing about the challenges that their government faced, and if democratic institutions were not vulnerable to distortions of the popular will, then the operation of those institutions would provide high-quality feedback. But that is not always the case, either. The proper mix of internal autonomy and capacity and external feedback and accountability is never clear.

Hong Kong is not the only political system that has become "disarticulated" or "disabled" or "disconnected" in the process of political transition, and has experienced a change in the balance of power between state and society. Taiwan, which moved from an authoritarian system to a democratic one from the late 1980s to the mid-1990s, faced similar challenges in adapting the old party-state to a pluralistic and competitive order. The system functioned adequately as long as the executive branch and the legislature were controlled by the old ruling party, the Kuomintang, in part because members of the bureaucracy and the military had been expected to join that party. But when the opposition Democratic Progressive Party gained control of the executive branch in 2000, disarticulation occurred. All such transitional systems require some degree of reengineering to create a new type of system integration. Per Synergynet, "It will be difficult to truly improve Hong Kong's governance if we simply change the SAR CE electoral system without reforming the system as a whole."[68]

Whatever the blueprint for a successful reengineering and whatever the recipe for an effective mix of state capacity, feedback, and legitimacy, one thing is certain: popular political participation is here to stay in Hong Kong, whether it is channeled through institutions or expressed outside them. Beijing inherited the British legacy of success at economic and social modernization, which had the predictable effect on the public's political attitudes and reform expectations. Democracy is certainly not a sufficient condition for a well-governed political system, but it has become a necessary one in Hong Kong. Continuing to restrict electoral choice will not induce a return to political quiescence, but will likely ensure a continuation of the protest culture. Popular election of the chief executive and all the members of the LegCo will not by themselves ensure policy effectiveness and performance legitimacy even if it might increase process legitimacy and broaden sources of feedback. But good, well-designed, and effective democratic institutions can increase good governance by enhancing incentives to channel most political participation through those institutions and restoring public trust in them. Johnny Mok, a Hong Kong barrister and member of the Law Committee of the PRC National People's Congress, may have a preference for the offices and bodies created by the Basic Law, but his reasoning applies to institutions more broadly: "The more effective [Hong Kong] institutions are in carrying out their duties, the more dynamic will they function as the engines of our autonomy.... It is the combined strength of all our key institutions that will guarantee our city's autonomy, up to 2047 and beyond."[69]

EIGHT

Hong Kong's Economy

More than anything, it was Hong Kong's economic success that turned a desperate refugee population into a stable and civilized society.[1] Although the government provided the necessary policy infrastructure, it was companies and workers that stimulated the transformative economic miracle. Sustaining economic growth and competitiveness may not guarantee social stability as it once did, if only because the city has become politicized, but it remains important. The question is how to sustain growth, given the power of globalization, rapid technological change, social change within Hong Kong, and the transformation of the Chinese economy across the border. As in the past, Hong Kong's future competitiveness will be determined primarily by market forces and the business acumen of private firms. Local firms cannot assume that the products or services they provide today will yield the same degree of profit tomorrow, because other firms will seek to take over the market niche they have dominated. So they will have to innovate in some way or go out of business. Government policy remains secondary but still critical, its aims being to design the policy environment and infrastructure in which Hong Kong firms act, to negotiate with Beijing on new avenues for local growth, and to remove Chinese regulations that are unfriendly to Hong Kong firms. Social and political trends within Hong Kong can both constrain and stimulate competitiveness.

171

The Hong Kong government is well aware of the need to maintain a competitive economy. Speaking in February 2014, John Tsang, Hong Kong's finance secretary, offered the government's view regarding the public concern that Hong Kong was "losing its edge," and warned, "Our competitors are also striving for excellence, [so] we have to work harder to stay ahead." But he emphasized that Hong Kong could rely in the future on the factors that had fostered past success: "grasping the opportunities presented by our country's [that is, China's] success, . . . our steadfast commitment to free market principles, and to our firm positioning as a world city." On the elements of the free market regime, Tsang cited the rule of law, a "level playing field promoting fair competition, an efficient public sector, and a simple and low tax regime."[2] The persistent question, then, is how to turn the aspiration of "grasping opportunities" into reality.

Historical Context

Hong Kong has been an interface between China and the international economy for almost two centuries. It was an entrepôt before World War II and from the 1950s to the 1980s, and when the Chinese economy was closed, it became a production-and-assembly platform for export-oriented companies, both local and international. Once China reopened to the global economy in 1979, Hong Kong companies shifted operations into China (mainly Guangdong Province) and so facilitated the rise of the mainland's labor-intensive export industries. Yet as the global and Chinese economies have changed, Hong Kong has constantly had to reengineer its interface with both of them to remain competitive.

Hong Kong's post-1979 relationship with Guangdong illustrates this challenge. Once China adopted its reform and opening up policies, Guangdong's Pearl River Delta region provided an optimal and cost-effective opportunity for Hong Kong firms facing rising local wage bills. They relocated their assembly and manufacturing operations to the Pearl River Delta while keeping business operations in Hong Kong. Guangdong was "the factory" and Hong Kong was "the shop," or front office. Before 2003, Guangdong received 30 percent of China's inbound foreign direct investment, with 90 percent of the province's foreign direct investment coming from Hong Kong. Hong Kong firms in Guangdong were prominent in "labor-intensive and pollution-heavy" industries such as leather tanning, shoemaking, and textile and garment production. As a result, Hong Kong helped lead an autarchic Chinese economy into the world of globalization. Its companies provided the capital, technology, management skills, and knowledge of markets in advanced economies, knowledge that, when transferred to mainland Chinese enterprises, allowed the Chinese economy to take off. And Hong Kong prospered as a result; it was a symbiotic, mutually beneficial relationship.

Then, in the middle of the 2000s, four things happened that altered this relationship. First, Hong Kong companies faced a changing economic environment in southern China, as labor shortages, rising wages, and new environmental regulations cut into their narrow profit margins.

Second, competition emerged from indigenous Chinese firms that sought to reap the advantages that Hong Kong firms enjoyed.[3]

Third, Chinese economic policy changed, with policymakers now preferring "clean, high value-added industries that can compete well in global markets" instead of production and assembly operations. "This new orientation ... eliminated most of [Hong Kong firms'] cost advantages in Guangdong, while also cancelling advantages in expertise." Guangdong began to move to an economy based on advanced manufacturing, innovation, services, and consumption.[4] The options of Hong Kong firms were to close down, move operations inland or to Southeast Asia, innovate, or shift into different sectors. According to a Federation of Hong Kong Industries report, the number of Hong Kong–financed factories in Guangdong declined by 40 percent from 2008 to 2013.[5]

Fourth, and most significant politically, there was a change in the direction of the flow of economic influence between Hong Kong and China. Instead of China's gaining economic benefits from Hong Kong, China began to provide benefits to Hong Kong. It was Beijing that helped lift Hong Kong out of its economic doldrums after the Asian financial crisis in the late 1990s, in three ways: permitting PRC citizens to go to Hong Kong as tourists, liberalizing trade with the territory in 2003 through the Mainland and Hong Kong Closer Economic Partnership Arrangement, and giving Hong Kong financial institutions the first crack at facilitating the internationalization of China's currency, the renminbi (RMB). Instead of Hong Kong's serving as the primary gateway to China, it has become one of China's gateways to the global economy. There was some fear in the Hong Kong SAR that Shanghai might regain its prewar position as the premier economic gateway into China and relegate Hong Kong to a secondary position.[6]

Can Hong Kong—the government, companies, employees, and consumers—engineer a new interface between it and China and the international economy? Can it retain the hybrid economic position that has served it well for almost two centuries? Or is it destined to become, as the saying goes, "just another Chinese city"? This chapter explores these questions by assessing Hong Kong's past economic performance and the debate over the key impediment to future success.

The Statistical and Ratings Picture

If we look at broad statistical measures of economic performance, Hong Kong appears to have little to worry about. According to 2014 estimates in the CIA's *World Factbook,* Hong Kong's gross domestic product (GDP), using purchasing power parity (PPP) methodology, was $414.5 billion, 45th worldwide, with a population just over 7 million people, 103rd worldwide. In 2015, the estimated real growth rate was 2.5 percent, a very respectful rate for a mature economy in which services have long since surpassed manufacturing and agriculture as the principal sector. Services accounted for 93 percent of GDP and manufacturing for the rest. Total trade was $1,023.7 billion, with China as the principal market for both exports (53.9 percent) and imports (47.1 percent). The stock of inbound and outbound direct foreign investment was about equal, $1.65 trillion more or less. Life expectancy at birth is 82.9 years, education expenditures in 2015 were 3.9 percent of GDP, and the total number of years of schooling (primary to tertiary) that a child can expect to receive ("school life expectancy") is sixteen years.[7]

But economic performance is about the past. How can one assess Hong Kong's future, its economic competitiveness? Several organizations have sought to define and measure economic competitiveness. The World Economic Forum (WEF) defines competitiveness as "the set of institutions, policies, and factors that determine the level of productivity of a country."[8] Competitiveness is therefore a means to the end of promoting growth and prosperity. Inherent in the idea of competition is that each economy exists within a global context in which all economies seek relative advantage while each one's factors for growth are constantly changing. Moreover, in advanced societies there is a general expectation that the benefits of growth should be distributed to all members of society, rather than just those who are better off. The WEF is among the organizations that periodically measure and rank the competitiveness of economies around the world. The International Institute for Management Development (IMD) is another. Each has its own methodology with a mix of objective and more subjective indicators. In all of these, Hong Kong ranks very well.

The WEF has identified twelve "pillars of competitiveness." Four pillars— "basic requirements"—are grouped together to compose one subindex: legal and administrative institutions, infrastructure, macroeconomic environment, and health and primary education. Six pillars concern enhancement of "efficiency" and form a second subindex: higher education and training; goods market efficiency; labor market efficiency; financial market development; technological readiness; and market size. The final two pillars are innovation and business sophistication and they combine to form a third subindex. In terms of overall index rankings for 2014–15, Hong Kong was ranked seventh worldwide with a score of 5.46 out of a total of 7 (the same rank as for 2013–14, and up two positions from ninth in 2012–13). For both "basic requirements" and "efficiency enhancement" subindices, Hong Kong ranked third in the world with scores of 6.19 and 5.58, respectively. Within these two, it received particularly high marks on infrastructure, financial market development, and efficiency of its goods and labor markets. On the third subindex, made up of innovation and business sophistication, Hong Kong was ranked twenty-third (4.75), still pretty high on a global basis but a drop of four slots since the last report.[9]

The IMD assessment is based on four major factors—economic performance, government efficiency, business efficiency, and infrastructure—and a variety of subordinate issues within each factor. Overall in 2014, Hong Kong ranked fourth worldwide, after the United States, Switzerland, and Singapore, which was a modest drop from first in 2011 and 2012, and third in 2013. Its ranking within each of the four factors:

- Economic performance: seventh, with prices as the only negative subfactor (below twentieth worldwide).
- Government efficiency: second, with "societal framework" as the only negative subfactor.
- Business efficiency: third with no negative subfactors.
- Infrastructure: twenty-first.
- Technological infrastructure: first.[10]

Despite strong economic performance data and competitiveness scores, Hong Kong is not performing as well as it might. Singapore provides an interesting comparison case because it has similar social and demographic characteristics as Hong Kong, and experienced rapid economic growth during the same time period. Its land mass is 63 percent of Hong Kong's and its population is 78 percent of the territory's. But Singapore's GDP (PPP) is over 10 percent higher than Hong Kong's at $445.2 billion. Singapore's real growth rate is 2.9 percent and its GDP per capita (PPP) was 47 percent higher ($81,300 versus $55,200).[11]

The WEF identified competitiveness problems related to Hong Kong's innovation and business sophistication. Comparing Hong Kong with other economies, the WEF warned that it "must improve on higher education (22nd) and innovation (26th, down three places in a year). In the latter category, the quality of research institutions (32nd, down one) and the limited availability of scientists and engineers (36th, down four) remain the two key issues to be addressed." The WEF also reported other problems: inefficient government bureaucracy, inflation, and policy instability.[12] Although the IMD placed Hong Kong in first place on technological infrastructure, it ranked worse than twentieth on all the other major indicators: basic infrastructure, scientific infrastructure, health and environment, and restrictive labor regulations.[13] Thus, the WEF and IMD agree in some areas (education and science) but not in others (basic infrastructure), no doubt reflecting differences in definition, methodology, and reliability of measurement. On the areas where the two diverge, the differences are modest for the factors measured objectively but far more likely on those that rely on subjective assessments. For example, the WEF uses questionnaires from local informants to compile some of its indicators, but the modest number of surveys returned likely skews the resulting factor values.[14]

Thus, Hong Kong faces challenges and limitations but also offers opportunities and advantages. Several issues remain the subject of ongoing debate: Which sectors can contribute to future growth? What are the advantages and risks of dependence on the Chinese economy? What is the proper level and allocation of government resources? How can the need for human capital be met? What can be done to reduce the high inequality of income and wealth, and increase access to education, employment, and housing?

Enduring Assets

There is general consensus in Hong Kong that two sources of its long-term competitiveness must be preserved at all costs. The first is the primacy of rule of law and independence of the judiciary—on this there is no dissent, for obvious reasons: a strong legal framework protects property rights of all kinds, provides due process of law and an authoritative resolution of disputes, and ensures business confidence. Hong Kong's strong rule of law is what leads mainland firms preparing initial public offerings to do them in Hong Kong rather than through their domestic system. Rule of law requires strong institutions to deter any attempts to bribe judges, and Hong Kong has those institutions.

The second element of economic success is fiscal prudence. Here the consensus is not as broad as with the rule of law, mainly because of differences in opinion on how much prudence is necessary. The danger of uncontrolled deficit spending is widely understood, but disagreements remain over the allocation of the government's fiscal resources, and the Hong Kong SAR government has been criticized for sacrificing public welfare to ensure balanced budgets. Article 107 of the Basic Law states that the Hong Kong government should "strive to achieve a fiscal balance, avoid deficits and keep the budget commensurate with the growth rate of its gross domestic product."[15] In line with that mandate, the unwritten rule is that the government's operating and capital budgets should constitute no more than 20 percent of GDP. For 2013–14, the total spent was $56 billion, around 19 percent of GDP.[16] The operating budget made up 78.1 percent of total expenditures and 21.9 percent was for capital costs.[17] Operating revenues are composed of direct taxes on individuals and companies (51.6 percent of the total), indirect taxes of which stamp duties are the largest (29.3 percent), and other revenues, of which investment income is most important (19.0 percent).[18] Total revenue for the 2013–14 fiscal year was $45.8 billion.

The rates for direct taxes are relatively low. After generous deductions and adjustments are taken as appropriate, the following tax rates apply:

- Profits tax: 16.5 percent for corporations and 15 percent for unincorporated businesses.
- Property tax: 15 percent, with 75 percent on any amount under $3,222 waived.
- Salaries tax: 2 percent on the first $5,155; 7 percent on the next $5,155, 12 percent on the next $5,155, and 17 percent on the remainder.[19]

In fiscal year 2013–14, 84 percent of revenues for the capital budget came from land premiums paid to the government by lessors of land when they sign the lease. For operating expenditures in the same year, 50.7 percent was spent on direct expenditures of the government departments; 33.4 percent on education, health, social welfare, and similar categories; and the remainder on one-time expenses such as tax rebates. The capital budget was $12.4 billion.

Some in Hong Kong would say that the problem with the Hong Kong government's fiscal management has been not deficits but recurring surpluses.

These critics point out that financial authorities have underestimated revenues and overestimated expenditures since the mid-2000s. For example, Financial Secretary John Tsang's original estimate for the 2013–14 fiscal year was for a deficit of $632 million. In February 2014 he revised that to a surplus of $1.546 billion, but the final accounts revealed a surplus of $2.706 billion![20] Some of the overestimation was understandable: a few expenditures did not occur as budgeted and revenues were sometimes higher than expected. Although the actual surplus was only around 5 percent of the total budget, the consistent lowballing of the surplus suggested a methodological bias, making Tsang the object of criticism and ridicule from politicians and the media. By 2015, the reserve fund, where operating surpluses are stored, was approximately $14.175 billion, not a small nest egg.[21] Tsang returned some of the surplus to taxpayers and businesses as an ad hoc payment, not by increasing recurrent expenditures. This windfall did not stop the ridicule.[22]

One reason for Tsang's fiscal conservatism was his belief that expenditures would soon balloon as Hong Kong's population aged. To better understand the problem—or to create a rationale for continuing to restrict government expenditures?—in the first half of 2013 he set up a Working Group on Long-Term Fiscal Planning whose members were all experts in public finance. The Working Group released its report in March 2014. Assuming that tax policy and tax rates would remain the same, the report estimated that government revenue would grow 4.5 percent for the next twenty to thirty years. It set out three different scenarios for expenditures in combined spending on education, social welfare, and health care. The scenarios were: continuing to spend at the current level; increasing spending by 1 to 2 percent per year; and increasing spending by an annual rate of 3 percent. Taking into account demographic and price factors, greater spending in the three categories would create permanent budget deficits after fifteen years under the first scenario, after eight to ten years under the second scenario, and after seven years under the third.[23] The Working Group recommended that the government "implement a combination of measures, including containing expenditure growth, preserving the revenue base and saving for future generations, to cope with the fiscal challenges ahead."[24] In his response to the report, Tsang recommended better tax-collection enforcement and increasing the fees the government charged for some of its services. Also, he called for greater cost control of government expenditures, but had no enthusiasm for increasing direct taxes. His only hint of flexibility was a proposal to consider using some of the accumulated surpluses for a "future fund," but these would be used to cover infrastructure projects should the budget go into deficit. Using the surpluses for the needs of the aging population was never actually mentioned.[25]

Capitalizing on China's Growth

Hong Kong has little choice but to ride the wave of Chinese economic growth. Its proximity to the mainland and small size of population and economic output make this inevitable. Historically, its opportunity has lain in the gap between the two economies, which varies depending on the economic sector, stage of development, and skill sets. The most telling measure of these differences is per capita GDP, which in 2013 was $6,747 for China in exchange rate terms and $37,777 for Hong Kong.[26] Because Hong Kong possesses skills and resources that China has lacked, it can export those northward to the benefit of both economies. This is what Hong Kong companies did in the field of consumer-goods manufacturing after 1979.

The China–Hong Kong development gap and the economic complementarity it facilitates mean that Hong Kong SAR's firms must think in terms of which sectors have the greatest potential to contribute to China's growth that Chinese firms cannot provide themselves. This is a moving target, of course, because the Chinese economy is changing significantly. The evolution of the Guangdong economy, which some analysts regard as "emerging as a globally important innovation zone and consumer market," is only a foretaste of a much broader shift.[27] The central reform goal of the current Chinese leadership is to simultaneously reduce the very high rate of investment and achieve higher levels of domestic consumption. The first tranche of reforms was announced at the third plenary session of the Chinese Communist Party's Eighteenth Party Congress in 2014, and included measures to stimulate innovation and productivity growth, rein in wasteful investment, and raise household income and consumption.[28]

In 2002, the Hong Kong government identified four "key industries" as the ones that had the greatest potential for future growth. The four key industries are financial services, tourism, trading and logistics, and professional and producer services. All four are part of Hong Kong's interface with the mainland economy. They have been "the driving force of Hong Kong's economic growth, providing impetus to growth of other sectors and creating employment." In 2013 they contributed 57.8 percent of GDP in terms of value added and employed 47.3 percent of the workforce, with trade and logistics leading both metrics.

In 2009, then chief executive Donald Tsang pinpointed six additional "selected emerging industries" as having "advantages for further development." These six are food and product safety, cultural and creative industries, medical services, education services, environmental industries, and innovation and technology. Clearly, the watchword here is diversity. Testing and certification services target the mainland, where food and product safety has been a serious problem. Cultural and creative industries and medical services address the needs of the Hong Kong SAR's aging middle-class society. Education services and environmental industries are needed both in Hong Kong and on the mainland. Innovation and technology is likely stimulated by the demands of a globalizing economy and China's own modernization. In 2013, these six sectors provided 9.1 percent of GDP in value added and accounted for 12.1 percent of employment, with culture and creative industries in the lead.[29]

Of the four leading industries, the continuing potential for financial services is most obvious. Hong Kong firms manage initial public offerings for mainland companies that wish to go public in an established international financial center. Hong Kong firms also are skilled at mergers and acquisitions and wealth management for PRC residents with substantial assets. The Hong Kong SAR government expressed hope that the territory's financial services industry could serve as the bond-issuing center for Beijing's regional infrastructure investment initiatives, such as the Asian Infrastructure Investment Bank.[30] In addition, any economic activity that is grounded in Hong Kong's superior legal system, such as legal and arbitration services, will benefit as long as China's own legal system remains procedurally unpredictable and subject to political interference.[31]

The most important finance-related task to which Hong Kong can contribute is the internationalization of the renminbi (RMB)—a point not lost on Chinese economic officials. This gives Hong Kong financial firms a huge advantage. Internationalization refers to "the use [of the RMB] in denominating and settling cross-border trade and financial transactions, that is, its use as an international medium of exchange."[32] Working to achieve this status for the RMB is PRC government policy, and it is a very complex task with many different aspects. It is closely linked to the larger objective of removing controls over capital markets and ultimately making the RMB a reserve currency. Sensibly, Beijing has decided to tackle internationalizing the RMB step by step and to use Hong Kong as its primary testing ground for identifying problems and working out solutions at each stage. In an August 2011 speech in Hong Kong, then Vice-Premier (now Premier) Li Keqiang said, "The Central

Government will actively support the growth of the RMB market in Hong Kong, expand RMB circulation channels between Hong Kong and the Mainland, and support the innovation and development of offshore RMB financial products in Hong Kong."[33] William H. Overholt, an expert on Asian politics and economics, observes: "A key reason for the extraordinary rise in the scale and sophistication of China's mainland capital markets has been its encouragement and high regard for Hong Kong's financial expertise, which China uses to an extraordinary extent."[34] And Beijing still has a long way to go on internationalization. Although the RMB ranks fifth among currencies used to settle international trade and financial transactions, it is less than 3 percent of the total. In global foreign exchange markets, the RMB's share of global turnover is less than 2 percent.[35]

Turning to the other three industries of high potential growth (tourism, trading and logistics, and professional and producer services), hotels (tourism) and high-end retail stores (trading) service over 50 million people a year—the great majority from the mainland—who visit the territory. The precondition is that the territory is stable enough for tourists to want to come and for Beijing to signal that it approves. Trade and logistics firms have established excellence in inventory management, regional distribution, and global supply-chain management. For example, Hong Kong leads the world in international air cargo throughput volume. Hong Kong firms capitalize on the Hong Kong SAR's sound legal system (professional and producer services) to provide services to mainland clients in mediation and arbitration, trust administration, and intellectual property trading.

Among the six emerging industries that were first recommended in 2009 by then Chief Executive Donald Tsang Yam-kuen, medical services appears best to meet expectations. Yue Chim Richard Wong, a Hong Kong University economist and newspaper columnist, predicts that domestic spending on health care as a share of GDP will likely double by 2041, from 5.12 percent in 2011 to 10.3 percent in 2041 (finance peaked in 2007, at 12.9 percent). Demography is the main driver here. The elderly's share of the population will double between 2011 and 2031, from 12.2 percent to 24.4 percent, and the elderly consume three times as much health-care services as the working-age population.[36] So the opportunities for new job creation could be very significant, particularly for small and medium-sized industries.

Hong Kong clearly understands that its economic relationship with the mainland is not static. This creates opportunities for new beneficial integration, and three initiatives from late 2014 and spring 2015 exemplify this dynamic. The first was the beginning of the Shanghai–Hong Kong Stock connect, which removed some obstacles facing investors in each of the two cities from trading stocks of the other economy. It was also a step to removing China's capital controls.[37] The second was an agreement between the Central People's Government and the Hong Kong SAR government, signed in December 2014, which liberalized firms' access to Guangdong Province's service sector, hitherto closed to Hong Kong.[38] The third initiative, announced in late May 2015, was an arrangement whereby mutual funds in each jurisdiction could be traded across the border.[39]

Meanwhile, Chinese firms are moving up the value chain—producing goods and services that are more demanding in terms of the technology and management skills required—as a result of business opportunity and government policy, and this, too, impacts Hong Kong's economic policy decisions. For instance, the opportunity that Hong Kong saw in promoting local testing and certification services disappeared more quickly than expected. When Chief Executive Donald Tsang proposed in 2009 that Hong Kong could benefit by marketing these services to mainland entities, Chinese consumers had lost confidence in the quality of numerous domestically produced items such as milk powder. By 2014, however, Chinese product standards were rapidly improving, at least for exported products.[40] This promising opportunity disappeared, and Hong Kong officials now barely mention it.[41] In fact, China has established a good record of gradually rectifying its weaknesses and capturing hitherto unavailable comparative advantage. Sectors once marked by complementarity have become competitive, forcing Hong Kong firms to adjust.[42] The very size of the Chinese economy and the scale of certain types of available resources only compound this problem for Hong Kong. Consequently, both the Hong Kong government and local firms must be nimble if they are to stay ahead of the competitive curve.

Even as Hong Kong adjusts its interface with the Chinese economy, it must also sustain its position as an international business hub, and in this it has recognized assets: the rule of law, high-quality infrastructure and international and domestic transport networks, and good financial infrastructure and services for business support.

The Hong Kong SAR government's strategy to preserve efficiency and enhance competitiveness includes "improving the efficiency in the flow of people, goods, capital and information, but also . . . enhancing the quality of our living environment and our position as an international hub." In practice this strategy has been translated into a large infrastructure program.[43] Some in Hong Kong have argued against over-reliance on services to ensure future growth. Nostalgic for the time before 1979 when the territory was one of the world's light manufacturing centers and seeing a niche for advanced manufacturing, they have called for an "industrial renaissance." What is now needed, writes the European economist Ken Davies, "is a move to state-of-the-art, high productivity, high-value-added, high-tech industries such as information technology and communications, biotechnology, robotics, 3D printing, or nanotechnology. Policymakers need to focus on providing an environment conducive to research and collaboration between academia and business."[44] The C. Y. Leung administration has been on the same wave length, enthusiastically promoting the expansion of the innovation and technology sector. In Leung's January 2014 policy address, he said that the sector could be a driver of growth and employment and enhance quality of life, and pledged that the government would continue to create an environment favorable for the growth of the industry. He specifically advocated enhancements in the government's innovation and technology fund to support applied R&D and the revival of a bureau-level unit in the government focused on supporting the sector.[45]

This is a worthwhile aspiration, but the difficulty comes in creating a proper business environment. Fostering a good research environment is certainly one element, but it is not the only one, and each factor of production to reach this goal is currently unfavorable:

- Land. High rents vastly increase the cost of doing business.
- Labor. There is some question as to whether the education system is creating the necessary skills. An innovation-based economy requires a large number of engineers, which Hong Kong's universities produced in large numbers in previous decades. Today, however, college students are far more likely to go into finance and other fields unrelated to science, technology, engineering, and mathematics.[46]
- Capital. Hong Kong does not attract venture capitalists: they do not see "Hong Kong start-ups having the potential to grow their business to a market size that would be big enough to generate a decent profit."[47] Hence, Hong Kong only received $15 million in venture capital in 2013, while Singapore received $1.71 billion, one hundred times as much, and China attracted $3.5 billion.[48] In the same year, the Hong Kong government spent 0.73 percent of GDP on research and development, while Singapore spent 2 percent and Shenzhen, across the border on the mainland, spent 4 percent.

More generally, Hong Kong's playing catch-up in this competitive environment risks wasting resources in order to gain entry into niches where others are already entrenched. Alan Ka-lun Lung, a director of the Asia Pacific Intellectual Capital Centre, based in Hong Kong, cautions, "We would be wise not to try to duplicate what the mainland and the rest of the world are already doing. Rather, we should focus on our niche—international connections, the last 10 per cent of research and development [the most difficult part], commercialization and the Closer Economic Partnership Arrangement with mainland China."[49]

The Role of Government

A more fundamental issue than the potential of specific economic sectors is the role that government should play in facilitating economic growth. There is broad agreement on some government steps, such as adjusting policies to enhance opportunities and remove obstacles for local firms. The finance secretary's annual budget speech usually includes mention of substantive yet fairly technical policy initiatives and incentives to help the four pillar industries continue their growth. No doubt many of these steps are recommended by the affected firms themselves.

Economists are likely to question the idea of picking winners and losers by government fiat. Facilitating the emergence of new sectors, particularly by quickly removing regulatory obstacles and easing the decline of sectors that are no longer competitive, is a proper role for government, but only if the market ultimately determines which sectors are truly competitive. Some Hong Kong experts question whether the government, even if it can both accurately pick future winners and successful start-ups, will then support them until they are established.[50] And, in a system like Hong Kong's, where the structure of political power creates privileged influence for certain established sectors, is there a danger of crowding out sectors that have true market potential but have limited access to government facilitation?

The same question applies to public agencies that have had a monopoly on the provision of certain public services and may limit market entry by private entities. The Hong Kong health-care system is a good example of a service provided by the public sector; it was modeled on the British system that was in place pre-reversion. As an aging population makes increasing demands for services, there is great potential for private-sector growth, but realizing this potential and the growth of business and employment that it would bring requires a "rezoning" of public-private roles and responsibilities.[51]

Another question concerns the Hong Kong SAR government's decision-making process. The Heritage Foundation has consistently placed Hong Kong at the top of its economic freedom ranking, but still saw fit to include this note of caution in its 2015 assessment: "Although Hong Kong maintains the features of an economically free society, economic decision-making has become somewhat more bureaucratic and politicized."[52] A significant example is the Legislative Council, where members of the Pan-Democratic opposition have engaged in filibusters to impede government action. For example, they filibustered to prevent the Leung administration's initiative to restore the government unit responsible for innovation and technology to bureau status. The tech industry supported it, as did the LegCo member for its functional constituency (who happened to be a Pan-Democrat). But more radical Pan-Democratic members opposed it for being a waste of money.[53]

The government's fiscal policy provokes additional questions. As noted, it returns some of the revenue surplus to the community in the form of one-off payments, but the benefit of these "sweeteners" has not been spread equally. A 2014 analysis by the Research Office of the LegCo Secretariat's Information Service Division found that the groups that benefitted most were relatively well-off owners of private housing units and those who paid the salaries tax. Together the two groups received 62.2 percent of the payments. Low-income groups received 3.9 percent and those who were otherwise disadvantaged got 7.6 percent. As one journalist commented: "This is obscene not only because the underserving got the most public subsidies, but that Tsang's pseudo-financial prudence wasted our surpluses that could have been used [on] schools, hospitals, universities, healthcare services and retirement funds."[54] Commentary from the other side of the issue would probably argue that the surplus should be eliminated by reducing tax rates.

Growth and Equity

Hong Kong is not alone when it comes to the politics of inequality (see discussion of inequality in chapter 4). Misdistribution and its political ramifications plague other developed societies, including the United States. The question to be answered: Is inequality an unavoidable consequence of the policies that advanced economies must follow to remain competitive in a globalized world where technology is rapidly changing? The answer from the conservative side of the spectrum is that facilitating growth is a government's top priority and that the benefits of growth will soon "trickle down" to society at large. The argument on the progressive side is that sustained growth is impossible without a better distribution of benefits. The latter view reflects not only a normative desire for equity but a pragmatic conviction about what works.

Progressives' main line of argument is that a highly unequal society cannot generate the mass demand that ensures full employment growth. The Brookings Institution economist Kemal Dervis has written, "So, if the dynamics fueling income concentration cannot be reversed, the super-rich save a large fraction of their income, luxury goods cannot fuel sufficient demand, lower-income groups can no longer borrow, fiscal and monetary policies have reached their limits, and unemployment cannot be exported, an economy may become stuck. . . . The broad trend toward larger income shares at the top is global, and the difficulties that it may create for macroeconomic policy [particularly weak mass demand] should no longer be ignored."[55] David Madland of the Center for American Progress goes beyond the issue of demand creation: "A strong middle class is a key factor in encouraging other national and societal conditions that lead to growth. It is a prerequisite for robust entrepreneurship and innovation, a source of trust that greases social interactions and reduces transaction costs, a bastion of civic engagement that produces better governance, and a promoter of education and other long-term investments."[56] A study undertaken by three economists for the IMF, based on a sophisticated methodology, concluded: "Extreme caution about [equality-promoting] redistribution—and thus inaction [by government]—is unlikely to be appropriate in many cases. On average, across countries and over time, the things that governments have typically done to redistribute do not seem to have led to bad growth outcomes, unless they were extreme. And the resulting narrowing of inequality helped support faster and more durable growth, apart from ethical, political, or broader social considerations."[57]

If this viewpoint is even half right, it suggests that current government policy on the distribution of growth benefits is generating two counterproductive effects. Inequality is causing the economy to perform below its growth potential and also fostering political instability that is helping to transform society in significant ways. Hong Kong's concentration of economic and political power has created consequences that are contrary, it would seem, to the interests of the very people it was designed to benefit.

NINE

What Hong Kong Can Do to Improve
Governance and Competitiveness

Hong Kong has had a long-running and inconclusive discussion on economics and politics and their relationship to each other. The debate on electoral reform and the turmoil of the Occupy period only reinforced contending views. Finance Secretary John Tsang offered the following position on behalf of the government: "Prolonged political bickering is detrimental to public administration and the international image of Hong Kong as a stable, law-abiding and efficient city. It may even dampen investors' confidence in Hong Kong. Such self-inflicted harm does not serve the city well."[1] Pang Yiu-kai, chairman of the Hong Kong General Chamber of Commerce, emphasized "the importance of a steady political environment."[2] Paul Yip, professor of social work and social administration at Hong Kong University, decried the fact that Hong Kong "is tied up in endless debates with no consensus emerging. From landfill expansion to the location of public housing, we can't seem to agree on anything. We need a workable solution for democracy. But where are the useful discussions in the legislature or the community as a whole?"[3] Democrats remain focused exclusively on democracy. Richard Wong of Hong Kong University offered a more nuanced view, writing, "Beijing and Hong Kong must appreciate the enormous importance of having a healthy opposition if our city is to thrive economically and socially." Yet he also noted, correctly, that a radical opposition that believes it can only get what it wants

187

through confrontation will provoke fears in Beijing and the Hong Kong establishment about how a democratic system would affect their interests.[4]

Hong Kong and Singapore: A Comparison

Comparing Hong Kong and Singapore provides one point of departure for assessing Hong Kong's options. Progressives would not wish to trade their political system, as deficient as they find it, for Singapore's version of a hybrid regime: elections conducted in the context of an essentially one-party state that restricts political freedoms. Bernard Chan, a member of Hong Kong's Executive Council, attributed Singapore's reputation for bold action to the government's "fundamentally authoritarian" character. He prefers Hong Kong's marriage of a "relatively weak government" and political freedoms.[5] But Hong Kong conservatives admire the Singapore government's ability to act decisively in formulating and implementing policies, because it does not face the same political obstacles as the Hong Kong SAR government.

Singapore has handled some issues better than others. One policy issue that Singapore has handled more successfully than Hong Kong is housing: as a matter of long-standing policy, the Singapore government makes it possible for most citizens to own quality, affordable apartments. Yet Singapore's high cost of living means that job-seekers who cannot find employment in high-paying professional, managerial, and technical jobs have a hard time staying afloat financially.[6] Singapore gets high marks for a government that is clean and competent owing to the selection of officials on the basis of merit. But even this good can lead to a negative complacency. Benjamin Wong of Singapore's Nanyang Technological University writes that even honest and competent leaders can succumb to an inflated sense of self-worth, and become "so distracted by success as to lose touch with the people." The ruling People's Action Party won a low 60 percent of the vote in the 2011 parliamentary elections; despite restricted political freedoms, this relatively low vote of confidence "demonstrate[s] the importance of democracy as a mechanism to check the excesses of a self-absorbed and overachieving meritocracy."[7]

In the colonial era the Hong Kong government probably was Singapore's equal when it came to government competence and official talent. Both systems were blessed with the strong rule of law; the colonial Hong Kong governments shared Singapore's fear of Communist-instigated disorder, and so, restricted political activities, at least into the 1970s. But there, the paths diverged. The British faced the unique challenge of returning Hong Kong over to China, an authoritarian, Leninist state, and sought to institute as many political freedoms and representative elections as they could before the handover. Those reforms led in a variety of ways to the "disarticulation" (unhinging) of the prior Hong Kong system (discussed in chapter 7): the civil service was weakened, both democratic and establishment politicians gained more influence, and the public turned to rallies and protests as its main political participation tool. If governance is to improve, the various elements of the political system will need to be "re-articulated."

There is certainly no going back to the system that existed before the Joint Declaration. "Becoming more like Singapore is not an option," Bernard Chan says.[8] Mass political participation is here to stay in Hong Kong; the only question is whether it can be channeled in ways that promote stability and good government. As discussed in chapter 7, experience elsewhere demonstrates that selection of leaders through competitive, popular elections does not by itself guarantee good governance, useful feedback, and a polity that enjoys public legitimacy. But the Hong Kong case suggests that without full electoral democracy, a stable and legitimate political system will not be possible. What John Tsang called "political bickering" can undermine good governance and investor confidence, but economic growth that does not benefit the broad majority of citizens leads to more than "political bickering," and to significant public protest against the concentration of power that Hong Kong's political system has fostered.[9]

Hong Kong differs from Singapore in another way, one that goes right to the nexus between economics and politics: it has a political economy built on rent-seeking. Scholars define rent-seeking as efforts by individuals, organizations, or groups to use their resources to secure a benefit, often from government, that does not generate benefits for society as a whole. When an industry lobbies and gets a protective tariff for its products, the benefit accrues only to the rent-seeker while consumers and taxpayers lose. There is no net increase in social resources, merely a redistribution of existing resources.[10] While rent-seeking is not a new feature in the Hong Kong system—it began under the British and has continued since reversion—it is at the heart of the system's oligarchic character. What are functional constituencies if not an institutionalized form of rent-seeking? Chapter 4 described in detail the special access that major property firms have to governmental decisionmaking. The Chinese government was happy to accommodate a political economy based on rent-seeking because it felt comfortable vesting power in the Hong Kong people who gained the most rents. But it is not just large firms that enjoy rents. Professionals like doctors and lawyers benefit from certification requirements that discriminate against foreigners. Taxi drivers and the companies behind them have enjoyed something of a monopoly, as the Hong Kong SAR government issued no new licenses for urban cabs after 1994 and so provided an exclusive benefit to those drivers who do have licenses. When challenges are mounted to this privileged position, cab drivers have engaged in strikes and go-slow tactics to get the government to protect the status quo. The opposition to high-tech car-hailing services such as Uber in the summer of 2015 was the most recent case of this kind of pushback.[11] Richard Wong of Hong Kong University precisely pinpoints the consequences of rent-seeking in a system like Hong Kong's: the government becomes "vulnerable as friends can no longer rally to its cause and everyone is a lobbyist and a rent-seeker.... Without policy accountability, to either an electorate or to a higher ideology, government loses authority much faster and ultimately legitimacy."[12]

Beijing was not opposed to the gradual change of the political system, but it arguably waited too long to propose meaningful electoral reforms, and so fostered a climate in which an increasingly radical democratic camp rejected a deal that was probably in its interest to accept. Because the "actual situation in the Hong Kong Special Administrative Region" has changed substantially in the years since the reversion project began, it is no longer possible for Beijing to engineer electoral progress in a manner that is both "gradual and orderly," as prescribed in articles 45 and 68 of the Basic Law.

What can Hong Kong do going forward in both the economic and political spheres to create a better Hong Kong system? Since the two spheres interact, reform will be required in each. Addressing only one or the other successfully will produce a suboptimal outcome, but poor execution of both will also create dire prospects. Only progress on both fronts best serves the interests of all parties concerned. Drawing on the ideas of many sensible and intelligent people who are grappling with these issues, in this chapter I explore reforms that Hong Kong could make on its own and that would be useful in bringing about effective and stable governance and a competitive economy with widely shared benefits. (Chapter 10 focuses on steps China can take to reengineer the Hong Kong system.)

Sustaining Economic Growth

General statistics demonstrate that Hong Kong's primary economic strategy of preserving competitiveness and prosperity through integration with the mainland has been quite successful. Sustaining that strategy will require government and business leaders to adjust to new changes in Chinese economic policy, but they have done this before. China has a large and growing economy, and the advantages it offers Hong Kong have complemented and not conflicted with those of Hong Kong itself. The city's firms were able to relocate their production and assembly operations across the border, capitalizing on the large supply of low-wage Chinese workers that entered the global labor market after 1979, just when Hong Kong companies were facing rising local cost pressures. Additionally, China's growing urban middle class creates demand for goods and services that Hong Kong and other economies can provide. Finally, the Chinese government has provided Hong Kong with privileged economic treatment in order to sustain its economic performance and, Beijing hopes, its political stability. Tens of millions of mainland tourists a year are the most visible example of Beijing's stance. Hong Kong has been quite successful in adjusting to the ongoing modernization of the Chinese economy, as mainland firms learn the business and technological skills from Hong Kong ethnic Chinese that they had been unable to access before the Communist regime adopted its policy of domestic reform and opening up to the international economy in 1979. The local financial services sector has "lent" its expertise to China's financial authorities as the latter have gradually worked to internationalize the renminbi and prepare to lift capital controls.

As outlined in the previous chapter, the World Economic Forum (WEF) and other organizations identify the many strengths of the Hong Kong economy that can sustain its growth in the future. The WEF gives Hong Kong high marks on "basic requirements," and "efficiency enhancement" variables. But it gives the economy lower marks for business sophistication and innovation. Innovation is particularly important because it is an essential capability to deploy if an advanced economy is to remain competitive. For example, innovation is necessary for Hong Kong to pursue advanced manufacturing.[13] Its ranking on innovation was particularly striking; at twenty-third, it ranked behind its major Asian competitors: Japan (fourth), Singapore (ninth), Taiwan (tenth), and Korea (seventeenth).[14] Specifically, Hong Kong fell short on various measures of secondary and tertiary education, science, engineering, and research and development.[15]

In the production of goods and services, Hong Kong has a lot of advantages, and yet there are areas of concern. First of all, there is reason for pessimism as well as optimism about the impact of the Chinese economy. On the optimistic side, Hong Kong may have opportunities to apply its talents to China's new regional infrastructure initiatives such as "One Belt, One Road," which seeks to improve transportation and trading links between East Asia and Europe, and the Asian Infrastructure Investment Bank.[16] Partnerships between Hong Kong science research centers and their mainland counterparts would provide the economies of scale that the Hong Kong SAR's institutions lack and create greater capacity for world-class scholarship.[17] On the pessimistic side, 2014 demonstrated that the growth of tourism is not guaranteed. Visitor arrivals grew at 16.4 percent annually from 2010 to 2013, but the rate of increase dropped to 12 percent in 2014 and then to *negative* 2.5 percent in 2015.[18] A Legislative Council (LegCo) report attributed the decline to fewer mainland tourists, who either stayed home because China's economic growth had slowed or sought travel opportunities elsewhere. Other reasons may have been political instability in the Hong Kong SAR and the dampening effect of Beijing's anti-corruption campaign on luxury consumption there. The report stressed the need "for Hong Kong to diversify its tourism source markets and product offerings."[19]

Of course, there is the prior question on how enhanced innovative capacity will be incorporated into the Hong Kong context. If advanced manufacturing is not the option that some suggest, then there may be less need for a robust innovation capacity.

MACROECONOMIC POLICY

Probably the greatest macroeconomic policy concern for Hong Kong is the peg of the Hong Kong currency to the U.S. dollar. The peg was set in October 1983 as a crisis measure at a time when Beijing had sent signals that its negotiations with Britain over the Joint Declaration were going badly, which led to a collapse of Hong Kong's stock market and the value of the Hong Kong dollar. At that time the Chinese economy was much smaller than it is today, and its place in global commerce was still modest, whereas the U.S. economy was relatively more significant than it is currently. As much as Americans may take pride in other economies' confidence in the U.S. dollar, Hong Kong's continued use of the peg in a very different global economy has serious consequences. The link to the U.S. dollar deprives the government of any control over interest rates—one of the principal reasons for the Hong Kong housing price boom was low interest rates after 2008. Some say that Hong Kong should tie its currency to the renminbi.[20] That may make sense in terms of national pride but it would open up the Hong Kong SAR to distortions similar to those it suffers from today. Another option, linking the Hong Kong dollar to a basket of currencies from major trading economies, would diversify risk.[21] An open and substantive discussion of alternatives to current policy is in order, even if it is ultimately decided to stick with the status quo.

EDUCATION AND MANPOWER

Hong Kong's education system presents a mixed picture. The territory's fifteen-year-olds usually score well on the OECD's Program for International Student Assessment: in 2012, Hong Kong ranked second in the world in reading and science and third in math (Shanghai ranked first in all three categories, but this result is somewhat suspect since Shanghai is China's most advanced city).[22] The 2014–15 World University Rankings (WUR) published by the *Times Higher Education Supplement* ranked two Hong Kong universities in the top 100 (the University of Hong Kong was forty-third and the Hong Kong University of Science and Technology was fifty-first) and five Hong Kong universities in the top 350.[23] Only two other Asian institutions, Tokyo University and the National University of Singapore, outranked them. Yet those rankings are not the whole picture. The WUR score is weighted toward research (scholarly citations, industry income, research, international outlook, and teaching). While Hong Kong University's teaching score is only marginally less than its overall score, the teaching score for Hong Kong University of Science and Technology is 20 percent less than its overall score.[24] These institutions' research strength is obviously important for Hong Kong's innovation capacity, but it is their teaching that affects their contribution to the economy's human capital. Overall, the WEF ranked the quality of Hong Kong's educational system twentieth worldwide.[25]

Within Hong Kong there are a variety of complaints over a growing mismatch between the skills employers need, the skills schools teach, and the jobs and income young people want.[26] In particular, people view the tertiary education system as biased too much toward academics and too little toward the vocational skills that are needed to produce a sufficiently diverse array of human capital.[27] In the academic track, the focus is on exams and absorbing the information needed to pass them, not on cultivating independent thinking. Thirty years ago, engineering was the most popular major; today, finance is the leader.[28] Curricular quality at the secondary level suffered as the share of secondary-school-aged students who attended school expanded. Standards for English and written Chinese have dropped and mathematics has been "dumbed down," with consequences for engineering and computer science programs.[29] There have been efforts to expand vocational training, but the efforts are handicapped by the general public view that pursuing the academic track confers more social status. Meanwhile, the politics of education loom as an increasingly salient issue.[30] Beijing and the local establishment clearly dislike it when students begin to think and act independently on issues such as electoral reform. But two Hong Kong University professors warn of moving too far in the direction of political control: "If the goal is to create a world-class university, then there is no better way to compromise the integrity of the institution than to create an atmosphere that promotes self-censorship."[31]

Even if reforms are introduced to address these problems and improve the quality of the educational system, they will have a limited impact on competitiveness if the total manpower pool is too small. Here, Hong Kong, like other Asian societies, must cope with the reality of an aging population. The fertility rate in Hong Kong in 2014 was 1.23 births per thousand, much lower than the level needed to ensure a stable indigenous working-age population. At current birth rates, even though the city's population will grow at a modest annual rate of 0.6 percent (reaching 8.47 million by 2041), the size of the labor force will fall, from an estimated 3.71 million in 2018 to 3.51 million in 2035.[32] The government recognizes that one way to increase the labor force is to encourage foreign labor to settle in Hong Kong. Yet there are a number of obstacles to this plan: resistance from political parties and unions, protectionist barriers to entry in professions such as medicine, and opposition to the presence in Hong Kong of too many workers from the mainland. The *South China Morning Post* notes the importance of making Hong Kong attractive to potential expatriate job seekers: "Those of the best caliber will pick and choose the place that suits them most. . . . [Our] living environment, work benefits, education for children and civil liberties—they are all crucial factors for consideration."[33]

INNOVATION

Regular commentaries appear in the Hong Kong media that call for the economy to transform itself into an innovation center. A sampling of headlines: "Hong Kong Has Potential to Become Start Up Hub of Asia Pacific Region"; "How Our Innovative Youth Can Make Hong Kong Even Greater"; "Hong Kong Needs More Tech Start Ups."[34]

The question is how to do that. The C. Y. Leung administration has proposed legislation to restore the government unit tasked with promoting innovation and technology to bureau level, and to increase the resources of its innovation and technology fund, which supports government-established research centers, collaboration between universities and private firms, and R&D work in small companies.[35] Yet Ron Hui Shu-yuen, a professor of electrical engineering at Hong Kong University, believes that more could be done than simply redrawing the government's organization diagram, suggesting that administration of the fund should be less bureaucratic, more resources should go to upstream projects that have no obvious immediate commercial use, and the government fund to support university research should receive more resources.[36] The legislation to create this government fund finally passed in November 2015 (Pan-Democrats in the LegCo had impeded the bill's passage, as discussed in chapter 8).

Three scholars, two of them members of the Hong Kong SAR government's Commission on Strategic Development, have identified five "pillars of our innovation economy" that are required:

- A political consensus that innovation in science and technology will be a priority for future competitiveness. This is necessary to ensure a proper government role in providing "thought leadership" and "facilitating collaboration between public and private sectors."
- Entrepreneurship, which requires that small and medium-sized firms get R&D support from universities.
- Ensured funding for R&D; Hong Kong's current spending on R&D is less than 1 percent of GDP, whereas China, Taiwan, and Singapore spend 2 to 3 percent, and Korea spends almost 4 percent.
- Enhancing education and training: "Our excellent universities must lead in fostering a culture of cross-fertilization with the private sector."
- Public consciousness of R&D's importance.[37]

Regina Ip makes the interesting observation that whereas the most advanced countries engage in "original innovation, China excels at making use of secondary innovation to stimulate economic growth." Hong Kong, she says, needs its own approach, presumably somewhere in between.[38]

Some in Hong Kong point to cultural or psychological factors impeding the greater role for innovation in the economy. Peter Guy, a financial journalist, has written that Hong Kong business has cultivated a conservative culture that depresses a willingness to take risks. Such a culture leads to a "steep learning curve [when it comes to] fostering innovation and entrepreneurship." What is needed, he says, is "a core brain trust" that fosters the sharing of experience, both positive and negative. Many of the areas cited by the WEF as Hong Kong's relative weaknesses for innovation stem from government policies.

Ron Hui Shu-yuen stresses that innovation is hard if students in universities, from which start-up talent often emerges, do not have "the ability to think freely."[39]

The entrepreneur Rex Sham Pui-sum, who had two start-up failures before he succeeded in building a successful robotics firm, agrees on the importance of an innovation culture and mind-set. "Hong Kong lacked an acceptance of failure" and an environment to "confront and discuss" projects that did not succeed.[40] But Sham also understands that as important as culture is, institutions and policies have a greater impact than culture on cultivating innovation. "Hong Kong's high rents, combined with relatively fewer opportunities compared to the 1980s and 1990s, and a plateauing economy, posed challenges for young people—the city's most well-educated generation."[41] For example, the Federation of Hong Kong Industries asked its members with operations in Guangdong's Pearl River Delta about the option of moving their R&D activities back to Hong Kong. Twelve of the 641 respondents had such plans, but they did not follow through because "the lack of land and high operating costs make it difficult."[42]

The best illustration of the limitations of Hong Kong's business environment for high-tech manufacturing is the Chinese company DJI—it's the "one that got away." In 2015 DJI sold more civilian drones worldwide than any other company. It was founded by Frank Wang Tao, who grew up in Shenzhen but graduated from Hong Kong University of Science and Technology, and wanted to start his company in Hong Kong. But, wrote George Chen in the *South China Morning Post,* "Wang's efforts went nowhere, due partly to a lack of funding, lack of government policy support and other operational issues in the city." Big banks would not lend him money in the early days. Also, mainlanders who graduate from a Hong Kong university cannot work in the Hong Kong SAR for more than a year without an employer's sponsorship and have difficulties registering a company or getting a bank account. Unable to surmount these obstacles, Wang relocated across the border in Shenzhen, and the rest is history.[43] Eden Woon Yi-teng, a vice-president at Hong Kong University of Science and Technology, offers a number of specific suggestions for creating a "business eco-system" that promotes the technology sector: increasing funding and tax concessions, and attracting large international companies to Hong Kong to be magnets for small firms and talent. "You need the whole atmosphere to be one where you announce to the world that Hong Kong is welcoming to technology personnel and we have policies to attract you to come here."[44]

Hong Kong does indeed have good prospects when it comes to the production of goods and services—if the city's government and companies are nimble enough to adjust to the inevitable changes in Beijing policy and if the performance of Chinese firms does not leave Hong Kong firms with too few opportunities to thrive alongside China's much larger economy. Improving human capital for various parts of the local economy is a challenge, but not an overwhelming one. Ideas exist for adapting the educational institutions to society's changing skill needs, and as hard as these tasks may be, reducing the politicization of secondary schools and universities may be the greater challenge. Hong Kong does not lack for gifted individuals who can be the entrepreneurs of the future. What is missing is a business environment that permits them to turn ideas into potential products and then to scale those products commercially. Both government and companies need to help create that environment.

Sharing the Wealth

The economy's fundamental problem is not on the production side but on the distribution side. The benefits of growth are not reaching society to a degree that sustains both economic growth and political stability. Maintaining adequate social welfare and avoiding extreme inequality have taken a backseat to preserving competitiveness and building sufficient infrastructure. Obviously, these various goals will always be in conflict to some degree; the question is how to achieve a balance that receives broad social acceptance. The current balance has not achieved this objective and instead has generated some counterproductive effects, even for the production side of the economic equation. The high rate of inequality has not only fostered chronic political protest but has also undermined competitiveness by suppressing mass demand.

There is no economic law stating that the benefits of growth for advanced, twenty-first-century economies must be distributed unequally, and the countries of northern Europe demonstrate that growth and equality can be compatible. How benefits are distributed is a function of the choices that societies make and of which sectors and policy priorities are empowered to influence the choices made. The discussion of social welfare policy in the previous chapter indicates the current priority of the Hong Kong government: maintain the low-tax regime, maintain government spending at 20 percent of GDP, and don't use continual budget surpluses to underwrite more generous benefits—despite the projected need. This shows small thanks for the generation of workers who made Hong Kong the prosperous place it is today.

COMPETITION POLICY

Competition policy is a key arena for reducing the search for and granting of rents. If existing firms have dominant market position because of policy favors or predatory behavior, it doesn't matter if market entry for new firms is easy in some sectors, as is the case in Hong Kong. Here, the record is not good. Key sectors are dominated by cartels that benefit themselves and not consumers. The columnist Howard Winn writes, "While Hong Kong may be competitive when it comes to trading in global markets, domestically it is hard to consume goods and services which don't come from a small number of conglomerates."[45] Chapter 4 discussed the eight large firms in the property sector that have the advantage in bidding for major projects because only they can afford the upfront premium. Some of those firms also control the two dominant supermarkets, ParknShop and Wellcome, as well as energy providers. When the French supermarket chain Carrefour tried to break into the market by cutting prices, the suppliers of ParknShop and Wellcome blacklisted the new entrant. Their suppliers would not trade with Carrefour, and in doing so, blocked the newcomer's strategy. The professions of law, accounting, and medicine make a laudable effort to maintain the quality of the services they provide—but they also keep certification requirements so high that foreign professionals cannot work locally.[46]

In the mid-1990s, discussions began in Hong Kong about enactment of a law to reduce monopolistic and oligopolistic behavior and to encourage competition, to be implemented by a Competition Commission. The law did not pass the LegCo until 2012 and finally went into effect in late 2015. The response to a long-standing problem took two decades. Along the way, the forces that stood to lose their rents sought to weaken the law through certain amendments, for example, increasing the minimum size of companies that would be affected, minimizing the penalties on those that are, and prohibiting private citizens from mounting their own civil actions.[47] Then, warning of "unmeritorious and vexatious complaints," they sought to shape the Competition Commission's implementation guidelines to make them less onerous for themselves.[48] Whether it will be effective in reducing price-fixing and other anti-competitive abuses remains to be seen. At least one long-time observer is skeptical because a number of statutory bodies and organizations linked to the government, many of which compete with private providers, were exempted from the requirements of the new law.[49]

THE TAX REGIME

At first glance, the Hong Kong tax system seems quite progressive. In the 2004–05 fiscal year, 1.27 percent of the working population were responsible for 35.8 percent of salary tax receipts (60 percent of the working population, particularly members of the working class, pay no salary tax). At the same time, 8 percent of all taxpayers contributed 57 percent of the total yield of the salary tax. This may seem like a heavy burden for the 8 percent, but Michael Littlewood, a law professor at Auckland University, points out, "Although the [salaries tax] burden is relatively heavy, it is in absolute terms very light, since liability is capped at 16 percent (and the definition of income is relatively very narrow)."[50] Neither dividends, capital gains, nor offshore income is taxed, and there is little double taxation.[51]

The Hong Kong SAR government extracts 19.7 percent of GDP in tax revenue. By way of comparison, Japan takes 34.7 percent, Korea 21.8 percent, Taiwan 16.8 percent, and Singapore 15.2 percent.[52] There are some apparent and legitimate reasons for this. The extraction rate for each economy correlates rather well with the percentage of population sixty-five years of age and older: Japan's population in that demographic is 26.6 percent; Taiwan's, 12.5 percent; Korea's, 13.02 percent; Hong Kong's, 15.3 percent; and Singapore's, only 8.9 percent.[53] Another reason that Singapore is an outlier may be that its political system is the least democratic, and so less open to demands for welfare expenditures.

In Hong Kong, the wealthy do provide much of the tax revenue that the government collects, but the low rates on what is taxed actually represents a rent that has as much to do with the elite's political power as it does with their contribution to the Hong Kong economy. There is speculation that in 2012, when Beijing officials insisted that pro-government members of the chief executive election committee abandon their support for Henry Tang and switch it to C. Y. Leung, corporate leaders on the committee agreed to do so on the condition that Finance Secretary John Tsang and his low-tax policies be retained.[54]

Another issue that is relevant to any discussion of the balance of tax responsibility is hidden taxes. For example, it can be argued that society as a whole pays hidden taxes because of the high price of housing and daily necessities, which take up most of an average family's budget but are a small portion of a wealthy family's budget.[55] High prices in turn are a consequence of the monopoly and oligopolistic character of the economy.

A broadening of the tax base will probably be necessary to bolster the government's budget resources as the needs of retirees increase. Broadening the tax base would very likely impact the middle class and probably would have to come with serious efforts to reduce "hidden taxes" to convince taxpayers that all burdens were being imposed more fairly. Of course, the middle class would likely be willing to shoulder a heavier direct and indirect burden only if the government also reduced the current degree of "taxation without [political] representation." The *South China Morning Post* editorialized, "The uncertainties and uneven spread of taxation have to be lessened so that there can be more reliable and sustainable streams of revenue." And, the *Post* advocated, "At the least, there has to be renewed debate."[56] In the mid-2000s, a goods and services tax was considered, but eventually it was abandoned. As of early 2016, the Hong Kong SAR government's tax policy was moving in the direction of narrowing the tax base (reducing the number of households that pay taxes), not expanding it.[57]

SOCIAL WELFARE AND PROPERTY

The Hong Kong government spends about 40 percent of its recurrent or operating budget on social welfare: education, health care, and welfare per se. For FY 2014–15 the estimates for these three categories came to about 7.7 percent of GDP: 2.9 percent for education, 2.3 percent for health care, and 2.5 percent for welfare. The amount for welfare was a 10 percent increase over FY 2013–2014, after some decline in the years prior to that.[58]

Taking health care as a "leading indicator" of welfare expenditures, the health-care spending estimate—2.3 percent of GDP—is at the lower end of actual expenditures for East Asian governments in 2013: Japan's was 8.5 percent; Taiwan's, 3.9 percent; Korea's, 3.8 percent; and Singapore's, 1.8 percent.[59] These figures make sense, since Japan's population has aged more and Singapore's less than those of the other three economies.

Whether to increase welfare expenditures at a rate greater than that of economic growth remains politically controversial. Secretary John Tsang is right to reject a spending binge on social welfare, and the business community agrees with him. Nevertheless, some changes in social welfare policy will require greater expenditures. For example, the public pension system for low-income retirees provides $90.85 a month for people over seventy years old.[60] There is a growing recognition that this level is quite inadequate and only creates more poverty. The only way to increase the pension in the near term is to change fiscal policy.

In other areas, a change in the institutional approach is required. Health care has hitherto been a government responsibility, and the system has provided good care without straining the public treasury. As the population ages, the only way to maintain a high level of care and not break the budget is to liberalize and deregulate the whole system. This will require creating a new private sector and working out a division of labor between the public sector and the new private sector. It will also require changing long-standing barriers and regulations that make it difficult for foreign doctors to practice in Hong Kong.[61]

The property sector is where policy change is most needed. The inadequate supply of housing is both a symptom and a cause of inequality, and thus fuels much of the middle class's alienation and protest. It is also a source of social distress, such as the elderly having to live far away from their children and grandchildren. In addition, high rents price small and medium enterprises out of the market and by doing so reduce an economy's competitiveness. Solving the property crisis will not end political alienation, since other issues such as the lack of electoral reform are in play, but failure to address it will keep social tensions at a higher level.

The Hong Kong government has recognized that property—both residential and business—is a problem that cannot be avoided or deferred. It has vowed to expand the housing supply, and there were signs in early 2016 that modest progress was being made, although obstacles remain.[62] For example, if developers wish to renovate an existing structure that truly needs renovation, they must contact and compensate a high percentage of existing owners of the structure in question. If the owners cannot be contacted for a variety of reasons (changing their residence without leaving contact information, for example), then nothing can happen. Protecting the interests of individual and absentee property owners to a high degree ultimately works against the public interest.

Even if the number of housing units is gradually increased and regulations are modified, building new dwellings and commercial spaces and renovating old ones will probably not eliminate the pent-up demand. More radical action is probably required to solve the housing crisis. The most promising proposal so far comes from Hong Kong University's Richard Wong. He advocates liberalization of the market to encourage more buying and selling of different public housing units so that tenants can become owners. The key impediment to implementing such a reform in the current housing ownership scheme (one-third of the public housing stock) is how Hong Kong's system of land premiums is applied to them. Normally, a buyer of property must pay the premium—essentially, a one-time tax on the use of the property, based on its value at the time of purchase. For participants in the housing ownership scheme, payment of the premium to the Housing Authority is deferred until the time they sell the property, but what they must pay is based on the property's current value, which has risen with the usual increase in asset prices, not what it was when the original purchase was made. This rule effectively becomes a prohibitive tariff that places true home ownership out of reach for most occupants of HOS dwellings. To enliven the market, Wong proposes radically reducing the land premium and easing the repayment scheme.[63]

Floating such ideas is a lot easier than carrying them out. Each policy area is a mare's nest of complexity, with a host of specific measures and legacy provisions that need to be addressed. With the proper leadership, substantive vision, and political will, confronting these issues and finding solutions, though challenging, would not be impossible. There is growing public consensus that initiatives in health care, education, and housing are in the best interests of the community and that criticism of the government for its fiscal caution is justified. Unlike many other places, Hong Kong does not lack resources to devote to solutions. Maintaining an allocation of resources with social welfare at current budget levels in the context of a low-tax regime, continuing surpluses, and an aging population may satisfy the 10 percent of citizens who pay about 60 percent of the government's revenue taxes—but it shortchanges the much larger lower- and middle-class shares of the population. And the middle and lower classes are not as well represented in the political system as are the wealthiest.

The fact is that there are unused resources. First, the land fund, to which the premiums on land sales go, has a large surplus. Currently it is dedicated to underwriting large infrastructure projects, but there is no inherent reason why some of this money could not be used for expanding the supply of housing. Second, the government proudly proclaims that it "maintains a strong fiscal position and does not need to finance its expenditures by issuing government bonds," but it could probably finance some infrastructure projects in this way without hurting the government's overall bond rating.[64]

Governance

There are steps that Hong Kong can take to "re-hinge" what Hong Kong University's Ian Scott has called the "disarticulation" of the Hong Kong SAR system (measures that involve Beijing are discussed in chapter 10). They would only require changes in local ordinances, regulations, and the rules and norms of institutions. Some changes would likely require an informal okay from Beijing, but securing that would be easier than for proposals requiring an amendment to the Basic Law.

CHANGES WITHIN THE LEGISLATIVE COUNCIL

Percy Luen-tim Lui, a political scientist at the Open University of Hong Kong, offers two ideas for improving the institutional capacity of the LegCo without changing the types of seats and the way representatives are selected.

The first is to reform the LegCo's system of committees and panels. It has only three standing committees, for finance, public accounts, and members' interests. All other business is reviewed by panels (a total of eighteen in 2012); they correspond to the chief executive's policy bureaus. Two related issues are at play. The first is the relative weakness of the panels vis-à-vis the standing committees. The standing committees have jurisdiction over the most important aspect of government: budget and spending. Panels are authorized to "monitor the performance of the Government [and] . . . deliberate on issues relating to specific policy areas."[65] The second issue is the degree of specialization of individual members. A system of established standing committees, as in the U.S. Congress, encourages legislators to develop specialized knowledge on a few policy areas, which enables them to exercise greater scrutiny over the executive's actions and thus gives them more clout. In the LegCo, however, members can change panel membership every year. Whether they do or not is a function of their time and level of interest, but the net effect is to reduce the incentive to specialize in a few policy areas. Lui concludes that "beyond a doubt the current underdeveloped committee system is insufficient to allow the LegCo to conduct its business proficiently," even as the volume of work grows.[66] He recommends that panels be turned into standing committees with no annual turnover in membership, in order to create incentives for members to specialize in specific policy areas.[67]

Second, Lui advocates improving the quantity and quality of LegCo's staff. As of 2016, members receive a monthly allowance of around $18,000 to cover the expenses of maintaining their legislative and district offices. All other administrative support for the council members—including legal, issue research, casework, publicity and information services, and more—is handled by the LegCo Secretariat. Because the Secretariat serves all members simultaneously, its freedom to serve any one member is limited. Lui believes that Hong Kong should emulate the three-tier system in the U.S. Congress: committee staff, personal staff, and support organizations.[68]

In addition to Lui's two proposals, many observers think changes in the filibuster rules could bring about positive change. The democrats' use—or abuse—of the filibuster during legislative proceedings has led to complaints that in turn have generated recommendations that the LegCo president be given greater power to restrict such delaying tactics. But there are reasons why the democrats have resorted to the filibuster. One observer remarked to me, "It's not necessary to reduce filibustering now, because it's the only mechanism by which LegCo members can function as legislators. The system as currently constituted is rigged. Once there is a change in dual voting and the restriction on private bills is lifted, then it will be time to address the filibuster."[69] Moreover, the prohibition against individual members' introducing bills unless they have the chief executive's agreement and the requirement for a majority vote by both geographic and functional-constituency members already place democratic members at a great disadvantage. LegCo's president has the powers to rule in or rule out amendments for consideration, and the current incumbent, Jasper Tsang Yok-sing, has used that authority but in a balanced way. To shut off all debate would likely invite different types of protest.

CHANGES IN THE RELATIONSHIP OF
THE LEGISLATIVE COUNCIL AND THE PUBLIC

Two relatively modest steps could markedly improve the current system. The first is to require functional constituencies to use a broad franchise within their sector for selecting their legislator(s). In effect, corporate voting should be terminated. Second—granting the point that they represent interests and not people—the functional constituencies could even so be made more representative. For example, occupants of public housing—people living in fully one-half of all residential units in Hong Kong—constitute a group whose interest deserves representation. This group has no representation in LegCo whereas members of the Heung Yee Kuk and the Agricultural and Fisheries constituencies have one member each. This is way out of proportion. In fact, if there had been agreement to these two changes in the summer of 2014, the reform package might have passed.

CHANGES WITHIN THE CIVIL SERVICE

Chapter 7 outlined both the central and autonomous role of the civil service before the 1990s and how its position had atrophied since then. Ian Scott is a professor at Hong Kong University and the city's foremost expert on the civil service. He has made suggestions for improving the position and capacity of the civil service; the changes require political will, but not amendments to the Basic Law.[70] He believes that a key to "re-articulation" lies in enhancing the LegCo's role in making the chief executive accountable. Three steps are necessary to increase accountability, mandated by article 64 of the Basic Law. Currently, accountability comes down to bureau directors answering formal questions in the LegCo. Bureau directors and other political appointees serve solely at the pleasure of their superiors in the executive. Accountability requires more. Scott would require that bureau directors bear ultimate responsibility to the LegCo for any mistakes made by their bureaus, the sanctions to include removal from their posts by a vote of no confidence. Second, the LegCo should subject public sector organizations that are funded by the government but are not a part of the civil service (such as the tourism board) to greater scrutiny. This oversight should ensure that appointment to these boards by the chief executive is based on merit (not used to reward political allies) and that public money is properly spent. Third, as LegCo takes on more duties, such as ensuring deeper accountability, its size should be increased commensurately.

Although Scott generally believes that the civil service is a sound and effective organization, he has two recommendations to rectify weaknesses resulting from the management "reforms" of the late 1990s. First, the earlier ethos of service in the public sector, which emphasized responsiveness and political neutrality, should be restored. Second, he recommends formation of a government commission to oversee the civil service and review the impact of cost-cutting measures on employee morale and agencies' ability to recruit (see chapter 7). Reduced salaries, misalignment of salaries with job responsibilities, and time in service should be considered for change.

CHANGES IN THE RELATIONSHIP OF
THE CIVIL SERVICE AND THE PUBLIC

As the balance of power shifted in the past two decades from the civil service to civil society, the bureaucracy has faced greater difficulties in formulating and implementing policies that command public support. Here, Scott writes, "There is a need for the government to build in specific implementation strategies which take account of the positions of the major stakeholders."[71] There is no single remedy. How to conduct civil engagement will depend on the nature of the specific issue under discussion—for example, whether it is has narrow or general public impact. At a minimum, civic engagement should not result in delays in formulating and implementing policy.

Ultimately, however, civic engagement should supplement and complement broader political representation; it is not a substitute for it. Absent full, representative democracy, all the mechanisms by which citizen feedback is

conveyed to government (the media, channels for seeking redress of grievances) should be made more effective and should also affect policymaking.
Scott's summary: "'Executive-led' government, unqualified by serious attention to public opinion, carries with it the danger of inappropriate policymaking, sometimes with disastrous results."[72]

CHANGING THE RELATIONSHIP OF
THE EXECUTIVE WITH MAJOR STAKEHOLDERS

Brian Fong of the Hong Kong Institute of Education observes that the government gets unnecessarily entangled with key stakeholders because it "fails
to engage in institutionalized negotiation and cooperation with major socio-
economic interests in its policy-making process." Before the 1990s, the colonial
executive council was structured in a way that facilitated such engagement,
but partial democratization and fraying of the business-government alliance
has taken a toll on those interactions. Fong's remedy is to transform the existing
Executive Council into a "core platform for forging a more broad-based governing coalition," a forum where policy initiatives are vetted before submis-
sion to the LegCo. The membership of the Executive Council should include
not only the government's three secretaries and the heads of policy bureaus,
but also legislators and social leaders. In addition, whether or not full electoral
democracy is established, the government should enable political parties to be
more effective intermediaries between the government and major social and
economic interests. Reducing the number of parties would facilitate this in-
termediary role.[73] Fong also believes that the post-1997 state needs to reassert
its autonomy vis-à-vis the business elites, which have institutionalized their
power within government. He understands, however, that business dominance
is at the heart of the Central People's Government's strategy for governing
Hong Kong, so enhancing the autonomy of the Hong Kong SAR government
could only come after Beijing makes a fundamental reassessment.[74]

Two significant aspects of the political system were instituted by local ordinance, and so hypothetically could be changed by votes in the LegCo (assuming sufficient support, of course). One is the prohibition on a serving chief
executive being a member of a political party. This is one reason for disarticulation between the executive and the legislative branches. The second is the
use of a proportional representation system for elections in the LegCo's geographic constituencies, which fosters fragmentation of the party system and
the radicalization of politics. Reform of each aspect deserves consideration,
yet making such changes would have an impact great enough to require more

than implicit approval from the Central People's Government (both changes are discussed in chapter 10).

If there is anything Hong Kong lacks it is a genuine political community—a sense of a shared reality and a common destiny. All that and a lot more is contested, and the divisions are deep.

As explained in chapter 6, localist and nativist sentiments have grown in post-1997 Hong Kong. Hong Kong residents have had a dual identity for some time, but now there is a deep generational divide when it comes to emphasis within the duality.[75] The origins of the Umbrella Movement demonstrated the political side of that difference; as noted in chapter 4, the young are most critical of government performance and most skeptical about the future. Some members of the movement have developed distinctive fundamental values, abandoning a material-oriented mentality for a post-materialistic one.[76] Thus, the fears in Hong Kong and Beijing about youth attitudes have some basis in reality.[77]

Yet it seems hardly productive to attribute young people's different perspective to their being "spoiled," being a source of "menace," or lacking in "civility."[78] Whatever truth such criticisms of youths' attitudes may possess, emphasizing them is unlikely to convince young people to do their part to bridge the social and political divide. Nor will asserting that the youths' political behavior stems from a lack of "patriotism," whatever the trends in youth identity might indicate. The idea that increasing "national education" instruction in Hong Kong schools will encourage moderation may be placing too much faith in a pedagogical solution to young people's disaffection.[79] Hong Kong SAR leaders have promoted "patriotic education" for a number of years, but the most recent attempt at it arguably divided society more than it united it.[80] And in any case, the local education system encourages some degree of independent thinking, so "national education" may not change minds.

Fact-based analysis of the problem may yield more constructive solutions. In 2009, the International Association for the Evaluation of Educational Achievement conducted its International Civic and Citizenship Education Study to assess the political views of fourteen-year-olds, including in Hong Kong. Some of the questions asked students about the forms of illegal protest they might engage in, such as spray-painting slogans, blocking traffic, and occupying public buildings. The share of Hong Kong respondents who said they might do such things was 10 percent or less, which was a lower rate than for some of Hong Kong's East Asian neighbors. In another study, two scholars in Hong Kong found that a student's readiness to engage in illegal protest was associated with a low level of civic knowledge, which in turn was associated with the quality of students' relationships with teachers and the openness of the classroom climate.[81] These findings suggest that the degree of alienation among Hong Kong young people and their tendency to engage in radical action is less than many believe, and offer some practical ways of defusing illegal protests by youths.

But not only young people are causing Hong Kong's political troubles. Although those under thirty are the most alienated from the political system and have the strongest Hong Kong–first identity, political disaffection extends to all demographics in the democratic camp. At least some adults share the sentiments of young activists, even though they may disagree with them on how to conduct political combat. Much of the social divide is the result of the Hong Kong SAR government's policies and its power structure. Two Singapore scholars even suggest, on the basis of survey results, that "Beijing has inadvertently contributed to the rise of Hong Kong identity and a concomitant decline of the Chinese identity." A top-down effort for "transplanting patriotic feelings and a sense of national identity have been fatally flawed."[82] Two Hong Kong University scholars argue that "liberal democratic values underlie Hongkongers' patriotism."[83] The implication here is that only if the Beijing government takes the lead in moving Hong Kong toward a fully democratic system and gains credit for doing so will it foster a stronger Chinese national identity.

Indeed, one might ask why young people and democrats are the ones who have to change in order to restore the sense of a stable community in Hong Kong. If it is to be a true "community," then perhaps others need to meet the young and the democrats halfway. An Institute of Education professor, decrying the rising level of incivility in Hong Kong public life, says that all groups have a shared responsibility to do the hard work of restoring "the core of common values that unite all Hong Kong people."[84] To focus on the character of youth ("spoiled") and activists ("radical") may identify one source of the city's turmoil, but it ignores policy and institutional factors that have genuine impact. Certainly the business community faces competitive challenges and the elite experiences the difficulties of governing in Hong Kong's hybrid system, yet the fact remains that the elite has reaped significant benefits from the system that Britain created and China sustained. Within this system the lower and middle classes have had to make their way. The elite certainly has a role to play in restoring community.

TEN

China, Hong Kong, and the Future of One Country, Two Systems

No political system is perfectly designed at the outset. The confederal system that the United States originally adopted was flawed from the start and was quickly converted into a federal system, which in turn went through significant transformations to cope with the challenges of slavery, the emergence of an industrial economy, and America's adoption of an active role in world affairs. Worldwide, the third wave of democratization that occurred in the 1980s occurred because various authoritarian rulers in Brazil, Chile, Taiwan, and South Korea recognized, or were forced to recognize, that their systems were no longer working. In some cases, the democratic successors, such as Brazil and Taiwan, didn't work well either. Given this history, it should not come as a surprise that the "one country, two systems" model that the People's Republic of China (PRC) crafted for Hong Kong in the 1980s is not performing as well as its designers expected. The Hong Kong that was the point of departure for creating one country, two systems has changed in profound ways, which the Central People's Government did not and probably could not have anticipated. Perhaps the time has come for the PRC government to consider adjusting the original model to adapt to contemporary circumstances.

Options for Adjusting One Country, Two Systems

So what can Beijing do? China is committed by treaty to preserve the Hong Kong Special Administrative Region (Hong Kong SAR) until July 1, 2047, so canceling the one country, two systems arrangement is not an option.

It is also unlikely that the central government would end Hong Kong's hybrid regime by restricting civil and political liberties. Technically it has the authority to do so under article 18 of the Basic Law, which states that if "turmoil" in Hong Kong "endangers national unity or security and is beyond the control of the government of the Region," the Standing Committee of the National People's Congress (NPC-SC) may decide that the Hong Kong SAR is in a state emergency, in which case the Central People's Government has the authority to "issue an order applying the relevant national laws in the Region."[1] In that event, and before issuing such an order, Beijing would no doubt ask how vigorously the local police and courts would enforce those laws. As well, Beijing would have to anticipate whether such a step would trigger an economic slump, massive social disorder, and alienation of the Hong Kong elite. Furthermore, the reputational costs to Beijing of such a step in Taiwan, in the rest of the East Asian region, and in the United States would be extreme.

The option that is more likely but still unproductive is to double down on past policy ("persist in sticking obstinately to the same course," to quote the Chinese historian Zhang Lifan).[2] Beijing could continue to act according to its existing playbook:

- View Hong Kong through a national-security lens.
- Interfere overtly and covertly in Hong Kong SAR affairs as needed and within an expansive definition of what the Basic Law allows.
- Explicitly define Hong Kong's degrees of freedom regarding political reform.
- Mobilize loyal elements in civil society at times of political conflict.
- Continue to provide economic benefits both to preserve the territory's prosperity and maintain political support for the Hong Kong SAR government.
- Nibble away at the political freedoms that currently exist.
- Use propaganda and the education system to foster a stronger sense of identification with China.

Although this approach has the purported virtue of consistency with past policy, its benefits have long since declined. The traditional playbook ignores the profound change that has occurred in the city since the early 1990s and the deep mistrust that PRC policies have spread among the Hong Kong public. Instead, Beijing seems to assume that recent turmoil is the work of "a small minority" that must be opposed because it has mounted a deliberate challenge to Beijing's rule. The Central People's Government may be correct in believing that the provocative behavior of local radicals has created serious political disruption, but it ignores how its own rigid stance and ill-considered actions have empowered those same radical forces and undermined the position of moderates who might, under the right circumstances, be prepared to support even modest reform. Nor has Beijing recognized that policies favoring the local oligarchy have, at least indirectly, contributed to the deep inequality that helps fuel political protest.

These failures of analysis suggest that whatever approach Beijing ultimately takes, first it must overhaul the way it collects information about Hong Kong developments and frames interpretations about the implications for PRC interests. Beijing likely receives information and analysis colored by a certain political correctness; inaccurate information can only complicate its relationship with Hong Kong and how it addresses challenges from the public. In addition, the Central People's Government would gain a more honest understanding of the policy context if it ended the reflexive tendency to blame the United States and the United Kingdom for Hong Kong's problems—this just distracts attention from more consequential local causes.

At least hypothetically, there are three more ambitious and transformative policy responses that the Central People's Government could adopt. I describe them in their ascending order of change to the status quo and the increasing degree of political resistance that each would meet with. The premise of this hypothetical exercise is that the Central People's Government is Hong Kong's sovereign. By its own declaration, the Hong Kong SAR's "local affairs" are to be run "as authorized by the central leadership. The high degree of autonomy of Hong Kong SAR is subject to the level of the central leadership's authorization."[3] The situation almost twenty years after reversion is the result of the political strategy the Central People's Government has employed and the associated policies it has implemented. That strategy created local winners and losers. Beijing sought to fortify its control by giving power to and relying upon the Hong Kong elite, which has certainly benefitted as a result. A more balanced strategy would shift some power to those who were the relative losers under the post-1997 arrangements and place more confidence in the political institutions dominated by the public rather than the oligarchy. None of these three alternatives will happen if the Central People's Government, as the sovereign, does not actually make the changes to secure the accommodation of its past allies to new arrangements.

GIVING THE GREEN LIGHT TO LOCAL REFORMS

A modest but meaningful alternative to sticking to the past game plan would be for the Central People's Government to approve and even encourage the steps outlined in the previous chapter, steps that do not require changes in the Basic Law but could be directed as necessary through NPC-SC decisions. These include strengthening education and talent creation; encouraging an economy based on innovation; sharing the benefits of economic growth more broadly, in part by expanding social welfare benefits; expanding the housing supply and reforming underlying housing policies regarding residential and commercial property; improving institutions in the Legislative Council (LegCo) and the civil service; making functional constituencies more transparent and representative; and facilitating a more effective governing coalition. Taken together, these represent incremental yet important changes to the current structure and policies. They would not resolve all the grievances that the public holds toward Beijing and the establishment, but they would be an important start. The emphasis here is on the word "start."

The main argument against these economic and political reforms is that the Hong Kong business elite would oppose them because they would harm their interests and reduce Hong Kong's competitiveness. That argument has an element of truth, but there are counterarguments. First of all, the elite's failure to share the benefits of growth, which it has enjoyed now for decades, has undermined the very stability on which competitiveness rests. Second, at some point the business elite should worry not only about its narrow economic interests but also the interests of the community as a whole. Third, how does the Central People's Government define its role as Hong Kong's sovereign? Is it to guarantee dominance for one part of society and minimize the role of the public at large— thus inadvertently empowering radical forces in society? Or has the time come for Beijing to begin to redistribute some of that dominance to the public, to rely less on individuals and groups that are powerful vested interests, and to place more confidence in institutions and the pragmatism of Hong Kong citizens?

"RE-SET" ONE COUNTRY, TWO SYSTEMS?

Under a re-set of the one country, two systems idea, Beijing would not only encourage or require all the steps that Hong Kong can take on its own hook, such as changing local ordinances, but also rectify elements of the Basic Law that have either outlived their usefulness or caused the disarticulation of the Hong Kong SAR system. The purpose would be to create better articulation of the elements of that system and, hopefully, to foster greater process and performance legitimacy.

For example, Percy Luen-tim Lui advocates repealing article 74 in the Basic Law, which requires that "the written consent of the Chief Executive shall be required before bills relating to government policies are introduced."[4] As Lui observes, this means that LegCo members are not "able to initiate bills of any political or policy significance."[5] Also ripe for reform is the system of dual voting, whereby a majority of members in both functional and geographic constituencies is required for "passage of motions, bills or amendments to government bills introduced by individual members."[6] These two provisions effectively prevent legislators from playing any constructive policymaking role. They also encourage tactics, such as filibustering, that impede the legislative process.

More generally, there is a nexus of issues that determines the method of selection of leaders and the role of political parties. The first is the electoral reform effort that was aborted in June 2015. Wherever blame is placed for that outcome, the consequences are bad for governance. Continuing the past methods for picking the chief executive and members of the LegCo feeds the sources of political instability. Indeed, the failure of reform may strengthen them further. One might hope that making the nominating committee more representative and transparent would be sufficient to split responsible moderate democrats off from their radical associates. Those adjustments might have worked in the spring of 2014, but subsequent developments only deepened mistrust. The chances of making progress through such limited changes may now be too small. Other concessions may well be necessary to restart discussions and produce an acceptable package for both selecting the chief executive and electing LegCo members. At this point, Beijing must take the initiative, first of all by dropping the Beijing-knows-best, take-it-or-leave-it stance it adopted from 2013 to 2015. To reduce democratic and public mistrust and marginalize the radicals, an approach that is surprising in its scope (positive "shock and awe," if you will) is probably necessary.

But that is only the starting point. Altering electoral procedures while retaining other aspects of the basic structure may be satisfactory in the short term but it will not be satisfactory in the medium and long term. Optimally, four issues should be addressed:

1. The chief executive and LegCo
2. Elections for the geographic constituencies
3. Elections for the functional constituencies
4. Greater flexibility within annual budgets

1. The chief executive: Above political parties? The first issue is the disarticulation between the chief executive and the legislature. Many Hong Kong observers are convinced that the legal requirement that the chief executive cannot be a political party member is a key reason for the disarticulation.[7] A newly elected chief executive who belongs to a party must resign the membership before inauguration.[8] Li Pang-kwong of Lingnan University identifies the consequence: "Not affiliated with any political party, the CE has to knit his supporting net by building coalition[s] with social and political groups in the society and in the legislature as well."[9] It frustrates the chief executive's efforts to enact policy initiatives and opens him or her to criticism even from legislators who generally share the same ideology. The restriction may have made sense in light of the principle of executive-led government as opposed to party-led government. It may have stemmed from Deng Xiaoping's April 1987 instructions to the Basic Law Drafting Committee that Hong Kong should not have "a British or American parliamentary system."[10] Whatever the theory, experience suggests that this requirement was a major factor in the disarticulation of the Hong Kong system. Successive chief executives have had no readily available support base within the LegCo. The executive-legislative hinge that is the basis of parliamentary systems has been lacking.

2. Elections in geographic constituencies. The second issue is the method used for designing geographic constituencies for LegCo elections. As described in chapter 4, the single-member-district, first-past-the-post system that Chris Patten instituted while he was governor was abandoned after reversion in favor of a multi-member-district proportional representation (PR) system. The goal was to improve the chances of the pro-business Democratic Alliance for the Betterment and Progress of Hong Kong (DAB) to gain seats in its contest for influence against the Democratic Party. It was much easier to do that in a multi-member, PR system than in a winner-take-all system. Generally, PR systems provide more accurate representation of various segments of the political spectrum. The problem was that what was good for the DAB goose was also good for the radical-democrat gander. The result was a proliferation of parties in the LegCo and the tendency of the League of Social Democrats and People's Power to play to their constituencies by engaging in provocative political tactics and intimidating moderate legislators.[11] Instituting the PR system sowed the seeds for the Occupy Movement and the rejection of the government's proposal for electoral reform.

No single electoral system is best for all contexts. Countries that have a historical British background tend to favor winner-take-all systems and two dominant parties. Continental European nations tend to favor PR and several parties. (There are also mixed systems—for example, Taiwan's—that give voters two votes: one in a single-member district and the other for their preferred party.)[12] Winner-take-all systems tend to be more adversarial and PR systems more consensual, because the latter force an array of parties to work together to form a majority. What is important are the priorities that the designers of an electoral system wish to achieve. Single-member districts tend to create governments with a small number of parties that have to appeal to a wide spectrum of opinion and legislators who are linked directly to their constituencies. They tend to be more decisive when it comes to adopting policies. But the winner-take-all feature grants the majority party a bonus in its number of parliamentary seats. Meanwhile, opposition parties and voters must be vigilant in rendering accountability. Multi-member districts tend to eliminate the winner's bonus and provide more precise representation of major political tendencies. They also create a large number of parties because each party can appeal to a narrow spectrum of views. As a result, the election of a majority party is less likely, coalition governments are the norm, and parties must cooperate in order to enact policies. Also, legislators are not responsible for a specific set of constituents, and so may be less responsive to their needs.[13]

Perhaps because the American political system has British roots, I have always had a bias in favor of a single-member, first-past-the-post system—in spite of the advantage it gives to the winning party in terms of legislative seats. The majority has both the opportunity to act on its program and the responsibility to be accountable for the results in the next election. Moreover, each legislator is tied to a specific constituency and must look out for constituents' interests, creating a form of feedback on how government policies affect individual citizens.[14] Recall that in Hong Kong, geographically elected legislators from any one electoral district represent the entire district together, which limits each legislator's ties and responsibility to any one group of constituents. Indeed, the voters in functional constituencies may get better representation from their legislators than do those in geographic constituencies.

Given the current fragmentation and polarization of Hong Kong's political system, I am inclined to believe that a British-American system would bring greater coherence, decisiveness, accountability, and stability than exists today. Moreover, the cleavages over policy issues appear to be more cumulative than cross-cutting. A single-member system is more appropriate when one party or a coalition of parties aligns on most issues, as Hong Kong's democratic camp tends to do on both constitutional and inequality issues. A PR system is better when the views on issues are more scattered along the political spectrum. A shift to a single-member system would produce a consolidation of parties. Doing so on the establishment side, with its mélange of corporate interests, a middle-class party (the DAB), and the Federation of Trade Unions, might be more difficult than the democratic camp. But the ultimate outcome would likely improve the quality of governance.

3. *Elections in functional constituencies.* The two steps just outlined may facilitate more centrist parties and better executive-legislative relations. Percy Luen-tim Lui's proposed reforms will give geographic-constituency LegCo members more opportunity to act as legislators, while restarting electoral reform on selection of the chief executive may bring local politics back to where they were in early 2013. But even taken together they will not address the structural reality of over-representation for the special interests that have their own functional constituencies (FC).

There have been a couple of different arguments for preserving FCs. One is what might be called the "original design" rationale. Johnny Mok, a barrister and member of the Basic Law Committee of the National People's Congress, offers a clear statement of this argument: preserving stability and prosperity has been the long-standing goal for Hong Kong, and the Hong Kong SAR "is constitutionally mandated to guard itself against any degeneration into an over-expanded and over-burdened economy." Exceptional representation for key sectors in the LegCo and in the election and nominating committees—both of them legacies of British rule—ensures that the interests of those sectors are protected. It is a check against populism and toxic instability in the future.[15]

The other argument, outlined by Man Mun-lam, a current affairs commentator on political affairs, is that FC LegCo members actually do a better job than their popularly elected colleagues. They are educationally and professionally more qualified, "calmly analyze issues and rationally seek solutions," and do not engage in "obstructing procedures." FC members have expertise across different fields, whereas directly elected members are "street-fighters" who "often lack professional knowledge and experience." The FC members ensure a balance among the interests of various social groups. "Additionally,

if the functional constituencies were abolished, representatives from industries and professions could not counter the often negative influence of career
politicians."[16]

These differences likely have less to do with the character and qualifications
of the two types of members than with the small size of their constituency
and power within the LegCo (democratic members are more confrontational
because they have little power). Most FC members are visible symbols of the
protection of narrow sectoral interests and Beijing's political strategy. Opinion surveys suggest that the public believes that the system is unacceptable
and should be changed. In twelve polls taken from November 2003 to January 2013, the share of respondents who favored direct election of all LegCo
members was below 70 percent in only one poll (66 percent in March 2006)
and was over 80 percent three times.[17] It might be possible to preserve a special
place for the interests that the FCs represent for a time—perhaps as an analogue
to the British House of Lords in a bicameral LegCo. Yet the time may have
passed when the public would accept such a solution. Sooner or later, it seems,
restoring the legitimacy of one country, two systems may require eliminating
the FCs.

4. Budgetary flexibility. Finally, Hong Kong's aging population and the
growing costs of caring for the elderly will require the Hong Kong SAR government to have greater flexibility in shaping annual budgets. Hypothetically,
there are ways of doing this within the current system. The relatively light tax
burden on individuals and companies could be increased in a modest but progressive way, which not only would generate more revenue but also, through
redistribution, would have a useful political effect. The government could
relax the unwritten rule that combined expenditures from its operating and
capital budgets should constitute no more than 20 percent of GDP. More of
the government's substantial reserves could be used in the short and medium
term instead of saving them for the long term. The purposes to which the capital
budget is applied, infrastructure, could be broadened beyond traditional projects such as roads, water systems, and tunnels to include more spending on
social welfare and poverty alleviation. David Akers-Jones, who served in a variety of positions in the colonial government, rising to chief secretary in the
mid-1980s, argues that the Basic Law's requirements for fiscal balance should
be reconsidered. "I just happen to think that if the Basic Law were written
today, those chapters on the economy could perhaps be written in a much more
imaginative way.... There wasn't an elderly population ... when the Basic
Law was being drafted."[18]

The LegCo does have the power to repeal the requirement that the CE cannot be a party member and to change the PR basis of the electoral system, although any major change in the FCs, including abolishing them, requires amendment of the Basic Law. Yet because each of the reforms suggested above is quite consequential for those who hold some power in the Hong Kong SAR government, there may be some value in having Beijing formally authorize the changes, if not through an amendment to the Basic Law, then as a decision by the NPC-SC. But, whatever the formal authorization, even attempting to make any of these changes would stimulate opposition in Hong Kong. The end of a PR system will likely spell the end of Hong Kong's minority parties, so they would naturally put up a bitter fight against ending the PR system. Meanwhile, FC members and the constituencies they represent would oppose an end to their superior political position. Parties with a minority presence in LegCo might be disinclined to support a system where the chief executive was the head of the majority party because it would be more difficult to check. On budget policy, change may require Beijing to send a strong signal that it wants a relaxation of fiscal prudence through an amendment or reinterpretation of article 107, which mandates "striving" for fiscal balance, avoiding deficits, and gearing expenditures toward GDP growth. It would do so not because it no longer cares about fiscal discipline but because too much past fiscal restraint has contributed to political instability.

As sensible as these four reforms may seem in light of democratic theory and practice, actually adopting them would require all those who benefit from the status quo, particularly the FCs, to accept a shrinkage of the representation of their interests. There may be tactical moves that would limit opposition to these reforms, such as packaging several together so that each of Hong Kong's political forces believes that it will receive some gain. Realistically, however, for a significant reform effort to be pushed through will require the Central People's Government to make clear that a significant re-set of one country, two systems is in the best interests of the community and the country, and must be passed. In particular, it will have to persuade the business community, which benefits the most from FCs, that defending the status quo is becoming unworkable and that politics must be put on a new basis.

REENGINEERING ONE COUNTRY, TWO SYSTEMS

Each of the suggested reforms is designed to deal with specific problems within the current political structures and policies of the government. Making each change will lead to some improvement in the relevant area, but it is not clear that the whole reform package will be greater than the sum of the parts. Because each of the outlined defects has contributed to the decline of governance in Hong Kong, it is a package of reforms that will improve governance significantly.

Take, for example, the idea of allowing the chief executive to be a member of a political party. The defects of the current system, which requires a supra-party executive, are obvious, but it is not clear that this step alone would resolve the underlying problem in the disarticulated political structure. The unstated but likely assumption of this reform is that, as in the current arrangements, there would be separate elections for the chief executive and the legislature. But if there are different political dynamics for chief executive and LegCo elections (similar to the difference in the United States between presidential and congressional races), the result could be the selection of a chief executive who is a member of a minority party in LegCo. That would create disarticulation of another kind. What creates the dynamic hinge of a Westminster system, in contrast, is that the leader of the majority party usually becomes prime minister and other party leaders, usually legislators, become ministers in the government.

The logic of reforming Hong Kong's political institutions while temporarily setting aside political constraints flows from two connected assumptions. The first is the need to vest a central role in the political system to healthy political parties. Whether in elections or the legislative process, parties are the key mechanism for aggregating public sentiments and political interests. They are also the training ground for political leaders. Parties are certainly not perfect (see the United States for evidence), but with the right institutional design they can reflect the major poles of political sentiment in society and provide a sort of political system coherence, something Hong Kong currently lacks. Parties or coalitions of parties should play the key role in nominating candidates for the chief executive election.[19] For LegCo, most, if not all, candidates should run as party candidates.

The second is the value of a Westminster-style parliamentary system.[20] Legislators would be picked in popular elections (with my preference being a single-member district system). Then the Central People's Government, as the sovereign, would invite the leader of the party that won the most seats—or a coalition of parties, if necessary—to form the Hong Kong SAR government. If that does not work, then the party leader most likely to be able to form a coalition government would be given the opportunity. Once a government is formed, Beijing would appoint both the chief executive and the heads of the various government departments. The government would then seek to enact its policy program based on its parliamentary majority. The chief executive and agency heads would be accountable to both the LegCo and the public for their performance. The voters would then judge the government's performance at the next election.

However far this reform is adopted, it would represent a major change in the Hong Kong political system. In theory, such significant reform would establish a stronger platform for governance, but it would require several things. First of all, Beijing would have to adopt a different approach in the exercise of sovereignty: give up behind-the-scenes control, place more faith in the pragmatism and good sense of Hong Kong citizens, and be confident that institutions are an effective way to channel and harmonize social conflict.[21] Second, it would require that business interests develop new ways to promote their interests (particularly if FCs are abolished at some point). They will have to engage more in electoral and media politics, either as their own political party (an expanded Liberal Party?) or by combining with the pro-Beijing DAB. Even in a new political mode, business would still have substantial resources to make its case to the public. Politicians in the democratic camp would have to seize the opportunity to gain a real share of power and to contribute to the governance of Hong Kong. Finally, there should be a working assumption that change will happen as the result of an incremental process and not as the result of a "big bang."

TRUST AND SEQUENCING

A focus on process—on devising an incremental process for change—must begin with the recognition that trust among Hong Kong political forces and between them and the Central People's Government is low. The virtue of an incremental reform process is that it can promote trust building without requiring any party to wager too much along the way. Success at one stage makes it easier to achieve progress at the next stage. The problem with an incremental process is that it raises questions about ultimate outcomes. Some actors will worry that gradualism could perpetually put off the goal they wish to achieve. Others will fear that a series of seemingly innocuous steps taken now will cumulatively produce an unwanted final outcome later.

Trust building is therefore connected to sequencing. The process employed between Taiwan and the mainland in the first term of Ma Ying-jeou's presidency adhered to the guideline "easy first, hard later." That made sense because the "easy" steps were mutually beneficial and enjoyed fairly strong support in democratic Taiwan. They enhanced mutual confidence. The process stalled after 2013, not because incrementalism was a bad approach but because there were fewer and fewer easy issues and the new agreements pursued had a negative effect on the interests of some parties on each side. Also, the Ma administration did not do an effective job of explaining to the public why further opening up Taiwan's economy to the mainland was actually in Taiwan's interest and would not ineluctably lead to what Taiwan citizens most feared: incorporation into the PRC on Beijing's terms.[22]

There is considerable scope for creative sequencing in Hong Kong. Some steps can be taken unilaterally by the government to demonstrate goodwill and regain legitimacy. A good place to start would be the property sector: the Hong Kong SAR government should increase the supply of residential and commercial space, and reform overly rigid regulations, particularly regarding public housing. Other steps can be phased in over time to ensure good implementation and head off unintended negative consequences—for example, phasing in expanded welfare benefits and phasing out functional constituencies. Whenever possible, the benefits of reform should be shared among various stakeholders. This is particularly important for the democrats, who have been disadvantaged under the current system. Indeed, Beijing could greatly enhance confidence among the opposition by signaling the changes that it would support and offering what it has never been willing to provide: a timetable about what new tranche of reforms it will offer later if the first tranche is enacted and does not destabilize Hong Kong.

Yet as of the end of 2015, the prospects that Beijing would demonstrate some degree of accommodation to Hong Kong seemed unlikely. In December, the Hong Kong Communist paper *Ta Kung Pao* reprinted an article that Wang Zhenmin had originally published in the Hong Kong monthly *Tzu Ching*. Wang was dean of the Tsinghua University Law School in Beijing and a major articulator of Central People's Government policy concerning the Hong Kong SAR. In his article, he identified four "deep-seated issues" that plague Hong Kong:

1. Hong Kong's original capitalism, which is in contradiction to the current hope of people to turn Hong Kong into a welfare society.
2. Hong Kong's inability to avoid the question of how to face the fact that it is part of its motherland.

3. The relationship between political conservatism and political radicalism.
4. The need to comprehensively and thoroughly implement one country, two systems and the Basic Law.[23]

The first, second, and fourth problems are hardy perennials in Beijing's caution regarding full democracy, namely, that forces within the democratic camp are unpatriotic, have reneged on obligations mandated in the Basic Law, and would end the policy of fiscal prudence. Each is either overstated or unfounded. Further to his point about political conservatism versus radicalism, Wang makes a disturbing allegation: "Political radicalism . . . no longer wishes to conserve and purposefully wishes to damage the rule of law and challenge tradition, and is itching to launch a full scale violent revolution, overthrow the current regime, and completely shatter the current institutional structure and government machinery."[24]

There is no doubt that Hong Kong has become radicalized since the mid-2000s. There is no question that radical elements in the democratic camp frustrated and blocked electoral reform. One effect of several reforms suggested in this chapter would be to defang radicalism and empower moderates. Yet Wang's placing all the blame for Hong Kong's troubles on the Hong Kong SAR and his unwillingness to acknowledge that Beijing's own policies may have empowered the very radicals he accuses of ill will toward the state suggest that creativity on the part of the Central People's Government is unlikely to be revealed anytime soon.

ELEVEN

Hong Kong and Taiwan

What happens in Hong Kong has implications not only for Hong Kong and the future of China but also for Taiwan and the United States. In this chapter I examine the implications for Taiwan of changes taking place in Hong Kong and in Beijing's stance toward the territory. The People's Republic of China (PRC) has used the same "one country, two systems" formula for Taiwan that it uses for Hong Kong in its quest to bring about Taiwan's incorporation into the PRC—in fact, the formula was first proposed in general terms in connection with Taiwan. Beijing elaborated the main elements of the Taiwan plan in September 1981 but met stiff rejection from Taiwan. So the first case for actually applying one country, two systems was Hong Kong, with the details fleshed out in late 1981.[1] But to this day Beijing has insisted that the formula remains the basis for resolving the differences with Taiwan, so one might assume that the Umbrella Movement would have had a profound impact on Taiwan's leaders and public. It is certainly true that the Umbrella protests grabbed the attention of people in Taiwan, particularly in the early stages when the standoff between the police and the protesters was most intense. But the implications drawn from them on Taiwan turn out to be more complicated than one might expect.

Background

After the PRC was founded in October 1949, there were three places that the government claimed as Chinese territory but did not capture: Hong Kong, Portuguese Macau, and Taiwan. Ending that state of division was always a goal of the Chinese Communist Party (CCP) regime, and it remained so when the post-Mao regime emerged in the late 1970s. Deng Xiaoping reaffirmed the importance of the national unification mission and formulated the one country, two systems model to initiate the process for all three territories.

But Deng approached this goal pragmatically. His main priority upon assuming power was to restore the economy and the authority of the Communist Party, and he correctly judged that the reincorporation of the three territories would have to be a long and gradual process. All three places were quite different from the mainland and from one another in their history and contemporary social and political systems. Whatever the pace of reversion, Beijing would have to accept preservation of the capitalist system in the three regions for an extended period of time and permit a system of indirect rule. For Hong Kong, the slogan was "Hong Kong people govern Hong Kong." In the meantime, the mainland hoped to draw on the resources of Hong Kong and Taiwan companies to speed its own economic development.

Although Deng established the same general one country, two systems formula for Taiwan, Hong Kong, and Macau, the eventual application varied. From the perspective of the Central People's Government, the most successful example of the formula has been Macau. The leftist government that assumed power in Portugal in 1974 decided to give up all of the country's colonies, including Macau. China chose to defer the reversion of Macau to a time of its choosing and it chose a later date. In the meantime Macau was designated Chinese territory under Portuguese administration and no longer a Portuguese colony. The formal transfer of sovereignty and control took place in December 1999, and the transition after that was relatively smooth.[2] Macau's local leadership and its social groups have so far accommodated to political co-optation by Beijing, and its China-friendly political institutions have developed gradually and without controversy.[3] Macau had also traveled an economic trajectory very different from Hong Kong's. As Hong Kong's industrialization gained speed in the 1950s and 1960s, Macau remained a sleepy Chinese town with Mediterranean characteristics. Today, Hong Kong is a world-class center of finance and other services. Macau is primarily a gambling mecca for mainland visitors and, some say, a convenient place for them to launder money—a service center of another sort.

If Macau was the easy case for one country, two systems and Hong Kong has been a mixed case, Taiwan has always been the hard case. Once Beijing began laying out the details of the plan in September 1981, Taipei's rigidly anti-Communist leaders had little interest in unification—and certainly not on Beijing's terms. Taipei may have been on the defensive in the early 1980s, since in 1979 the United States established diplomatic relations with the PRC and no longer recognized the Republic of China (ROC), based in Taipei, as the government of China. But Taiwan still had U.S. political and security support, so it stood on its principles and told Beijing that unification would only occur on the ROC's terms. Deng Xiaoping accepted that reality and quickly shifted attention to adapting one country, two systems to Hong Kong.

Early on, Beijing retained the hope that a successful transition in Hong Kong would create a positive demonstration effect for Taiwan and gradually reduce the latter's recalcitrance. Observers often cite this calculation to explain why the Central People's Government is restrained—or should be restrained—in its handling of Hong Kong. But Beijing's hope in a Hong Kong demonstration effect has not been realized, primarily because Taiwan—like Hong Kong—has changed dramatically in the decades since the initial enunciation of one country, two systems. Most important, in the late 1980s and early 1990s the island moved from an authoritarian regime to a democratic political system that gave the public a say in its government's policies toward China. (Hong Kong residents did not have a similar voice, and so decisions on their fate were made from afar.) When it arrived, democracy in Taiwan exposed intense opposition by over a majority of the population, in contrast to Hong Kong, where there was much stronger confidence that reversion would work, particularly on the part of the anti-British, pro-Chinese nationalists who welcomed unification. The reasons for Taiwan's opposition to one country, two systems have changed over the years, but its basic opposition persists.

Taiwan's Responses to One Country, Two Systems

Taiwan has opposed unification under the one country, two systems formula for two very different reasons. One stems from a long-standing ideology and the other from the island's more recent democratization.

IDEOLOGICAL REGIME RIVALRY

Initially, the reason Taiwan's leaders rejected one country, two systems was inevitable, given China's twentieth-century history. Since the 1920s, the Nationalist Party, called the Kuomintang, and the Chinese Communist Party had been bitter ideological and military rivals. In 1928, the Kuomintang (KMT), led by Chiang Kai-shek, gained control of the ROC government, which had been founded by Dr. Sun Yat-sen in 1912 after the fall of the Qing dynasty on the mainland. After 1928 the Kuomintang, with only brief interruption, fought a civil war with the CCP until 1949, when the Communists emerged victorious on the mainland and founded the People's Republic of China. The Nationalist armies retreated to Taiwan, and for many years Taipei was called the ROC's "provisional capital." The ROC and PRC now contended as rival governments of China. They fought for the right to represent China in the international community, with each dismissing the idea that the other was a legitimate government with an international identity. Chiang Kai-shek famously described the zero-sum rivalry in moral terms: *Hanzei buliangli* ("A legitimate government cannot coexist with bandits"). But by 1980, after the United States officially recognized the PRC as the legal government of China and representative of the Chinese nation, Beijing had essentially won that battle.[4]

Consequently, when Beijing first enunciated one country, two systems, Taipei had no interest in being unified under what it still regarded as a bandit regime, and it rejected Beijing's formula out of hand. Instead, Taiwan announced that unification would take place on the basis of the "three people's principles" espoused by Dr. Sun Yat-sen, the founder of the Kuomintang as well as the Republic of China. In the meantime there would be no official contact, negotiations, or direct trade and shipping between Taiwan and the mainland. This ideological approach to unification colored the ROC government's view of Hong Kong. The ROC's president, Lee Teng-hui, bluntly remarked one year after Hong Kong's reversion: "The 'one country, two systems' formula is in essence deceptive, contradictory and anti-democratic: deceptive because the two systems, though seemingly equal, are in fact absolutely unequal; contradictory because communism is practiced alongside capitalism; and anti-democratic in the sense that power in a democracy is bottom-up, while on the mainland it is top down. Basically, the 'one country, two systems' formula is nothing less than 'peaceful annexation.' "[5]

Economically, however, Taiwan had to be pragmatic, and it was here that Hong Kong was useful. Since the early 1980s Taiwan companies had faced rising labor costs and U.S. pressure to strengthen the island's currency, so the business opportunities on the mainland created by Deng's post-1978 policies of economic reform and opening were a godsend. Because the ROC government had forbidden its companies to engage in direct trade or shipping with China, Hong Kong assumed a key role. It became the ideal trans-shipment point for Taiwan components, finished goods, and people entering the Chinese market.[6] Once reversion occurred in 1997 and Hong Kong was no longer a possession of the United Kingdom but a formal part of the PRC, pragmatic adjustments were required. Taiwan's legislature had already passed the Hong Kong–Macau Relations Act in 1994, which authorized continuity in economic, cultural, legal, and law enforcement matters and on entry and exit procedures once the two territories reverted to the PRC.[7] Special arrangements were soon made for aviation and shipping.[8]

Beijing and Taipei may have learned to coexist economically since the 1980s, but they still differ on the political and legal status of the governing authorities on Taiwan. The consistent traditional position of the Taiwan government is that those authorities are a sovereign state, the Republic of China, which was founded in 1912 and has existed continuously since then. The formal position of the PRC is that the ROC ceased to exist on October 1, 1949, the day that Mao Zedong proclaimed the founding of the PRC. Since then, Beijing says, the institutions governing Taiwan are merely "local authorities." From Taipei's point of view, its claim that the ROC both exists and has a sovereign character is in fundamental conflict with Beijing's formula: the one country, two systems approach to unification would create a Taiwan Special Administrative Region of the PRC—a subordinate part of the PRC. This problem did not exist in the case of Hong Kong, because Hong Kong had been a subordinate part of the United Kingdom and thus had no basis for claiming sovereignty. For Taipei its case is conceptually very different from that of Hong Kong, and to this day the ROC's claim that it exists as an "independent sovereign state" has been and continues to be the fundamental obstacle to reconciliation across the Taiwan Strait.[9]

Two other points are also worth noting. First, Taipei's claim for the ROC's sovereignty does not necessarily rule out national unification on terms other than one country, two systems. It would no doubt be very difficult to construct and sustain such an arrangement, particularly given the PRC's self-identity as a unitary state and the evolution of very general attitudes on Taiwan away from identification with China and toward identification with Taiwan alone. But political systems, such as the United States, the European Union, and, increasingly, the United Kingdom, based on the idea of dual sovereignty

(sovereignty at both a central and subcentral level), and specific dual-sovereignty models for Taiwan have never been explored.

Second, there are differences of opinion within Taiwan regarding unification. Generally the KMT does not rule out the right kind of unification at some time in the future, but it has also had no domestic political incentive to discuss the issue publicly. Taiwan's other principal party, the opposition Democratic Progressive Party (DPP), has a different point of departure. In its early, most anti-KMT and anti-ROC phase, it adopted the formal goal of a Republic of Taiwan completely divorced from China politically. Its current position, adopted in 1999, is more nuanced and hinges on what territory is actually covered by the Republic of China. It agrees that "Taiwan" is a sovereign independent country and rejects the idea that Taiwan is "subject to the jurisdiction of the People's Republic of China." But it acknowledges that only Taiwan is "named the Republic of China under its current constitution." This leaves the implication that the current constitution, the name of the country, and its territory might be changed sometime in the future. The two Taiwan political parties also have disagreed over the territorial scope of "the Republic of China" and "Taiwan." KMT governments have usually said that the Republic of China is both the mainland and Taiwan. The DPP's position in the 1999 resolution was that "Taiwan's jurisdiction covers Taiwan, Penghu, Kinmen, Matsu, its affiliated islands and territorial waters."[10]

These arcane yet fundamental differences aside, the basic conceptual difference between the positions of the PRC and of Taiwan (both KMT and DPP) over the latter's legal and political character have made any kind of political negotiations between the two sides very difficult. It also severely limits any positive demonstration effect that Hong Kong might have for Taiwan. If Taiwan's government and public believe the two places have nothing in common, then there is no effect to be had.

TAIWAN'S DEMOCRATIZATION AND COMPETING IDENTITIES

Back in the 1980s, Chinese leaders still retained some hope that these conceptual obstacles could be removed. After all, Taiwan's leaders in the Kuomintang were mainlanders who had moved to Taiwan after World War II. Beijing could make appeals to Chinese patriotism and cite prosperity and stability in Hong Kong to bring the Kuomintang around. In Taiwan, the KMT's long-term goal was also unification; it just differed with Beijing over the terms. Thus, in response to the CCP's proposal in the fall of 1981, Taipei countered early in 1982 that unification had to occur according to the "three people's principles" of

KMT founder Sun Yat-sen: democracy, the nation, and the people's livelihood. Beijing may also have assumed that if persuasion did not work, leverage and intimidation might be more effective. Their key strategies were deepening economic ties across the Taiwan Strait and breaking Taipei's cord to Washington.

But this strategy would succeed if and only if the authoritarian system that Chiang Kai-shek had created on Taiwan continued, because it denied the Taiwan public a voice in any negotiations. Chiang Ching-kuo, Chiang Kai-shek's son and successor, negated that possibility by beginning a process of democratization in 1986.[11] After his death in January 1988, his successor, Lee Teng-hui, gradually implemented political reforms. By 1996 it could be said that Taiwan's transition to democracy was complete.

This political transformation profoundly complicated matters from Beijing's point of view due to two game-changing effects. First, elections for president and the Legislative Yuan, Taiwan's parliament, would now be competitive and the results would reflect the general sentiments of voters. Competition meant that the KMT soon faced a challenge from the DPP, which was founded in 1986. The DPP was the principal political force that capitalized on resentment of the KMT's authoritarian rule and the "mainlanders" who dominated it. The DPP reflected the sentiments of many Taiwan citizens whose families had been on the island for generations (the "native Taiwanese"). The idea that the KMT, which was Beijing's preferred interlocutor, might lose power to the DPP alarmed Beijing because it believed the DPP was committed to de jure independence and did not acknowledge that Taiwan was a part of China. Beijing's greatest difficulties with Taiwan would occur during the 2000–2008 period, when Chen Shui-bian of the DPP was president.

Second, liberalization permitted political expression and activity on Taiwan that hitherto had been prohibited. Political parties formed, demonstrations and rallies became common, and public political expression was soon prevalent. In particular, democratization released a long-suppressed view on who Taiwan people were and where they thought the island should go that was contrary to that of Kuomintang leaders. For instance, in 1994 26.2 percent of people surveyed as to their ethnic and political identity said they were Chinese, 20.2 percent said they were Taiwanese, and 44.6 percent said they were both. Two decades later, in 2014, only 3.5 percent of those polled said they were Chinese, 60.6 percent said they were Taiwanese (triple the 1994 share), and 32.5 percent said they were both.[12]

The formation of a Taiwan identity, first subterranean and later above ground, had a unique cause. When the ROC took over Taiwan in 1945, pursuant to decisions made by Franklin Roosevelt and other allied leaders during World War II, the predatory actions of its officials and soldiers quickly alienated the local population. Occupying soldiers willfully seized the property of long-time residents, and official corruption grew. These abuses provoked an islandwide rebellion in February and March 1947 that was quickly and brutally suppressed by ROC army units. Around 20,000 people lost their lives in the "228 Incident" (short for February 28 when the conflict began), countless more were imprisoned, and a deep resentment pervaded the whole society. When the ROC government officially moved to the island in 1949, its working assumption was that fifty years of Japanese colonial rule over the island, which was annexed from the Qing dynasty in 1895 after the first Sino-Japanese War, had leached away the Chinese soul of the population and that special measures were needed to restore a national consciousness. The regime transformed the education system into a tool to impose "Chineseness," which included requiring Mandarin Chinese as the language of instruction in schools, even though the overlap between it and the local spoken dialects was minimal. Students were forbidden to speak their native dialect in class and the focus of social studies and literature was exclusively on China as a whole; local history, geography, and literature were deliberately neglected. For young Taiwanese men, mandatory military service was another occasion for the involuntary imposition of national consciousness. Finally, the authoritarian political system harshly punished words and actions that it deemed a Taiwanese challenge to political orthodoxy and used the ongoing conflict with the CCP and the fiction that the ROC was the only legal government of China to deny islandwide elections.

In response, most Taiwanese just sought to avoid trouble and made the best of a bad situation for themselves and their families, principally by taking advantage of the rapid economic growth that the ROC government had the good sense to promote. A very small minority overtly provoked the regime, and lost their freedom in the process. Simultaneously, many Taiwanese resented the regime's efforts to impose a national identity upon them. The logic seems to have been, "If the treatment I have received is what it means to be Chinese, I am not Chinese but something else. I am Taiwanese." It was dangerous to express this contrarian thought under authoritarian rule, but once repression was lifted the seeds of Taiwan identity germinated and quickly bloomed.[13] The result was the mix of previously latent public attitudes revealed in the opinion surveys cited earlier. Memories of the harsh authoritarianism period had another effect, one that is relevant to PRC unification policy today: a general fear of mainlander outsiders. At least some Taiwanese who recall all the cruel policies that came with KMT-style unification are not eager to try a PRC version.

In the meantime, the growth of a strong Taiwan identity had a significant impact on politics. By the mid-1990s, two political camps emerged that differed in their emphasis on identity and in their approach to China. The "Blue" camp, dominated by the KMT, is ambiguous regarding Taiwanese identity. Those in the Blue camp currently believe that Taiwan can benefit from engaging China economically, but are cautious about moving forward on political issues, in part because they must secure the support of some native Taiwanese to win elections. The "Green" camp, dominated by the DPP, draws electoral support from the Taiwanese majority, has capitalized on a localist identity, and remains fearful of China's intentions toward Taiwan and skeptical about any economic engagement.

Promoting Taiwan identity and feeding fears of China has been a staple in most presidential election campaigns, a tool that even the KMT cannot avoid. Although Lee Teng-hui was the leader of the KMT, he used identity issues and fear of China successfully in his 1996 reelection campaign. Candidates of the DPP generally try to raise the salience of local identity, and parties and candidates who advocate unification get no traction in electoral politics. Candidates on the KMT side who see value in improving relations with Beijing must still tread carefully in order to avoid the charge of selling out Taiwan, and yet tend to believe that economic interchange is the only safe area of cross-Strait interaction. Ma Ying-jeou, Taiwan's president from 2008 to 2016, stressed repeatedly during his incumbency that unification was off the agenda; he also realized that political talks with Beijing on issues even well short of unification were too unpopular with the public to undertake. The opposition DPP, which took an explicit position in favor of de jure independence in 1991, retreated to a less provocative but more ambiguous stance in 1999.[14] It made this shift in order to secure electoral support from a populace that has no interest in either unification or independence.

The general public, too, has taken a centrist stance on the outcomes it does and doesn't want. Survey after survey has demonstrated that people's default preference is the status quo (the exact outlines of the status quo go undefined). In 2014, for example, 59.5 percent of those surveyed were wedded to the status quo, either forever or for a long time; 25.9 percent wanted to maintain the status quo for an unspecified period and then move to an ultimate outcome: 18.0 percent for independence and 7.9 percent for unification. Only

5.9 percent of respondents wanted to move toward independence right away, and just 1.3 percent desired unification right away. These percentages have not changed significantly since the late 1990s, even as Taiwan identity has strengthened.[15] Although the options offered in surveys on ultimate outcomes are fairly general and undefined, the Taiwan public's strong preference for "the devil we know" is clear. This mainstream sentiment is a mixed blessing for Beijing: it serves as a bulwark against what China fears—independence—but remains an obstacle to what it has long sought—unification.

The substance of identity has evolved over time. As economic opportunities on the mainland grew and democracy in Taiwan strengthened, younger generations adopted a less strident type of Taiwanese nationalism and their fears of PRC outsiders slightly diminished, especially when they realized that job opportunities were greater on the mainland than in Taiwan.[16] This was not a fundamental or irreversible trend, however, as most Taiwan residents had no doubt that the island was their home and that the mainland was a different society. Further, fears that China might swallow up Taiwan continued to gain currency in some parts of society, particularly among young people.[17]

TAIWAN POLITICS AND THE BASIC LAW

Taiwan's transition to democracy widened the gap between the island's political system and the system projected for Hong Kong under one country, two systems. The key difference concerned electoral processes and Beijing's ability to control Hong Kong election outcomes. In crafting the provisions of the Hong Kong Basic Law on how the chief executive and members of the Legislative Council were to be selected, Beijing had made sure that it retained significant control over who was picked and who, thereafter, dominated the legislative process. The nominating committee mandated in the universal suffrage proposal had much the same character. Clearly, Beijing's initial purpose was to ensure that no political leader from the democratic camp could be selected, and no opposition political party or coalition of parties could win control of the Legislative Council and then set the legislative agenda.[18]

Consequently, anyone in Taiwan who bothered to read the election provisions of the Hong Kong Basic Law and studied how they have been applied would have deep concern about the implications for a Taiwan that agreed to unification on the basis of one country, two systems.[19] Concretely, replication of Hong Kong's electoral arrangements in Taiwan would likely make it difficult or impossible for a DPP leader to become president and for the DPP to gain control of the legislature. Given Beijing's belief that the DPP is a Taiwan independence party, it would likely be even more insistent in denying it real power than it is regarding Hong Kong's democratic camp. At least one Taiwan scholar, John Lim of Academia Sinica in Taipei, understood the implications of Hong Kong's electoral arrangements for Taiwan, writing: "Beijing is very concerned about how, on the thorny issue of universal suffrage in Hong Kong, it is to control the [nomination] commission and the territory's whole electoral mechanism to block prodemocracy forces from fielding a candidate for the post of chief executive."[20]

Of course it is possible that Beijing would be more liberal in drafting the analogous provisions in a Taiwan Basic Law than it was in the case of Hong Kong. After all, democracy on Taiwan is a fait accompli, whereas Hong Kong had only begun a transition of sorts when the Basic Law was drafted. But if it comes time for Taiwan to decide whether to negotiate on unification, there is no reason to assume that China will *not* try to control electoral outcomes as it has in Hong Kong. Establishing full democracy was a source of pride and international prestige within Taiwan. On this important issue, therefore, Hong Kong's demonstration effect is again decidedly negative.

Since the late 1980s, there have been a couple of interesting points of convergence and divergence between Taiwan and Hong Kong. Concerning political systems, Taiwan removed the pillars of the authoritarian system and created democratic institutions in the late 1980s and early 1990s, at the same time that Hong Kong was contending within itself and with Beijing over how much democracy to allow. The Basic Law imposed limits on electoral competition, which Chris Patten tried to work around, but to no avail. Hong Kong residents likely began to acquire a sense of local identity in the 1980s, at a time when it was still dangerous in Taiwan to talk openly about the subject. By the mid-to-late 1990s, in both places people increasingly identified with where they lived, and their attachments to China became more and more ambivalent. In both places there was, perhaps, a growing sense that one's ethnicity or place of birth and residence was less important than the vital aspects of the political system. Hong Kong had its liberal institutions and some competitive elections, whereas Taiwan's residents had both freedoms and the ability to choose all their political leaders.[21]

Taiwan and the Umbrella Movement

Hong Kong's debate over universal suffrage and the Umbrella protests during the fall of 2014 opened a recent and useful window on Taiwan sentiments about one country, two systems.

Actually, the struggle over electoral reform in Hong Kong created a double demonstration effect between Hong Kong and Taiwan, one that was decidedly contrary to Beijing's interests. There was a demonstration effect from Taiwan to Hong Kong—what Sonny Lo of the Institute of Education calls the "Taiwanization of Hong Kong politics."[22] As noted in chapter 1, the Umbrella Movement drew some inspiration and borrowed some political tactics from Taiwan's Sunflower Movement six months before. There the issue was not free and fair elections, but the process by which the Legislative Yuan was reviewing the agreement on trade-in-services that the Ma Ying-jeou government had negotiated with Beijing. The opposition party and student activists alleged that the process was a "black box" closed to comment and critiques from the general public. The students suddenly seized the legislative complex, bringing legislative review to an end. The crisis would preoccupy Taiwan politics before being brought to an unsatisfactory end after twenty-three days.[23] Not surprisingly this exaggerated mainland fears of the dangers of separatism.

There was also a demonstration effect from Hong Kong to Taiwan, which played out in different ways and at two levels. The Taiwanese public at large had relatively little interest in Hong Kong, believing that these were two different cases. Hong Kong protests were not the lead story in the Taiwan media's news reporting after the initial vivid clashes between the Occupy Movement and the police. The *Taipei Times*, a Green camp newspaper, did cover the major episodes of the electoral reform saga, but it relied significantly on foreign news services such as Reuters and Agence France Press, with only a relatively small number of stories written by its own reporters.[24] This likely reflects the greater salience of domestic issues for most media organizations. One Taiwan friend bluntly put it to me in the midst of the Occupy Movement, "People in Taiwan don't care at all what is happening in Hong Kong."[25]

After the protests were over, a scholar friend of mine put it somewhat differently: "Taiwan didn't pay much attention to events in Hong Kong.... Presumably, people here assume that China will not attack Taiwan, let alone occupy it. The pro-DPP *Liberty Times* more often than not used Hong Kong demonstrations for its headlines, apparently in the hope of fanning up the [already strong] anti-China attitude in Taiwan."[26] That is, Hong Kong events did prompt a vigorous debate between the KMT and the DPP and in the editorial and commentary pages of media outlets that reflect their views. One part of the story that did get covered was the position the two Taiwan political camps took toward the protests. Generally, the DPP and the Green camp supported the protesters and agreed with them that Beijing's August 31 decision and the Hong Kong SAR government's final proposal denied voters any semblance of a democratic choice. On October 1, 2014, Tsai Ing-wen, the chair of the DPP, said, "We call on the Hong Kong government to display self-restraint in protecting the people of Hong Kong's right to assemble and in ensuring that conflict does not take place again.... Human rights, democracy and freedom are universal values, and people should have an inalienable right to pursue them, free from threats, coercion and violence."[27] The *Taipei Times* asserted in an editorial that the actions of the Hong Kong government in the early days of the protests (tear gas, pepper spray) reflected the authorities' attempt to grapple with a sudden crisis as well as Beijing's "brutal" intentions on electoral reform.[28] Speaking for the government on October 10, President Ma Ying-jeou expressed his "strong support for the people of Hong Kong." Citing Deng Xiaoping's view from the 1980s that some Chinese should get rich first, Ma asked why Beijing couldn't "let some people go democratic first?" That is, Beijing should allow Hong Kong's people to enjoy full democracy before others in the PRC. Moreover, Ma suggested that democratization in Hong Kong would be "strongly welcomed by the people of Taiwan ... [and] be a huge boost for the development of cross-strait relations."[29] For his convictions, Ma earned a rebuke from the Taiwan Affairs Office in Beijing, which said that he should "not make irresponsible remarks, respect the choice and pursuit of the 1.3 billion people on the mainland, [and] do more things that advance the development of cross-Strait relations, rather than going the opposite way."[30]

Beijing's criticism of Ma was mild compared to the invective he received from Taiwan's Green camp media. In the cutthroat thrust and parry of Taiwan politics, his opponents seized on any issue that might weaken him and his party in the eyes of the public. The Umbrella Movement period was particularly contentious because it happened to coincide with the last two months of campaigning for local elections in Taiwan. A September 11, 2014, *Liberty Times* editorial, "Ma Deaf to HK's Call to Democracy," was typical of this criticism. It said that Ma's response to Beijing's August 31 decision, which he conveyed at a KMT meeting, was "slow and inappropriate" and that he shied away from "a dignified and forthright expression as the president of a nation." It also challenged his fundamental intentions and loyalty to Taiwan: "Ma does not believe that sovereignty belongs to the people. As he continues to oppress Taiwan's democracy through the KMT's party-state system, sovereignty is distorted, as it no longer belongs to the people, but to Ma himself. Ma is probably preparing for the next phase, in which sovereignty will belong to Xi."[31]

Beneath the polemics, the Green camp did have a narrative composed of several elements. First, Beijing had broken the promises it had made to Hong Kong. By insisting on a nominating committee, it was violating its pledges to preserve autonomy, let the Hong Kong SAR's people govern themselves, and institute universal suffrage (the Green camp media never fully explored in their reports exactly what Beijing had promised). The *Taipei Times* (of the Green camp) wrote: "Prior to 1997, the CCP gave assurances that it would maintain a 'one country, two systems' administration in Hong Kong, with a high degree of autonomy, democratic governance and no change to the system for 50 years. However, it has reneged on these promises."[32] (The implication here was that the Ma administration was naive to negotiate cross-Strait agreements with Beijing.)[33]

Second, how China was implementing the one country, two systems model in Hong Kong was an important reference point for Taiwan, since China had proposed the same approach for both entities. John Lim's assessment on the implications of Beijing's efforts to control Hong Kong's electoral outcomes has already been mentioned. But Lim believed that the implications went beyond that in ways relevant to Ma's mainland policy: "Almost every progressive measure taken to expand cross-strait exchanges over the past few years, from easing restrictions on Chinese tourists, to relaxing regulations on Chinese students studying in Taiwan, were tried out between Hong Kong and China first. Only after being tested in these ways were such measures implemented between Beijing and Taipei."[34] Lim implied that Beijing's efforts to control elections via the nominating committee in Hong Kong would be replicated in Taiwan if it ever accepted one country, two systems.

A third element in the Green camp's narrative is that Taiwan should be clear-eyed about the consequences of slipping slowly but inexorably into China's orbit under one country, two systems—promises of autonomy notwithstanding. Hong Kong itself had little or no choice in choosing its relationship with the Central People's Government, and its people are now caught in a situation that combines China's growing economic presence and political control. Taiwan has more choice in choosing its future; the lesson of Hong Kong is that too much economic dependence creates growing political vulnerability. Thus, the *Taipei Times* editorially criticized the Ma administration for reacting "rather nonchalantly" to developments in Hong Kong. "Such reactions may be appropriate if the chaos happens in a faraway place that has nothing to do with Taiwan. However . . . the 'one country, two systems' framework—originally designed for Taiwan—is not working in Hong Kong. It is time for the government to be responsible and learn from the developments in Hong Kong, and reflect on its China-leaning policies to prevent Taiwan from being dragged into the same predicament."[35] The Green camp's slogan was "Today's Hong Kong is tomorrow's Taiwan." Tung Chen-yuan, a respected scholar in the Green camp who is a professor at National Chengchi University in Taipei, concurred: "Beijing's intervention, manipulation and even obstruction to Hong Kong's democracy makes people in Taiwan more reluctant to accept the so-called one country, two systems scheme."[36]

The Blue camp actually agreed with the Greens on some parts of its narrative. An early September 2014 editorial by the Blue-leaning newspaper *Lien Ho Pao* warned that "the failure of the 'one country, two systems' in Hong Kong will spontaneously lead to the conclusion that it will also fail in Taiwan." The main reason was the undemocratic character of the election system proposed for Hong Kong: "How can Taiwanese people appreciate and accept a model under which Taiwan's presidential candidates are to be named only by a few autocratic members of a communist 'nominating committee'?"[37] About a month later, Xi Jinping, meeting with pro-unification visitors from Taiwan, emphasized the formula of one country, two systems even though PRC officials had generally given it limited attention. This prompted intense speculation across the Taiwan political spectrum about Xi's motivation. One explanation was that Beijing was worried about the civil disobedience tactics used during the Sunflower Movement and the outlook for Taiwan's presidential election in January 2016, which the DPP was then favored to win (it ultimately did). Another was that Beijing's difficulties in Hong Kong led to a greater stress on the "one country" part of the formula. Chang Ya-chung, a strong proponent of the right kind of unification, drew the implication of Xi's remarks in an open letter to Xi: his policy, Chang wrote, would place China and Taiwan "in a father-son relationship, rather than one guaranteeing equal status to both," something Taiwan could not tolerate.[38] But the KMT government rejected the Green idea that Hong Kong was Taiwan's canary in the China mineshaft. Instead, Taiwan's premier, Jiang Yi-hua, reiterated the fundamental political difference between Hong Kong and Taiwan, specifically that the ROC had "complete sovereignty" while Hong Kong was just a part of the PRC—"So there is no need to worry that we could be subject to pressure from Beijing, as Hong Kong is now." He thought the slogan should be, "Today's Taiwan, tomorrow's Hong Kong."[39]

A Lingering Question

Looking outward from Beijing, Hong Kong and Taiwan are far away, not only geographically but also politically and psychologically.[40] Their reunification with mainland China has been the PRC's goal since the founding of the regime in 1949 (it was the ROC's goal as well). Mao Zedong and his colleagues judged early on that seizing the two territories and then ruling them like the provinces that the CCP already controlled was not a top priority (in Taiwan's case, conquest was a military impossibility). The reunification goal rose in salience in the post-Mao period, but even Deng Xiaoping understood that direct rule was impractical—hence his formulation of the one country, two systems approach. Deng's likely calculation was that indirect rule would work for China if accommodating elites were found to whom it could delegate authority over local affairs and by trusting the assumed "patriotism" of the people in both territories.

It hasn't worked out that way, of course. Hong Kong's response to Tiananmen and the flowering of Taiwan identity were the early warning signs that Beijing had misread the tea leaves. By 2016 the two societies had been totally transformed, and in ways that called into question the wisdom of one country, two systems. In both places, generational change fostered political mentalities that were quite alien to CCP assumptions. In particular, majority opinion in both Hong Kong and Taiwan is that the people themselves should pick their leaders. (One might even argue that the most important demonstration effect at work today, one that Beijing leaders may not be willing to take on board, is the way modernization transforms middle-class attitudes, especially among the young, raising the possibility that the same transformation will occur on the mainland.) Hong Kong may now have some "buyer's remorse" about one country, two systems and Taiwan is very much in the mode of "buyer beware," yet China's leaders may have their own case of "seller's remorse"—a belief that these two geographically and politically peripheral areas are moving in directions that undermine China's sense of security as it defines it.

Beijing has been less than skillful in the way it has promoted one country, two systems and responded to the desire for full democracy in Hong Kong and the power of Taiwan identity. One might even question the wisdom of the basic approach, at least in retrospect. Yet the question still lingers: Are there ways that Hong Kong and Taiwan could reassure Chinese leaders that their worst fears are not justified and that creative adaptations of one country, two systems might foster a more stable basis for their relationship with Beijing?

These are complicated issues, especially when it comes to Taiwan. Certainly, the fears of Chinese leaders are magnified by the way the PRC system conducts threat assessments. Even Ma Ying-jeou's proactive steps to reassure Beijing did not negate the belief in Beijing that his ultimate goal was not national unification consistent with one country, two systems, but "peaceful separation."[41]

Why would a small country give up autonomy to come under the power of a huge neighbor? The only remotely relevant analogous situation in recent history is the relationship of Finland and the Soviet Union during the Cold War, a relationship dubbed "Finlandization" by Hans Mouritzen, the leading authority on the concept. He describes it as "adaptive acquiescence" in interstate relations, a focus that would seem to negate its value at least for Hong Kong (since Hong Kong is not an independent state), but the core elements of the concept are still worth exploring. In adaptive acquiescence, Mouritzen argues, the weak state must meet the following requirements:

> First and foremost is [the weak state's] maintaining an overarching commitment to [its own] core values. Statements [of those values] . . . must be repeated over and over again in order to be effective. Second, such statements must be given credibility, which depends on the presence of a civil society historically committed to democracy. Third, to sustain this credibility, [there must be leadership] by a politician with nationalist credentials who cannot be suspected of selling out the state's core values. Fourth, Finlandization requires an elitist approach to foreign policy: only a small number of top politicians should be kept adequately informed and involved in major decisions. Finally, governments pursuing Finlandization cannot always afford the luxury of free and frank democratic debate, since that could rock the boat in relations with the bigger neighbor; the media may therefore have to act as "co-diplomats" by endorsing the government's policy line.[42]

Adaptive acquiescence in the Finnish-USSR case was essentially a bargain between a weak state (Finland) with one set of values and a great-power neighbor animated by a very different ideology. Finland recognized that it was part of Moscow's sphere of interest, abjured a security relationship with a rival great power (the United States), but insisted that the Soviet Union respect its core values and allow Finland to preserve its preferred social and political system. Finland's way of preserving its national independence was to impose demands on its own political system by discouraging all political parties from making a divisive political issue out of policy toward the Soviet Union.

The unique features of Beijing's relationship with Hong Kong and Taiwan and its belief that Hong Kong is a subordinate unit of the PRC, and that Taiwan should be one, make a direct application of the Finlandization model to this situation impossible. The political evolution of the Hong Kong SAR and of Taiwan may rule out any possibility of placing limits on how each system would define its relationship with Beijing. The purpose of the analogy is both to be suggestive and to reveal the difficulties involved. Probably most relevant to the PRC is the requirement Mouritzen identifies for the big-power entity in the relationship: Finlandization "requires Bismarckian restraint on the part of the great power, which must resist the temptation to simply impose its own puppet regime."[43]

Conclusion

Taiwan's politicians and public have a variety of reasons for resisting the idea that Hong Kong has any relevance for their future. First is the belief that the two places are fundamentally different in nature. Hong Kong was a colony whose people were deprived of any say in determining their future by both Britain and China, whereas Taiwan is seen as a sovereign entity whose people insist on having a say through their democratic system. Second, what happens in Hong Kong can serve as a useful flail for the Green camp to use in criticizing the Blue camp. For the Greens, the leaders of the KMT have been naive at best, and traitorous at worst. A third reason is the setup of the Hong Kong political system, which observers in Taiwan correctly attribute to a Chinese desire to restrict the range of outcomes as a way to maintain control. This gap between the limited competition in the Hong Kong system and more open elections in Taiwan creates a strong allergy in Taiwan to one country, two systems.

When the PRC government addressed the process of electoral reform in Hong Kong, it had an opportunity to begin to close this political gap between Taiwan and Hong Kong. If Beijing had changed the Hong Kong political system enough to permit genuine competition for the chief executive and later had ended the undemocratic character of the legislature (the functional constituencies), it would have eliminated an obvious argument made by the anti-unification forces in Taiwan. As Ma Ying-jeou told the *New York Times* during the protests, "If mainland China can practice democracy in Hong Kong, or if mainland China itself can become more democratic, then we can shorten the psychological distance between people from the two sides of the Taiwan Strait."[44] Even if that had occurred, an enduring positive demonstration effect would have required that competitive elections in Hong Kong contribute to political stability and good governance, with higher levels of process and performance legitimacy (see chapter 7).

But the first lost opportunity to begin closing the gap was Beijing's failure to demonstrate greater flexibility and a better sense of timing in 2014, before the protests ever began. As it was, the white paper, the August 31 decision, and the PRC's subsequent actions only confirmed for people in Taiwan that the Central People's Government was more concerned with political control in Hong Kong than with using elections to provide better feedback for the government or with winning hearts and minds in Taiwan. Taiwan's first minister of culture, Lung Ying-tai, who had lived and worked in Hong Kong for nine years, clarified the issue when she called on Beijing to regard the Hong Kong protests as the majority sentiment in the territory and not "the longings and pursuits of only a handful of people," as Beijing seemed to claim. For both Taiwan and Hong Kong, she emphasized, "Beijing has to win hearts and minds of the people with civility."[45]

TWELVE

United States Policy toward Hong Kong

America has had a presence in Hong Kong since virtually the colony's founding in 1842, and its role in Hong Kong affairs has grown significantly over time. Hong Kong has had a presence in the United States since the beginning of the Cold War, when residents of the territory began emigrating to America. Hong Kong has been one element in U.S. policy toward East Asia since World War II; although the mix of interests and values has changed over time, with commercial interests always at the fore, and other objectives waxing and waning in their importance. Since World War II, policy toward Hong Kong has often been a function of Washington's relationship with the People's Republic of China (PRC), and not necessarily in ways that benefit the territory. As a matter of general principle, Americans and their government have supported the idea of a more democratic political system for Hong Kong, but the objective has never been at the top of the agenda. Moreover, U.S. domestic interests and politics sometimes distort American foreign policy objectives. Additionally, the fact that the United Kingdom was Hong Kong's sovereign before July 1997 and the People's Republic of China has been its sovereign since then has had its own impact on the U.S. stance toward Hong Kong. Consequently, the question of how and how much the United States should promote democracy in Hong Kong—or anywhere, for that matter—has no easy or obvious answers. That became apparent in the debate over electoral reform.

The United States in Hong Kong: Hong Kong in the United States

The ties between American and Hong Kong societies have been broad and deep since the mid-twentieth century. Between 1950 and 2013, 496,455 Hong Kong residents secured permanent residence in the United States. Between 1991 and 2013, 101,875 people born in Hong Kong were naturalized as American citizens.[1] In 2014, around 65,000 American expatriates lived and worked in Hong Kong (compared to 21,146 Japanese and 13,607 Korean expatriates) and over a million American tourists visited or transited Hong Kong.[2] In the 1950s and 1960s the American missionary presence was considerable but is much smaller now: ethnic Chinese long ago assumed leadership of local churches, and the city's government needed less and less help from the local or foreign private sector to provide social services. The visibility in Hong Kong of Western culture, which includes American culture, makes Hong Kong a very cosmopolitan place.

In 2014, Hong Kong was the ninth-largest export market for the United States and the sixth-largest for agricultural goods. The United States is Hong Kong's second-largest trading partner after China. American companies have had a presence in the territory since the nineteenth century, but the number grew substantially after 1979, when China liberalized its economic policies and the city became an important portal through which foreign companies could enter and thrive in the mainland market. As of 2015, more than 1,300 American firms had a presence in the Hong Kong Special Administrative Region (Hong Kong SAR), and the local American Chamber of Commerce plays an active role in the business community.[3] From 1966 to 2013, the cumulative American direct investment in Hong Kong grew from $126 million to $58.83 billion (the stock of Japanese investment in Hong Kong in 2014 was $29.1 billion, and the stock of Korean investment in 2012 was $11.6 billion).[4]

Although the Hong Kong SAR is only one small part of the PRC, the official American presence there is quite large. The U.S. consulate general has eighty-five American officers, more than double the size of the next-largest foreign mission in the territory and probably larger than the staff of a number of U.S. embassies around the world.[5] The personnel includes representatives from a variety of executive-branch agencies, all of whom work with their Hong Kong counterparts on a regular and substantive basis on a wide range of issues. In addition to economic matters, U.S. officials interact with their counterparts in the Hong Kong SAR government on issues such as counterterrorism, counternarcotics, customs issues, law enforcement, money laundering, corruption, and so on. For the most part, they do so on a routine basis, and often below the radar screen of media publicity. The U.S. Navy makes on average thirteen port calls a year, taking advantage of the city's excellent harbor.[6] As a sign of the special status that Washington accords to Hong Kong, the consulate reports directly to Washington and not through the embassy in Beijing, as do the American consulates in Shanghai, Chengdu, Shenyang, and Wuhan.

The U.S. commercial interest in Hong Kong is strong and of long standing. It developed as the Hong Kong economy grew and has reengineered itself since the 1950s. Although the U.S. government facilitates business ties as it deems appropriate, American companies do most of the actual work.

Yet there are other U.S. policy issues vis-à-vis Hong Kong that require special finesse, and some of which entail American domestic politics. Most of these are a function either of Hong Kong's special position in the Chinese political system or of U.S. relations with China. Between 1949, the year of the PRC's founding, and 1971–72, the year of Nixon's opening to China, U.S. policy toward Hong Kong followed a Cold War template. Since reversion, in 1997, in some policy areas, such as technology transfer, the United States has treated Hong Kong differently from, and better than, it has treated the rest of China. On these issues, Washington's bottom line is that the Hong Kong SAR continues to enjoy the autonomy promised by the Central People's Government in the policy areas of particular interest to the United States and that its government retain the institutional competence to preserve that autonomy and maintain the legal competence to honor its international obligations. In the matter of Hong Kong's political development, Washington has walked a narrow line between its support for democracy in principle and the reality of China's sovereignty over the city.

Historical Background (1843–1992)

The United States was not always so important in Hong Kong affairs. Prior to World War II, its relationship with the territory was modest. Washington established a consulate in 1843, not long after the formation of the British colony, and a small American community resided there into the twentieth century. American firms took advantage of Hong Kong's proximity to the

Chinese market and the insulation it provided from the vagaries of both the imperial and republican political systems. After World War II, however, Hong Kong was the subject of a series of disputes between Washington and London.[7]

The first was the colony's postwar future. In 1942, in the initial aftermath of Hong Kong's fall to the Japanese, London came under pressure from both the Republic of China (at that time the legitimate government of China) and the United States to pledge to return the colony to China after the war. At that point, even Winston Churchill was inclined to agree. Franklin Roosevelt strongly supported decolonization, and he continued to send signals that Hong Kong should be returned to China, which was now the ally of the United States and Britain in the fight against Japan. In February 1943, he suggested to Madame Chiang Kai-shek, who was visiting Washington at the time and staying at the White House, that it should become a free port. In the fall he floated the idea that Britain return Hong Kong to China as a "gesture of generosity," after which the ROC would quickly declare it a free port under international trusteeship. Yet once London saw the tide turning against Japan in the war, it became convinced that regaining the colony would be vital to Britain's interests in East Asia. The disagreement surfaced at the Cairo Conference, in December 1943, where Roosevelt, Churchill, and Chiang met to discuss postwar arrangements. At Chiang Kai-shek's suggestion, Roosevelt raised the matter of returning the colony to China with Churchill, but Churchill rejected it out of hand.[8] In the summer of 1945, the American commander in China, Albert Wedemeyer, worked to facilitate a takeover of Hong Kong by Chiang's forces, but London mounted a full-court press to derail it. Harry Truman, who had succeeded FDR in April, did not share his predecessor's passion for decolonization; he decided, and made clear to Chiang, that Britain, not China, should accept the Japanese surrender of Hong Kong and it would revert to its status as a British colony. Chiang complied. It appears that he was more interested in blocking Communist guerillas from taking over Hong Kong than he was in doing so himself; conversely, the guerillas' priority had been to block Chiang's troops.[9]

THE COLD WAR

The Communists' victory in the Chinese civil war raised a new issue: Hong Kong's security. Even though the People's Liberation Army stopped at the Hong Kong border in 1949, it was always possible that it might resume a southward march into the colony. The British government lacked the military capability to defend Hong Kong, so it sought a guarantee of defense support from the Americans. The American response was generally coy. In public, American officials sounded supportive, but they did not make a specific pledge of military support to defend Hong Kong's border. Privately, U.S. commitments were guarded at best. A 1950 internal National Security Council document stated that the United States would provide military aid in accordance with "commitments and capabilities"—this was when the Truman administration was consumed with mobilizing forces for the war in Korea.[10] Dwight Eisenhower occasionally made statements of general support for Hong Kong's defense, but again with no specifics. There is some evidence that London assumed that the U.S. commitment was more explicit than Washington believed it had stated. Some U.K. military planners even hoped for a short while that Washington would go so far as to use nuclear weapons to help defend the colony.[11] In March 1957, Prime Minister Harold Macmillan puzzled Eisenhower and Secretary of State John Foster Dulles by floating the idea of abandoning Hong Kong all together, because it was becoming too expensive to keep it. In the end, Britain took greater comfort from intelligence that Beijing had no intention of taking Hong Kong, because, presumably, the colony was proving useful as a conduit of needed goods and money.[12] Washington, too, found the colony useful as a center for its various intelligence agencies to collect information about China and for CIA case officers to run agents into the PRC.[13] Apparently Washington paid no attention to Beijing's warnings to London that China's forbearance regarding the status of Hong Kong was a function of London's restraining U.S. agencies from using the territory as a platform for provocative activities.[14]

The late Georgetown University professor Nancy Tucker, who wrote the seminal book on the history of U.S. policy toward Hong Kong, trenchantly pointed out, "United States pressure on the People's Republic in practice jeopardized the survival of Hong Kong far more than [Chinese] military threats."[15] When China entered the Korean War in the latter half of 1950, the United States imposed a ban on trade and financial transactions with the PRC and pushed its allies to join the embargo. This had an immediate impact on Hong Kong, which had always depended on economic ties with China for its survival and already bore the added burden of a large refugee population. In 1951, both British and Hong Kong officials sought relief from Washington and asked that the embargo be lifted. Although the State Department was sympathetic, officials of both the Defense and Commerce Departments successfully blocked them. A year later, however, the Truman administration accepted that the embargo's cost to Hong Kong outweighed whatever specific benefits it yielded in containing China and agreed that Hong Kong firms could sell goods to the countries adhering to the ban as long as they were free of any inputs from China. Hong Kong agreed to ensure that no imports from those nations would find their way into the mainland market.[16] (Much of the embargo was lifted gradually during Richard Nixon's opening to China in the early 1970s.)

The next episode that contributed to trade tensions concerned Hong Kong textile exports to the United States. This issue was not so easy to resolve. Spinning yarn and weaving cloth are usually the first stages of any economy that is building a manufacturing sector. That had been true of China in the first half of the twentieth century, and it was now true of Hong Kong in the second half. In fact, China's leading textile firms had established Hong Kong's mills, financed by investments from banks such as the Hong Kong and Shanghai Bank, and staffed by plentiful refugee Cantonese labor.[17] The success of those firms initiated Hong Kong's economic miracle, but their exports threatened the competitive position of American textile companies, which pressured the U.S. government to impose import restrictions. As a result, Hong Kong had to live with a succession of agreements limiting access to the American market for its textiles and apparel. (The restrictions also encouraged Hong Kong to move up the product quality ladder, where U.S. restrictions were not so severe.) These trade tensions subsided after 1979 as Hong Kong firms moved their production and assembly facilities across the border into Guangdong. According to U.S. Customs Service rules, the goods produced in these new Hong Kong–owned factories were now PRC products, because they were physically assembled or produced in China. That the facilities where assembly and production occurred were owned by Hong Kong firms and that China added only modest value to these goods was immaterial. So by moving factories to the mainland, Hong Kong had effectively exported the American import restrictions on its textiles to China.

In the 1980s, the American agenda concerning Hong Kong shifted from economics to politics. Although the United States had little involvement in the U.K.-PRC interactions concerning Hong Kong's reversion, American diplomats tended to echo the relative optimism of their British counterparts that Hong Kong would survive economically and politically after reversion to China.[18] Once the Joint Declaration was concluded in 1984, the United States offered rhetorical support for the new arrangements. U.S. officials accepted the reality that Hong Kong would become PRC territory politically, and made a commitment to treat Hong Kong as an economic entity separate from the PRC.[19]

During the Cold War the Americans may have held up Hong Kong rhetorically as the "Berlin of the East," but actual American policy did not favor the colony, either economically or militarily. There was no clear or binding U.S. defense commitment. Washington saw Hong Kong as a place where the PRC could circumvent the embargo, which was not totally dismantled until Richard Nixon began the U.S. rapprochement with China.

THE AFTERMATH OF TIANANMEN

The next occasion for intense U.S. government attention to Hong Kong came after Tiananmen. The PRC crackdown on the 1989 protests in Beijing and other Chinese cities transformed U.S.-China policy and altered the American approach to Hong Kong as well. Initiative in U.S. policymaking shifted from the executive branch to Capitol Hill. For Hong Kong, three issues came to the fore: immigration, China's most-favored-nation trading status, and broad U.S. policy toward Hong Kong after reversion.

On immigration, members of Congress who followed the Hong Kong issue grew concerned that Hong Kong people would not have sufficient opportunities to emigrate if they found post-reversion restrictions too constraining, by which time it might be too late. So these members added provisions to the Immigration Act of 1990 to address that contingency.[20] This legislation gradually increased the U.S. immigration quota for Hong Kong by a factor of more than ten and gave those who were given immigrant visas the option of waiting until 2002 (five years after reversion) to actually relocate to the United States. The legislation also created a special category for employees of American businesses in Hong Kong. In the event, there was not a huge demand for the delayed-action immigrant visas, perhaps because political life in Hong Kong did not deteriorate after 1997 as much as anticipated. But the congressional intent to create an "escape hatch" for Hong Kong residents was clear.[21]

Second, after Tiananmen, some members of Congress sought to use economic leverage against the PRC to force it to make changes in its policy on human rights and other similar matters. This was possible because provisions of U.S. trade law required that the application of normal tariffs to Chinese products entering the American market be approved by the president every year. This happened without controversy during the 1980s, but Congress did have the option of canceling most-favored-nation status altogether or passing legislation to place conditions on its future continuation. Rejecting the president's action was never a serious option, because the interdependence between the Chinese and American economies had already reached a significant level, and it would have required a two-thirds vote of both houses in Congress to accomplish. But conditional most-favored-nation legislation was undertaken several times in the 1990s. If these bills had ever become law, the impact on Hong Kong's prosperity would have been indirect but painful, because Hong Kong firms increasingly used the mainland as their production platform.

The Hong Kong government, the various chambers of commerce in the territory, and business executives all mounted an aggressive lobbying campaign to remind Congress that if most-favored-nation conditionality bills became law they would severely damage the very people that the United States wished to help and protect. The high point of this annual lobbying campaign occurred in May 1993, when Hong Kong's governor, Christopher Patten, made the rounds in Washington, talking primarily about the danger that economic sanctions on China presented for Hong Kong. At a session at the Brookings Institution that I attended, Patten noted that Hong Kong was at the center of an economic reform process in China—a process that should continue; he reiterated that it was "impossible to restrict trade with China without hurting Hong Kong."[22] When congressional committees held hearings concerning most-favored-nation legislation, they usually included a witness from Hong Kong, typically the president of the local American Chamber of Commerce (John Kamm in a May 1990 hearing).[23] Of all the arguments against most-favored-nation legislation, the one that had the greatest impact was the damage it would do to Hong Kong.[24] That did not stop the legislation from passing one or both houses of Congress because other, more powerful motivations were in play. But the Hong Kong argument was still the hardest to refute. Ultimately, these bills never became law.

The third initiative was the effort to enact comprehensive legislation regarding U.S. ties with Hong Kong after 1997, which led to passage of the U.S.–Hong Kong Policy Act of 1992. Members from both Hong Kong's business community and the democratic camp were lobbying U.S. political leaders for its passage.[25] Senator Mitch McConnell of Kentucky took the lead in this effort, reportedly at the suggestion of Martin Lee, a member of Hong Kong Queen's Counsel and an early leader of the democratic movement. Lee strongly supported the key provision of the "U.S.–Hong Kong Policy Act" (Senate bill 1731), which McConnell introduced in the Senate in September 1991 and Representative John Edward Porter of Illinois introduced in the House of Representatives the following month.[26]

The original draft of McConnell's bill had included a provision that would have required the U.S. executive branch to report on a periodic basis to the

Congress on, among other things, "the degree to which the Joint Declaration is being implemented in Hong Kong."[27] (Indeed, the first version of the bill in early draft form, which I have in my files, has the title "The Hong Kong 'One Country Two Systems' Act.") Such wording would have placed the U.S. government in the position of judging whether the People's Republic of China had fulfilled the obligations undertaken in a diplomatic instrument it had concluded with the United Kingdom. Setting this standard ignored the possibility that the obligations inhering in the Joint Declaration might be superseded in the Basic Law enacted in 1990. Beijing's response to the bill as conveyed via the Communist media in Hong Kong was, predictably, critical: "The Joint Declaration does not give any right or power to the United States to meddle in Hong Kong's affairs in the transition period. . . . It is hoped that the relevant American politicians will carefully reconsider these simple facts and will not repeat the same mistake committed by McConnell and his company."[28]

Actually, it was Senator McConnell who reconsidered his own "mistake." After a trip to Hong Kong in the spring of 1992, when he heard from a broad range of local stakeholders, he decided to moderate the key reporting requirement. Support for the bill within Hong Kong reportedly increased.[29] The new version of his bill, which passed the Senate on May 21, required that the report, which was to be issued every year through 2007, only cover "significant developments in United States relations with Hong Kong, including a description of agreements that have entered into force between the United States and Hong Kong; . . . other matters, including developments related to the change in the exercise of sovereignty over Hong Kong, affecting United States interests . . . or relations; . . . [and] the development of democratic institutions in Hong Kong."[30] After resolving some uncontentious technical issues, the House of Representatives passed a revised version of the bill on August 11, 1992, which the Senate accepted a month later. President Bush signed the bill on October 5.[31]

Probably the most important aspect of the bill concerned the continued application of U.S. law to Hong Kong after 1997, and the continuation of all treaties, international agreements, and multilateral conventions between the United States and Hong Kong as well as the accords reached with the United Kingdom before 1997 or China thereafter that were then applied to Hong Kong. On the application of U.S. law, the standard that the Hong Kong legislation established was whether Hong Kong was "sufficiently autonomous" to justify treatment under the law in question. If the executive branch determined that Hong Kong was not sufficiently autonomous to be treated differently

than China under a specific American law, it was permitted—but not required—
to suspend application of the law through an executive order. An important
example here is technology transfer. If Hong Kong Customs did not have
the capacity and will to block technology approved for Hong Kong but not
for China from leaking to the mainland, it could have serious consequences
for U.S. interests. Suspension of special treatment would hurt Hong Kong
economically.

Concerning the application of treaties, agreements, and conventions, the
standard was whether Hong Kong was "legally competent" to carry out its obligations under those international instruments. If the executive branch determined that it was not legally competent, or that "the continuation of Hong
Kong's obligations or rights under any such treaty or other international agreement is not appropriate under the circumstances," it was to inform Congress
of that determination through an annual reporting requirement.[32] In practice,
this annual report served more of a symbolic purpose. It certainly sent a signal
that the U.S. government was watching, which the Chinese government resented because it regarded Hong Kong as an internal affair. Yet Congress had
not required the executive branch to actually *do* anything if or when Hong Kong
developments were negative. In that event, the principal check on arbitrary or
excessive actions by Beijing would have to come from the people of the territory.

To sum up, American responses to Tiananmen were a mixed bag for Hong
Kong. Treating it as a special immigration case was generous but probably not
necessary. Enacting conditions on China's most-favored-nation trading status
on human rights grounds would have seriously damaged the city's economy.
The U.S.–Hong Kong Policy Act would have offended Beijing's sensibilities as
originally drafted, but the final language of the legislation was toned down. In
the issue of China's most-favored-nation status, at least, American members of
Congress were more intent on sending a message to China than on protecting
the interests of Hong Kong's residents.

Post-Reversion U.S.–Hong Kong Relations

After 1997, the conduct of U.S. relations with Hong Kong was fairly routine,
and was accomplished without much media or congressional attention. The
State Department issued its annual report through 2007, when the requirement
in the U.S.–Hong Kong Policy Act expired.

Recently, however, two high-profile episodes demonstrated the dilemmas
that can face U.S. decisionmakers. The first was the presence in Hong Kong in

May and June 2013 of Edward Snowden, the former National Security Agency contractor who was accused of stealing countless government secrets. In Washington's eyes, this called into question just how much autonomy the Hong Kong SAR actually had. It was also an instance in which the U.S. government uncharacteristically pushed very hard and very publicly to get what it wanted from the Hong Kong government. The second episode was the Umbrella Movement and how much electoral reform the Central People's Government was prepared to grant the Hong Kong SAR. In both cases, Hong Kong received extraordinary public attention in the United States, at least for a while, and some in Congress weighed in for the first time in more than two decades.

EDWARD SNOWDEN

Up until the Occupy Movement, the Snowden case probably brought Hong Kong the most media coverage it had ever received in America. Much of that attention was unwanted in the city, because it created the impression that the Hong Kong SAR government was acting at the behest of Beijing and therefore not autonomously.

Snowden arrived in Hong Kong on May 20, 2013. He went there because he believed it was a place beyond the reach of the American legal system. His confidence in Hong Kong as a haven was probably exaggerated, since Hong Kong's rule of law for this kind of issue was not as strong as he thought. He may have been unaware of the degree of cooperation between the U.S. and Hong Kong SAR governments on the surrender of criminals, pursuant to the U.S.–Hong Kong Extradition Treaty, which was negotiated in 1996 and ratified by the Senate in 1997. He may also have underestimated how aggressively the American authorities would try to secure his return, even though he should have anticipated this. His revelations concerning the National Security Agency's surveillance of American citizens created immediate shock and alarm in the intelligence community, which did not know how many secrets he had stolen and how many documents he was prepared to release. In the American government's eyes he was a traitor, a criminal of the worst kind. The sooner he was returned to the United States, they thought, the faster the government could limit the damage. Hong Kong became a target in this American crusade to secure Snowden's return.

Two questions would dictate the outcome of the Snowden affair. First, would legal or political factors take precedence in determining the outcome? Second, would Hong Kong or Beijing make the final decision on returning Snowden? Washington believed that Hong Kong should make the decision based on legal criteria. Under the U.S.–Hong Kong Extradition Treaty in place, the Hong Kong government was obligated to surrender fugitives who were accused of violating American laws if the alleged crime in question was also a crime in Hong Kong. The extradition treaty did stipulate that the Hong Kong SAR had the right to refuse to surrender a PRC national wanted by the United States if the case involved foreign affairs, defense, or public interest of the PRC, but there was no such right of refusal regarding nationals of other countries simply because of their nationality. On Friday, June 21, the U.S. Department of Justice sent a request, with legal justification, to the Hong Kong SAR government that it issue a provisional warrant of arrest for Snowden. The Hong Kong SAR responded somewhat belatedly by identifying what it believed were defects in the U.S. request. Some of these were rather technical, but the critical one concerned whether the statute under which Snowden would be charged in Washington was compatible with Hong Kong law and, therefore, whether it was covered by the treaty.[33]

As Hong Kong and Washington exchanged legal points, the question of China's role loomed larger. There was the general principle in the Basic Law that Beijing retained full authority over Hong Kong's foreign affairs and defense. The implication, which was more political than legal, was that the Snowden case fell within the gray area between Hong Kong's judicial autonomy and Beijing's powers as the sovereign. U.S. diplomats likely presumed that China would have a behind-the-scenes role in Hong Kong's deliberations, but they hoped its actions would facilitate getting Snowden back into American jurisdiction.

In the end, it appears that Snowden himself and the Chinese government combined to make the final decision and preempt any moves Washington was planning. Snowden came to realize, on the basis of information from his advisors, that if the Hong Kong government did not reject the American request for his transfer back to the United States, he would get caught in the Hong Kong judicial process. As a result, he would be detained and lose access to his laptop—and maintaining that access was one of his highest priorities. So he left Hong Kong as soon as he could, on Sunday, June 23. As for China, it appears that Beijing decided that having Snowden in Hong Kong for a long period of time would excessively complicate U.S.-China relations. It was certainly the consensus view of the American media that Beijing directed the Hong Kong SAR government to speed up Snowden's departure from Hong Kong.[34]

Whatever Beijing's role, Hong Kong bore the brunt of the Obama administration's immediate wrath, and after Snowden's departure from the city,

U.S. officials warned that Hong Kong would suffer "serious consequences" for its handling of the case. Hong Kong certainly suffered at least a temporary blow to its reputation. The U.S. government decided that it had a lot at stake in what happened to Snowden, and Hong Kong was a key target of American diplomacy for a few weeks. Whether Washington had a realistic sense of what Hong Kong was free to do legally and politically given its subordinate political status was another matter.

By the time the State Department issued its reinstated Hong Kong policy report in April 2015, the U.S. judgment on the episode had moderated. In general, the report judged that Hong Kong had demonstrated a degree of autonomy "sufficient to justify continued special treatment by the United States for bilateral agreements and programs." Also, in general, the report applauded the "robust law enforcement relationship" that the two sides had developed. In the abstract, at least, the Snowden affair had raised the question of whether Hong Kong had the "legal competence" (the wording of the U.S.–Hong Kong Policy Act) to carry out its obligations under the 1996 extradition treaty. Perhaps the Hong Kong SAR government had the necessary legal competence, including the ability to raise legal questions concerning the Justice Department's request. Yet at the end of the day, it lacked the political freedom to exercise that competence. In any event, the 2015 report rendered the final U.S. judgment on the affair: "The [Snowden] incident strained our relations with Hong Kong and, due to its intersection with issues related to foreign affairs and security, revealed a limit to Hong Kong's autonomy in law enforcement cooperation."[35]

The United States and the Umbrella Movement

Hong Kong's extended debate over universal suffrage began to intensify as attention to Snowden died down. Yet compared to the very high-pitched and public stance that the United States took regarding its "man on the run," its approach toward electoral reform was guarded and low-key. Clifford Hart, in his first public address after becoming the U.S. consul general in July 2013, broke no new ground on political matters: "The United States Government has repeatedly made clear that it supports Hong Kong's progress toward genuine universal suffrage as laid out in the Basic Law and the National People's Congress's 2007 decision. . . . The United States will always stand for our core democratic values. We have no prescription for Hong Kong's electoral process [and do] not take a position for or against any particular electoral formulation on how genuine universal suffrage is achieved."[36]

AN AMERICAN "BLACK HAND"?

The CCP had its own view of the American role in the Umbrella Movement. A hardy perennial of China's statecraft is to blame a foreign country for the problems that it faces. As early as 1952, Beijing had charged that Washington was using Hong Kong as a base for aggression against the PRC regime.[37] In October 1955, Premier Zhou Enlai warned Hong Kong's governor, Alexander Grantham, that Beijing would tolerate the British presence in Hong Kong only if the colony was not used as an anti-Communist base.[38] (This warning was not without a basis in fact, coming as it did just six months after Taiwan intelligence agents had plotted to assassinate Zhou by planting a bomb on his aircraft when it transited Hong Kong on the way to Indonesia.)

Since the 1950s, Beijing has held fast to the principle of noninterference by other states in its internal affairs, and by the 2000s its fears of a U.S. plot to foment a "color revolution" and overturn CCP rule began to grow. In 2011, China identified several "core interests" that it expects other countries to re-spect, one of which was the preservation of the PRC's political system.[39] So it came as no surprise that China accused both the United States and the United Kingdom of covertly supporting the Umbrella Movement in order to promote a local color revolution and "Hong Kong independence." The purported goal to be furthered by these activities was to use Hong Kong as a base against China. For example, in early 2014, Jiang Rongdiao, a scholar associated with the Institute of East Asian Studies in Shanghai, wrote an assessment in which he asserted that "the United States, the United Kingdom and other foreign forces interfered in Hong Kong affairs, and have already moved from their hiding place into the open, and from behind the screen to stage-front."[40] If China's charges were true, it would point to a violation of another PRC core interest, that of preserving its sovereignty and territorial integrity. Of course, accusing outsiders of creating problems within China deflects attention from the possibility—real in this case—that Beijing's own policies were the source of its difficulties with the Hong Kong SAR. The *New York Times* reported that Chinese officials believed the United States and the U.K. "wield so much influence" in Hong Kong that opening the electoral process too much would allow the foreign forces to seduce the public into allowing their political allies in the city to take power.[41] Hong Kong's chief executive, C. Y. Leung, also made the charge of foreign support of the Umbrella Movement in a media in-terview: "There are external forces, yes, from different countries in different parts of the world. I shan't go into details but this is not entirely a domestic movement."[42] Accusations of a U.S. role can serve a local, instrumental purpose by implicitly targeting Hong Kong political actors whose objectives are similar to the principles and goals that the U.S. government enunciates rhetorically.[43] Some prominent Hong Kong citizens cast similar accusations. In the summer of 2014 I laid out my ideas for a compromise approach to universal suffrage to a well-known Hong Kong tycoon. He replied that my approach had merit but that Pan-Democrats would never agree to it until they got a green light from the U.S. government.[44]

On almost a daily basis, the Communist media in Hong Kong "exposed" America's nefarious activities in the territory. One particularly precious example reflects the broader narrative. The article, in *Ta Kung Pao,* purported to present the conclusions of an "analytical report" on how a congressionally funded American organization and a subsidiary have been "intervening in Hong Kong's internal affairs" with students as the primary target. The article is worth citing at length:

> The exposure [of U.S. intervention] enables one to see the light suddenly: how come some of Hong Kong's young students, known as refined in manner, hard-working and law-abiding, have in recent years become increasingly radical, lost and restless and inclined to resort to violence. How come they blame the government for everything unsatisfactory in their education, employment and daily life, and hence become inclined to take to the streets to protest, and even vent their dissatisfaction on their families or parents, resulting in family tragedies? It turns out that, since Hong Kong's handover, the American "Uncle Democracy" on the other side of the Pacific Ocean has taken a fancy to young people in the HKSAR, putting in a large sum of money to "guide" and "foster" them into anti-government, anti-society and anti-establishment "vanguards" in hopes that they could become the "kindling" and hope to promote a "color revolution" in Mainland China in the future. A pity, and risky! Such good and promising young Hong Kong people in fact have been placed under such a complicated and evil political plot. As long as the goal to change and manipulate young people's thinking and view of values can be attained, financial support in U.S. dollar will keeping flowing in.[45]

An article in *Wen Wei Po* exhibited the analytical weakness of many of these screeds. The author argued that *Fortune* magazine's naming of Joshua Wong, the head of Scholarism, as one of the fifty greatest leaders in the world proved that he was an agent of the United States as it pursued its subversive goals.[46]

(Here, Chinese analysts are victims of mirror imaging. The Leninist playbook for destabilizing another society includes working through nongovernmental organizations and the media.)

Evaluating these allegations requires a deeper understanding of the activities of American organizations such as the National Endowment for Democracy and the National Democratic Institute. For Beijing to target them makes more sense than trying to make the case that the U.S. government actively supports the protests, at least superficially. It is true that the Congress created the National Endowment for Democracy along with four other organizations and continues to fund them. The four organizations are the National Democratic Institute for International Affairs and the International Republican Institute, which are linked to the two major political parties; the American Center for International Labor Solidarity, an organization connected to organized labor; and the Center for International Private Enterprise, which is tied to business. It is also true that these organizations take very seriously their mission of building indigenous organizations around the world that promote and sustain democracy. They and other American nongovernmental organizations have invited Hong Kong citizens to conferences on democracy and democracy building. But the National Endowment for Democracy and its affiliated organizations are legally independent and value that independence. Each has a board of directors that sets their agendas, so institutionally it would be difficult for the U.S. government to use them as tools for subversion.

In any case it is important to understand how little these organizations spend on activities in Hong Kong. The National Endowment for Democracy has given an annual grant of about $150,000 a year to the Hong Kong Human Rights Monitor to conduct a variety of activities related to civil and political rights. The American Center for International Labor Solidarity has given about the same amount of money annually to the Confederation of Trade Unions in order to "advance worker rights by building the capacity of democratic trade unions in Hong Kong." The National Democratic Institute for International Affairs provided two grants totaling over $700,000 to an organization at Hong Kong University for Design Democracy, an Internet-based platform where citizens, particular university students, could offer proposals and exchange ideas concerning Hong Kong's political institutions and constitutional reform process, so that they could "more effectively participate in the public debate on political reform." Design Democracy had no agenda of its own; it merely created a platform. No doubt the Chinese government would prefer for these American democracy organizations to spend their money elsewhere, but the public descriptions of their work hardly seem subversive. No one has made the case that these activities are undertaken at the direction of the U.S. government. And no one on the PRC side has sought to evaluate the effect of these activities on Hong Kong politics relative to other likely factors.

So those who believe that the United States is the "black hand" behind Occupy Central must fall back on anecdotes and pseudo-evidence to make their case. One such piece of pseudo-evidence was the fact that a staffer from the Hong Kong America Center, located at Chinese University of Hong Kong, had interactions with student activists. The second was that Louisa Greve, a vice-president of the National Endowment for Democracy, met with a leader of Occupy Central. Third and most pointed was a story in *Wen Wei Po* that alleged that the National Democratic Institute for International Affairs increased funding "by ten times" to an entity at Hong Kong University with which Benny Tai was said to be affiliated, and did so after Tai launched Occupy Central. I have looked into the first two allegations and there is no basis for either the facts or interpretations presented. On the third, a representative of the National Democratic Institute for International Affairs informed me that they gave no money to Occupy Central. The project referred to in the article was Design Democracy, and funding to Hong Kong programs actually fell substantially from 2010 to 2014.[47] The consulate's spokesperson, Scott Robinson, rebutted these accusations, "What is happening in Hong Kong is about the people of Hong Kong, and any assertion otherwise is an attempt to distract from the issue at hand, which is the people of Hong Kong expressing their desire for universal suffrage and an election that provides a meaningful choice of candidates representative of the voters' will."[48]

President Obama himself sought to set the record straight in November 2014, when he met with President Xi Jinping at a bilateral summit in Beijing on the margins of the annual leaders' meeting of the Asia-Pacific Economic Cooperation forum. The public exchange between the two leaders at their joint press conference likely indicates what they said privately. President Obama said that he was "unequivocal in saying to President Xi that the United States had no involvement in fostering the protests that took place there; that these are issues ultimately for the people of Hong Kong and the people of China to decide."[49]

Obama's assurance seemed to have little impact on the frequency of propaganda attacks, which continued virtually without interruption after his meeting with Xi. For example, in March 2015 a senior officer in the People's Liberation Army charged that "external forces . . . orchestrated a Hong Kong version of a color revolution.["50] This sort of rhetorical statement was something that Xi Jinping, in his capacity as general secretary of the CCP and the ultimate boss of the Party propaganda department, had the authority to stop. But he did not, perhaps because he believed either that Obama was deceitful in making his statement or that he did not know what the agencies of his government were doing. Perhaps Xi thought that insulting the United States was a low-cost way of maintaining the support of pro-Beijing segments in the Hong Kong public. Another possible explanation is that Chinese analysts who cover Hong Kong believed that blaming China's own policies for the Hong Kong SAR's troubles would not be a career-enhancing move.

The larger issue is whether China's leaders believe that the United States was behind the Occupy protests and base their policy decisions on that belief. An absence of information makes it very difficult to answer the factual question, but an American scholar who has regular contact with senior Chinese leaders concludes that they genuinely think the U.S. government was in fact instigating the protests.[51]

"GOOD COP, BAD COP": THE EXECUTIVE BRANCH AND CONGRESS

Washington's response to the Hong Kong protests is an interesting case study in how different branches of the U.S. government—the executive branch and the Congress—deal with foreign policy issues. The executive branch is usually guided by pragmatism: what works in furthering its objectives. Congress is motivated by a range of views, including, often, moral positions.

For the White House and the State Department, the key executive branch agency for conducting relations with Hong Kong, Beijing's "big lie" about the United States as a "black hand" in Hong Kong may have been annoying, but it helped create the context in which they formulated and implemented policy. If Washington actually had sought to pursue the subversive goals that Beijing and some in Hong Kong believed, that would likely heighten the Chinese leadership's paranoia about the purported threat that the Hong Kong SAR poses to China's national security (see chapter 5). That in turn would make it less likely that the United States could achieve the goals it declares in public statements. In addition, the United States has other interests in Hong Kong, such as business and law enforcement, which must be balanced against the desire for a more democratic system. Finally, the United States is somewhat constrained by the strategies, tactics, perceptions, and passions of key actors in Hong Kong. Because those actors have imperfections, taking one side or another may not help produce the outcome that American policymakers would like to see.

The U.S. government, therefore, had to walk a fine line on universal suffrage. It tended to confine its interventions to public statements and private diplomatic messages (as opposed to siding with one side in Hong Kong's domestic debate or the exercise of economic leverage) that advanced its objectives. For example, the statements that Josh Earnest, the White House press secretary, made on September 29, 2014, the first workday after the Occupy protests began, conveyed both explicit and implicit messages:

- "The United States supports internationally recognized fundamental freedoms, such as the freedom of assembly and the freedom of expression." That is, Washington believes that Hong Kong people should exercise the political rights that even the Basic Law confers.
- "The United States urges the Hong Kong authorities to exercise restraint and for protestors to express their views peacefully." That is, each side in the struggle shares responsibility to exercise proper restraint.
- "The United States supports the universal suffrage in Hong Kong in accordance with the Basic Law and we support the aspirations of the Hong Kong people." That is, Washington respects both Beijing's right to set certain electoral parameters and the Hong Kong people's political desires.
- "We believe an open society with the highest degree of autonomy and governed by the rule of law is essential to Hong Kong's stability and prosperity." That is, the United States supports stability and prosperity as worthwhile goals (as does Beijing), but believes that those depend on an open society, maximum autonomy, and the rule of law.
- "We believe the basic legitimacy of the chief executive in Hong Kong will be greatly enhanced if the Basic Law's ultimate aim of [selecting the] chief executive by universal suffrage is fulfilled. We also believe the legitimacy of the chief executive will be enhanced if the election provides the people of Hong Kong a genuine choice of candidates that are representative of the people's and the voters' will." That is, the chief executive will be more legitimate if he or she is the winner of a genuinely competitive election.
- "We have been very consistent in voicing our support to the People's Republic of China for universal suffrage and for the aspirations of the Hong Kong people and we are going to continue to do so." That is, we make our views known via official channels, not just for public consumption in the United States or Hong Kong.[52]

In November, President Obama coupled his assurance to Xi Jinping that the United States was not instigating the protests with a broader pledge that the United States would speak out for the right of free expression and "encourage [that] the elections that take place in Hong Kong are transparent and fair and reflective of the opinions of people there." (Xi Jinping's response: Occupy Central was an "illegal movement"; law and order were paramount in all systems; Beijing supported the effort of the Hong Kong government to restore order and stability; and Hong Kong was an internal Chinese affair into which "foreign countries should not interfere in any form or fashion.")[53]

The U.S. Congress plays a very different role on foreign policy. Members hold a range of views, and some members are more active than others on particular issues. Congress has the luxury and constitutional requirement of focusing on only some aspects of foreign policy, and there are few mechanisms to reconcile competing interests and agendas to ensure consistent implementation. On certain issues at least, morality sets the tone rather than pragmatism.

When it came to universal suffrage for Hong Kong, some in Congress clearly believed that the U.S. government had not adopted a sufficiently robust stance. Representative Chris Smith of New Jersey argued, "A status quo U.S. policy is unsustainable if Beijing continues to insist that Hong Kong become like mainland China.... The special privileges the U.S. grants to Hong Kong can only endure if Beijing fulfills its longstanding obligation under international law to maintain Hong Kong's autonomy, guarantee human rights and allow free and fair elections in 2017 and beyond."[54]

Congress's most tangible response to the Umbrella Movement and the Hong Kong SAR government's response came at the end of November and in early December. Two hearings were held, the first convened by the Congressional-Executive Commission on China (created by Congress to monitor human rights in China with representatives and senators among its members) and the second by the Subcommittee on East Asia, the Pacific, and International Cybersecurity Policy in the Senate Committee on Foreign Relations. The theme in both these sessions was broken promises. The members who had convened the hearings—Congressman Chris Smith, Senator Sherrod Brown, Senator Ben Cardin, and Senator Marco Rubio—all claimed that China had reneged on its promise to grant Hong Kong full democracy.[55] Senator Brown: "China made a promise . . . to the people of Hong Kong that they could enjoy certain freedoms and freely elect their leaders." Senator Rubio: "The Chinese government . . . has proven to be . . . an untrustworthy partner. . . . They basically signed this agreement and now have found interesting ways to circumvent it."[56] Their argument appeared to be that China had signed the Joint Declaration with Britain and now had violated its commitments. This allegation ignores two pertinent points. First, the Joint Declaration was general and its provisions were subject to a variety of interpretations. On the selection of the Hong Kong SAR chief executive, the Joint Declaration says, "The chief executive will be appointed by the Central People's Government on the basis of the results of elections or consultations to be held locally." Nowhere did the term "universal suffrage" appear, and nowhere was it specified how elections, if that was the method chosen, would take place. Indeed, an "election committee" was the mechanism employed for the first four selections of the chief executive, and Beijing claimed that it was "highly representative." Second, the Joint Declaration was to some extent superseded by the Basic Law and subsequent decisions of the Standing Committee of the National People's Congress (NPC-SC), which mandated specific arrangements for selecting leaders. And in these later documents, too, the terms and provisions were subject to competing definitions (see, for example, the discussion of "universal suffrage" in chapter 5). So Chinese officials could argue that they were observing the provisions of the Joint Declaration and were observing the mandates of the Basic Law and subsequent decisions—as Beijing defined them.

At the Senate subcommittee hearing, Daniel Russel, assistant secretary of state for East Asian and Pacific affairs, offered the Obama administration's view, stating that the NPC-SC August 31 decision "does not necessarily contravene the letter of the Basic Law, but the decision could have and should have gone much, much further," to allow "the people of Hong Kong to have a meaningful say in the selection of the Chief Executive." He did not accept that the game was over. "How to define membership [of] and the procedures of the nominating committee is very much still underway; it is still a work in progress."[57]

The more serious congressional activity had to do with legislation updating the U.S.–Hong Kong Policy Act. A bill to do that was introduced late in the 2014 congressional session, but there was no time for committee consideration. Instead, there was a stopgap measure: an amendment to the annual appropriations bill that required the State Department to submit a report regarding the situation in Hong Kong as of late 2014.[58] Then on February 27, 2015, Representative Chris Smith introduced H.R. 1159 "To reinstate reporting requirements related to United States–Hong Kong relations." After a long series of findings, the bill stated the sponsors' rendering of U.S. policy: to reaffirm the principles and objectives of the 1992 act; to support Hong Kong residents' democratic aspirations; to urge Beijing to "uphold its commitments to

Hong Kong"; and to support genuine electoral arrangements and press freedom. The legally binding provisions of the bill took the form of two amendments to the 1992 act: one requiring resumption of the annual State Department report on Hong Kong, the other requiring an additional, annual certification by the Secretary of State determining "whether Hong Kong is sufficiently autonomous to justify separate treatment different from that accorded the PRC in any new laws, agreements, treaties, or arrangements entered into between the United States and Hong Kong."[59] The authorization in the original act to suspend the special application of laws and the possibility of a presidential determination concerning treaties and international agreements would continue in force.

These policy updates contained both positive and negative aspects. On the negative side, the term "arrangements" was not defined, so it might mean any manner of formal or informal understandings between the U.S. and the Hong Kong SAR governments. Second, the certification sloppily used "autonomy" as the standard to judge Hong Kong's fulfillment of its obligations under treaties and agreements whereas the original act used "legal competence" as its criterion.[60] But these defects could be remedied as the legislative process went forward. On the positive side, the draft legislation confined the scope of the certification to only "new" laws, agreements, and so on. The source of the certification was not the president but the secretary of state, who was also authorized to waive the certification if the "national interest" justified it. And all the secretary had to do was issue a certification. To be sure, officials in the executive branch would have to spend precious time examining "new laws" to ensure that Hong Kong had the autonomy to justify U.S. application of those laws to the territory, and China would likely be offended that the American secretary of state was judging internal matters in the Hong Kong SAR at all. But the legislation did not require the executive branch to actually do anything to Hong Kong. More consequentially, as of early 2016 the chances that Congress would actually pass the legislation were slim.[61]

Meanwhile, the executive branch continued its restrained yet pointed approach to developments in Hong Kong. In mid-April 2015, the State Department sent Congress a report concerning Hong Kong that reiterated—with some new supplemental wordings—the basic U.S. stance concerning electoral reform: "The United States has called for the conduct of a multi-candidate competitive [note inclusion of this word] election for Chief Executive in 2017, which would enhance the legitimacy of Hong Kong's Chief Executive, would be a major step forward in Hong Kong's political development and would bolster Hong Kong's stability and prosperity."[62] Following the April 22, 2015, release of the Hong Kong government's detailed plan on the selection of the chief executive, the U.S. consul general, Clifford Hart, released a statement: "The legitimacy of the chief executive will be greatly enhanced if the chief executive is selected through universal suffrage and Hong Kong's residents have a meaningful choice of candidates."[63] The statement artfully did not indicate whether Washington believed that the plan met its standard of "meaningful choice." At the end of June, not long after the defeat of electoral reform, Hart urged the Hong Kong SAR government, Beijing, and the Hong Kong people to continue working "together towards the goal of achieving universal suffrage" and "local friends of all perspectives [to] fall back on their hallmark civility, forbearance, and patience in dealing with one another as they address the myriad challenges of governance before them."[64] This admonishment implicitly criticized the absence of these hallmarks in the political conflict leading up to LegCo's rejection of the plan in June.

Promoting Democracy in Hong Kong

Promoting democracy around the world has always been part of the American foreign policy impulse. More precisely, making other countries "more like us" is one of four broad and competing streams of American foreign policy.[65] Woodrow Wilson was the United States' democracy champion in the first half of the twentieth century; Ronald Reagan was the champion of the second half. Reagan's speech to the British Parliament in June 1982 helped forge a consensus in Congress that placed more emphasis on promoting democracy in authoritarian countries and less on the protection of specific human rights.[66] The National Endowment for Democracy and its affiliated organizations were created and the Department of State and the U.S. Agency for International Development adopted democracy promotion as a policy objective.[67]

When President Bill Clinton met with Governor Chris Patten at the White House in May 1993, Clinton reportedly said, "I think the democracy initiative in Hong Kong is a good thing, and I'm encouraged the parties have agreed to talk about it. . . . The idea of trying to keep it an open and free society after 1997 is in the best interests of the Chinese. . . . I support [democracy in Hong Kong]. And I hope it doesn't offend anybody, but how can the United States be against democracy? It's our job to go out there and promote it."[68] Yet stating this general aspiration offered no guidance on how to "go out there and promote it" in a specific context. And Hong Kong was in a very special context, one that created a multilayered dilemma for the United States.

COMPETING INTERESTS

First of all, there is the generic tension between American security and economic interests on the one hand and the objectives of human rights and democracy on the other. At any point in time, policymakers must strike a balance among these competing issues. For example, the regimes of Ferdinand Marcos in the Philippines and the Chun Doo Hwan military regime in South Korea faced serious challenges from pro-democracy opposition movements in 1986 and 1987, respectively. Yet the Reagan administration was reluctant to push the two dictators very hard because of the fundamental security interests at stake. American bases in the Philippines were seen as essential to the strategy of forward deployment, and sustained instability in South Korea risked an intervention by North Korea. It was only toward the end of each crisis that the administration acted, urging Marcos to accept the results of the 1986 elections and leave the country, and urging the post-Chun leadership to accept direct presidential elections. But the pressure from executive branch agencies might not have been effective without personal communications from Reagan, who Marcos and Chun thought was more tolerant of their authoritarian ways.

The U.S. government has no comparable security interests in Hong Kong, but some of its agencies see Hong Kong as a potential hub for narcotics trafficking and money laundering, and so they work intensively with counterparts in the Hong Kong government to contain those problems. Moreover, the American economic interest in the Hong Kong SAR is significant and contributes to the city's political stability.

AMERICAN DOMESTIC POLITICS

In addition to balancing foreign policy priorities, U.S. administrations sometimes have to cope with internal political pressures for changes in policy. Constituencies that favor different sets of concerns will contend with each other and press the executive branch for action. Human rights and democracy groups advocate a robust U.S. stance in support of their causes, while the American business community cautions against steps that might affect its economic interests. Both constituencies were involved in the struggle over China's most-favored-nation trading status. Another example of competing domestic interests was Taiwan: during the Cold War the United States had a security interest there, and American conservative groups sympathetic to the authoritarian Kuomintang regime were a key force in convincing like-minded congressional leaders to restrain successive U.S. administrations from pressing the regime to reform. Only when other, liberal members of Congress emerged in the early 1980s and pushed for democracy and greater promotion of human rights through hearings and resolutions did the Kuomintang regime begin to move in a reformist direction.[69] As a general matter, the priority that Washington places on democracy promotion abroad will partially be determined by the balance of political forces in the United States' own democratic system.

There is obvious sympathy in the United States for Hong Kong and the democratization project. For some people, the Hong Kong SAR is David to the PRC's Goliath. Some human rights groups are relatively active on the issue, and some democratic politicians in Hong Kong, particularly Martin Lee and Anson Chan, have good access to American lawmakers. Yet the impact of this sentiment on U.S. policy is fairly modest. It may be broad, but it is neither deep nor sustained.

HONG KONG AS A PART OF CHINA

A unique and dominating consideration for U.S. policy is the fact that the People's Republic of China has sovereignty over the Hong Kong territory. This fact plays out in two ways. Beijing consistently rejects the idea that Hong Kong's internal political arrangements are a legitimate subject of American diplomacy. Xi Jinping said in November 2014, "Foreign countries should not interfere in any form or fashion" in Hong Kong. China would prefer that the United States treat the Hong Kong SAR as merely an economic entity—just as the one country, two systems framework treats it. Beijing, not the Hong Kong SAR government, is the ultimate arbiter of the pace and scope of political reform in the territory. How Beijing assesses the reasons for and extent of U.S. support of democracy in Hong Kong can affect its choices—whether those assessments are correct or not. At the time of the 2014 Xi-Obama summit, Xi also said, "We will protect the lawful rights and interests of foreign citizens and business organizations in Hong Kong, as well."[70]

Another important point is the centrality of China to American foreign policy. The two economies have become closely integrated since the 1990s, and American states and localities now look to China as a source of investment. China's growing material power and its desire to expand its strategic depth in East Asia automatically creates tension with the United States, which bases its policy in the region on forward deployment of U.S. forces. The growing frictions in the East and South China Seas are only the most obvious case in point.[71] Yet there are issues on which Beijing and Washington can and do cooperate, such as containing North Korea, restraining Iran's nuclear program, and limiting climate change. Hong Kong's political system is only one issue among many. How it fits within Washington's overall diplomacy toward Beijing is never simple, and assigning priorities among these is a daily challenge for U.S. officials, particularly since different agencies have different priorities. The question of whether and how to link one issue to another becomes critical.

Hong Kong policy can be tailored to fit the needs of the fundamental U.S. policy approach toward China. Successive administrations have employed a two-sided approach to China: Engage China where possible, reaping the benefits of closer economic ties and cooperation on global and regional foreign policy problems where interests overlap (such as North Korea, Iran, and climate change), and at the same time, manage points of friction such as Taiwan, with whom the United States has a security relationship that Beijing has always opposed, and the South China Sea, and seek to shape the growth of Chinese power and influence. When it comes to the democratization of China, U.S. policymakers generally assume any political change will be the result of internal dynamics over which outside parties have little direction or control. America may be able to support those dynamics when they occur, but it cannot create them. This stance can affect the approach on the more modest issue of democracy in Hong Kong.

If American policymakers were to elevate as a priority the promotion of democracy in China relative to other objectives, it would reshuffle the deck, both for the PRC and Hong Kong. If Chinese leaders regard that shift as threatening to the durability of CCP rule, as they probably would, then they would likely put at risk certain types of bilateral cooperation that they believe are important to U.S. interests. The one time that the United States in fact moved to raise the priority of human rights in China was early in the Clinton administration: on May 28, 1993, Clinton signed an executive order that linked the annual renewal of China's most-favored-nation trading status to improvement in its protection of human rights. China threatened to retaliate if Washington imposed this economic sanction, and the Clinton administration backed down. Beijing also employed economic and political coercion in response to Chris Patten's effort to enhance the democratic features of the system created by the Basic Law (see chapter 2). One reason China was confident in deploying these tactics was its knowledge that the business communities in the United States and Hong Kong would support it.

In the summer of 2015, Senator Marco Rubio of Florida, then a presidential candidate, called for a major shift in priorities for China policy:

> Our approach to China in this century relates to the last pillar of my foreign policy: the need for moral clarity regarding America's core values. Our devotion to the spread of human rights and liberal democratic principles ... is ... a strategic imperative that requires pragmatism and idealism in equal measure. The "rebalance" to Asia needs to be about more than just physical posturing. We must stand for the principles that have allowed Asian economies to grow so rapidly and for democracy to take root in the region. As president, I will strengthen ties with Asia's democracies, from India to Taiwan. Bolstering liberty on China's periphery can galvanize the region against Beijing's hostility and change China's political future. China will likely resist these efforts, but it is dependent on its economic relationship with the United States and, despite angry outbursts, will have no choice but to preserve it.[72]

Bill Clinton had assumed in 1993, as did Rubio in 2015, that China's dependence on the U.S. economy would lead it to accommodate to U.S. pressure to improve human rights. It turned out Clinton was wrong, at a time when the Chinese economy was much smaller than it is today. That Beijing would respond more than two decades later with no more than "angry outbursts" does not seem plausible.

If a future administration were to give democracy promotion a higher place on the U.S. agenda for China policy, Hong Kong would be a likely place to start. With its liberal order, it has a shorter distance to go than the rest of the PRC, where the Leninist state lacks the rule of law and severely restricts political freedoms. In Hong Kong, a significant share of the public, political parties, and civil society groups already favor rapid movement to "genuine universal suffrage." Given the Hong Kong SAR's preexisting foundation of social and economic development, democracy advocates would likely argue that competitive elections are long overdue. Those who would place a high priority on democratizing China would say that, at a minimum, a democratic Hong Kong should serve as an example for the rest of the country. More ambitiously, they might say that it could be a useful platform for activities across the border. The downside, of course, is that using Hong Kong in this way would only confirm Beijing's long-standing fears about American intentions.

POLICY EFFECTIVENESS

Even if we stipulate that the United States should do something to promote democracy in Hong Kong, there is the question of how to do so effectively—an issue that has always bedeviled U.S. human rights diplomacy. Effectiveness is least likely in "hard authoritarian" systems, whose rulers firmly resist progressive political change (China and Saudi Arabia come to mind). No U.S. initiatives are liable to be successful. Soft authoritarian systems can present a greater opportunity because their leaders begin to understand that the repression that used to keep them in power no longer works to preserve stability. During the "third wave" of democratization that began in the 1970s, some authoritarian leaders were able to preserve a significant degree of initiative in leading the process of political reform (as in Taiwan and Brazil). In other cases, the leaders acted under duress, usually from public protest (as in Korea and Pakistan). In most cases, there was some degree of negotiation between the regime and the forces of change; the balance of power dictated which side had the negotiating advantage.[73]

But authoritarianism does not always give way to democracy, and two important intermediate factors come into play. The first factor is preexisting social and economic conditions. Although democracy scholars reject the hypothesis that democracy is impossible in societies with deeply divided economic classes or ethnic and religious cleavages, they acknowledge that in the presence of those cleavages, designing a political system that performs well is more difficult. The political scientist Francis Fukuyama would argue that promotion of democracy by the United States is likely to be ineffective in countries that lack a strong state structure, the rule of law, and at least some institutions for accountability. Moreover, a focus on elections in the absence of other requisite institutions is unlikely to have enduring and positive results. For outside parties such as the United States to spend time and energy in trying to build a liberal democracy in such situations is liable to yield meager results, as the Iraq case amply demonstrates.

Yet most of these considerations do not apply to Hong Kong. Social and economic modernization has created a population that is capable of sustaining democracy once it is established. Significant state capacity, the rule of law, and some mechanisms for accountability already exist. Ethnic and religious cleavages are absent. The gap between the wealthy and the rest has become so politically significant that many of those who are not wealthy believe only electoral democracy can provide a check against abuse of power. At the same time, the decline of the Hong Kong SAR's civic culture and the growing allergy to compromise does not portend well for democratic development. In sum, on balance, Hong Kong's preexisting conditions are relatively positive and do not present obstacles to effective American involvement—but they do not define what form it might take.

A second factor is the depth of division in an authoritarian society: between those who hold power and those who want it, and among internal factions within those two contending camps. The prospects for any significant and constructive American role are likely to be severely limited in situations where there is a power asymmetry between the regime and the opposition. China itself is a case where the regime's superiority leaves little incentive to take American suggestions about political reform seriously. Outside actors may have greater opportunities when there is more of a balance of power. Those may increase when both the regime and the opposition are split into moderate and radical factions and the moderates have the power advantage in each camp. That creates more favorable conditions for the negotiation of a democratization pact. Even more favorable is when the leader of the regime is not unalterably opposed to reform.

Taiwan in the mid-1980s was such a case. The Kuomintang regime and the nonparty opposition were each split, and Chiang Ching-kuo, Taiwan's president from 1978 to 1988, had decided that the time had come for political change. He had come to the counterintuitive conclusion that survival of the regime—or key parts of it, such as the military—would be better served by liberalizing the political system than by continuing and intensifying repression. He also saw the opportunity to create a new, values-based foundation for inducing U.S. support for Taiwan's security. The United States was able to insert itself into this process: the executive branch provided rhetorical support for peaceful political change and sought behind the scenes to moderate overreactions by the regime. Meanwhile, liberal members of Congress both criticized repression and promised support for a democratic Taiwan. Chiang led the reform effort until his death in January 1988, and Lee Teng-hui, his successor, engineered a process of incremental and mutual accommodation between regime reformers and opposition moderates.[74]

For Hong Kong, the balance and division of power is somewhat different. The democratic camp has become more divided as time goes on, with radicals gaining the upper hand in 2014–15. But the divided democrats do have the capacity to mobilize large crowds for controlled marches or civil disobedience actions. On the establishment side, the Central People's Government, the Hong Kong SAR government, and the business community have their differences, in terms of both roles and policy stances. Beijing clearly sets the broad parameters of policy, and Hong Kong SAR officials must live within the parameters Beijing lays down. But Hong Kong officials do have flexibility in translating general guidelines into specific policies. Still, PRC officials always display an aversion to losing control (there is apparently no Chiang Ching-kuo in Beijing who might see the value of giving up some control for the sake of stability). The business community looks out for its economic interests but does have some enlightened members. The overall and objective balance of power favors Beijing, and could have been more accommodating to moderate democrats during the electoral reform struggle without undermining its fundamental interests. However, it chose not to do so or to act in a timely manner. This is due in part to the subjective, exaggerated fear the PRC government has of the threat posed by the democrats.

This imbalance affects the effectiveness of the U.S. role. What would be conceivable is some kind of below-the-radar intermediation between the two camps led by the United States that stops short of its being a mediator and the broker of a deal. There is no absence of communication channels; most useful may be the more limited exercise of "intellectual facilitation." This entails listening to and probing the views of each side separately, offering analytical perspectives that reflect the "art of the possible," and feeding the perspectives gained generally from one side to the other. Effective intellectual facilitation requires not only that the United States not take sides in the Hong Kong political struggle but also that it be seen by all concerned parties as not taking sides. But Beijing and many of its local supporters already believe that Washington has taken the wrong side, while the democratic camp would like to induce it to take its side. These perceptions impede U.S. intermediation.

Moreover, as noted in earlier chapters, the primary cause of the establishment-democrat breakdown in 2014–15 was not a dearth of ideas but a serious absence of trust. Hong Kong does not lack smart specialists on politics who understand, among other things, the pros and cons of proportional representation and single-member electoral systems. There may be specific areas on which local experts are deficient, and filling those gaps is an appropriate role for organizations such as the National Democratic Institute for International Affairs, the International Republican Institute, and their European counterparts, such as Germany's Friedrich Ebert Foundation and Great Britain's Westminster Foundation. More broadly, the current state of the American political system does not vest U.S. diplomats with presumptive wisdom on how to design a good democratic system. Given the relationship that the authorities in Beijing and Hong Kong on the one hand and the territory's democratic camp on the other have constructed for themselves, no substantive pact can be negotiated unless these two sides are willing to take risks to engage each other, which in turn could alter each camp's calculations over the fundamental intentions of the other. But minimal mutual trust and some acceptance of risk have been missing, not only between the establishment and the democrats, but within the democratic camp as well. The democrats' decades-long history of disappointment and fear that political freedoms are in atrophy are germane here, as is Beijing's fear of a "color revolution" and of "Hong Kong independence." Even if both sides trusted Washington's intentions (which they do not), it is not clear exactly how the U.S. government can insert itself in a productive way into this context, where mutual mistrust and fear cloud assessments of substantive positions and make it hard to begin a negotiating process. But without "inserting itself," the United States can still support democracy in Hong Kong:

- There is good value and little harm in the U.S. executive branch offering rhetorical support for democratization and the emergence of a system in which candidates representing the principal streams of political thinking are able to compete for office on a free and fair basis. The same can be said about conducting annual reports on developments in Hong Kong. The Obama administration has done that.
- It is appropriate for Congress to express strong support for democracy, as some members have done, and to indicate that what happens in Hong Kong will have implications for the American people's support for U.S.-China relations. Yet Congress should not take legislative steps that set too high a standard in judging Hong Kong's autonomy, and in so doing undermine its economy.
- Periodic visits to Hong Kong by senior U.S. officials and members of Congress send a signal to the Hong Kong elite and public of continued concern.
- The American business community in Hong Kong should continue to provide its informed and balanced perspective on the Hong Kong SAR government's policies regarding the economy.
- It is not appropriate and probably not effective for the United States to align itself with any specific pro-democracy proposal or group. The U.S. interest is in the future of Hong Kong as a whole and not in any one actor or faction in the community.

- It is not appropriate for Washington to gratuitously speak or act in ways that would confirm Beijing's misperception that the U.S. government—either directly or indirectly, overtly or covertly—is the cause of Hong Kong's instability. The PRC tendency to deflect blame away from its own policies creates the possibility that greater U.S. activism on behalf of Hong Kong democracy would only harden Beijing's resistance to meaningful reform and thus make the situation worse.

To sum up, the U.S. government has long cared about Hong Kong, but not always in ways that Hong Kong appreciates. During the recent protests, Washington probably took the strongest position of any foreign government, mainly through statements that boiled down to support for a truly competitive election. American scholars and other observers have watched what has happened in Hong Kong for clues about China's more general course. But how the U.S. government should act on the values and sentiments that it states rhetorically is not clear-cut. In addition to standing for certain principles, Washington also wishes to be effective, and that requires an assessment of what tactics will lead Beijing to choose the right course. Americans believe that a more democratic Hong Kong would be in China's own interest, but getting Beijing to understand that is not easy.

THIRTEEN

Conclusion

THE FUTURE AND VALUE OF THE HONG KONG HYBRID

Hong Kong is a very small place, its surface area smaller than that of West-chester County, New York (426 square miles to 500 square miles). The struggles over its political system don't get much attention in the global media unless and until protests erupt and tear gas fills the air. The most recent epi-sode, over reform of the method for electing the chief executive, may have begun with something of a bang but it ended with a whimper, resolving noth-ing and reinforcing the prior stalemate.

Nonetheless, Hong Kong actually occupies an interesting place in the long and serious debate over how to construct a political order that works well for both rulers and the ruled. Every great civilization occupies a different position on the autocracy-to-democracy continuum at any point in time, and that po-sition changes over time. Ultimately, none end up being pure democracy or pure autocracy. Each is a mix of strengthening the power of the state and then checking excessive use of that power. Within each civilization a debate occurs over what the position on the continuum should be, and from that spectrum of views, each will come to at least a temporary mainstream view. In pre-imperial China, in the sixth to third centuries BCE, the legalist school emphasized the power of the state, and most imperial dynasties tried to reflect that emphasis. But the Confucian philosopher Mencius stressed that successful kingship rested on the acceptance of the sovereign's rule by the subjects of the realm.

His disciple Huang Zongxi argued in the fourteenth century that the Ming dynasty failed because it was too autocratic.[1] More than five centuries later, Presidents Chiang Ching-kuo and Lee Teng-hui of Taiwan abandoned the (in their culture) long-time mainstream preference for authoritarian rule and made an unprecedented choice in Chinese history, successfully engineering a transition from a version of autocracy to democracy.[2]

As this ideological debate played out in the twentieth century, the argument was over whether states organized on totalitarian and authoritarian principles or those that rested on a democratic foundation could better ensure external safety and internal prosperity and stability. The democratic camp won the major battles of that struggle because the United States had superior resources, national will, and an array of allies, whereas adversaries such as Nazi Germany and imperial Japan were reckless and the Soviet Union could not sustain itself for the long term.

The ideological struggle continues into the twenty-first century, with China and the United States as the main protagonists as each pursues a different approach to cultivating political and social order and promoting economic prosperity. Reflecting a long Western tradition, the United States approach rests on autonomous, impersonal institutions that channel discontent, mute social conflicts, and limit government abuse. These institutions include the rule of law, liberal freedoms, mechanisms to control corruption, and the checks on the abuse of power (whether those institutions work well in practice is another question). The approach of the Chinese Communist Party (CCP), which draws on a century of Leninist practice, relies on a powerful and ideally clean and effective vanguard party. ("The Communist Party of China is the vanguard both of the Chinese working class and of the Chinese people and the Chinese nation.")[3] Organizationally, the party has a presence and leadership role in all major institutions, including government agencies and the judicial system. Ideologically, it seeks within the Party to establish authoritative or orthodox positions on all policy and organizational issues, and outside the Party it uses a robust propaganda apparatus to propagate that orthodoxy. For organizations and networks it does not completely control, it relies either on outright repression or United Front methods: co-optation of local groups that share its interests, placement of loyalists in key positions, demonization of opponents, and the use of propaganda to win over the undecided, all to bias the scope and actions of institutions and protect the party's interests.[4] In the end different types of regimes' performance, not just their process, will affect their value, and each society, or at least its political elite, will establish its own balance between process and performance legitimacy.

In the early twenty-first century, hybrid political systems have become more common and this has made the democracy-autocracy contest more complicated.[5] These systems possess features of democratic systems but are subverted by authoritarian institutions and practices that undermine popular accountability. To varying degrees, Russia, Venezuela, and Singapore come to mind as systems that have "elections without democracy," in Larry Diamond's formulation. Implicit in the debates about how leaders are selected is a parallel discussion on how well different types of political systems perform. Legitimacy can flow from both process and performance.

Even among hybrids, the Hong Kong Special Administrative Region (Hong Kong SAR) is uncommon, being a product of both Chinese and British traditions. Constitutionally, it is a unit of the People's Republic of China (PRC), an authoritarian system that takes only rhetorical bows toward democracy. Politically Hong Kong enjoys the strong liberal foundation that the rest of the PRC lacks—the rule of law and political freedoms—yet its mechanisms for selecting most key political leaders do not reflect the popular will, but instead permit the Central People's Government in Beijing to maintain control of the outcomes. Previous chapters detailed how this system came about and the periodic efforts to shift it in one direction or the other.

The intriguing question for the future is whether a hybrid system of this type can continue indefinitely—to paraphrase Abraham Lincoln's "House Divided" speech of 1858, will it "become all one thing or all the other"? The politicization of Hong Kong society that has occurred since the early 1990s and the radicalization of politics since around 2005 have exposed the strains and contradictions within a hybrid that combines political freedom with only partial popular rule. As Hong Kong's "actual situation" has changed, Beijing's long-stated desire for an electoral transition that is both gradual and orderly seems less and less feasible. The Central People's Government's heightened concern about national security and Hong Kong's potential to undermine it suggest[s] that Beijing's tolerance for the ways that Hong Kong people use (some might say abuse) their political freedoms could decline. And hanging over the stalemate of the mid-2010s is the cloud of 2047, when the one country, two systems arrangement is set to expire, and Hong Kong might become like Shanghai, a special municipality of the PRC.

The Failure of Political Reform, 2013–15

Hong Kong's political struggle over universal suffrage was the most significant and recent attempt to readjust its hybrid political system. Electoral reform evoked two conflicting narratives about what happened and why. In one narrative, a coalition of politicians, academics, spoiled adolescents, and radical activists sought to block adoption of the latest act of generosity by the Central People's Government, the city's sovereign. Driving this obstructionism, it was said, were two underlying public attitudes: a general unwillingness to accept that the Hong Kong SAR is a part of the PRC, and so a willingness to entertain the possibility of political independence; and a lack of gratitude for all that the motherland had done for the city since its return in 1997, and with it, a disregard for Beijing's interests. A subplot of this narrative is the role of the United States, which was alleged to have manipulated the local opposition in order to advance America's purported goal of subverting the authority of the Chinese Communist Party in both the Hong Kong SAR and the rest of the PRC. This was a struggle between chaos and order, treason and patriotism, and a few against the many.

The second narrative was about the struggle of courageous fighters for democracy against a repressive Chinese government. Activists such as Martin Lee, Benny Tai, and Joshua Wong campaigned in Hong Kong for "the right of all citizens to choose their leaders and shape their future" and thus to challenge a Beijing government that has a "fierce determination to curtail self-rule and direct elections." Beijing sought to restrict political freedoms and ordered the Hong Kong government to abandon "the planned shift to direct elections of Hong Kong's chief executive." In response, young Hong Kong democrats led "dynamic, informal, nonviolent movements . . . to demand change."[6] This was a contest between good and evil, democratic values versus Leninist realpolitik, and Hong Kong's David versus Beijing's Goliath. In this narrative, the United States refused to stand up for its democratic ideals in favor of accommodating a rising China to preserve economic ties.

These two narratives—both of them morality plays—distort reality as much as they illuminate it. My analysis and the evidence upon which it rests suggest a different interpretation. Electoral reform failed in Hong Kong not because the Hong Kong SAR government's ultimate plan was fundamentally flawed but because each side mistrusted the intentions of the other. The government's plan was certainly not perfect: the pathway to competitive elections that it offered was indeed narrow and required democrats to make at least a modest and moderating leap of faith. But it did offer a path. Beijing's tactics were indeed heavy-handed and ill-timed, and it should have offered more concessions earlier in the game. But at the end of the day the PRC approved a mechanism that could have produced a moderate democrat as chief executive and, later on, a Legislative Council (LegCo) without members representing functional constituencies. In the opposition camp, some clearly preferred to oppose for the sake of opposition or to seek a perfection that could not be realized (the most extreme fantasy was Hong Kong independence). But the great majority of people who just wanted a wider democracy were as idealistic and sincere as they were frustrated by Hong Kong's entrenched inequality—which the Central People's Government seemed not to recognize. It was far from foreordained that the LegCo would reject the government's proposal; the rejection was the unnecessary product of misperception, miscalculation, mistrust, and missed opportunities within and between the establishment and democratic camps. Key actors on both sides failed at key points to engage realistically with each other to construct a mutually acceptable solution. Process overwhelmed product.

The failure of electoral reform was doubly tragic because it delayed needed governance and competitiveness reforms into the indefinite future. If each political camp had had enough trust in the other to allow compartmentalization of electoral reform from other issues, there might have been majorities in LegCo to pass some of the items suggested in chapter 9. For example, repealing the prohibition on the chief executive's being a member of a political party would have allowed greater coherence between the executive and the legislature. This may still be possible in the future. As a current practical matter, however, it appears that the scars of battle over universal suffrage are still too raw to permit such differentiation. If such reforms are to go forward, genuine democratization must be part of the package. Democracy, by spreading the benefits of growth more widely, is a necessary precondition for good governance and economic competitiveness.

Yet facilitating competitive elections for the chief executive and all LegCo seats—the key missing element of Hong Kong's democratization—is not a sufficient condition for achieving these objectives. Without at least some of the changes outlined in chapters 9 and 10, the Hong Kong political system is unlikely to perform well. In particular, the LegCo must be transformed into a more genuinely representative institution in its own procedures, so that opposition members are free to introduce bills that the Hong Kong SAR government does not like. Without wide-ranging reform, contention will persist and the government's performance legitimacy will continue to lag behind expectations. If, for example, the fragmentation of political support into a number of parties and the disarticulation between legislature and civil service are not reduced, then more competitive elections might make the formulation of policy more contentious and the implementation of policies less effective.

Whether it is possible to reform the Hong Kong political system and political economy depends ultimately on Beijing. A number of steps that should arguably be a part of the necessary reform require amendment to the Basic Law by the National People's Congress, or a new interpretation by its Standing Committee. Even the changes that only need LegCo approval still require the initiative of the Hong Kong SAR government, which is unlikely to undertake them without some signal of approval from Beijing. Formally or informally, these reforms really are the prerogative of the sovereign. The Central People's Government claims to want social stability, equitable prosperity, and governmental effectiveness for Hong Kong. To secure that, it must take the lead on forward-looking change rather than standing in the way. CCP General Secretary Xi Jinping has demonstrated a relatively high tolerance for risk and established a record for taking risks in an assertive mode, which has put his internal and external adversaries on the defensive. Hong Kong represents one relevant case of this tactic. Might Xi also be willing later in his tenure to take risks in the Hong Kong SAR, in order to restore momentum to the political reform process?[7]

The central government's reasons for pursuing a hard-line strategy and employing tactics that alienated the democratic camp and made an impasse more likely remain something of a mystery. One likely reason is the dysfunction of some democratic systems in East Asia and around the world. But these real problems do not reflect a fundamental defect of democracy, but failures of design in the systems that are experiencing difficulty. And democracies are not alone in suffering from dysfunction; so do many authoritarian systems. A more likely explanation is that the CCP leaders continued to assume that the methods of political control that they thought made sense in the 1980s—combining a liberal oligarchy with United-Front-from-below support mechanisms—were still effective in an advanced middle-class society with a high level of political participation, when in fact that recipe no longer works. Essentially, Beijing has yet to reach the (counterintuitive) conclusion that Taiwan's President Chiang Ching-kuo reached in the mid-1980s: that in the circumstances he faced it would be easier to stay in power by opening up the political system and fashioning open institutions to channel political participation may enhance stability and legitimacy more than by undermining them.

A Different Approach to Hybrids

In an April 2015 essay, Simon-Hoey Lee, a Hong Kong lawyer and consultant to the government, observed that two very different types of politics coexisted in the Hong Kong SAR's political system. The first type—top-down, elite-dominated, executive-led, and meritocratic—had been dominant through the colonial period and into the 1990s. The second type, which he called "mass politics," emerged in the 1990s and took the form of public participation and electoral politics. It was a bottom-up process dominated by political parties and civil society. The first way was more consensus-based while the second thrived on political competition and conflict. The two types reflected the different social backgrounds of those who were politically active in them (the elite versus the public at large) and also different attitudes toward the Central People's Government (tolerant to deferential versus skeptical to hostile).[8]

The conflict over electoral reform was essentially one in which Lee's first type of politics was on the defensive and the second was on the offensive. It was a contest over political participation: Who gets to play in politics, in which arenas, and under what rules? Hong Kong citizens did what they had done for more than a decade: they use the political freedoms that the Basic Law had granted them to press Beijing and the Hong Kong SAR government to expand political participation by instituting competitive, universal suffrage elections to pick senior leaders.

Simon Lee's distinction reminds us that participation is not all there is to politics, and that the executive governmental agencies will have a job to do however the question of electoral reform is resolved. He thus looks more at broader issues of governance, including how policy is made and implemented (see chapter 7) and the two types of political legitimacy, process and performance. Lee's dichotomy directs attention to a more fundamental issue of how, in Francis Fukuyama's terms as set forth in his recent two-volume study of political development, advanced societies reconcile state capacity with political accountability.[9] The answer does not lie in marginalizing one form of politics at the expense of the other. That only creates counterproductive effects. Nor is it helpful to pose false choices between democracy and meritocracy or democracy and technocracy. John Fitzgerald, who is a member of the faculty of business and law at Swinburne University of Technology, points out in a trenchant review of Daniel Bell's *The China Model: Political Meritocracy and the Limits of Democracy* that merit-based selection of officials was developed not so much as an alternative to elections but to limit patronage and

corruption. Specifically about China he writes, "Arguably, the critical constitutional question facing China today is not the choice between meritocratic
autocracy and electoral politics but the question of who constitutes the political nation and who therefore is entitled to participate in public political life."[10]

The reality of advanced society is that both state capacity and political
accountability are necessary, along with the rule of law. Effective government
requires the application of expert, often scientific, knowledge. Policy solutions
to complex social problems that rely on ideological simplicity are doomed to
failure. Therefore, although reliance on objective measures of merit and expertise in picking the people who will carry out the routine work of government
does not ensure superior performance all the time, it is more effective than
appointment by patronage or personal connections. Governments must include strong institutions that deter officials from using their decisionmaking
positions to secure personal gain.

Yet mechanisms that increase the odds that the experts vested with the
authority and power to govern complex societies will do so efficiently and fairly
does not ensure good governance. Large organizations are subject to pathologies such as "group think," careerism, and arrogance, even when they are staffed
by experts. Coordinating the overlapping policies of technocratic agencies
when they are of similar bureaucratic rank is not always easy. Although experts may be able to anticipate and mitigate many of the negative consequences of changed policies, they are not omniscient. Most of all, feedback
mechanisms for measuring performance are never completely accurate, nor
even complete.

As a result, as strong states with civil services staffed by experts emerged in
Western Europe and North America from the eighteenth century on, it was
all but inevitable that demands for institutions to be broadly accountable
would grow. Those demands may have begun in the West, and Western history and culture may have shaped the particular form of those institutions.
But the demands that spread through Latin America, Asia, and Africa in the
twentieth century were less the result of any Western example and more the
consequence of the emergence of strong states and the need to control abuses
of executive power through democratic institutions and the rule of law. These
accountability institutions include using elections to pick political leaders
who provide broad direction for the experts who make up the "permanent"
government and representatives to serve in legislatures that appropriate funds
for executive agencies and oversee policy implementation. Inevitably, the institutions created to provide accountability suffer their own pathologies that

can undermine their core purpose. The United States has become an example in this regard, such as the "pay to play" culture in the U.S. Congress, where individuals and organizations seeking support for legislative initiatives must make a campaign contribution just to have their request considered.

However imperfectly they function, the coexistence of meritocratic and technocratic state structures on the one hand and institutions to ensure accountability on the other is a fact of modern political life. The task of governance is to design state agencies and accountability mechanisms as well as the interface between them so that each performs well and strengthens the effectiveness of the other. Although Hong Kong has suffered a weakening of state capacity since the early 1990s, and accountability institutions are only partly established—fostering the temptations to radical political action—it still has the potential to provide what Ian Scott would call a new "articulation" among the elements of the political system.

THE 2047 FACTOR

The changing nature of the Hong Kong hybrid isn't academic, as the political combat of 2014 and 2015 demonstrated. And the longer the question is not answered one way or another, the more fraught it will become. The reason is the inexorable month-by-month, week-by-week, day-by-day drawing closer of July 1, 2047—the day on which the pledge in article 5 of the Basic Law to preserve Hong Kong's "previous capitalist system and way of life" for fifty years expires. Anyone who owns property in Hong Kong or plans to will be concerned about their property rights if there is a lack of clarity about the future Hong Kong legal system, just as there was in the early 1980s. Yet another local constituency more volatile than property owners is also watching the clock: for activists such as Joshua Wong, who were not yet twenty at the beginning of the 2014 protests and who had already formed very definitive ideas about the PRC political system and its government's intentions, 2047 will be a very large part of their life experience.[11]

It is perfectly conceivable that Beijing will decide in a moment of good sense to simply extend the deadline by another fifty years and in doing so will deflate public anxiety about the future. Far more likely is that it will do so only on the basis of its assessment of circumstances at that particular time and when there is less and less excuse for a delay. For people in Hong Kong, the longer that uncertainty is prolonged, the greater the temptation will be to act upon their anxieties in public and demonstrative ways. Yet one lesson of the failed effort to enact electoral reform in 2014–15 was that the more contentious

Hong Kong politics become, the less likely it is that Beijing will show good sense. Alternatively, the earlier Beijing shows itself willing to accommodate the public's desire for greater accountability in government, the less the likelihood that the expression of public anxieties will become difficult to manage.

What Might Hong Kong Do for China?

It is worth noting that the contemporary PRC has its own hybrid character when compared to the more uniformly totalitarian nature of the Mao period. By the late 1970s, Deng Xiaoping came to the conclusion that if the CCP was to regain its legitimacy and strengthen China, it would have to reduce its deep penetration of some aspects of national life. He did not opt for democracy, but he did lead a transition to a selective authoritarianism that preserved tight controls in the political arena but liberalized many aspects of economic and social life. The level of repression of political dissent has varied over time: the post-Tiananmen period was the most repressive and Xi Jinping is certainly no liberal. On balance, however, selective authoritarianism has been the CCP's default approach, not only to stimulating economic growth and the growth of a middle class but also to sustaining the hegemony of the vanguard party. The CCP has sometimes made adaptations to cope with new challenges even as it continues to place its highest priority on maintaining control.[12] Although there is selective nostalgia for the Mao period, something that Xi Jinping encourages for his own reasons, no one in China who knows anything about the reality of the chairman's harsh rule would want to return to it.

Even though the CCP has made some adaptations to the political system that it leads, it is not making them fast enough. As J. Stapleton Roy, a former U.S. ambassador to China, has written, "The fundamental contradiction facing China's leaders is that they are attempting to modernize China while retaining a pre-modern form of governance. The more China modernizes, the more acute this contradiction will become."[13] Hong Kong, on the other hand, despite its hybrid character, has a modern form of government. That raises the question of whether there are ways that Hong Kong might lead the way toward better governance on the mainland, even if electoral democracy is not on the agenda.

The Xi Jinping regime has not ignored political reform, broadly defined, even as it tightened the screws on political dissent. Part of the program that Xi Jinping unveiled at the third plenary session of the Eighteenth Central Committee in November 2013 focused mainly on economic reform. The document

targeted defects in China's governance and spoke of institutional weapons
that just happen to be sources of strength in Hong Kong. These included property rights protection; "upholding the authority of the constitution and the law;
deepening the reform of administrative law enforcement; ensuring the independent and equitable exercise of judicial and prosecutorial power; . . . perfecting
the judicial system for the protection of human rights; . . . strengthening the system for restraining and supervising the [state's] use of power." The latter item
included "punishment and prevention of corruption; . . . clean politics . . .
and . . . diligent efforts to achieve the honesty of cadres." Clearly, how the regime
crafts and implements such initiatives will determine the degree of convergence, if
any, with Hong Kong. The frequent use of the catch-all term "in accordance
with law" in the plenum's document indicates that it may be more rhetoric than
a prediction of future reality. But at least on the rhetorical level, the mainland
appears to be pointing toward the direction of Hong Kong.[14]

Whenever the CCP does make adaptations, it follows its long tradition of
testing policy initiatives on an experimental basis in a limited number of settings before scaling them up to national implementation.[15] Beijing's use of
Hong Kong's financial sector for internationalization of the RMB is effectively part of that tradition. It is quite possible that the CCP could use Hong
Kong as a test bed on issues of governance as well as economics.

The fact is that Hong Kong has already made a contribution to China,
although Chinese officials concentrate on what the mainland has done for the
territory rather than the other way around.[16] A more objective inventory of
the city's contributions was created by Peter T. Y. Cheung, a Hong Kong University professor in the department of politics and public administration, who
notes the positive example that the Hong Kong SAR's public service provides
the mainland and the specific contributions in training and building governance capacity. "Focal points include the appointment of Hong Kong advisers, the training of Chinese civil servants, and lessons to learn from Hong
Kong's experience in anti-corruption and public management." Training
mainland lawyers and judges is another significant contribution. Clearly, China's post-1978 economic takeoff could not have occurred without investment
and know-how from Hong Kong as well as Taiwan, even if Cheung is correct
that the Hong Kong SAR influence was greater in neighboring South China
than in the country as a whole.[17]

Two areas for continued and expanded Hong Kong contribution to Chinese
governance deserve special attention: controlling corruption and strengthening the rule of law.

CONTROLLING CORRUPTION

Transparency International's global Corruption Perceptions Index for 2014 ranked China 100th among 175 ranked countries and regions, with a score of 36 out of 100.[18] Various types of corruption—graft, rent-seeking, the purchase of official positions, and so on—have reached endemic proportions in the PRC. It was to excise this cancer that Xi Jinping in late 2012 undertook an unprecedentedly ambitious campaign to investigate, prosecute, and punish officials who have undermined the prestige and effectiveness of the vanguard party by using their official positions for personal enrichment. In this campaign, both the prominent and not-so-prominent (both "tigers and flies") have been targets. The most prominent casualties were Zhou Yongkang, a former member of the Politburo Standing Committee, who controlled both the energy and public security sectors, and Generals Xu Caihou and Guo Boxiong, members of the Politburo. Xi and Wang Qishan, his chief corruption fighter, have no doubt made many enemies, but as of early 2016 the campaign had not let up and appeared to be popular with the public.[19]

Hong Kong had its own corruption problems in the 1950s and 1960s that alienated the common people who were its victims. In 1973, the colonial government undertook a vigorous enforcement campaign to try to bring the problem under control. The campaign was almost too vigorous and created morale problems in the police and civil service, and the authorities eventually declared an amnesty. But to deter future wrongdoing and retain the threat of enforcement, the government, smartly, created a set of institutions to sustain the effort, particularly the Independent Commission Against Corruption (ICAC). The ICAC proved to be a great success, fostering anti-corruption norms both within the government and in the public at large. In 2014, Hong Kong ranked seventeenth on the Corruption Perceptions Index with a score of 74.[20] Could an institution similar to the ICAC be adapted to the mainland context?

Probably the most comprehensive analysis of whether and how the Hong Kong experience might be applied to the mainland is a 2004 article by Melanie Manion of the University of Wisconsin–Madison.[21] She identifies three parts of the ICAC's strategy that were fortified through the agency's institutional design: The Operations Department carried out enforcement (investigation and prosecution). The Community Relations Department undertook education both to set a new moral standard and to ensure that the public understood anti-corruption laws but had a low-risk role in enforcement. The Corruption Prevention Department worked to reform government practices to reduce the ways civil servants could use their offices for private gain.[22] Manion also pointed out, however, that these operational agencies would have been less effective absent the strong signal from the colonial governor that he recognized corruption as a serious problem and was willing to create a single institution vested with independent power and authority to fight it. The public received that signal and was prepared to act upon it, thus ensuring the ICAC greater success.[23]

The PRC system as it evolved in the post-Mao period lacks the key features that made Hong Kong's ICAC so effective but has counterproductive features. For example, the leadership created not one agency but two, and gave them overlapping jurisdictions, which meant that neither one had sufficient authority to act credibly. The CCP's discipline inspection commissions are responsible for monitoring the actions of all leaders of the Party hierarchy down to the grassroots; the state procuratorates are responsible for government officials at three administrative levels—national, provincial, and county—but not the grassroots. In theory, there is a division of labor between the two: the CCP's commissions are responsible for Party members' infractions against Party rules and norms; the state procuratorates are responsible for actions by government officials that violate criminal laws. But the realities of the Leninist system effectively blur these distinctions: many government officials are Party members, and the nature of the infraction—whether it is criminal in character—is not immediately clear. The inspection commissions and prosecutors often work at cross purposes, with each ignorant of what the other is doing.

Another problem is the formal and informal constraints on discipline inspection commissions at the local level. Before 2004 they were under the joint authority of both the Party committee at their own level of the hierarchy and the discipline inspection commission at the next higher level. Party committees had a reputational interest in hiding their misdeeds.[24] In 2004, this dual leadership system came to an end, and Party committees had no formal authority over discipline inspection commissions. Yet one specialist on the subject asserts that informal constraints still come into play, and Party committees can impede discipline inspection commissions from doing their job—for example, by withholding information needed to corroborate allegations. Thus, he writes, "The dominance of local party committees and the [investigation commissions'] lack of independence contribute to the ineffectiveness of the disciplinary organizations."[25]

A further weakness in PRC anti-corruption efforts is that they are implemented not through sustained institutionalized effort but in campaigns that occur outside normal bureaucratic processes. They are not anchored in existing norms of due process (to the extent that these exist in the first place), and create great fear and uncertainty among those who are targets and others who worry that they may become targets. Campaigns are politically disruptive while they occur and whose deterrent effect declines once normalcy returns. Because they are so clearly driven by political imperatives, campaigns do not promote respect for and confidence in the rule of law.[26] An economist who writes under the pseudonym James Leung has written, "If Xi's fight against corruption becomes disconnected from systemic reforms, or devolves into a mere purge of political rivals, it could backfire, inflaming the grievances that stand in the way of the 'harmonious society' the party seeks to create."[27]

Institutional design contributes to the mixed signals that the regime puts out both to its agencies and to the public, something that the absence of the rule of law and respect for civil liberties only reinforces. Finally, Manion argues, the mere fact that an anti-corruption agency is independent is not a guarantee of success: "An independent agency answerable only to a chief executive is as credible as the chief executive, unless he or she is constrained by some mechanism to respond responsibly."[28]

Three scholars, two from Hong Kong and one from the mainland, offered a similar analysis by examining the contextual and operational factors behind the success of the ICAC. Regarding context, first the economy must be sufficiently developed so that the government has the resources to pay decent salaries to civil servants and thus to reduce their motivation to solicit bribes in return for properly implementing the government policies under their control. Second, public attitudes must be supportive of anti-corruption policies. In Hong Kong, the formation of the ICAC at the same time that residents had begun to accept Hong Kong as their home and not a place of temporary sojourn was important. These newly identified residents had more skin in the game and therefore were willing to work with the government to help fight corruption. Third, senior officials need to set an example not only through their own behavior but also through their relatives' actions. On the operational side, the ICAC succeeded because it was truly independent, made possible partly through the careful screening and intensive training of its personnel. A public that hitherto had reason to believe that corruption was a fact of life was socialized to the conviction that "zero-tolerance" was the new norm. Last, the authorities made the strategic decision to not attempt a root-and-branch purge of the civil service, which would have damaged morale. Implementation of the new policies certainly required the successful and very public prosecution of a number of exemplary cases, but amnesty for lesser infractions improved morale and commitment to new norms.[29]

The Hong Kong system is not perfect. Ian Scott of Hong Kong University fully recognizes the achievements of Hong Kong's anti-corruption institutions, but he also notes something of a mismatch between ends and means. The focus of the ICAC's approach is to create rules to deter corruption and mechanisms to hold violators accountable if deterrence fails. The ongoing public education campaign has created a context in which rules are more likely to work, but, as Scott points out, there remains a zone of discretion wherein officials find new ways to use their public positions for private gain, despite the system of rules. One way to reduce this zone is to add even more rules. But that can lead to caution or even paralysis in the formulation and implementation of decisions and a tendency for decisions to be pushed up the hierarchy. Another way, hypothetically, is to socialize officials with values that preserve their zone of discretion, but bias their choices in directions that sustain the goal of controlling corruption. In Hong Kong, however, "The introduction of value-based elements is still in its infancy."[30] Scott notes that controlling misbehavior by Hong Kong's chief executives is particularly difficult because some of the agencies that have the job of ensuring accountability report to the chief executive. But under one country, two systems, the chief executive, though selected in Hong Kong, is appointed by Beijing, and is therefore subject to dual accountability.[31]

Despite these weaknesses, the ICAC and its operations have been remarkably successful and have contributed to the legitimacy of the Hong Kong SAR government. Yet it is premature to hope that the ICAC might be an effective model for China. The Beihang University professor Ren Jianming explains: "The ICAC succeeded because it is an autonomous investigation unit in a society with judicial independence. The mainland first needs to tackle the problems of an excessive concentration of power, and it is highly unlikely its disciplinary watchdogs will copy the ICAC system because of the judiciary's lack of independence or transparency."[32] To the need for judicial independence if effective anti-corruption measures are to work one might add freedom of the press and channels for citizens to convey complaints without fear of exposure and retribution.

THE RULE OF LAW

The fourth plenary session of CCP Eighteenth Central Committee went beyond the general goals stated in the third plenary session, for political reform, and was dedicated exclusively to the subject of "rule according to law" (*yifa zhiguo*). This focus was significant in and of itself and suggested that perhaps the Party might be moving the PRC system in the direction of Hong Kong's. It appeared to represent a positive swing of the pendulum toward judicial autonomy and capacity after almost a decade of retrogression away from reforms instituted in the 1990s.[33]

Still, the proposed changes were a mixed bag, providing evidence for both optimists and pessimists. Donald Clarke, a specialist on the PRC legal system at the George Washington University School of Law, divides the proposals, contained in a "Decision" document of the Fourth Plenum, into four categories. In the first are "major meaningful reforms," which included the creation of a career civil service for judges and the creation of circuit tribunals covering several provinces. In the second are "minor meaningful reforms" that are technical in nature but would still increase judicial autonomy if followed. Also included in this category are steps that would be highly significant if carried out but are unlikely to be carried out. These include reaffirmation of presumption of innocence of the accused, exclusion of unlawfully secured evidence, and movement to more of a jury system along British and American lines. In the third category is "feel good language": reiteration of past changes that were not put in practice. In the fourth are "dogs that didn't bark," most significant being silence regarding "a long-standing feature of China's legal-administrative system" that impedes movement to rule-based governance: "the centralization of rule-making power coupled with the decentralization of administrative power."[34]

The balance of expert opinion inclined toward pessimism. It is clear that nothing in the principle of "rule according to law" will change the fundamental fact that the CCP will continue to rule as it chooses. And the area where it continues most to use law to preserve its monopoly of power is the area of political freedoms. There is no hint that Chinese courts would, like Hong Kong courts, protect the freedom of citizens to exercise those rights when the state seeks to abridge them.

The legal system's role in the economy is different, as Jacques deLisle of the University of Pennsylvania Law School usefully clarifies. In this arena, the Fourth Plenum's rule-of-law reforms are designed to adapt the role of the legal system to a changing economic system: create more robust protection of property rights, facilitate movement toward a "mixed ownership economy" and reform state-owned enterprises, and reduce the current phenomenon of legal protectionism, whereby local courts issue judgments that favor local stakeholders. These changes, if implemented, are not trivial and would continue the slow convergence of the PRC and Hong Kong systems when it comes to economic affairs.

Legal reforms are also designed to better serve the anti-corruption campaign, which has been waged principally by the Party institution, the discipline inspection commissions, with the courts acting only after basic outcomes have been determined.[35] Finally, changes in the management of judicial personnel are designed to strengthen central control, not to enhance judicial autonomy.[36]

Instituting an autonomous legal system and an independent judiciary provides a check on abuses of power by the state and creates a set of institutionalized rules and norms for social action. But the rule of law is analytically and institutionally distinct from democratic institutions. The history of Hong Kong demonstrates that a robust judiciary can coexist with a regime of limited political freedoms. At the same time the rule of law is inherently incompatible with a system dominated by a vanguard party. The Chinese legal system may act effectively in some areas, but only as the CCP gives it scope to do so. Ultimately, it is the Party that decides what the law means. The day may come when the CCP decides to reduce its Leninist penetration of the judiciary, and when it does, Hong Kong can provide some guidance on how to do that. The fact that the Hong Kong SAR legal system has a common-law basis and the mainland has a civil-code basis renders impossible an exact and comprehensive one-to-one transference. Richard Wong of the University of Hong Kong clarifies: "Civil law, which originated with the French, is 'policy implementing' and embraces socially-conditioned private contracting, while common law, which originated in England, is 'dispute resolving' and supports unconditioned private contracting."[37]

Despite these institutional and philosophical differences, a reform-minded Beijing could learn much from Hong Kong if it decided to do so. What Hong Kong has accomplished concerning the rule of law and controlling corruption could also be viewed by Beijing as successful experiments in those areas. Regrettably, the CCP is unlikely to apply the lessons learned in Hong Kong to the rest of China as long as it places primary emphasis on the CCP's vanguard role. If that role were adjusted or eliminated for the sake of more effective governance, then the Hong Kong SAR could serve as a point of reference for reform of the Chinese political system.

To engineer a shift in the PRC's legal and anti-corruption systems toward Hong Kong's institutions would constitute significant reforms. Even more fundamental would be facilitating a transition toward an open, pluralistic, and competitive political system. This would entail an end to the CCP Organization Department's control over a long list of personnel appointments in partial favor of popular elections. It would imply empowering people's congresses at all levels of the political system vis-à-vis their relevant executive departments. It would likely mean moving from a centralized and unitary system to a federal one, in which at least some levels of subnational administrative units would possess their own autonomous authority. The prospect that the CCP would divest itself of much of its power seems to be a pipedream, however dearly political idealists might like to see it. But then again, this was precisely the transition that Taiwan's Kuomintang decided to make—from a political system based on Leninist principles of control to a genuine democracy. If the CCP were ever to choose to go down this road, it would surely wish to experiment with institutional designs before applying them nationwide. The Hong Kong hybrid already has almost two decades of experience with the protection of political freedoms. When it comes to electoral politics, it could provide Beijing with a testing ground—if Beijing were prepared to take a chance on allowing popular rule in the Hong Kong SAR.

The Issue of Reputation

Another drama is unfolding parallel to the contest between authoritarian and democratic systems. This drama is the revival of China as a great power and the place it creates for itself in the East Asia region and the world. In this drama, too, Hong Kong may play a bit part. This is not the first time that a rising or reviving great power has challenged the international status quo, but it will likely be the defining dynamic of the twenty-first century.

This drama will be played out at the macro-level, as China continues its buildup of military capabilities and projects its power—military, political, and economic—in its home region and more broadly. Those trends challenge the interests of states that created the current status quo in the decades since World War II and have benefitted from their position in that order; their response will help determine the ultimate outcome. They can accommodate growing Chinese capabilities, actively seek to match them, or find a hedging option in between. China sees the United States as the principal obstacle to its revival, not only because of its great power but also because it has maintained a dominating forward position on China's littoral since the Korean War.

But the interplay between China as the rising power and America as the status quo power takes place at a micro-level as well. Beijing and Washington will face off on a large number of specific issues, some cooperatively, others competitively, and still others with conflict. The results of these specific encounters can affect the relative advantage that each enjoys on the regional and global chessboard. Cumulatively these micro-level encounters will shape each country's assessment of the long-term intentions of the other, either benign or malign. But there will also be a cumulative reputational effect. What China does regarding North Korea, the Senkaku Islands, the Spratly Islands, Taiwan, Tibet, and Hong Kong, too, will help define for China's neighbors and for the world what kind of great power China is becoming, and so alter their assumptions about corresponding policy. Hong Kong is certainly not the most important issue on this list, but it is on the list. What happens there may have little effect on China's reputation if the city continues to muddle through. But initiatives by the PRC either to move the Hong Kong SAR to a full democracy or to significantly limit political freedoms would be noticed, by two audiences in particular.

The first audience is Taiwan. The Taiwan public does not currently believe that what happens in the Hong Kong SAR is relevant to the island's ultimate future, including the relationship with China (discussed in chapter 11). But what happens in Hong Kong will loom larger if and when leaders in Taipei decide it is in their interest to begin talks with Beijing on core political issues or feel that they have no choice but to do so. One might speculate on the result in Taiwan if, vis-à-vis Hong Kong, Beijing had made modest concessions earlier, during the electoral reform process, and so had created a certainty that it would allow clearly competitive elections for the chief executive and all LegCo seats and would also accept full democracy for the city over time. It *might* have led opinion leaders on Taiwan to rethink what has always been a key obstacle to the island's consideration of one country, two systems: how Hong Kong's political system was designed to prevent outcomes that Beijing did not wish to risk. Because Taiwan already has a democratic system, even a slightly dysfunctional one, turning back the clock to a system with controlled outcomes was always a nonstarter. In contrast, for Beijing to continue to bias electoral results in favor of itself and its local allies in Hong Kong only confirms long-established assumptions in Taiwan.

The second key audience is the American public and the political leadership of the United States. Human rights and democracy have always been issues in U.S.-China relations. They were muted during the 1980s, when American liberals and centrists assumed that the reform occurring in China would have to be gradual and would target the economy before political freedoms. That assumption disappeared in the late 1980s and early 1990s when events in the Soviet Bloc demonstrated that fundamental political change could occur quickly. In 1989, the CCP's suppression of the Tiananmen protests ended any illusions in the United States that this was a benign and tolerant regime. Since the mid-1990s, China's domestic political arrangements have not been a priority issue in U.S. diplomacy but they persist, and some American leaders advocate raising democracy to the top of Washington's China agenda.[38]

Here again, Taiwan led the way. One of the reasons that Chiang Ching-kuo decided during the 1980s to begin the process of democratization was to create a values basis for relations with the United States where none had existed before. Taiwan is small in geographical size and global power compared to China, but the island's democratic system remains a reason for its claim on assured American support. If Beijing were to choose a grand strategy that included coexistence with the United States in East Asia (rather than trying to drive it from the region), it could strengthen U.S. confidence that this was in fact genuine Chinese policy by moving gradually in the direction of a more open and political system. Completing that process in Hong Kong would certainly be a good place to start.

Notes

Chapter One: The Hong Kong Hybrid

1. Jermain T. M. Lam, "Political Decay in Hong Kong after the Occupy Central Movement," *Asian Affairs: An American Review* 42 (April–June 2015), p. 104.

2. Support for the protests broke along educational and generational lines. People fifteen to twenty-four years old and those with a tertiary education were much more likely to support the cause. Ibid., p. 114.

3. Professor In Joo Song, Hong Kong University, personal communication to the author, April 15, 2015.

4. For authoritative Chinese government statements at the beginning of the crisis see "Resolutely Implement '3 Unswervinglys,'" *Renmin Ribao*, October 2, 2014 (Open Source Center [hereafter OSC] CHO2014100207212050); "Resolutely Maintain the Decision of the Standing Committee of the National People's Congress," *Renmin Ribao*, October 3, 2014 (OSC CHR2014100312837820); and "Resolute Maintenance of Rule of Law in Hong Kong," *Renmin Ribao*, October 4, 2014 (OSC CHO2014100408422221558).

5. Keith Bradsher, "Some Chinese Leaders Claim U.S. and Britain are Behind Hong Kong Protests," *New York Times*, October 10, 2014 (www.nytimes.com/2014 /10/11/world/asia/some-chinese-leaders-claim-us-and-britain-are-behind-hong -kong-protests-.html).

6. Deng Xiaoping, "Speech at a Meeting with the Members of the Committee for Drafting the Basic Law of the Hong Kong Special Administrative Region," April 16, 1987, *Selected Works of Deng Xiaoping* 3 (https://dengxiaopingworks.wordpress.com /2013/03/18/speech-at-a-meeting-with-the-members-of-the-committee-for-drafting -the-basic-law-of-the-hong-kong-special-administrative-region).

7. When I lived in Hong Kong in the early 1960s, those were certainly my impressions.

8. Adrian Roon, *Place Names of the World*, 2nd ed. (Jefferson, N.C.: MacFarland, 2005), p. 168.

9. Kevin Bishop and Annabel Roberts, *China's Imperial Way: Retracing an Historical Trade and Communications Route from Beijing to Hong Kong* (Hong Kong: Guidebook Company, 1997), p. 218.

10. Fanny W. Y. Fung, "Excavation at MTR Site Could Help Prove Song Dynasty's Links to Hong Kong," *South China Morning Post*, June 2, 2014 (OSC CHR2014060201808929).

11. GDPs are in terms of purchasing power parity. The eight economies were Russia, Britain, France, Prussia, Italy, the United States, Japan, and Spain. See Angus Madisson, *Contours of the World Economy, 1–2030 A.D.* (Oxford University Press, 2007), p. 379.

12. For a solid history of Hong Kong, see Steve Tsang, *A Modern History of Hong Kong* (London: I. B. Tauris, 2004).

13. James Hayes, *The Great Difference: Hong Kong's New Territories and Its People, 1898–2004* (Hong Kong University Press, 2006).

14. Business and community leaders served this same linkage role in cities in imperial China and in Chinese minority communities in Southeast Asia and the United States. See Brian C. H. Fong, "State-Society Conflicts under Hong Kong's Hybrid Regime: Government Coalition Building and Civil Society Challenges," *Asian Survey* 53 (September–October 2013), pp. 854–82.

15. On this subject, see Suzanne Pepper, *Keeping Democracy at Bay: Hong Kong and the Challenge of Chinese Political Reform* (New York: Roman & Littlefield, 2008).

16. For the comprehensive treatment of the wartime period, see Philip Snow, *The Fall of Hong Kong: Britain, China, and the Japanese Occupation* (Yale University Press, 2003). Snow provides a vivid account of the humiliation of the British (pp. 91–148).

17. Leo F. Goodstadt, *Uneasy Partners: The Conflict between Public Interest and Private Profit in Hong Kong*, 2nd ed. (Hong Kong University Press, 2009), pp. 159–66; David Faure, *Colonialism and the Hong Kong Mentality* (Hong Kong University, Center of Asian Studies, 2003), pp. 32–33.

18. Siu-Keung Cheung, "Reunification through Water and Food: The Other Battle for Lives and Bodies in China's Hong Kong Policy," *China Quarterly* 220 (December 2014), pp. 1012–32.

19. Census and Statistics Department, Hong Kong SAR Government (henceforth: Census and Statistics Department), "GDP by Major Expenditure Component, in Chained (2012) Dollars," Table 1(c), *2014 Gross Domestic Product*, February 2015 (www.censtatd.gov.hk/hkstat/sub/sp250.jsp?productCode=B1030002), p. 14.

20. Fong, "State-Society Conflicts under Hong Kong's Hybrid Regime."

21. Christine Loh, *Underground Front: The Chinese Communist Party in Hong Kong* (Hong Kong University Press, 2010).

22. On the riots and the colonial government's response, see Robert Bickers and Ray Yep, eds., *May Days in Hong Kong: Riot and Emergency in 1967* (Hong Kong University Press, 2009).

23. For an excellent series of articles on Hong Kong's contribution to transforming various economic sectors in China, see *Asian Survey* 51 (July–August 2011).

24. Census and Statistics Department, "GDP by Major Expenditure Component, in Chained (2012) Dollars."

25. John Darwin, "Hong Kong in British Decolonisation," in *Hong Kong's Transitions, 1842–1997,* edited by Judith M. Brown and Rosemary Foot (London: Palgrave Macmillan, 1997), p. 16.

26. "Vital Principle to Hong Kong," *China Daily Asia-Pacific,* May 20, 2014 (OSC CHR2014052013985002).

27. See Pepper, *Keeping Democracy at Bay.*

28. Wm. Roger Louis, "Hong Kong: The Critical Phase, 1945–1949," *American Historical Review* 102 (October 1997), pp. 1052–84 (cited passage on p. 1065).

29. Goodstadt, *Uneasy Partners,* p. 57; Chi-kwan Mark, *Hong Kong and the Cold War: Anglo-American Relations, 1949–1957* (Oxford University Press, 2004), p. 29.

30. Ambrose Yeo-chi King, "Administrative Absorption of Politics in Hong Kong: Emphasis on the Grass Roots Level," *Asian Survey* 15 (May 1975), p. 431.

31. Steve Tsang of the University of Nottingham goes so far to conclude that "the people of Hong Kong did not [demand democracy in the 1970s] because they did not need to." The British administration "possessed the characteristics of a [benign] traditional Chinese political order: efficiency, fairness, honesty, benevolent paternalism, and non-intrusion into people's lives." See Tsang, *A Modern History of Hong Kong,* p. 197.

32. Dan Slater of the University of Chicago concludes that Malaya and Singapore "had literally become police states" by the early 1950s. See Dan Slater, "Strong-State Democratization in Malaysia and Singapore," *Journal of Democracy* 23 (April 2012), p. 21.

33. Steve Yui-sang Tsang, *Democracy Shelved: Great Britain, China, and Attempts at Constitutional Reform in Hong Kong, 1945–1952* (Oxford University Press, 1988), pp. 103–04.

34. Goodstadt, *Uneasy Partners,* p. 51.

35. Ibid., pp. 37–47. On policing, Hong Kong mixed the civil policing model common in Britain and the paramilitary model found in Northern Ireland and many colonies. See Georgina Sinclair, "'Hong Kong Headaches': Policing in the 1967 Disturbance," in *May Days in Hong Kong: Riot and Emergency in 1967,* edited by Robert Bickers and Ray Yep (Hong Kong University Press, 2009), pp. 89–104.

36. Mark, *Hong Kong and the Cold War,* p. 70.

37. Stephan Ortmann, *Politics and Change in Singapore and Hong Kong* (New York: Routledge, 2010), pp. 46–69.

38. Loh, *Underground Front.*

39. Goodstadt, *Uneasy Partners;* Ortmann, *Politics and Change in Singapore and Hong Kong,* pp. 49–70, 97–100.

40. The only other British examples are Gibraltar and Cyprus. Spain ceded Gibraltar to Britain in 1703, but still claims it. Cyprus belonged to the Ottoman Empire up until 1914, when it became part of the British Empire. As the successor state to the Ottomans, Turkey therefore has a historical connection to the island. But Britain did

not return Cyprus to Turkey; instead it granted it independence in 1960. The situation was complicated because a majority of the population was Greek. Pro-Greece forces carried out a coup in 1974. Turkey invaded the island in 1975 and still occupies the northern portion to this day.

41. Louis, "Hong Kong: The Critical Phase," p. 1069. Although London asserted that legally Hong Kong Island and Lower Kowloon had been ceded by China outright and in perpetuity, some British officials had recognized even before World War II that the three parts of the colony were too integrated socially and economically to attempt to return only the New Territories.

42. Mark, *Hong Kong and the Cold War,* p. 29.

43. There was only a grain of truth in Zhou's fear. Singapore was indeed moving to self-government, but the stimulus was the demand of local political forces, which Britain accommodated. See "People's Action Party," in *Singapore: A Country Study* (Washington, D.C.: Library of Congress Federal Research Division, 1991) (https://cdn .loc.gov/master/frd/frdcstdy/si/singaporecountry00lepo/singaporecountry00lepo .pdf). The pressures in Hong Kong for more democracy were tepid by comparison (see Pepper, *Keeping Democracy at Bay,* pp. 135–36). An extract of the key document suggests that Zhou's message was not a formal and official PRC government demarche, but more of an alert. See also Gwynn Guilford, "The Secret History of Hong Kong's Stillborn Democracy," *Quartz,* October 10, 2014 (www.qz.com/279013/the_secret _history_of_hong_kongs_stillborn_democracy).

44. Mark Roberti, *The Fall of Hong Kong: China's Triumph and Britain's Betrayal,* 2nd ed. (New York: John Wiley, 1996), p. 10.

45. Ibid., p. 10. UN norms, expressed in Article 73 of the Charter and General Assembly Resolution 1514, established that colonial powers had the obligation to facilitate self-government and political independence. See United Nations Charter, "Chapter XI: Declaration Regarding Non-Self-Governing Territories" (www.un .org/en/documents/charter/chapter11.shtml); United Nations, General Assembly Resolution 1514, "Declaration on the Granting of Independence to Colonial Countries and Peoples," December 14, 1960 (www.un.org/en/decolonization/declaration .shtml).

46. Lawrence Durrell, *Bitter Lemons of Cyprus* (New York: Open Road Integrated Media, 1957).

47. Alvin Y. So, "Hong Kong's Problematic Democratic Transition: Power Dependency or Business Hegemony?" *Journal of Asian Studies* 59 (May 2000), pp. 359–81. See also Shiu-hing Lo, *The Politics of Democratization in Hong Kong* (New York: St. Martin's Press, 1997), pp. 121–31, 137–72.

48. Lau Siu-kai, ed., *The First Tung Chee-hwa Administration: The First Five Years of the Hong Kong Special Administrative Region* (Chinese University Press, 2002); Ming K. Chan and Alvin Y. So, eds., *Crisis and Transformation in China's Hong Kong* (Armonk, N.Y.: M. E. Sharpe, 2002).

49. Hong Kong Transition Project, *Constitutional Reform in Hong Kong: Round Three* (Hong Kong, June 2013) (www.hktp.org/list/round-3-of-constitutional.pdf), pp. 57, 65.

50. Hong Kong's economy was not immune from the 2008 financial crisis, although it was able to recover faster than the Asian financial crisis, hitting 6 percent average annual GDP growth from 2010 to 2014. See Census and Statistics Department, "Table 030: Gross Domestic Product (GDP), implicit price deflator of GDP and per capita GDP" (www.censtatd.gov.hk/hkstat/sub/sp250.jsp?subjectID =250&tableID=030&ID=0&productType=8).

51. Alvin So, "The Development of Post-Modernist Social Movements in the Hong Kong Special Administrative Region," in *East Asian Social Movements: Power, Protest, and Change in a Dynamic Region,* edited by Jeffrey Broadbent and Vicky Broadbent (New York: Springer, 2011), p. 366–69; Joseph Y. S. Cheng, *The July 1 Protest Rally: Interpreting a Historic Event* (City University of Hong Kong Press, 2005).

52. Census and Statistics Department, "Hong Kong 2011 Population Census— Summary Results" (www.censtatd.gov.hk/hkstat/sub/sp170.jsp?productCode=B112 0055).

53. Liu Yang, "Influx of Mainland Visitors Adds Fuel to Hong Kong's Political Warfare," *Global Times,* March 30, 2014 (OSC CHO2014400130453493).

54. Those in Hong Kong who fear the consequences of populism have something of a point: democratization tends to foster demands for more budgetary resources and for social welfare. See Stephan Haggard and Robert R. Kaufman, *Development, Democracy, and Welfare States: Latin America, East Asia, and Eastern Europe* (Princeton University Press, 2008).

55. I am grateful to one of the anonymous reviewers of an early manuscript of this work for suggesting the category of peripheral territories.

Chapter Two: Negotiating Hong Kong's Political System

1. For good accounts, see Robert Cottrell, *The End of Hong Kong: The Secret Diplomacy of Imperial Retreat* (London: John Murray, 1993); Steve Tsang, *Hong Kong: An Appointment with China* (London: I. B. Tauris, 1997); Mark Roberti, *The Fall of Hong Kong: China's Triumph and Britain's Betrayal,* 2nd ed. (New York: John Wiley, 1996); Jonathan Dimbleby, *The Last Governor: Chris Patten and the Handover of Hong Kong* (London: Warner Books, 1997).

2. Cottrell, *The End of Hong Kong,* p. 95.

3. Percy Craddock, *Experiences of China* (London: John Murray, 1994), p. 178. The Hong Kong governor Edward Youde was another person who felt a responsibility to the people of the territory. Percy Craddock, the principal architect of the British negotiating position, wrote that Youde "was driven to move from the centre position to one more nearly corresponding to that of his constituents" (186).

4. Ibid., p. 185. Craddock referred to this as the "first finesse," but in bridge, a finesse is a move designed to present one's opponent with a no-win choice. What Craddock did was cover Britain's retreat from its own no-win situation.

5. Roberti, *The Fall of Hong Kong,* p. 55.

6. Ibid., p. 97.

7. Ibid., p. 117–18.

8. Cottrell, *The End of Hong Kong,* pp. 158, 173.

9. Ibid., 106.

10. Craddock, in *Experiences of China,* reports that the Chinese "objected to us citing Hong Kong opinion, insisting that they knew its people better than we did" (211).

11. Roberti, *The Fall of Hong Kong,* pp. 98–99. At this time, there was also confusion on the meaning of the word "accountable" in the draft provision that the chief executive should be accountable to the legislature. The Chinese had a narrow meaning (as in accounting for expenditure) while the British had a broader and more metaphorical definition.

12. Cottrell, *The End of Hong Kong,* pp. 164–66; Roberti, *The Fall of Hong Kong,* p. 111.

13. Roberti, *The Fall of Hong Kong,* p. 112.

14. Ibid., p. 142.

15. "Speech at a Meeting with the Members of the Committee for Drafting the Basic Law of the Hong Kong Special Administrative Region," April 16, 1987, *Selected Works of Deng Xiaoping* 3 (https://dengxiaopingworks.wordpress.com/2013/03/18/speech-at-a-meeting-with-the-members-of-the-committee-for-drafting-the-basic-law-of-the-hong-kong-special-administrative-region).

16. Roberti, *The Fall of Hong Kong,* pp. 252–58, 265.

17. Ibid., p. 271, 278, 283.

18. Ibid., p. 277.

19. Craddock, *Experiences of China,* p. 228.

20. The Basic Law of the Hong Kong Special Administrative Region of the People's Republic of China (website; henceforth: Basic Law), "Basic Law Full Text, Annex I: Method for the Selection of the Chief Executive of the Hong Kong Special Administrative Region" (www.basiclaw.gov.hk/en/basiclawtext/images/basiclaw_full_text_en.pdf), pp. 53–55.

21. Basic Law, articles 45 and 68 (www.basiclaw.gov.hk/pda/en/basiclawtext/chapter_4.html).

22. UN, Human Rights, Office of the High Commissioner, International Covenant on Civil and Political Rights (www.ohchr.org/en/professionalinterest/pages/ccpr.aspx), and the International Covenant on Economic, Social and Cultural Rights (www.ohchr.org/Documents/ProfessionalInterest/cescr.pdf).

23. Basic Law, article 39, p. 13.

24. Roberti, *The Fall of Hong Kong,* pp. 171–72, 180–81.

25. Basic Law, article 19, pp. 7–8. Questions of fact concerning acts of state would be secured from the Central People's Government through the chief executive.

26. James Hayes, *The Great Difference: Hong Kong's New Territories and Its People, 1898–2004,* paperback edition (Hong Kong: Hong Kong University Press, 2012), pp. 123, 16–65.

27. Roberti, *The Fall of Hong Kong,* p. 100.

28. Ibid., pp. 101, 119.

29. Ibid., p. 102.

30. Ibid., p. 102.

31. Ibid., pp. 119–20, 156.

32. Ibid., pp. 158–63, 179, 187, 190–91, 195, 213.

33. Craddock, *Experiences of China*, p. 219.

34. Roberti, *The Fall of Hong Kong*, pp. 259, 260, 265, 268–70, 280 (cited passage on p. 259). For Craddock's ambivalent yet on balance pessimistic view of the proposal, see his *Experiences of China*, p. 228.

35. "Chapter 383: Hong Kong Human Rights Ordinance" (June 30, 1997 version) (www.legislation.gov.hk/blis_pdf.nsf/6799165D2FEE3FA94825755E0033E5 32/AE5E078A7CF8E845482575EE007916D8/$FILE/CAP_383_e_b5.pdf).

36. Tony Carty, "Hong Kong's Electoral Standoff: the Bigger Picture," *South China Morning Post*, May, 12, 2015 (OSC CHR2015051235425955).

37. Roberti, *The Fall of Hong Kong*, pp. 295, 299.

38. The author heard Patten's report of this colloquy when the governor met with members of Congress in Washington, D.C., in the spring of 1993.

39. Dimbleby, *The Last Governor*, p. 291.

40. Roberti, *The Fall of Hong Kong*, pp. 296–301.

41. Anthony B. L. Cheung, "The Changing Political System: Executive-Led Government or 'Disabled' Governance?," in *The First Tung Chee-hwa Administration*, edited by Lau Siu-kai (Chinese University Press, 2002), p. 49.

42. For an analysis that reaches a similar conclusion, see Richard Baum, "Britain's 'Betrayal' of Hong Kong: A Second Look," *Journal of Contemporary China* 8 (March 1999), pp. 9–28.

43. This discussion is based on Ma Ngok, "Negotiating Democracy and 'High Autonomy': The 2010 Political Reform," in *Negotiating Autonomy in Greater China: Hong Kong and Its Sovereign Before and After 1997*, edited by Ray Yep (Copenhagen: Nordic Institute of Asian Studies, 2013), pp. 242–68.

44. "The Interpretation by the Standing Committee of the National People's Congress of Article 7 of Annex I and Article III of Annex II to the Basic Law of the Hong Kong Special Administrative Region of the People's Republic of China," adopted April 6, 2004, in Hong Kong Special Administration Government, "Methods for Selecting the Chief Executive in 2016 and for Forming the Legislative Council in 2017: Consultation Document," December 2013 (www.legco.gov.hk/yr13-14 /english/panels/ca/papers/ca1209-cdoc20131204-e.pdf), pp. 48–50.

45. Decision of the Standing Committee of the National People's Congress on Issues Relating to the Methods for Selecting the Chief Executive of the Hong Kong Special Administrative Region in 2007 and for Forming the Legislative Council of the HKSAR in 2008, adopted April 26, 2004, National People's Congress website (www.npc.gov.cn/englishnpc/Law/2007-12/12/content_1383886.htm).

46. Ibid, pp. 250–51. The Hong Kong journalist Frank Ching argues that Beijing, by dictating this five-step process, reneged on a 1993 commitment by the then director of the PRC Hong Kong and Macau Affairs Office that Hong Kong itself would decide on its own when the whole of the Legislative Council would be chosen by universal suffrage. See Frank Ching, "Beijing's Broken Promise on Hong Kong Democracy

Shattered Our Trust," *South China Morning Post,* December 16, 2014 (OSC CHR2014121623718631).

47. Ho-fung Hung and Iam-chong Ip, "Hong Kong's Democratic Movement and the Making of China's Offshore Civil Society," *Asian Survey* 52 (May–June 2012), pp. 512–13 (cited passage on p. 513).

48. Ma, "Negotiating Democracy and 'High Autonomy,'" pp. 261–62.

49. *Wikipedia,* s.v. "Democratic Party (Hong Kong)," last modified February 28, 2016 (http://en.wikipedia.org/wiki/Democratic_Party_(Hong_Kong)).

50. The elections were done on a party-list proportional representation basis, using the largest remainder method and the Hare quota.

51. Based on research by Maeve Whelan-Wuest, Foreign Policy program, Brookings Institution; documentation available in the author's files.

52. Ngok, "Negotiating Democracy and 'High Autonomy,'" p. 58.

53. Lauren Higgers, "Hong Kong's Umbrella Revolution Isn't Over Yet," *New York Times Magazine,* February 18, 2015 (www.nytimes.com/2015/02/22/magazine /hong-kongs-umbrella-revolution-isnt-over-yet.html).

54. Keith Bradsher, "Beijing Switches Sides in the Race for Hong Kong's Chief Executive," *New York Times,* March 22, 2012 (www.nytimes.com/2012/03/22/world /asia/beijing-switches-support-in-race-for-hong-kong-chief.html). In dictating the outcome, Beijing ironically accommodated to the public will as measured by polls, even as it continued to deny universal-suffrage elections.

55. Guillermo O'Donnell and Philippe C. Schmitter, *Transitions from Authoritarian Rule: Tentative Conclusions about Uncertain Democracies* (Johns Hopkins University Press, 1986), pp. 17–28.

56. On the difficulties in the democratic camp, see Joseph Y. S. Cheng, "Introduction: Causes and Implications of the July 1 Protest Rally in Hong Kong," in *The July 1 Protest Rally: Interpreting a Historic Event,* edited by Joseph Y. S. Cheng (City University of Hong Kong Press, 2005), pp. 13–18.

57. "Cheng Minzhudang buhui yu Beijing Jiu Zhenggai Dandu Tanpan: Ho Chun-ren: Puxuan Xufu Guoji Biaojun" [Hu Chunyan declares that the Democratic Party will not negotiate separately with Beijing on political reform; universal suffrage must be consistent with international standards], *Apple Daily,* September 19, 2013 (OSC CHL2013091920970563); Tanna Chong: "'I Won't Negotiate on Chief Executive Screening,' Says Lawmaker Fung," *South China Morning Post,* October 10, 2013 (OSC CHR2013101003971468).

Chapter Three: Hong Kong's Liberal Oligarchy: Civil and Political Rights

1. Larry Diamond, "Elections without Democracy: Thinking about Hybrid Regimes," *Journal of Democracy* 13 (April 2002), pp. 21–35.

2. Benjamin Wong, "Political Meritocracy in Singapore: Lessons from the PAP Government," in *The East Asian Challenge for Democracy: Political Meritocracy in Comparative Perspective,* edited by Daniel A. Bell and Chenyang Li (Cambridge University Press, 2013), pp. 288–313.

3. Tanna Chong, "How a Handful of Voters Elect 30 Lawmakers," *South China Morning Post,* February 6, 2014 (OSC CHR2014020601873029); "Structural Defects in Constitutional System," *Ming Pao,* January 7, 2014 (OSC CHR2014010721525510). Five additional functional-constituency members are drawn from members of the district councils and are picked by a citywide ballot. So indirectly their selection reflects the sentiments of the total electorate.

4. Website of Freedom House, "Territorial Rankings and Status FIW 1973–2013" (spreadsheet), 2013 (https://freedomhouse.org/report/freedom-world/2015/hong-kong).

5. For example, during the debate over reform of the electoral system, there was a steady stream of statements from PRC and Hong Kong officials and articles in the pro-Beijing media on how any change had to be consistent with the Basic Law; see Carrie Lam, "Hong Kong Must Accept Basic Realities to Achieve Universal Suffrage in 2017," *South China Morning Post,* March 3, 2014 (OSC CHR2014030301222887). Carrie Lam is the chief secretary of the Hong Kong SAR government.

6. Kang-chung Ng, "Hong Kong's Rule of Law Ranks 16th in the World," *South China Morning Post*, March 6, 2014 (OSC CHR2014030601523224).

7. U.S. Department of State, "China (Includes Tibet, Hong Kong, and Macau) 2014: Human Rights Report" (www.state.gov/documents/organization/236648.pdf), pp. 97–102 (cited passages on p. 102).

8. Hong Kong expert on the judicial system, author's interview, May 2015.

9. Website of Transparency International, "Corruption Perceptions Index 2014: Results" (www.transparency.org/cpi2014/results).

10. Leo F. Goodstadt, *Uneasy Partners: The Conflict between Public Interest and Private Profit in Hong Kong*, 2nd ed. (Hong Kong University Press, 2009), pp. 139–57.

11. Tsang, *A Modern History of Hong Kong* (London: I. B. Tauris, 2004), p. 276.

12. Ian Scott, "Institutional Design and Corruption Prevention in Hong Kong," *Journal of Contemporary China* 22 (2013), p. 92.

13. Ibid., pp. 88–91.

14. U.S. Department of State, "China 2014 Human Rights Report," p. 114.

15. Ibid., pp. 104–5.

16. The Liaison Office of the Central People's Government in Hong Kong is the sole stakeholder of a holding company, Guangdong New Culture, that controls various PRC-origin publishing outlets, including *Wen Wei Po, Ta Kung Pao,* and three publishing and distribution companies. See "Zhonglianban Wokong Lianhe Chuban, Jituan Yong Sanda Shuju, Jian Longduan Faxing; Yiyuan Zhi Shewei Jibenfa" [Liaison Office controls Sino United Publishing and the three big book stores; also monopolizes publishing; legislator charges this violates the Basic Law], *Apple Daily,* April 9, 2015 (OSC CHR2016040923812833).

17. Alex Lo, "Hong Kong Protesters Attack Leung Chun-ying with Impunity," *South China Morning Post,* January 29, 2014 (OSC CHR2014012900953373).

18. Jeffie Lam, "Mainland Authorities Seize Thousands of Rolls of Toilet Paper Printed with Hong Kong Leader's Face," *South China Morning Post,* February 7, 2015 (OSC CHR2015020663317186).

19. The papers were *South China Morning Post, Apple Daily, Ming Pao, Sing Tao Jih Pao,* and *Wen Wei Po.*

20. Chris Buckley, "Exposés of China's Elite a Big Lure in Hong Kong," *New York Times,* May 19, 2013 (www.nytimes.com/2013/05/19/world/asia/exposes-of-chinas -elite-a-big-lure-in-hong-kong.html).

21. On tightened restrictions at the border, see Wang Xiangwei, "A Tall Tell All Tale from the Dark Side of Chinese Power," *South China Morning Post,* February 9, 2015 (OSC CHR2015020877747258). On Bao Pu's publishing activities and how he evaluates mainland pressure, see Louisa Lim, *The People's Republic of Amnesia: Tiananmen Revisited* (Oxford University Press, 2014), pp. 161–64. Hong Kong Christian leaders who sponsor activities on the mainland face similar problems. Unrestricted in the Hong Kong SAR, they are sometimes picked up by the authorities in the PRC. See Javier C. Hernandez and Crystal Tse, "Hong Kong Christian Groups Feel New Scrutiny from Mainland," *New York Times,* August 26, 2015 (www.nytimes.com /2015/08/27/world/asia/hong-kong-christian-groups-feel-new-scrutiny-from -mainland.html).

22. Hong Kong has an array of commercial broadcast and cable television and radio stations, for which profit considerations are paramount. The concern about censorship and self-censorship applies to print media.

23. U.S. Department of State, "China 2014 Human Rights Report," p. 109.

24. "Number of Society [*sic*] Registered under Society Ordinance, Cap.151 (Running Total)," Social Indicators of Hong Kong, accessed January 6, 2014 (http:// socialindicators.org.hk/en/indicators/strength_of_civil_society/3.1). It is not clear from this source whether the running total takes account of organizations that have been dissolved.

25. U.S. Department of State, "China 2014 Human Rights Report," p. 123.

26. Ibid., p. 126. See also U.S. Department of State, "Trafficking in Persons Report, June 2014" (www.state.gov/documents/organization/226846.pdf), pp. 198–200.

27. Amnesty International, *Exploited for Profit, Failed by Governments: Indonesian Migrant Domestic Workers Trafficked to Hong Kong,* 2013 (www.amnesty.org/en /documents/asa17/029/2013/en/).

28. Michael Forsythe, "Hong Kong Woman Sentenced to 6 Years for Abusing Indonesian Maid," *New York Times,* February 27, 2015 (www.nytimes.com/2015/02 /28/world/asia/hong-kong-woman-sentenced-to-6-years-for-abusing-indonesian -maid.html).

29. "Racist Hong Kong Is Still a Fact," *South China Morning Post,* May 25, 2013 (OSC CHR2013112220112334).

30. U.S. Department of State, "China (Includes Tibet, Hong Kong, and Macau) 2013 International Religious Freedom Report" (www.state.gov/documents /organization/222339.pdf), p. 39.

31. According to James Tong, professor of political science at UCLA, the regime's crackdown on Falun Gong "was a powerful show of force that testifies to the centrality of state monopoly of coercive and propaganda institutions and the efficacy of the

sanctioning and monitoring capacity of the communist state." See James W. Tong, *Revenge of the Forbidden City: The Suppression of the Falungong in China, 1999–2005* (Oxford University Press, 2009), p. 225.

32. U.S. Department of State, "China 2013 International Religious Freedom Report," p. 41.

33. U.S. Department of State, "China 2014 Human Rights Report," p. 110.

34. Edmund W. Cheng, "How Feedback Matters: The Diffusion of Vigorous Activism in Postcolonial Hong Kong," conference paper presented at conference "The Boundaries of Democracy: New Developments in Hong Kong and Taiwan Relations with China Mainland," Contemporary China Studies Workshop, Hong Kong University, October 10, 2014 (author's collection), pp. 6–7.

35. For example, website of Hong Kong SAR, "Special Traffic Arrangements on Hong Kong Island for Public Procession," February 28, 2014 (OSC 2014022837834901).

36. "Tiananmen Square Anniversary Prompts Campaign of Silence," *New York Times*, May 27, 2014 (www.nytimes.com/2014/05/28/world/asia/tiananmen-square-anniversary-prompts-campaign-of-silence.html).

37. See, for example, Tan Wen-tien, "Harmony Will Lead to Peace; Perversity Will Lead to Hostility," *Ta Kung Pao*, June 29, 2006 (OSC CPP20060705715034), which charged that Falun Gong had an "anti-China motive."

38. Severn Anderson, "Hong Kong 2005: Changes in Leadership and Issues for Congress," Congressional Research Service, Report RL33013, July 15, 2005, pp. 12–13.

39. U.S. Department of State, "China 2014 Human Rights Report," p. 112.

40. The Basic Law of the Hong Kong Special Administrative Region of the People's Republic of China (website), "Basic Law Full Text, Chapter VIII: Interpretation and Amendment of the Basic Law" (www.basiclaw.gov.hk/en/basiclawtext/chapter_8.html).

41. Website of Hong Kong SAR government, "Interpretation: A 'Legal and Constitutional Option,'" May 18, 1999 (www.info.gov.hk/gia/general/199905/18/0518159.htm).

42. Eric C. Ip, "Constitutional Competition between the Hong Kong Court of Final Appeal and the Chinese National People's Congress Standing Committee: A Game Theory Perspective," *Law & Social Inquiry* 39 (Fall 2014), pp. 824–48.

43. Kemal Bokary, "The Rule of Law in Hong Kong Fifteen Years after the Handover," *Columbia Journal of Transnational Law* 51 (May 2013), pp. 294, 299.

44. Stuart Lau, "Hong Kong Justice Chief Slammed in Row over Judicial Rulings Related to Occupy Protests," *South China Morning Post*, March 31, 2015 (www.scmp.com/news/hong-kong/article/1752316/hong-kong-justice-chief-slammed-row-over-judicial-rulings-related).

45. Dennis Kwok, "Overworked Justice System at Risk," *South China Morning Post*, September 13, 2013 (www.scmp.com/comment/insight-opinion/article/1308849/overworked-justice-system-risk).

46. Joseph Y. S. Cheng, *The July 1 Protest Rally: Interpreting a Historic Event* (City University of Hong Kong Press, 2005).

47. U.S. Department of State, "2013 Human Rights Report: China (Includes Tibet, Hong Kong, and Macau)" (www.state.gov/documents/organization/220401.pdf), p. 110.

48. Jeffie Lam, "Press Freedom in Hong Kong at 'Low Level,' Journalists' Study Finds," *South China Morning Post,* April 23, 2014 (OSC CHR2014042332716525); Joanna Chiu, "Foreign Journalists Call for Greater International Scrutiny of Hong Kong Press Freedom," *South China Morning Post,* April 1, 2014 (OSC CHR2014040134507084).

49. Stuart Lau, "Beijing Blamed as Hong Kong's Press Freedom Declines," *South China Morning Post,* February 13, 2014 (OSC CHR2014021301526734); Jennifer Ngo, "Public's Trust in Hong Kong Media Sinks to All-Time Low, Credibility Poll Shows," *South China Morning Post,* January 2, 2014 (www.scmp.com/news/hong-kong/article/1395930/publics-trust-hong-kong-media-sinks-all-time-low-credibility-poll).

50. Chiu, "Foreign Journalists Call for Greater International Scrutiny of Hong Kong Press Freedom."

51. "Threatened Harbor: Encroachments on Press Freedom in Hong Kong" (www.pen.org/sites/default/files/PEN-HK-report_1.16_lowres.pdf).

52. Chris Buckley and Michael Forsythe, "Press Freedom in Hong Kong under Threat, Report Says," *New York Times,* January 17, 2015 (www.nytimes.com/2015/01/17/world/asia/press-freedom-in-hong-kong-under-threat-report-says.html).

53. Jake van der Kamp, "Some Myths About Self Censorship and Threats to Press Freedom," *South China Morning Post,* May 3, 2015 (OSC CHL2015050268036739).

54. Ho Lok-Sang, "HK Needs to Set Limits on Freedom of Speech and Press," *China Daily (Asia-Pacific),* May 7, 2014 (OSC CHR2014050705134877).

55. Cathy Holcombe, "Internet Now Subsidising Struggling Newspapers," *South China Morning Post,* May 25, 2015 (OSC CHR2015052603342967); former Hong Kong journalist, author's interview, May 2015.

56. Francis L. F. Lee and Joseph M. Chan, "Professionalism, Political Orientation, and Perceived Self-Censorship: A Survey Study of Hong Kong Journalists," *Issues & Studies* 44 (March 2008), pp. 205–238.

57. Michael Forsythe and Neil Gough, "Hong Kong Media Worries Over China's Reach as Ads Disappear," *New York Times,* June 11, 2014 (www.nytimes.com/2014/06/12/business/international/hong-kong-media-worries-over-chinas-reach-as-ads-disappear.html).

58. Duihua Foundation, "Hong Kong Residents Adrift in Mainland Prisons?" *Human Rights Journal,* April 9, 2014 (www.duihuahrjournal.org/2014/04/hong-kong-residents-adrift-in-mainland.html).

59. Angela Meng, "Shenzhen Court Gives Hong Kong Publisher Yiu Man-tin 10-year Prison Sentence," *South China Morning Post,* May 8, 2014 (OSC CHR2014050801257995); Chi-fai Cheung, "New Paper Has No Link to Mainland, Owners Insist," *South China Morning Post,* February 8, 2014 (www.scmp.com/news/hong-kong/article/1423381/new-paper-has-no-link-mainland-owners-insist); "Hong Kong Paper Ousts Top Editor, Stirring Concern," *New York Times,* January

30, 2014 (www.nytimes.com/2014/01/31/world/asia/hong-kong-paper-ousts-top -editor-stirring-concern); "Hong Kong Editor Whose Ouster Stirred Protests Is Slashed," *New York Times*, February 25, 2014 (sinosphere.blogs.nytimes.com/2014 /02/25/hong-kong-editor-whose-ouster-stirred-protests-is-reported-stabbed); "Hong Kong Man Seeking to Issue Book About Xi Is Held in China," *New York Times*, January 28, 2014 (www.nytimes.com/2014/01/29/world/asia/publisher-of -book-critical-of-chinas-leader-is-arrested.html).

60. Ian Johnson, "Lawsuit Over Banned Memoir Asks China to Explain Censorship," *New York Times,* April 25, 2015 (www.nytimes.com/2015/04/26/world/asia /china-lawsuit-over-banned-li-rui-memoir-censorship.html).

61. Kin-man Chan, "Uncertainty, Acculturation, and Corruption in Hong Kong," *International Journal of Public Administration* 24 (2001), pp. 900–928.

62. "Complaints to Hong Kong Graft Buster Agency Drop for the Third Year," *South China Morning Post,* December 17, 2014 (www.scmp.com/news/hong-kong /article/1663941/complaints-hong-kong-graft-buster-agency-drop-third-year).

63. Samuel Chan, "More Civil Servants Abusing Power for Personal Gain: ICAC Watchdog," *South China Morning Post,* January 27, 2014 (OSC CHR2014012720431838); Tony Cheung, "Timothy Tong Scandal Deals 'Distressing' Blow to ICAC: Carrie Lam," *South China Morning Post,* February 19, 2014 (OSC CHR2014022038275501); Lana Lam, "Government urged to boost junior ICAC salaries to police levels," *South China Morning Post,* March 9, 2014 (www.scmp.com/news/hong-kong/article/1443822/government-urged-boost -junior-icac-salaries-police-levels).

64. Stuart Lau and others, "Raphael Hui and Thomas Kwok Found Guilty of Bribery in Hong Kong's Biggest Graft Trial," *South China Morning Post,* December 19, 2014 (OSC CHR2014121941109176).

65. Phillip Bowring, "Raphael Hui Trial Leaves Nagging Questions," *South China Morning Post,* December 28, 2014 (www.scmp.com/news/article/1668430 /rafael-hui-trial-leaves-nagging-questions).

66. U.S. Department of State, "2009 Human Rights Report: China (Includes Tibet, Hong Kong, and Macau)" (www.state.gov/j/drl/rls/hrrpt/2009/eap/135989 .htm).

Chapter Four: Hong Kong's Liberal Oligarchy: Economic and Political Inequality

1. Census and Statistics Department, Government of the Hong Kong Special Administrative Region (henceforth: Census and Statistics Department), "Hong Kong Annual Digest of Statistics" (2010, 2011 and 2015 editions) (www.censtatd.gov.hk /hkstat/sub/sp140.jsp?productCode=B1010003). Hong Kong's currency, the Hong Kong dollar, has been pegged to the U.S. dollar since 1983. If context requires specifying which currency is meant, HK$ or US$ will be used.

2. Ibid., "2011 Census: Thematic Report: Household Income Distribution in Hong Kong," June 2012 (www.censtatd.gov.hk/hkstat/sub/sp440.jsp?productCode =B1120057), p. 8.

3. Ibid., "Table 030: Gross Domestic Product (GDP), implicit price deflator of GDP and per capita GDP" (www.censtatd.gov.hk/hkstat/sub/sp250.jsp?tableID =030&ID=0&productType=8); see longer data series table.

4. Social Indicators of Hong Kong, "Real Wage Index of Wage Workers" (www.socialindicators.org.hk/en/indicators/low_income/17.9 [accessed January 4, 2014]).

5. Informational Services Department, Hong Kong SAR government, "Hong Kong: The Facts" (www.gov.hk/en/about/abouthk/factsheets/docs/population.pdf).

6. James Davies, Rodrigo Lluberas, and Anthony Shorrocks, "Global Wealth Report," prepared for Credit Suisse Research Institute, 2014 (https://publications .credit-suisse.com/tasks/render/file/?fileID=60931FDE-A2D2-F568 -B041B58C5EA591A4), p. 33.

7. High net worth individuals are defined as "those having investable assets of US$1million or more, excluding primary residence, collectibles, consumables, and consumer durables." See Capgemini and RBC Wealth Management, "2014 Asia-Pacific Wealth Report" (www.worldwealthreport.com).

8. The Gini coefficient "is calculated from the Lorenz curve, in which cumulative family income is plotted against the number of families arranged from the poorest to the richest"; *CIA World Factbook,* Hong Kong, "Field Listing: Distribution of Family Income—Gini Index" (www.cia.gov/library/publications/the-world-factbook/fields /print_2172.html).

9. Forbes, "The World's Billionaires: 2015 Ranking" (www.forbes.com/billionaires /list [accessed March 23, 2015]).

10. "Hong Kong Poverty Line Shows Wealth Gap with One in Five Poor," *Bloomberg News,* September 29, 2013 (www.bloomberg.com/news/articles/2013-09-29 /hong-kong-poverty-line-shows-wealth-gap-with-one-in-five-poor).

11. Census and Statistics Department, "Hong Kong Poverty Situation Report 2012," September 2013 (www.povertyrelief.gov.hk/pdf/2012_Poverty_Situation_Eng.pdf); Richard Wong, "Demystifying Hong Kong's Poverty Rate," *South China Morning Post,* October 27, 2015 (www.scmp.com/business/article/1872735/demystifying-hong-kongs -poverty-rate).

12. Jennifer Ngo, "Bad Government Policy Worsens Poverty, Says Ex-Adviser Goodstadt," *South China Morning Post,* September 28, 2013 (www.scmp.com/news /hong-kong/article/1319571/bad-government-policy-worsens-poverty-says-ex -adviser-goodstadt).

13. Social Indicators of Hong Kong (website), tables for various categories of household expenditures (https://socialindicators.org.hk/en/indicators/basic_statistics [accessed January 4, 2014]).

14. Ibid., "Average Monthly Household Expenditure for a Family of Four" (http:// socialindicators.org.hk/en/indicators/basic_statistics/12.6 [accessed January 4, 2014]).

15. Ibid.

16. Hong Kong Transition Project, "Constitutional Reform in Hong Kong: Round Three" (survey results), June 2013 (www.hktp.org/list/round-3-of-constitutional.pdf), p. 34.

17. Website of Hong Kong SAR government, "Hong Kong: The Facts—Education" (www.hk.gov/education.pdf).

18. Census and Statistics Department, 2011 Census, Report F304, "Persons from the Mainland Having Resided in Hong Kong for Less Than 7 Years (PMRs) Aged 15 and Over by Sex, Age Group" (www.census2011.gov.hk/en/main-table/F304.html).

19. IndexMundi, "School Enrollment, tertiary (% gross)—Country Ranking" (www.indexmundi.com/facts/indicators/SE.TER.ENRR/rankings [accessed March 23, 2015]).

20. Central Intelligence Agency, *CIA World Factbook,* China and Hong Kong "Economy" pages (https://www.cia.gov/library/publications/the-world-factbook /geos/hk.html; https://www.cia.gov/library/publications/the-world-factbook/geos/ch .html).

21. Census and Statistics Department, Quarterly Report on General Household Survey, October to December 2014, "Table 2.4: Employed Persons by Detailed Industry of Main Employment and Sex" (http://www.statistics.gov.hk/pub /B10500012014QQ04B0100.pdf), p. 27.

22. Ibid., "Table 4-3A: Employed Persons by Educational Attainment, Age and Sex (Excluding Foreign Domestic Helpers)."

23. Census and Statistics Department, 2011 Census, Report C131, "Working Population by Industry and Educational Attainment (Highest Level Completed)" (www.census2011.gov.hk/en/main-table/C131.html).

24. Ibid., "Median Monthly Wage Analysed by Sex, Age Group, Educational Attainment, Occupational Group and Industry Section (2011–2013)" (www.censtatd .gov.hk/hkstat/sub/sp210.jsp?productCode=D5250017).

25. Ibid.

26. Phila Siu, "Salaries of Hong Kong's University Graduates Dropped 20 Percent in Last 20 Years, Study Finds," *South China Morning Post,* July 29, 2015 (www .scmp.com/news/hong-kong/economy/article/1844661/salaries-hong-kongs -university-graduates-dropped-20-cent-last); Jeffie Lam, "Fewer Hong Kong Youngsters with Degrees Land Middle Class Jobs, While More Work as Clerks," *South China Morning Post*, August 3, 2015 (Open Source Center [hereafter: OSC] CHR2015080357935623).

27. Census and Statistics Department, Quarterly Report on General Household Survey, First Quarter 2015, "Unemployed Persons with a Previous Job by Detailed Previous Industry" (link to table at www.censtatd.gov.hk/hkstat/sub/sp200.jsp ?productCode=D5250022).

28. Census and Statistics Department, "Unemployment Rate by Sex and Age," August 2015 (www.censtatd.gov.hk/hkstat/sub/sp200.jsp?tableID=011&ID=0 &productType=8).

29. Social Indicators of Hong Kong, "Percentage of Youth Aged 15–19 in Low Income Households" (www.socialindicators.org.hk/en/indicators/youth /30.13).

30. University of Hong Kong, "Global Admissions Profile, 2012" (www.als.hku .hk/pdf/HKU130131.pdf), p. 4; John Tsang budget speech, "Hong Kong Budget

Speech by the Financial Secretary 2014–15," Hong Kong Special Administrative Region of the PRC website, February 26, 2014 (www.info.gov.hk/gia/general/201402 /26/P201402260264.htm).

31. Census and Statistics Department, 2011 Census, Report A106, "Population by Place of Birth, 2001, 2006, and 2011" (www.census2011.gov.hk/en/main-table /A106.html); University of Hong Kong, "Global Admissions Profile, 2012."

32. Census and Statistics Department, "Hong Kong Annual Digest of Statistics" (2014, 2008, 2007, 2006, 2005, 2004, 2003, 2002 editions) (www.censtatd.gov.hk /hkstat/sub/sp140.jsp?productCode=B1010003).

33. Census and Statistics Department, 2011 Census, Report F301, "Persons from the Mainland Having Resided in Hong Kong for Less Than 7 Years (PMRs) by Sex and Age Group, 2001, 2006 and 2011" (www.census2011.gov.hk/en/main-table /F301.html).

34. Ng Kang-chung and Mandy Zuo, "Mainland Chinese Immigrants to Hong Kong May Get Chance to Move Back," *South China Morning Post,* January 13, 2015 (OSC CHR2015011274724991).

35. See Vicky Feng, "Are Mainland Students 'Robbing Hong Kong Locals of School Places and Jobs'?" *South China Morning Post,* June 3, 2014 (OSC CHR2015011370216783).

36. In Joo Sohn (Hong Kong University), communication with the author, April 15, 2015.

37. Feng, "Are Mainland Students 'Robbing Hong Kong Locals'?"

38. Bettina Wassener and Mary Hui, "Hong Kong Rents Push Out Mom and Pop Stores," *New York Times,* July 3, 2013 (www.nytimes.com/2013/07/04/business /global/soaring-rents-in-hong-kong-push-out-mom-and-pop-stores.html).

39. Ironically, it is middle-class people who tend to participate in these movements, and the effect, perversely, is often to limit the supply of housing for themselves and people like them.

40. Hong Kong Housing Authority and Housing Department, Housing in Figures 2014, "Distribution of Population by Type of Housing" (www.housingauthority .gov.hk/en/common/pdf/about-us/publications-and-statistics/HIF.pdf). Less than 1 percent of the population lived in temporary housing in 2014.

41. Yue Chim Richard Wong, *Hong Kong Land for Hong Kong People: Fixing the Failures of Our Housing Policy* (Hong Kong University Press, 2015), p. 22.

42. Ibid., pp. 30–31.

43. Richard Wong, "Why Hong Kong's Public Housing Estates Should be Sold to Sitting Tenants," *South China Morning Post,* September 16, 2015 (www.scmp.com /comment/insight-opinion/article/1858624/why-hong-kongs-public-housing -estates-should-be-sold-sitting).

44. Ibid., pp. 83–90, for a brief history of the program.

45. Ibid., p. 30.

46. Ibid., p. 19.

47. This is the subject of Alice Poon, *Land and the Ruling Class in Hong Kong,* 2d ed. (n.p.: Enrich Professional Publishing, 2010).

48. The major firms in the market are Cheung Kong Holdings (Li Ka-shing and his family); Sun Hung Kai (the Kwok family); Henderson Land and Henderson Investment (the Lee family); New World Development (the Cheng family); Wharf Holdings, Wheelock, and i-Cable Communications (the Pao and Woo families); and the CLP Group (the Kadoorie family). In 2010, the companies controlled by the large conglomerates reportedly held 14.7 percent of the market capitalization on the Hong Kong Stock Exchange. See ibid., pp. 11–35.

49. Fanny Fung, "Three Biggest Hong Kong Developers Occupy 80pc of MTR Residential Sites, Study Shows," *South China Morning Post,* February 23, 2015 (OSC CHR2015022263936895).

50. Alex Lo, "The Forced Necessity of Hong Kong's Current Housing Target," *South China Morning Post,* January 27, 2015 (OSC CHR2015012666037961).

51. Fanny W. Y. Fung, "Only 1 in 60 Chance to Win in Great Hong Kong Flat Rush," *South China Morning Post,* January 23, 2015 (OSC CHR2015012362718421).

52. Rating and Valuation Department, Hong Kong SAR Government, "Hong Kong Property Review Monthly Supplement," April 2015 (www.rvd.gov.hk/en /property_market_statistics/index.html).

53. Social Indicators of Hong Kong, "Expenditure on Housing as Share of Total Household Expenditure" (http://socialindicators.org.hk/en/indicators/housing/8 .13 [accessed February 6, 2015]).

54. Amy Nip, "Hong Kong's 'Tiniest Flats Ever' Go on Sale for HK$2 Million," *South China Morning Post,* December 14, 2014 (www.scmp.com/property/hong -kong-china/article/1661820/modest-reception-tiny-new-flats).

55. Amy Nip, "Hong Kong Property Prices out of Reach for Most Would-Be Flat Buyers, Survey Says," *South China Morning Post,* March 23, 2015 (www.scmp.com /news/hong-kong/article/1745251/hong-kong-property-prices-out-reach-majority -would-be-flat-buyers).

56. Wong, *Hong Kong Land for Hong Kong People.*

57. Philip Bowring, "Raphael Hui Trial Leaves Nagging Questions," *South China Morning Post,* December 28, 2014 (www.scmp.com/news/article/1668430/rafael -hui-trial-leaves-nagging-questions).

58. Stephen Vines, "Housing Policy Makes Hong Kong One of World's Most Unequal Societies," *South China Morning Post,* January 22, 2015 (OSC CHR2015012170227108).

59. Tyler Cohen, "It's Not the Inequality; It's the Immobility," *New York Times,* April 3, 2015 (www.nytimes.com/2015/04/05/upshot/its-not-the-inequality-its-the -immobility.html).

60. Research Council, Legislative Office Secretariat, "Social Mobility in Hong Kong," Research Brief, Issue No. 2, 2014–2015 (January 2015) (www.legco.gov.hk/research -publications/english/1415rb02-social-mobility-in-hong-kong-20150112-e.pdf).

61. Ibid., see pp. 2, 3, 4, 5, 8–9, 1.

62. The classic treatment of the co-optation is Ambrose Yeo-chi King, "Administrative Absorption of Politics in Hong Kong: Emphasis on the Grass Roots Level," *Asian Survey* 15 (May 1975), pp. 422–39.

63. Synergynet, Governance Review Project, "Review of the Governance Performance of the HKSAR Government 2014" (in Chinese) (www.synergynet.org.hk/wp-content/uploads/2013/09/governance_2014.pdf), p. 22.

64. Leo F. Goodstadt, *Uneasy Partners: The Conflict between Public Interest and Private Profit in Hong Kong* (Hong Kong University Press, 2009), pp. 97–98, 108, 117, 126.

65. Much of this discussion is based on Anthony B. L. Cheung, "Who Advised the Hong Kong Government: The Politics of Absorption before and after 1997," *Asian Survey* 44 (November–December 2004), pp. 874–94; Christine Loh, *Underground Front: The Chinese Communist Party in Hong Kong* (University of Hong Kong Press, 2010).

66. Brian C. H. Fong, "The Partnership between the Chinese Government and Hong Kong's Capitalist Class: Implications for HKSAR Governance, 1997–2012," *China Quarterly,* no. 217 (March 2014), pp. 195–220.

67. Wing-Chung Ho, Wan-lung Lee, Chun-man Chan, Yat-nam Ng, and Yee-hung Choy, "Hong Kong's Elite Structure, Legislature and the Bleak Future of Democracy under Chinese Sovereignty," *Journal of Contemporary Asia* 40 (August 2010), pp. 466–86.

68. Cheung, "Who Advised the Hong Kong Government," p. 891.

69. Jermain T. M. Lam, "District Councils, Advisory Bodies, and Statutory Bodies," in *Contemporary Hong Kong Government and Politics,* 2nd ed., edited by Lam Wai-man, Percy Luen-tim Lui, and Wilson Wong (Hong Kong University Press, 2012), pp. 121–27.

70. Ibid., p. 893.

71. Tai-lok Lui, "Government and Business Relations since the 1997 Handover," *Hong Kong Journal Archive,* no. 10, April 2008 (www.carnegieendowment.org/hkjournal/archive/2008_summer/5.htm).

72. Christopher Jackson, "Business and Politics in Hong Kong," *Hong Kong Journal Archive,* no. 4, October 2006 (www.carnegieendowment.org/hkjournal/archive/2006_fall/jackson.htm).

73. Fong, "The Partnership between the Chinese Government and Hong Kong's Capitalist Class"; Goodstadt, *Uneasy Partners,* p. 136. One Hong Kong informant noted that the effectiveness of this lobbying depended on the protocol level of the lobbyist. The higher the level, the better the access. National People's Congress members were more likely to be successful than Chinese People's Political Consultative Conference members, and so on.

74. James Pomfret and Greg Torode, "China Extends Reach into Hong Kong to Thwart Democrats," Reuters, June 19, 2015 (www.reuters.com/article/2015/06/19/us-china-hongkong-unitedfront-insight-idUSKBN0OZ19R20150619).

75. Lyman P. Van Slyke, *Enemies and Friends: The United Front in Chinese Communist History* (Stanford University Press, 1967), p. 3.

76. Suzanne Pepper, "For Beijing, Vilifying Foreign Forces Is a Useful Strategy for Hong Kong," *South China Morning Post,* October 21, 2013 (OSC CHR20131100210310172). For a useful discussion of how the CCP uses the United

Front on the mainland, see Gerry Groot, "Chinese Growing Social Inequality Prompts Stronger Social Control," *China Brief* 16, February 23, 2016 (www.jamestown.org /programs/chinabrief/single/?tx_ttnews%5Btt_news%5D=45126&tx _ttnews%5BbackPid%5D=828&no_cache=1#.Vth0bPkrK1s).

77. Shiu-hing Lo, Wing-yat Yu, and Kwok-fai Wan, "The 1999 District Councils Elections," in *Crisis and Transformation in China's Hong Kong,* edited by Ming K. Chan and Alvin Y. So (Armonk, N.Y.: M. E. Sharpe, 2002), pp. 148–55 (cited passage on p. 154).

78. Lam, "District Councils, Advisory Bodies, and Statutory Bodies," pp. 115–18; *Wikipedia,* s.v. "Hong Kong local elections, 2011" (http://en.wikipedia.org/wiki /Hong_Kong_local_elections_2011). There was little change in the balance of forces in the district council elections held in November 2015; see also Jennifer Lo, "Hong Kong District Elections: Pan Democrats Make Gains after 'Umbrella Movement,'" *Nikkei Asian Review,* November 21, 2015 (OSC JPR2015112372649687).

79. Tony Cheung, "Hong Kong District Council Elections: The top 4 Surprises and What They Mean to the Future of Politics in the City," *South China Morning Post,* November 24, 2015 (www.scmp.com/news/hong-kong/politics/article/1881970 /hong-kong-district-council-elections-top-4-surprises-and).

80. In addition, one-quarter of election committee members are individuals who serve ex officio: all members of LegCo and all Hong Kong's members in the PRC National People's Congress, plus some Hong Kong members of the Chinese People's Political Consultative Conference, some district council members, and some members of the Heung Yee Kuk, the rural committees. One FC, the District Council (Second), in LegCo since 2012, is made up of five individuals who are picked in a territorywide contest by Hong Kong voters who do not vote in any other FC election.

81. With the creation of the District Council (Second) FC, the number of LegCo members who were in some way popularly elected was now forty, compared to the thirty-five from the existing FCs.

82. Mark Roberti, *The Fall of Hong Kong: China's Triumph and Britain's Betrayal,* 2nd ed. (New York: John Wiley, 1996), p. 285.

83. Census and Statistics Department, *Hong Kong Monthly Digest of Statistics,* April 2015, table 2.6, "Number of Establishments, Persons Engaged and Vacancies (Other Than Those in the Civil Service) by Industry Section/Industry Division" (www.censtatd.gov.hk/hkstat/sub/sp30.jsp?productCode=B1010002).

84. Christine Loh and Civic Exchange, eds., *Functional Constituencies: A Unique Feature of the Hong Kong Legislative Council* (Hong Kong University Press, 2006).

85. Simon N. M. Young and Richard Cullen, *Electing Hong Kong's Chief Executive* (Hong Kong University Press, 2010), p. 75.

86. Ibid., appendixes 10–13, pp. 135–222.

87. Stuart Lau and Gary Cheung, "The 300 Who Are Used to Voting for Hong Kong's Leader," *South China Morning Post,* May 11, 2015 (OSC CHR2015051075927822).

88. Website of Legislative Council, Members Biographies, "Hon Tommy Cheung Yu-yan, SBS, JP" (www.legco.gov.hk/general/english/members/yr12-16/cyy.htm).

89. Ibid., "Hon Steven Ho Chun-yin" (www.legco.gov.hk/general/english /members/yr12-16/hcys.htm).

90. Fanny W. Y. Fung, "Lau Wong-fat's Portfolio Grows Bigger by the Day," *South China Morning Post,* October 10, 2010 (www.scmp.com/article/727046/lau-wong -fats-portfolio-grows-bigger-day).

91. Alex Lo, "The Political Genius of Hong Kong Rural Kingpin Lau Wong Fat," *South China Morning Post,* June 3, 2015 (OSC CHR2015060272328314); John Chan, "Time to Thoroughly Overhaul Hong Kong's Small House Policy and Root Out Those Who Abuse It," *South China Morning Post,* January 5, 2016 (OSC CHR2016010533930860).

92. Ng Kang-chung, "Heung Yee Kuk Chairman Steps into Father's Shoes Saying He'll Seek His Advice," *South China Morning Post,* June 1, 2015 (www.scmp.com /news/hong-kong/politics/article/1814463/heung-yee-kuk-chairman-steps-fathers -shoes-saying-hell-seek).

93. Goodstadt, *Uneasy Partners;* Fong, "The Partnership between the Chinese Government and Hong Kong's Capitalist Class."

94. Gordon S. Wood, *The Creation of the American Republic, 1776–1787* (New York: W. W. Norton, 1969), pp. 206–22.

95. Suzanne Pepper, *Keeping Democracy at Bay: Hong Kong and the Challenge of Chinese Political Reform* (New York: Rowman & Littlefield, 2008), p. 51.

96. Simon Young (Faculty of Law, Hong Kong University), author interview, May 27, 2015.

97. In 2012, the democrats also won three of the seats in the District Council (Second) FC, but its members are elected on a mass basis, like members from geographic districts.

98. This is a major theme of Brian C. H. Fong, *Hong Kong's Government under Chinese Sovereignty: The Failure of the State-Business Alliance after 1997* (New York: Routledge, 2015), especially pp. 121–59.

99. Stuart Lau, "Parties' Legco Voting Records Show a Blurring of Political Lines, Post Finds," *South China Morning Post,* July 22, 2014 (OSC CHR2014072175922895); Albert Cheng, "Hong Kong's Biggest Trade Union Is Failing Workers by Giving Up on Working Hours Legislation," *South China Morning Post,* April 2, 2015 (OSC CHR2015040238114291).

100. Hong Kong Transition Project, "Constitutional Reform in Hong Kong: Round Three," pp. 59, 65, 95.

101. Ibid., p. 108.

102. Ibid., pp. 127, 128, 115, 5.

103. Ibid., p. 3.

104. Yun-han Chu and Bridget Welsh, "Millennials and East Asia's Democratic Future," *Journal of Democracy* 26 (April 2015), pp. 149–63.

105. Richard Wong, "Hong Kong's Soul Is Central but Remote," *South China Morning Post,* December 30, 2014 (www.scmp.com/business/article/1670673/hong -kongs-soul-central-remote).

106. Janet Pau, "Lack of Opportunities in Hong Kong Creating a Generation without Hope," *South China Morning Post,* October 21, 2014 (OSC CHR2014102150710766).

107. Perry Lam, "Occupy Sites the Front Line for a Generation That Got Ripped Off," *South China Morning Post,* November 7, 2014 (www.scmp.com/news/hong -kong/article/1633701/occupy-sites-front-line-generation-got-ripped)

108. Siegfried Sin, "The Source of Hong Kong Youth's Frustration," *South China Morning Post,* December 12, 2014 (www.scmp.com/comment/insight-opinion/article /1661412/source-hong-kong-youths-frustration).

109. Bernard Chan, "Hong Kong's Prosperity Must Benefit All—Not Just a Few," *South China Morning Post,* December 11, 2014 (OSC CHR2014121134226244).

110. Hong Kong police officer, author interview, October 2013. For a case in which demonstrators violated a "letter of no objection" to which the event organizer had agreed, see website of the Hong Kong SAR, "Police Condemn Violent Acts," May 4, 2014 (www.info.gov.hk/gia/general/201405/04/P201405040962 .htm).

111. Alvin So, "The Development of Post-Modernist Social Movements in the Hong Kong Special Administrative Region," in *East Asian Social Movements: Power, Protest, and Change in a Dynamic Region,* edited by Jeffrey and Vicky Broadbent (New York: Springer, 2011), pp. 365–77.

112. Ibid., p. 368.

113. Edmund W. Cheng, "How Feedback Matters: The Diffusion of Vigorous Activism in Postcolonial Hong Kong," paper read at Contemporary China Studies Workshop, "The Boundaries of Democracy: New Developments in Hong Kong and Taiwan's Relations with China Mainland," Hong Kong University, October 10, 2014, p. 7 (in author's collection).

114. Cheng, "How Feedback Matters," pp. 7–8.

115. For an early analysis of the use of social media for political mobilization, see Rikkie L. K. Yeung, "Digital Democracy: How the American and Hong Kong Civil Societies Use New Media to Change Politics," Brookings Center for East Asia Policy Studies working paper, April 2008 (www.brookings.edu/research/papers/2008/04 /digital-democracy-yeung).

116. Ho-fung Hung and Iam-chong Ip, "Hong Kong's Democratic Movement and the Making of China's Offshore Civil Society," *Asian Survey* 52 (May–June 2012), pp. 506–14; Alex Lo, "Social Media Amplifies Hate and Despair," *South China Morning Post,* June 11, 2015 (OSC CHR2015061137242121); Kin-man Chan, "Civil Society and the Democracy Movement in Hong Kong: Mass Mobilization with Limited Organizational Capacity," *Korea Observer* 36 (Spring 2005), pp. 167–82 (cited passage on p. 168). Professor Chan, of the Chinese University of Hong Kong, emerged as one of the leaders of Occupy Central.

117. Cheng, "How Feedback Matters," pp. 11–12. The protest I observed in October 2013 appeared to be a hybrid of these two types. The orderly conduct of the participants suggested some degree of coordination between organizers and the police.

But the number of people mobilized in just a few days was more likely to have been accomplished through social media rather than more traditional methods.

118. Mike Rowse, "Hong Kong's Colonial Era Postboxes Should be Treasured, Not Covered Up or Destroyed," *South China Morning Post*, October 11, 2015 (OSC CHR2015101134128361).

119. Ngok Ma, *Political Development in Hong Kong: State, Political Society, and Civil Society* (Hong Kong University Press, 2007), p. 199.

120. Gary Cheung, "How Hong Kong's Electoral System Only Discourages Political Moderates," *South China Morning Post*, November 16, 2015 (OSC CHR2015111632713526).

121. League of Social Democrats leader, author interview, October 8, 2013.

122. Chris Yeung, "New Group Could Enliven Democracy Movement," *South China Morning Post*, October 1, 2006 (OSC CPP20061002701005); Steven Chen, "Brief Protest Disrupts Tsang's Address," *China Daily* (Hong Kong edition), October 12, 2006 (OSC CPP20061012067032); "Protester Hurls Pinocchio Effigy at Hong Kong Leader," NBC News, July 16, 2012 (http://photoblog.nbcnews.com/_news/2012/07/16/12765706-protester-hurls-pinnochio-effigy-at-hong-kong-leader).

123. Keith Bradsher, "Hong Kong Retreats on 'National Education' Plan," *New York Times*, September 8, 2012 (www.nytimes.com/2012/09/09/world/asia/amid-protest-hong-kong-backs-down-on-moral-education-plan.html).

124. Ho Lok-sang, "Universal Suffrage Only Possible within the Bounds of the Law," *China Daily*, January 9, 2014 (OSC CHL2014010907245751).

125. Hong Kong Federation of Students, "The Choice of Time, the Voice of People—Letter to Prime Minister Li Keqiang," November 15, 2014, reprinted in *Epoch Times*, November 16, 2014 (www.theepochtimes.com/n3/1084812-in-open-letter-hong-kong-students-invite-chinese-premier-to-visit).

126. Chu and Welsh, "Millennials and East Asia's Democratic Future," 161, 154–55. See also Min-hua Huang, "The Rise of the Internet and Changing Political Participation in Asia," Brookings Institution Working Paper, draft, June 2015 (in author's collection).

127. Karl Marx and Frederick Engels, *The Manifesto of the Communist Party*, chapter 1 (www.marxists.org/archive/marx/works/1848/communist-manifesto/ch01.htm#007).

128. Marx and Engels might also be alarmed that power in the Chinese Communist Party today is distributed, says the dissident Bao Tong, according to "hereditary privilege deriving from revolutionary bloodlines. . . . What's that got to do with Marx and the proletariat? . . . It's more feudal than feudalism." Bao Tong quoted in Louisa Lim, *The People's Republic of Amnesia: Tiananmen Revisited* (Oxford University Press, 2014), p. 171.

Chapter Five: Debating Universal Suffrage Before Occupy

1. Hong Kong SAR government, Consultation Document, "Let's Talk and Achieve Universal Suffrage: Methods for Selecting the Chief Executive in 2017 and for Forming the Legislative Council in 2016," December 2013 (www.2017.gov.hk /filemanager/template/en/doc/Con_Doc_e_(FINAL)_with_cover.pdf), p. 44.

2. Website of the Hong Kong SAR, "Chapter 383, Hong Kong Human Rights Ordinance," June 30, 1997 version (http://www.legislation.gov.hk/blis_ind.nsf /CurEngOrd/45005C093DC38DA1C825648300293CC4).

3. Also, Beijing and its Hong Kong partisans asserted that the United States and Great Britain were additional characters plotting in the wings to promote a "color revolution." Keith Bradsher, "Some Chinese Leaders Claim U.S. and Britain Are behind Hong Kong Protests," *New York Times,* October 10, 2014 (www.nytimes.com /2014/10/11/world/asia/some-chinese-leaders-claim-us-and-britain-are-behind-hong -kong-protests-.html).

4. Alice Miller, "The CCP Central Committee's Leading Small Groups," *China Leadership Monitor,* no. 26, September 2008 (www.hoover.org/sites/default/files /uploads/documents/CLM26AM.pdf).

5. Joseph Y. S. Cheng, City University of Hong Kong, communication with author, April 7, 2014.

6. Gary Cheung and Stuart Lau, "China's Hold on Hong Kong: Who Makes the Policy Decisions for the City?" *South China Morning Post,* May 15, 2016 (OSC CHR2016051524313451).

7. David M. Lampton, "Xi Jinping and the National Security Commission: Policy Coordination and Political Power," *Journal of Contemporary China* 24 (September 2015), pp. 759–77 (cited passage on p. 763).

8. Yuhua Huang and Carl Minzer, "The Rise of the Chinese Security State," *China Quarterly,* no. 222, June 2015, pp. 339–59.

9. State Council Information Office, "Full Text: China's Peaceful Development," Xinhua, September 6, 2011 (OSC CPP20110906968009).

10. David Shambaugh, *China's Communist Party: Atrophy and Adaptation* (Washington, D.C., and Berkeley: Woodrow Wilson Center Press and University of California Press, 2008), pp. 65–73, 74–75.

11. Cary Huang, "Paranoia from Soviet Union Collapse Haunts China's Communist Party, 22 Years On," *South China Morning Post,* November 18, 2013 (www .scmp.com/news/china/article/1359350/paranoia-soviet-union-collapse-haunts -chinas-communist-party-22-years).

12. "Document 9: A ChinaFile Translation: How Much Is a Hardline Party Directive Shaping China's Political Climate?" *ChinaFile,* November 8, 2013 (www .chinafile.com/document-9-chinafile-translation). The seventh "peril," questioning Deng Xiaoping's policies of "reform and opening up," was a bit out of place alongside the other six. It came not from the West but from China's own neo-Maoist Left. Document Number 9 was one of a series of numbered "central documents" issued each year to officials at lower levels of the hierarchy that address issues of significant concern to the leadership. This one was the ninth to be issued in 2013.

13. Zhao Kejin, "China's National Security Commission," Carnegie-Tsinghua Center for Global Policy, July 14, 2015 (www.carnegietsinghua.org/2015/07/09 /china-s-national-security-commission/id7i).

14. "The CPC Central Committee Political Bureau Opens a Meeting to Study and Decide the Organizational Structure of the Central National Security Committee and Review the Implementation of the Central Authorities' Eight Regulations; CPC Central Committee General Secretary Xi Jinping Chairs the Meeting," Xinhua, January 24, 2014 (OSC CHR2014012440983881).

15. "Xi Jinping Vows to Fight Terrorism, Secession at Politburo Study Session," Xinhua, April 26, 2014 (OSC CHR2014042647052109).

16. Lampton, "Xi Jinping and the National Security Commission," pp. 12–13.

17. "Full Text: China's Military Strategy," *China Daily,* May 26, 2015 (OSC CHR2015052612653330).

18. State Council Information Office, "The Practice of the 'One Country, Two Systems' Policy in the Hong Kong Special Administrative Region," Xinhua, June 10, 2014 (OSC CHR2014061013966806).

19. "Full Text of PRC National Security Law," Xinhua, July 1, 2015 (OSC CHR2015070152887690).

20. David Zweig, "How China's Very Real National Security Fears Shaped Its Reform Plan for Hong Kong," *South China Morning Post,* September 24, 2014 (www .scmp.com/comment/article/1599574/how-chinas-very-real-national-security-fears -shaped-its-reform-plan-hong).

21. Alex Lo, "Give Beijing Security and It May Give Hong Kong More Democracy," *South China Morning Post,* May 9, 2015 (OSC CHR2015050869044954).

22. Bruce Ackerman and James Fishkin, *Deliberation Day* (Yale University Press, 2004).

23. Joshua But and Gary Cheung, "Occupy Central Pioneer Outlines Its Four-Stage Plan to Achieve Democracy," *South China Morning Post,* March 28, 2013 (OSC CPP20130328695010).

24. Joshua But, "Pan-Democrats to Seek Public Opinion on Three Proposals for 2017 Election," *South China Morning Post,* July 10, 2013 (www.scmp.com /news/hong-kong/article/1279121/pan-democrats-seek-public-opinion-three -proposals-2017-election). People's Power and the Federation of Students had proposed that signatures from 1 percent of the electorate would be sufficient for nomination. See Tanna Chong, "Radicals Admit Moderate Proposals Would Give Voters 'Genuine Choice,'" *South China Morning Post,* May 8, 2014 (OSC CHR2014050817113754).

25. Richard Wong, "Way Out Still Open for Stalemated Hong Kong Politics," *South China Morning Post,* May 26, 2015 (OSC CHR2015052664221090).

26. Website of the U.K. Parliament, "Glossary: White Papers" (www.parliament .uk/site-information/glossary/white-paper/), "Glossary: Green Papers" (www .parliament.uk/site-information/glossary/green-papers/), and "Consultation Principles 2016" (www.gov.uk/government/uploads/system/uploads/attachment_data/file /492132/20160111_Consultation_principles_final.pdf).

27. John P. Burns, *Government Capacity and the Hong Kong Civil Service* (Oxford University Press, 2004), p. 174; author interview with John P. Burns, May 25, 2015.

28. "'Beijing's Opponents Cannot Become Chief Executive,' Says Li Fei," *South China Morning Post,* November 22, 2013 (OSC CHR2013112230014344); "Puxuan Chengbai Guanjian Zaiyu Shifou Yifa Panshi" [The key factor for success or failure of universal suffrage is whether matters are managed according to law], *Wen Wei Po,* November 22, 2013 (OSC CHR2013112219552636); Michael C. Davis, "Hong Kong Government Must Not Blindly Follow Electoral 'Instructions,'" *South China Morning Post,* November 25, 2013 (www.scmp.com/comment/insight-opinion/article /1365398/hong-kong-government-must-not-blindly-follow-electoral). Davis is a scholar of constitutional law at the University of Hong Kong.

29. Stuart Lau, "Latest Reform Consultation Paper 'Dishonest': Anson Chan," *South China Morning Post,* January 2, 2014 (OSC CHL2014010701233277); Frank Ching, "Political Reform Consultation Fails the Test of Open Debate," *South China Morning Post,* December 31, 2013 (OSC CHL2013123111210555).

30. "Structural Defects in Constitutional System," editorial, *Ming Pao,* January 7, 2014 (OSC CHR2014010721525510).

31. The Hong Kong Transition Project surveyed 1,007 permanent residents of Hong Kong. See Hong Kong Transition Project, "Constitutional Reform: Confrontation Looms as Hong Kong Consults," April 2014 (www.hktp.org/list/constitutional -reform.pdf), pp. 117–18, 120–21, 124, 152.

32. Tony Cheung and Gary Cheung, "Zhang Dejiang Rules Out Public Nomination for Chief Executive Poll," *South China Morning Post,* March 4, 2014 (OSC CHR2014030501225456).

33. Kahon Chan, "President Calls for Consensus on HK Constitutional Reform," *China Daily (Asia-Pacific),* December 19, 2013 (OSC CHL2013121902438128); Jeffie Lam, "Political Reform in Hong Kong Only Possible through Consensus, Says Wang," *South China Morning Post,* December 19, 2013 (OSC CHL2013121933612378).

34. On questioning sincerity, see Tanna Chong, "Liaison Official Questions 'Ulterior Motives' for Raising Opposing Views," *South China Morning Post,* March 14, 2014 (OSC CHR2014031001531295); "Pan-Democrats See Scare Tactics on Reform," *The Standard,* March 20, 2014 (OSC CHR2014032001527798). On predictable conclusions: "Consensus Is the Key to Achieving Meaningful Electoral Reform for 2017," *South China Morning Post,* February 9, 2014 (www.scmp.com /comment/insight-opinion/article/1424233/consensus-key-achieving-meaningful -electoral-reform-2017); "The Opposition Must Answer Three Questions," *Ta Kung Pao,* March 14, 2014 (OSC CHR2014031423936721).

35. Anson Chan, Johannes Chan (dean of the Law Faculty at Hong Kong University), Frank Ching, the legal scholar Michael Davis, the Civic Party leader Ronny Tong Ka-wah, and a separate group of eighteen scholars had their own proposals along these lines. See Tony Cheung, "Academic's Reform Plan Receives Muted Response," *South China Morning Post,* March 17, 2014 (OSC CHR2014031701255758), about a proposal of Johannes Chan of Hong Kong University Law School; Tony

Cheung, "Pan-Democrats' Demands Omitted from Chan Proposal," *South China Morning Post,* March 20, 2014 (OSC CHR2014032036305477); Jeffie Lam, "2017 Debate Widens Rift between Ronny Tong Ka-wah and Civic Party," *South China Morning Post,* December 30, 2013 (OSC CHL2013123008751304); Frank Ching, "How to Make Nominating Committee 'Broadly Representative' for 2017 Vote," *South China Morning Post,* December 17, 2013 (www.scmp.com/comment/article/1384227/how-make-nominating-committee-broadly-representative-2017-vote); Tanna Chong, "Academics Asked to Explain Reform Principles in Election Plan," *South China Morning Post,* April 9, 2014 (OSC CHR2014040932743826); Michael Davis, "The Middle Way to Electing the Next Chief Executive," *South China Morning Post,* March 24, 2014 (www.scmp.com/comment/article/1456235/middle-way-electing-next-chief-executive).

36. Jeffie Lam, "Why Says Pan-Democrats Can't Be Patriots? Jasper Tsang," *South China Morning Post,* March 31, 2014 (OSC CHR2014033101819886).

37. Tony Cheung, "Unite or Fail, Alliance Leader Joseph Cheng Tells Pan Democratic Parties," *South China Morning Post,* January 11, 2014 (OSC CHL2014011101578841).

38. "Long Hair" Lueng Kwok-hung guaranteed that he would be denied entry into China by traveling in a T-shirt printed with a message of support for the mothers of participants in the Tiananmen protests in Beijing in 1989. The meeting may have been less contentious as a result of his absence. Jeffie Lam, "Long Hair Leung Kwok-hung Flies Back to Hong Kong after Row at Shanghai Airport," *South China Morning Post,* April 11, 2014 (OSC CHR2014041201538606).

39. Wang's speech was quickly published in full in Hong Kong in the Communist newspaper *Wen Wei Po.* See "Jian Neihao, Mou Fazhan, Qun/Ning Gongshi, Da Puxuan: Gangao Banzhujen Wang Guangya zai Lifahui Yiyuan Zuotanhuishang Fayan Quanwen" [Reduce internal strife, strive for development, forge consensus, achieve universal suffrage: complete text of Hong Kong and Macao Affairs Office director Wang Guangya's speech to the forum of Legislative Council members], *Wen Wei Po,* April 14, 2014 (OSC CHR2014041424379121).

40. "Timinghui Timing Jiang Sanfengxian: Quanguo Renmin Daibiao Dahui Fumishuzhang jian Jibenfa Weiyuanhui Zhuren Li Fei zai Zuotanhuishang Quanwen" [Minimize three risks in nominations by the Nominating Committee: complete text of speech by Li Fei, National People's Congress Standing Committee deputy secretary general and director of the Basic Law Committee to the Forum of Legislative Council members], *Wen Wei Po,* April 14, 2014 (OSC CHR2014041424684566).

41. One Hong Kong University professor concluded, "These bloc submissions are clearly orchestrated, presenting a single, unified opinion. We should not take these reports at face value." See Calvin Liu, Brian Yap, and Joyce Ng, "Hong Kong Political Reform Consultation Was Dominated by 'Orchestrated' Responses," *South China Morning Post,* August 18, 2014 (www.scmp.com/news/hong-kong/article/1575617/consultation-dominated-bloc-responses).

42. Website of the Hong Kong SAR, "Submissions on Constitutional Development Consultation," May 5, 2014 (OSC CHR2014050542906832); "Electoral Reform in Hong Kong: Your Guide to the Chief Executive Nomination Plans," *South*

China Morning Post, May 13, 2014 (OSC CHR2014051402421833), summarizes each of the eighteen proposals; website of the Hong Kong SAR, "SCMA Answers Media Questions on Constitutional Development," April 23, 2014 (OSC CHR2014042327306283).

43. Michael Rowse, "Missed Opportunities from Both Sides of the Political Reform Divide," *South China Morning Post,* May 12, 2014 (OSC CHR2014051201522356).

44. "Constitutionalism in Danger," *Ming Pao,* May 8, 2014 (OSC CHO2014050821016865); "Let Moderatism Prevail," *Ming Pao,* May 13, 2014 (OSC CHO2014051306940393); "Occupy Central Accused of 'Disenfranchising' Moderates in Vote," *South China Morning Post,* May 7, 2014 (OSC CHR2014050801273872).

45. Regina Ip, "Occupy Central Should 'Deliberate' on the Effectiveness of Its Campaign," *South China Morning Post,* May 25, 2014 (OSC CHR2014052501230869).

46. State Council Information Office, "The Practice of the 'One Country, Two Systems' Policy in the Hong Kong Special Administrative Region," Xinhua, June 14, 2014 (OSC CHR2014061013966806).

47. Michael Rowse, "Overreaction to White Paper on Hong Kong Not Supported by the Facts," *South China Morning Post,* June 23, 2014 (www.scmp.com/comment /insight-opinion/article/1537020/overreaction-white-paper-hong-kong-not -supported-facts).

48. Sonny Lo, "White Paper on Hong Kong Underlines Beijing's Firm Stance on Sovereignty," *South China Morning Post,* June 12, 2014 (www.scmp.com/comment /article/1530867/white-paper-hong-kong-underlines-beijings-firm-stance -sovereignty).

49. Michael C. Davis, "With White Paper, Beijing May Have Achieved the Opposite of What It Wants," *South China Morning Post,* June 16, 2014 (OSC CHR2014061601256529).

50. "The Occupy Central Vote and Beijing's HK Policy," *Ming Pao,* June 25, 2014 (OSC CHR2014062521145488).

51. Jeffie Lam, "Beijing's White Paper Makes Passing Reforms Tougher, Carrie Lam Says," *South China Morning Post,* June 20, 2014 (OSC CHR2014062001529188).

52. Jeffie Lam, "Electronic Poll on Electoral Reform Opens, Despite Billions of Cyberattacks," *South China Morning Post,* June 20, 2014 (OSC CHR2014062017119781). According to one expert, the attacks came from the computers of mainland companies in Hong Kong. See Jeffie Lam, "Cyberattacks against Occupy Central Poll Traced to Mainland Firms' Computers in Hong Kong," *South China Morning Post,* June 23, 2014 (OSC CHR2014062339008368).

53. "Alliance for True Democracy Proposal Wins Occupy Central Poll as Nearly 800,000 Hongkongers Vote," *South China Morning Post,* June 29, 2014 (OSC CHR2014063007993963).

54. "It's One Form of Giving Opinions, Insists Lam," *The Standard,* June 30, 2014 (OSC CHR2014070101237522).

55. Tony Cheung and others, "Democrats Pull Out of Alliance for True Democracy," *South China Morning Post,* June 30, 2014 (OSC CHR2014063058210982).

56. "Huge Crowds Turn Out for Hong Kong Pro-Democracy March," *New York Times,* July 1, 2014 (www.nytimes.com/2014/07/02/world/asia/hong-kong-china-democracy-march.html).

57. "Most Marchers Surveyed Motivated by Desire for Public Nomination of 2017 Poll Candidates," *South China Morning Post,* July 2, 2014 (OSC CHR2014070200645277).

58. Clifford Lo and others, "Police Used Physical 'Pressure Point Tactics' to Clear Chater Road," *South China Morning Post,* July 3, 2014 (OSC CHR2014070309013942).

59. Gary Cheung and others, "Beijing Unmoved by Massive Rally Turnout, Say Advisers," *South China Morning Post,* July 3, 2014 (OSC CHR2014070302130153).

60. Ng Kang-chung, "US Voices Support for 2017 Election Method That Is 'Credible' to Hong Kong People," *South China Morning Post,* July 11, 2014 (OSC CHR2014071130013858).

61. Website of Hong Kong SAR, "Opening Remarks by CS at LegCo House Committee Special Meeting on Constitutional Development Public [consultation]," July 15, 2014 (OSC CHR2014071539928002); Chris Buckley and Alan Wong, "Hong Kong Leader Says 'Mainstream' Opposes Direct Nominations," *New York Times,* July 16, 2014 (www.nytimes.com/2014/07/16/world/asia/hong-kong-leader-says-mainstream-opposes-democracy-activists-key-proposal.html).

62. Carrie Lam, "Electoral Reform Must Be Based on Proper Understanding of Its Context," *South China Morning Post,* July 18, 2014 (OSC CHR2014071802180850); Jeffie Lam, "Lawmakers Slam Carrie Lam's Report on Public Views of Political Reform," *South China Morning Post,* July 15, 2014 (OSC 2014071561133862); Emily Tsang and Jeffie Lam, "Ambiguous and Unscientific: Critics Scornful of Reports on Electoral Reform," *South China Morning Post,* July 16, 2014 (OSC CHR2014071569622908).

63. Emily Lau, "Time for Beijing to Trust Hongkongers in Their Quest for Democracy," *South China Morning Post,* July 15, 2014 (www.scmp.com/comment/article/1554059/time-beijing-trust-hongkongers-their-quest-democracy); Jeffie Lam and Austin Chiu, "Business Chambers Liken Occupy Central to Thai Protests, Say Tourism Will Plummet," *South China Morning Post,* July 29, 2014 (OSC CHR2014072907697140).

64. "Beijing and Pan-Democrats Should Throw Off Shackles of Extremism," *Ming Pao,* July 25, 2104 (OSC CHR2014072511597878); "Need to Increase Common Ground," *Ming Pao,* July 17, 2014 (OSC CHR2014071720160159).

65. Dai Yanting (Benny Tai), "Beijing Yao Shenma? Yuan Fuchu Shenma?" [What does Beijing want? What is it willing to pay?], *Ping Kuo Jih Pao,* July 8, 2014 (OSC CHR2014070810506920).

66. Carrie Lam, "Electoral Reform in Hong Kong."

67. Jeffie Lam, "Pan-Democrats Can Be Patriots, NPC Chief Tells Loyalists in Shenzhen Visit," *South China Morning Post,* July 20, 2014 (OSC CHR2014072043303217); Jeffie Lam, "'Patriotic' Chief Executive Candidates Should Never Question One-Party Rule: Zhang Dejiang," *South China Morning Post,* July 21, 2014 (OSC CHR2014072121913071).

68. Tony Cheung, "Talks between Liaison Office and Pan Democrats 'Far More Frank Than Expected,'" *South China Morning Post,* August 19, 2014 (OSC CHR2014081939909845).

69. Michael Forsythe and Keith Bradsher, "On Hong Kong, Democracy and Protecting the Rich," *New York Times,* August 29, 2014 (http://sinosphere.blogs.nytimes .com/2014/08/29/wang-zhenmin-on-hong-kong-democracy-and-protecting-the -rich/); George Chen, "Rumbling PLA Carriers in Hong Kong Set Minds Rolling," *South China Morning Post,* September 1, 2014 (www.scmp.com/business/article /1582406/rumbling-pla-carriers-hong-kong-set-minds-rolling).

70. "Full Text of NPC Decision on Universal Suffrage for HKSAR Chief Selection," Xinhua, August 31, 2014 (OSC CHR2014083130700158); "Full Text of Explanation of NPC Decision on HKSAR Chief Selection by Universal Suffrage," Xinhua, August 31, 2014 (OSC CHR2014083132986645).

71. "'One Man, One Vote' Is a Big Step Forward after All," editorial, *Sing Tao Jih Pao,* September 2, 2014 (OSC CHR2014090213812998); Alex Lo, "More Political Instability Now Inevitable in Hong Kong," *South China Morning Post,* September 1, 2014 (OSC CHR2014083172030254).

72. Joyce Ng, "SCMP: Basic Law Committee Chairman Li Fei Outlines Remaining Issues to Be Sorted," *South China Morning Post,* September 2, 2014 (OSC CHR2014090171419296); Tony Cheung, "Hong Kong's Candidate Nominating System Out of Balance, Says Beijing Scholar," *South China Morning Post,* August 31, 2014 (OSC CHR2014083104843794); Joyce Ng, "Moderate Pan-Democrat Can Still Run for Chief Executive, Rita Fan Says," *South China Morning Post,* September 2, 2014 (www.scmp.com/news/hong-kong/article/1586859/moderate-pan-democrat -can-still-run-chief-executive-rita-fan-says).

73. For example, see Sonny Lo, "Democrats Still Have Room to Manoeuvre within Nominating Committee for 2017 Election," *South China Morning Post,* September 14, 2014 (OSC CHR2014091433331341).

74. "Full Text of Former Chief Executive Tung Chee Hwa's Speech on Hong Kong's Political Reform," *South China Morning Post,* September 3, 2014 (OSC CHR2014090357320329).

75. "Zhichi 'Yiren Yipiao Xuan Teshou' Caishi Zuida Minzhupai" [Supporting one person, one vote to select the chief executive is the largest democratic camp], *Wen Wei Po,* September 8, 2014 (OSC CHR2014090813315983).

76. Jeffie Lam, "Pan Democratic Lawmakers in Joint Pledge to Kill Election Reform Plan Backed by Beijing," *South China Morning Post,* August 31, 2014 (OSC CHR2014083148927285).

77. Michael DeGolyer, "'Mistakes Were Made': Analyzing Pan-Democratic and Pro-Beijing Negotiation Tactics and Errors During the Current Round of Constitutional Reform," presentation at a meeting of the Hong Kong Political Science Association, August 30, 2014 (http://hktp.org/weblog/mistakes-were-made -analyzin.html).

78. Ibid.

79. Ibid.

Chapter Six: Electoral Reform After Occupy

1. "Xi Urges Legal, Orderly Political Development in HK," *China Daily*, December 26, 2014 (OSC CHR2014122712929611). Xi said that political reform should be carried out in a "legal and orderly manner." That formulation was different from the Basic Law, where the word "gradual" was paired with "orderly." Was this a hint that gradualism was no longer required, and that a compromise was possible as long as it was within Beijing's "legal" parameters?

2. Ng Kang-chung, "Hong Kong, Macau Need 'Enlightenment' on Law and Identity, Says NPC Official after Protest," *South China Morning Post*, December 14, 2014 (OSC CHR2014121433660072).

3. Cheung Chi-fai, Fanny W. Y. Fung, Emily Tsang, and Tony Cheung, " 'Small Fixes' not Enough to Solve Hong Kong's Big Problems, Says Beijing Adviser," *South China Morning Post*, December 12, 2014 (www.scmp.com/news/hong-kong/article /1661358/next-fight-hong-kong-students-winning-over-disapproving-public-says).

4. Wang Ping, " 'Zhanzhong' Kuohou Hsiangkang Xu Zhanchu 'Xinmo' " [In the wake of 'Occupy Central' Hong Kong must abandon 'bias'], *Renmin Ribao Haiwaiwang (People's Daily Overseas Online)*, December 16, 2014 (OSC CHR2014121611440612).

5. Ho Lok-sang, "The Most Important Lesson from 'Occupy,' " *China Daily (Asia-Pacific)*, December 15, 2014 (OSC CHR2014121514720040).

6. Guo Zhongxing, "Zhichi Zhenggai shi Wenho Fanduipai di Weiyichulu" [Supporting political reform is the only way to moderate the opposition faction], *Wen Wei Po*, December 15, 2014 (OSC CHO201412151300401).

7. "Leave the Streets within 20 Hours, Carrie Lam Warns Hong Kong Protesters Ahead of Clearance," *South China Morning Post*, December 10, 2014 (OSC CHR2014121033958946).

8. C. Y. Leung, "2015 Policy Address": Uphold the Rule of Law, Seize the Opportunities, Make the Right Choices, Pursue Democracy, Boost the Economy, Improve People's Livelihood," January 14, 2015 (www.info.gov.hk/gia/general/201501 /14/P201501140331.htm).

9. Regina Ip, "Protesters Must Abandon Fantasy of a 'Hong Kong Race' Free from Mainland," *South China Morning Post*, December 7, 2014 (OSC CHR2014120733922630).

10. "Government Must Tread Cautiously," *Ming Pao*, December 15, 2014 (OSC CHO2014121510109178); "Let's Now Find a Way Forward on Hong Kong's Political Reform," *South China Morning Post*, December 12, 2014 (OSC CHR2014121234835035).

11. Leung Kwok-leung, "Spoiled Young People Are a Menace to Society," *South China Morning Post*, January 22, 2015 (OSC CHR2015012219081884); Lauren Higgers, "Hong Kong's Umbrella Revolution Isn't Over Yet," *New York Times Magazine*, February 18, 2015 (www.nytimes.com/2015/02/22/magazine/hong-kongs -umbrella-revolution-isnt-over-yet.html).

12. Philip Bowring, "Hard Lessons of the Occupy Protests," *South China Morning Post*, November 16, 2014 (OSC CHR2014111581926971); Mike Rowse, "Whatever

Happens with Political Reform, Pan Dems Have Already Triggered De Facto Paralysis," *South China Morning Post,* February 16, 2015 (OSC CHR2015021572022246).

13. Richard Wong, "Next Year No Time for Brinksmanship in Universal Suffrage Debate," *South China Morning Post,* December 16, 2014 (OSC CHR2014121617187570).

14. "Zhuanjia: Zhongyan Fangren Yanlun Fanchangtai" [Expert: It's abnormal for the center to permit freedom of expression], *Ming Pao,* February 28, 2015 (OSC CHL2015022832886841). Freedom of expression "concerning Hong Kong" is implied.

15. "Jingguan Xuezhe Ziwopiping 'Huihen' Dui Xianggang Taikuanrong" [Beijing officials and scholars conduct self-criticism and 'deeply regret' too much lenience toward Hong Kong], *Ming Pao,* March 31, 2015 (OSC CHL2015033112684212).

16. "CPPCC Enhances Great Unity with Compatriots from Hong Kong, Macau, and Taiwan," Xinhua, March 3, 2015 (OSC CHR2015030352734060).

17. Yahoo! Finance, "Hang Seng Index, Historical Prices" (http://finance.yahoo .com/q/hp?s=%5EHSI&a=06&b=1&c=2014&d=02&e=3&f=2015&g=d&z=66 &y=0).

18. *MarketWatch.com,* "Hang Seng Index, Historical quote for: HSI, Tuesday, March 31, 2015" (www.marketwatch.com/investing/index/hsi/historical?CountryCode=hk).

19. Census and Statistics Department, Hong Kong SAR government, National Income statistics, "Table 030: Gross Domestic Product (GDP), implicit price deflator of GDP and per capita GDP" (www.censtatd.gov.hk/hkstat/sub/sp250.jsp?tableID =030&ID=0&productType=8 [accessed March 3, 2015]).

20. Timmy Sung, "Hong Kong Posts Worst Retail Sales Figures Since Sars in 2003," *South China Morning Post,* February 3, 2015 (OSC CHR2015020267516585); Sandy Li, "Pacific Place Sales Down 6pc Last Year Due to Occupy Central Protest," *South China Morning Post,* February 23, 2015 (OSC CHR2015022351610522).

21. "Xianggang Zhengzhi Guangpu Bianhua ji qi dui 'Houzhanling' de qishi" [Changes in Hong Kong's political spectrum and their message for the post-Occupy period], *Ming Pao,* December 31, 2014 (OSC CHR2014123114019801).

22. Gary Cheung and Peter So, "Post Occupy Central Public Views of Hong Kong Reform Little Changed: SCMP Poll," *South China Morning Post,* January 27, 2015 (OSC CHR2015012670551862).

23. Peter So, "Pan-Dems Say They Won't Back Down on Political Reform," *South China Morning Post,* December 10, 2014 (www.scmp.com/news/hong-kong/article /1659170/pan-dems-say-they-wont-back-down-political-reform).

24. Joyce Ng, "Occupy Groups to Start 'Non-Cooperation Movement' as Follow-Up to Mass Protests," *South China Morning Post,* December 14, 2014 (OSC 2014121433631641); Fanny Fung and Tony Cheung, "Hong Kong Protest Leaders Say Will Try to Win Over Disapproving Public, but Warn of 'More Radical Actions,'" *South China Morning Post,* December 12, 2014 (OSC CHO 2014121236155403); Jennifer Ngo, "James Tien Sends Conciliatory Message in Dialogue with Student Leaders," *South China Morning Post,* December 12, 2014 (OSC CHR2014121233642348).

25. Joyce Ng, "5 More Universities Face Calls to Quit Hong Kong's Union of Student Unions," *South China Morning Post,* March, 2, 2015 (OSC CHR2015030259725069).

26. For more information on these groups see their Facebook pages (www
.facebook.com/StudentFrontHK; www.facebook.com/ChildeaHK).

27. "Joshua Wong: Scholarism on the March," *New Left Review,* no. 92, March–
April 2015 (www.newleftreview.org/II/92/joshua-wong-scholarism-on-the-march).

28. Higgers, "Hong Kong's Umbrella Revolution Isn't Over Yet."

29. Mary Hui, "Occupy Insiders Give Their Verdict on the Protests," *South China
Post Magazine,* February 7, 2015 (www.scmp.com/magazines/post-magazine/article
/1701641/occupy-insiders-give-their-verdict-protests).

30. All survey results included a 5 percent margin of error. Hong Kong University Public Opinion Program, "Poll on Identity" (http://hkupop.hku.hk/english
/popexpress/ethnic/eidentity/poll/datatables.html [accessed June 15, 2015]).

31. Hong Kong Transition Project, "Constitutional Reform in Hong Kong: Round
Three," June 2013 (www.hktp.org/list/round-3-of-constitutional.pdf), pp. 19–21. The
two groups were about equal on the category of "Chinese Hong Konger," and the views
of those sixty to eighty-five were about the same as those thirty to fifty-nine. The same
poll (see p. 18 of report) found that more than 70 percent of those under sixty had
been born in Hong Kong (with some decadal groups over 80 percent); over 70 percent
of those seventy and older had been born on the mainland; and the group in their
sixties more or less evenly split.

32. Yiew Chiew Ping and Kwong Kin-ming, "Hong Kong Identity on the Rise,"
Asian Survey 54 (November–December 2014), pp. 1088–1112.

33. Hong Kong Transition Project, "Constitutional Reform in Hong Kong:
Round Three," pp. 21–22.

34. Jeffie Lam, "Is the Rise of Localism a Threat to Hong Kong's Cosmopolitan
Values?" *South China Morning Post,* June 2, 2015 (OSC CHR2015060205186439);
Thomas B. Gold, "Occupy Central/Sunflower: Popular Resistance in Greater China,"
Foreign Policy Research Institute e-note, October 2014 (www.fpri.org/articles/2014
/10/occupy-centralsunflower-popular-resistance-greater-china).

35. Mike Rowse, "Treatment of 'Stateless' Boy Shames Hong Kong," *South China
Morning Post,* June 8, 2015 (OSC CHR2015060810824562).

36. Suzanne Sataline, "Meet the Man Who Wants to Make Hong Kong a
City-State," *Foreign Policy,* May 18, 2015 (www.foreignpolicy.com/2015/05/18/hong
-kong-china-protests-democracy-nativism).

37. " 'Dugang' Waiguo Zhuce Chengdang Tumou 'Dahan Yichang' " ['Hong Kong
Independence movement' registers party formation overseas; planning to 'make an all-
out effort'], *Wen Wei Po,* April 14, 2015 (OSC CHO2015041625022189).

38. Ibid. On assistance from Taiwan: Huang Min-hua (National Taiwan University), communication with author, June 2015.

39. "Faxue Jijinhui Fangjing Tuixiao 'Fangang Dufa'; Wu Li Fei, Zhang Rongxun;
Chang 'Raoluan' Dingzui" [The Legal Exchange Foundation visits Beijing to promote their anti-Hong Kong independence law; they see Li Fei and Zhang Rongxun
and advocate criminalizing sowing chaos], *Sing Tao Jih Pao,* April 2, 2015 (OSC
CHL2015040212939339).

40. "'No Market' for Talk of Hong Kong Independence, Jasper Tsang Says," *South China Morning Post,* April 9, 2015 (www.smp.com/news/hong-kong/politics /article/1762537/no-market-talk-hong-kong-independence-jasper-tsang-says).

41. Leung, "2015 Policy Address."

42. "Who Has the Last Word on Hong Kong Affairs," *Ming Pao,* January 15, 2015 (OSC CHL2015011221843836); Gary Cheung, "Lessons on Chinese History, Both the Good and the Ugly, Would Benefit Hong Kong Students," *South China Morning Post,* January 26, 2015 (OSC CHR2015012724020293).

43. Website of Hong Kong SAR, "Consultation Document 2017, Seize the Opportunity: Method for Selecting the Chief Executive by Universal Suffrage" (hereafter: "Consultation Document 2017"), January 2015 (www.2017.gov.hk/en/second /document.html).

44. Ibid., pp. iv, vi.

45. "'This Is a Sad Day for Hong Kong and Democracy': Scholar Slams Beijing's Reform Plan," *South China Morning Post,* September 1, 2014 (OSC CHR2014090150719298).

46. Suzanne Maloney, "Iran Surprises Itself and the World: A New President May Take His Country in a New Direction," Brookings Essay, September 11, 2013 (www.brookings.edu/research/essays/2013/iran-surprises-itself-and-the-world-a).

47. "Consultation Document 2017," pp. 10–11.

48. Ibid., pp. 14–15.

49. Jeffie Lam and others, "Second Key Democrat Encourages Pan Dems to Accept Beijing's 2017 Vote Plan," *South China Morning Post,* February 4, 2015 (OSC CHR2015020362141178); "Let's Be Pragmatic about 2017 Poll," editorial, *South China Morning Post,* January 8, 2015 (www.scmp.com/comment/insight-opinion /article/1676775/compromise-no-confrontation-will-help-hong-kong-achieve-one).

50. Bernard Chan, "Tolerance Key to Hong Kong's Search for New Unity," *South China Morning Post,* January 8, 2015 (OSC CHR2015010833913384).

51. Tony Cheung and others, "Politicians Condemn Public Consultation That Gives 'Little Leeway' for Reform Debate," *South China Morning Post,* January 8, 2015 (OSC CHR2015010776820666); "Youhua Wubuyushi Pouxi Teshou Bushu Lianren Daji" [Improvements are useless; analyzing the chief executive's scheme to gain a second term], *Ming Pao,* January 31, 2015 (OSC CHO2015020231291995).

52. Jeffie Lam and others, "Hongkongers Still Divided over Beijing's Reform Plan for 2017, Poll Finds," *South China Morning Post,* February 9, 2015 (OSC CHR2015020877470248).

53. Jeffie Lam, "Democratic Party Warns Members against Launching Hong Kong Political Reform Petition," *South China Morning Post,* April 3, 2015 (OSC CHR2015040320412507); Jeffie Lam, "Pan Democrats Stand Firm on Reform Veto amid Moderates' Calls to Pocket Beijing's Proposal," *South China Morning Post,* April 6, 2015 (OSC CHR2015040615612903).

54. Joyce Ng, "27 Pan Democrat Lawmakers United in Pledge to Veto Political Reforms," *South China Morning Post,* March 10, 2015 (OSC CHR2015030963342877);

"Fanmin Lianshuhou, Li Fei Che Laigang; Beizhi Taozhan Xianzhihquan Fanmin: Zhongyang Ju Goutong Tuxieze" [After the Pan-Democrats' joint declaration, Li Fei cancels his trip to Hong Kong; responds to the Democrats' challenge to Beijing's constitutional power: The center will not have contacts with those who plan to shirk their responsibility], *Ming Pao*, March 11, 2015 (OSC CHR2015031129294324).

55. Ronny Tong, "Until There's Mutual Trust, Hong Kong Won't See Universal Suffrage," *South China Morning Post*, April 23, 2015 (OSC CHR2015042342628603).

56. Michael Chugani, "Hong Kong Must Decide Why It Wants Democracy," *South China Morning Post*, May 1, 2015 (OSC CHR2015050121933296).

57. Jeffie Lam and Ng Kang-chung, "Anson Chan's Think Tank Suggests Easing 'Majority Support' Rule in Hong Kong's Chief Executive Race," *South China Morning Post*, March 4, 2015 (www.scmp.com/news/hong-kong/article/1729254/hong-kong-political-reform-framework-unshakeable-say-top-beijing). In the Hong Kong 2020 plan, there would be a run-off of the top two vote-getters in the general election if no candidate received over 50 percent, or if only recommended candidates did so.

58. Website of Hong Kong SAR government, "LC: Statement by CS on Consultation Report and Proposals on the Method for Selecting the Chief Executive by Universal Suffrage," April 22, 2015 (http://www.info.gov.hk/gia/general/201504/22/P201504220392.htm).

59. "Central Gov't Says HK Universal Suffrage Package 'Legal,' 'Practical,'" Xinhua, April 22, 2015 (OSC CHR2015042218772661).

60. In this respect, the government's proposal conformed to that of Hong Kong 2020.

61. Lai Ying-kit, "Anson Chan Calls for Law Allowing Future Changes to Election Process," *South China Morning Post*, May 11, 2015 (OSC CHR2015051137999802); Joyce Ng, "Top Mainland China Official Says Hong Kong Election Method Could Be Changed after 2017," *South China Morning Post*, April 29, 2015 (OSC CHR2015042934515114); Joyce Ng, "2017 Electoral System Must Be Put to the Test Before Changing It, Beijing Official Tells HK Barristers," *South China Morning Post*, April 29, 2015 (OSC CHR2015042872022943).

62. Jeffie Lam, "Wooing the Moderates: Democrats Stand Firm," *South China Morning Post*, May 7, 2015 (www.scmp.com/news/hong-kong/politics/article/1787819/wooing-moderates-democrats-stand-firm); Gary Cheung, Joyce Ng, and Peter So, "Moderates Urge Fresh Thinking on Post Veto Reform Negotiations," *South China Morning Post*, May 8, 2015 (OSC CHR2015050771429818); "Dissent Is Part of Democracy," editorial, *South China Morning Post*, May 24, 2015 (www.scmp.com/comment/insight-opinion/article/1807859/dissent-part-democracy).

63. For the editorials, see "For Hong Kong's Sake, Legco Must Pass Reform Package for 2017 Chief Executive Election," editorial, *South China Morning Post*, April 23, 2015 (OSC CHR2015042264255974); "Can We Achieve Democracy by Vetoing the Government's Plan?" *Ming Pao*, April 24, 2015 (OSC CHR2015042421562487).

64. Regina Ip, "Hong Kong's Political Reform Package Will Put Real Power in the Hands of the People," *South China Morning Post*, April 26, 2015 (www.scmp

.com/news/article/1775169/hong-kongs-political-reform-package-will-put-real
-power-hands-people).

65. Frank Ching, "Pan-democrats Must Play No Part in Perpetuating Hong
Kong's Small-Circle Election Committee," *South China Morning Post,* May 5, 2015
(OSC CHR2015050525890189).

66. "Beijing Vows to Fight Separatist Elements," editorial, *Ming Pao,* June 3, 2015
(OSC CHR2015060314078624); Tony Cheung and Jeffie Lam, "Legco Vote on Re-
form Will Show Who's Loyal to 'One Country, Two Systems,' Warns Basic Law Panel
Chief," *South China Morning Post,* May 31, 2015 (OSC CHR20150531471213440).

67. Du Liangmou, "Zhenggai Qiji: Jianzhi Mouduo Zhixuan Xiwei" [Political
reform pivot: the establishment maneuvers to secure a majority of directly elected
seats], *Sing Tao Jih Pao,* June 4, 2015 (OSC CHL2015060521525343).

68. Jennifer Lo, "Hong Kong District Elections: Pan Democrats Make Gains
after 'Umbrella Movement,'" *Nikkei Asian Review,* November 21, 2015 (OSC
JPR2015112372649687); Gary Cheung, "Hong Kong's Pro Beijing Parties Should
Brace Themselves for a Tough 2016," *South China Morning Post,* November 30, 2015
(OSC CHR2015113071122309).

69. Opinion expressed by Hong Kong citizens well informed about LegCo elections and operations, author interviews, May 2015.

70. Li Xianzhi, "Fuhao Fencheng Zhenggai Zhenxinjiayi Bingcun" [Tycoons in
disarray over political reform; sincerity and hypocrisy coexist], *Ming Pao,* June 9,
2015 (OSC CHL2015060928429147).

71. Tony Cheung, "Democratic Party's Wu Chi Wai Blasts Carrie Lam's Defence of Nomination Plan," *South China Morning Post,* May 25, 2015 (OSC
CHR2015052509620441).

72. Jeffie Lam and Stuart Lau, "Hong Kong Public Opinion Now Split Equally
on 2017 Reform, Rolling Poll Shows," *South China Morning Post,* June 11, 2015
(OSC CHR2015061085541220).

73. Pan-Democratic member of the LegCo, personal communication with author, May 2015.

74. "Hong Kong's Universal Suffrage Bill Is Constitutional, Legal, Sensible, and
Reasonable," *People's Daily,* June 10, 2015 (OSC CHR2015061011712973).

75. Hong Kong political scientist, personal communication with author, May
2015.

76. "Biggest Study on Hong Kong Political Reform Shows Majority Support Passage of Bill," *South China Morning Post,* June 16, 2015 (OSC CHR2015061572922339).

77. "Hong Kong Reform Package Rejected as Pro-Beijing Lawmakers Walk Out
before Vote," *South China Morning Post,* June 18, 2015 (OSC CHR2015061823486890).

78. Shirley Zhao, "China's Leaders Fear 'Subversion' in Hong Kong: Professor Lau Siu-kai," *South China Morning Post,* December 29, 2014 (OSC
CHR2014122872026777); David Zweig, "How China's Very Real National Security Fears Shaped Its Reform Plan for Hong Kong," *South China Morning Post,* September 24, 2014 (www.scmp.com/comment/article/1599574/how-chinas-very-real
-national-security-fears-shaped-its-reform-plan-hong).

79. Chris Buckley, "Communist Leadership Approves Security Goals for China, *New York Times,* January 23, 2015 (www.nytimes.com/2015/01/24/world/asia /communist-leadership-approves-security-goals-for-china.html); Andrew Jacobs and Chris Buckley, "In China, Civic Groups' Freedom, and Followers, Are Vanishing," *New York Times,* February 26, 2015 (www.nytimes.com/2015/02/27/world/asia/in -china-civic-groups-freedom-and-followers-are-vanishing.html).

80. Steve Vickers & Associates, "Hong Kong Post Occupy Central: The Likely Consequences," report, January 8, 2015 (http://www.pressenza.com/2015/01/hong -kong-post-occupy-central-likely-consequences/).

81. Dennis Kwok, "In Defense of Hong Kong's Judiciary," *South China Morning Post,* April 21, 2015 (OSC CHR2015042128209400).

82. David Lague, Greg Torode, and James Pomfret, "Special Report: How China Spies on Hong Kong's democrats," Reuters, December 15, 2014 (www.reuters.com /article/2014/12/15/us-hong-kong-surveillance-special-report -idUSKBN0JT00120141215).

83. Gao Liangjie, "Zhi Liuzhao Yingdui 'Houzhanzhong' " [Take six moves to deal with the 'post–Occupy Central' situation], *Ta Kung Pao,* December 12, 2014 (OSC CHL2014121214166216).

84. Danny Mok, "Firebombs Hurled at Home of Hong Kong Media Tycoon Jimmy Lai and Next Media HQ," *South China Morning Post,* January 12, 2015 (OSC CHR2015011208438643).

85. Cliff Buddle, "Hong Kong's Article 23 Obligations Are Already in Our Legal Armoury," *South China Morning Post,* January 29, 2015 (OSC CHR2015012939912488); " 'No Market' for Talk of Hong Kong Independence, Jasper Tsang Says," *South China Morning Post,* April 9, 2015 (www.scmp.com/news /hong-kong/politics/article/1762537/no-market-talk-hong-kong-independence -jasper-tsang-says); "LCQ19: Article 23 of Basic Law," Hong Kong Special Administrative Region Website, April 22, 2015 (OSC CHR2015042231213019).

86. Thomas Chan, "Accusation of Occupy Bias 'Unfair to City's Judges,' " *South China Morning Post,* May 3, 2015 (OSC CHL2015050282679539).

87. Samuel Chan and Clifford Lo, "Hong Kong Police Stress Use of Public Order Law Against 'Fishy' Gatherings," *South China Morning Post,* March 19, 2015 (OSC CHR2015031964507430); "Challenges Await Hong Kong's New Police Chief," editorial, *South China Morning Post,* May 1, 2015 (OSC CHR2015043064219353).

88. Chow Chung-yan, "Alibaba Buys the South China Morning Post: Full Q&A with Executive Vice Chairman Joseph Tsai," *South China Morning Post,* December 11, 2015 (www.scmp.com/news/hong-kong/article/1890057/alibaba-buys-south -china-morning-post-full-qa-executive-vice-chairman).

89. Michael Forsythe and Alan Wong, "Timing of Editor's Firing Has Hong Kong Worried About Press Freedom," *New York Times,* April 20, 2016 (www .nytimes.com/2016/04/21/world/asia/hong-kong-ming-pao-editor.html).

90. For a good summary of the episode, see Eddie Li, "The Road to Sedition: the Legal Debate at the Root of Hong Kong Independence Controversy," *South China Morning Post,* April 22, 2016 (OSC CHR2016042300362143).

91. Public Opinion Programme, Hong Kong University, poll on Degrees of Freedom (http://hkupop.hku.hk/english/popexpress/socind/socq46/poll/datatables .html; accessed June 15, 2015).

92. Phila Siu, "Hong Kong Demands Answers from Mainland Chinese Police After Five Booksellers Go Missing," *South China Morning Post*, January 3, 2016 (OSC CHR2016010354926871).

93. Simon Denyer, "After Mysterious Disappearance, Hong Kong Publisher Claims He Is in China 'Cooperating with Authorities,'" *Washington Post*, January 4, 2016 (www.washingtonpost.com/news/worldviews/wp/2016/01/04/hong-kong-angry -at-china-over-booksellers-disappearance/).

94. "Singapore: China Slams Britain for 'Interfering' in Hong Kong Bookseller Case," *Channel News Asia* (Singapore), February 12, 2016 (OSC SER2016021271122619).

95. Chris Buckley, "Britain Accuses China of Violating Treaty in Hong Kong Bookseller's Case," *New York Times,* February 12, 2016 (www.nytimes.com/2016/02 /13/world/asia/britain-china-hong-kong-bookseller.html). A U.S. State Department spokesman said that the case raised "serious questions" about China's commitment to Hong Kong's economy and to protection of international human rights. "US State Department Says Disappearance of Hong Kong Booksellers Raises Serious Questions About 'One Country, Two Systems,'" *South China Morning Post,* February 2, 2106 (OSC CHR2016020214740951).

96. U.S. Department of State, "China (Includes Tibet, Hong Kong, and Macau) 2015: Human Rights Report" (http://www.state.gov/documents/organization/252967 .pdf), p. 95.

97. "After Mysterious Disappearance," "Greater Confidence in 'One Country, Two Systems,'" editorial, *Ming Pao*, January 7, 2016 (OSC CHR2016010725363231).

98. "A Matter of the Greatest Moment," editorial, *Ming Pao,* January 5, 2016 (OSC CHR2016010624678792).

99. Siu, "Hong Kong Demands Answers from Mainland Chinese Police After Five Booksellers Go Missing."

100. "The Basic Law of the Hong Kong Special Administrative Region of the People's Republic of China" (www.basiclaw.gov.hk/en/basiclawtext/images/basiclaw _full_text_en.pdf), pp. 8, 11, 13.

101. Danny Mok and Christy Leung, "Booksellers' Release in 'Few Days' after Televised Confessions," *South China Morning Post,* March 3, 2016 (OSC CHR2016030311341819).

102. "Leading Columnists Purged at Hong Kong's Paper of Record," *Asia Sentinel,* May 20, 2015 (OSC CHO2015052049901242).

103. The newspaper sought to rebut those fears in a statement issued on July 22, 2015; "SCMP Website Carries Statement Defending New Editorial Page Practices," *South China Morning Post,* July 22, 2015 (OSC CHL2015072202247580).

104. Tony Cheung, "Central Government Researcher Warns of 'Radicalized' Hongkongers," *South China Morning Post,* February 17, 2015 (OSC CHR2015021671124975); Tony Cheung, "HKU Students Branded 'Brainwashed Radicals' by Chinese Government Mouthpiece 'People's Daily,'" *South China Morning*

Post, August 3, 2015 (OSC CHR2015080318621105); "Chanchu Jijin Duliu; Huo-gan Ranrong Wending" [Eradicate the radical cancer; attain prosperity and stability for Hong Kong], editorial, *Wen Wei Po,* July 2, 2015 (OSC CHO2015070216438452); "Xu 'Fanmin' Qianzheng Liluo yu 'Gandu' Qiege" [The 'Pan-Democrats' must make a clean break with 'Hong Kong independence'], *Ta Kung Pau,* June 30, 2015 (OSC CHR2015063023760403).

105. Clare Baldwin, James Pomfret, and Jeremy Wagstaff, "On China's Fringes, Cyber Spies Raise Their Game," Reuters, November 30, 2015 (www.reuters.com /article/us-cybersecurity-hongkong-insight-idUSKBN0TI0WF20151130).

106. Jeffie Lam, "Hong Kong Education Chief 'Risks Eroding HKU Autonomy' in Probe of Occupy's Benny Tai," *South China Morning Post,* May 21, 2015 (OSC CHR2015052114138639).

107. Timmy Sung, "Pro Democracy Academic Joseph Cheng Yu Shek De-moted by Hong Kong's City University," *South China Morning Post,* May 27, 2015 (OSC CHR2015052715912473); David Matthews, "Unsafe Harbour? Academic Freedom in Hong Kong," *Times Higher Education,* September 10, 2015 (www .timeshighereducation.com/features/academic-freedom-in-hong-kong-unsafe -harbour).

108. Danny Mok and Gary Cheung, "Hong Kong's 'Godfather of Localism' Hor-ace Chin Set to Lose Job at Lingnan University," *South China Morning Post,* Febru-ary 24, 2016 (OSC CHR2016022412144750).

109. Ernest Kao, "Former Ming Pao Editor Kevin Lau Calls for Answers from HKU over Delayed Appointment of Pro Vice Chancellor," *South China Morning Post,* June 2, 2015 (OSC CHR2015060205192702); website of Hong Kong SAR, "Chief Executive's Office Statement," February 8, 2015 (OSC CHR2015020852544108). By tradition, Hong Kong's chief executive serves as chancellor of all of the territory's public universities.

110. Shirley Zhao and Joyce Ng, "University of Hong Kong's Council Votes 12–8 to Reject Professor Johannes Chan's Appointment," *South China Morning Post,* Sep-tember 29, 2015 (OSC CHR2015092954666192).

111. Joyce Ng, "Five Points to Note in Johannes Chan's Appointment Vote at University of Hong Kong," *South China Morning Post,* September 29, 2015 (OSC CHR2015092938447155).

112. "University of Hong Kong Vice-Chancellor Condemns 'Mob Rule' by Stu-dents," *South China Morning Post,* January 28, 2016 (OSC CHR2016013012781486).

113. Jeffie Lam, "Two HK Government Ministers Replaced in 'Shock' Cabinet Reshuffle after Beijing Had Qualms," *South China Morning Post,* July 22, 2015 (OSC CHL2015072218574961); Joyce Ng, "Pro-Beijing Newspaper Backs Former Chief Editor Tsang Tak-sing after his Ousting," *South China Morning Post,* July 24, 2015 (OSC CHR2015072423827712); Jeffie Lam and others, "Removal of Tsang Tak Sing from Hong Kong Government Is a Sign That Leftists Are Out in the Cold," *South China Morning Post,* July 23, 2015 (OSC CHR2015072280244295).

114. Jeffie Lam and Gary Cheung, "Hong Kong's Main Pro-Beijing Party Meets Zhang Dejiang and Is Given Mission—Win Two-Thirds of Legco Seats," July 24,

2015 (www.scmp.com/news/hong-kong/politics/article/1843309/unite-hong-kong
-and-win-wider-recognition-top-beijing).

115. Alex Lo, "Hong Kong's Pro Establishment Parties Show Their Disregard for Ordinary People," *South China Morning Post,* October 23, 2015 (CHR2015102437226714).

116. Damien Ma, "The Year the Training Wheels Came off China," *Foreign Policy,* December 31, 2014 (www.foreignpolicy.com/2014/12/31/the-year-the-training
-wheels-came-off-china-economic/reforms-gdp). The summer 2015 crash of the Shanghai stock market was a reminder to Hong Kong investors that the PRC government was much more likely to arbitrarily intervene in the operation of markets than was their own government. See Stephen Vines, "Hong Kong a Free Market and Mainland China? Not Really," *South China Morning Post,* July 15, 2015 (OSC CHR2015071525817684).

117. "Hong Kong, Mainland Sign New Trade Liberalization Deal," Xinhua, December 18, 2014 (OSC CHR2014121831838155).

118. Benjamin Robertson, "Hong Kong Financial Stocks Up on Cross Border Fund Scheme News," *South China Morning Post,* May 26, 2015 (OSC CHR2015052623717319).

119. "HK Chief Executive Proposes 11 Initiatives to Improve Livelihood, Propel Economic Growth," Xinhua, June 19, 2015 (OSC CHR2015061936824977).

120. "Yu Zhengsheng Stresses National Identity among HK, Macao Youth," Xinhua, July 17, 2015 (OSC CHR2015071739409659).

121. "CY Urges Young 'to Do Their Duty,'" *The Standard,* July 27, 2015 (OSC CHR2015072703934048).

122. "Signs of a Thaw? Hong Kong Democratic Party Members Hold Behind Closed Doors Talks with Top Beijing Official," *South China Morning Post,* August 27, 2015 (OSC CHR2015082740512257).

123. Jeffie Lam, "Beijing Hopes Hong Kong's Moderate Pan Democrats Can Help Secure Legislative Majority," *South China Morning Post,* September 10, 2015 (OSC CHR2015091022858037).

124. Gary Cheung and Jeffie Lam, "Has Beijing Set the DAB on Mission Impossible?" *South China Morning Post,* July 25, 2015 (OSC CHR2015072481095235).

125. Gary Cheung and Tony Cheung, "Exclusive: Hong Kong Legco Chief Says Urgent Review Needed on Beijing's Enactment of 'One Country Two Systems,'" *South China Morning Post,* August 30, 2015 (OSC CHR2015083078037532).

126. Mike Rowse, "No Mystery about Who Murdered Hong Kong's Reform Plan," *South China Morning Post,* June 22, 2015 (OSC CHR2015062179228176).

127. Yue Chim Richard Wong, *Hong Kong Land for Hong Kong People: Fixing the Failures of Our Housing Policy* (Hong Kong University Press, 2015).

128. Stuart Lau, "Focus of Reform Debate on 2017 Election All Wrong, Laments Academic Michael De Golyer," *South China Morning Post,* June 15, 2015 (OSC CHR2015061651029779).

129. Richard Wong, "Way Out Still Open for Stalemated Hong Kong Politics," *South China Morning Post,* May 26, 2015 (OSC CHR2015052664221090).

130. Jacques deLisle, "Blurring Borders: National, Subnational, and Regional Orders in East Asia," Foreign Policy Research Institute e-Note, July 2015 (www.fpri .org/articles/2015/07/blurring-borders-national-subnational-and-regional-orders -east-asia).

131. Wong, "Way Out Still Open for Stalemated Hong Kong Politics"; Gary Cheung, "Lessons on Hong Kong Politics, from Game Theory Pioneer John Nash," *South China Morning Post,* June 14, 2015 (OSC CHR2015061407843016). For a brief summary of the security dilemma concept, see Robert Jervis, "Was the Cold War a Security Dilemma?" *Journal of Cold War Studies* 3 (Winter 2001), pp. 36–37.

Chapter Seven: Democracy and Good Governance

1. Pippa Norris, *Making Democratic Governance Work: How Regimes Shape Prosperity, Welfare, and Peace* (Cambridge University Press, 2012), pp. 23–29.

2. Lam Woon-kwong, "Democracy Is Only Option to Offer Relative Stability," *South China Morning Post,* February 14, 2014 (OSC CHR2014021401536717). Michael Davis of Hong Kong University agrees; see Michael C. Davis, "Constitutionalism and the Politics of Democracy in Hong Kong," *Fletcher Forum of World Affairs* 30 (Summer 2006), p. 166.

3. George Cautherley, "Despite Its Limitations, Democracy Beats Other Types of Government," *South China Morning Post,* January 24, 2014 (OSC CHR2014012416220751).

4. Andrew J. Nathan, *Chinese Democracy* (New York: Knopf, 1985), pp. 45–66.

5. Ho Lok-sang, "People Need to Understand Chinese Model of Democracy," *China Daily (Asia-Pacific),* June 17, 2014 (OSC CHR2014061714435317).

6. Ho Lok-sang, "HK Needs Democratic Culture," *China Daily (Asia-Pacific),* October 8, 2013 (OSC CHR2013100803128035).

7. Alice Wu, "Hong Kong Is Stuck—with or without Political Reform," *South China Morning Post,* March 30, 2015 (OSC CHR2015032962420854).

8. The best summary of this scholarly work is by Larry Diamond, particularly his synthesis in *The Spirit of Democracy: The Struggle to Build Free Societies throughout the World* (New York: Times Books, 2008), pp. 88–112.

9. Diamond, *Spirit of Democracy,* p. 99. Harvard University's Samuel Huntington posited that modernizing countries are likely to move toward democracy during the middle phase of development. For East Asia, the boundaries of this middle phase, as expressed by the United Nations Development Programme's Human Development Index, are roughly .650 to .750. Hong Kong reached an index of .712 in 1980, while South Korea, which began its transition to democracy in 1987, had only reached .064 in 1980. See Samuel P. Huntington, *The Third Wave: Democratization in the Late 20th Century* (Oklahoma University Press, 1993); website of United Nations Development Programme, "Table 2: Human Development Index Trends" (https://data.undp.org/dataset/Table-2-Human-Development-Index -trends/efc4-gjvq).

10. Diamond, *Spirit of Democracy,* p. 103.

11. For example, a study by the Council on Foreign Relations that reviewed the literature on transitions to democracy was skeptical about any causal relationship. See Isabel Coleman and Terra Lawson-Remer, eds., *Pathways to Freedom: Political and Economic Lessons from Democratic Transitions* (New York: Council on Foreign Relations, 2013), p. 23.

12. Diamond, *Spirit of Democracy,* p. 97.

13. Ibid., pp. 51–54.

14. Ibid., p. 96.

15. Anar K. Ahmadov, "Oil, Democracy, and Context: A Meta-Analysis," *Comparative Political Studies* 47 (August 2014), pp. 1238–1267.

16. Website of the United Nations Development Programme, Human Development Reports, "Table 1: Human Development Index and Its Components" (http://hdr.undp.org/sites/default/files/hdr_2015_statistical_annex.pdf).

17. Ma Ngok, "Value Changes and Legitimacy Crisis in Post-Industrial Hong Kong," *Asian Survey* 51 (July–August 2011), pp. 683–712.

18. Yu-tzung Chang, Yun-han Chu, and Frank Tsai, "Confucianism and Democratic Values in Three Chinese Societies," *Issues and Studies* 41 (December 2005), pp. 1–33. The study was based on data from the Asian Barometer Survey.

19. Larry Diamond, "Why China Will Democratize," PowerPoint presentation at School of Advanced International Studies, Johns Hopkins University, April 24, 2014 (in author's collection).

20. Tai-lok Lui, Hsin-chi Kuan, Kin-man Chan, and Sunny Cheuk-wah Chan, "Friends and Critics of the State: The Case of Hong Kong," in *Civil Life, Globalization, and Political Change in Asia: Organizing between Family and State,* edited by Robert P. Weller (New York: Routledge, 2003), pp. 58–75; Ho-fung Hung and Iam-chong Ip, "Hong Kong's Democratic Movement and the Making of China's Offshore Civil Society," *Asian Survey* 52 (May–June 2012), pp. 504–27.

21. Stephen D. Krasner, *Sovereignty: Organized Hypocrisy* (Princeton University Press, 1999).

22. Lam Woon-kwong, the convener of the Executive Council, made this point in a commentary that examined Hong Kong from the perspective of the 1977 democratic transition in Spain. See Lam, "Hong Kong Can Learn from Spanish Experience on Road to Democracy," *South China Morning Post,* March 20, 2015 (OSC CHR2015031963622511).

23. Perhaps Beijing took comfort from a study done not long after it agreed upon the Joint Declaration with Britain. The 1988 study concluded that Hong Kong residents were apolitical when it came to either challenging the initiatives of the powers that be or taking action themselves to put issues on the policy agenda. See Siu-kai Lau and Hsin-chi Kuan, *The Ethos of the Hong Kong Chinese* (Hong Kong University Press, 1988).

24. For the comprehensive and pessimistic diagnosis of the American system, see Thomas E. Mann and Norman J. Ornstein, *It's Even Worse Than It Looks: How the American Constitutional System Collided with the New Politics of Extremism* (New York: Basic Books, 2012).

25. Larry Diamond, "Facing Up to the Democratic Deficit," *Journal of Democracy* 26 (January 2015), pp. 141–55 (cited passage on p. 152).

26. Steven Levitsky and Lucan Way, "The Myth of Democratic Recession," *Journal of Democracy* 26 (January 2015), pp. 45–58.

27. On Thailand, see Richard Bernstein, "Thailand: Beautiful and Bitterly Divided," *New York Review of Books,* November 20, 2014 (www.nybooks.com/articles/archives/2014/nov/20/thailand-beautiful-and-bitterly-divided/), and William Klausner, James Stent, Robert Fitts, Danny Unger, "Thailand Needs a Democratic, Just Society," *Bangkok Post,* April 2, 2015 (www.bangkokpost.com/opinion/opinion/515323/thailand-needs-a-democratic-just-society). On Taiwan, see Richard C. Bush, *Uncharted Strait: The Future of China-Taiwan Relations* (Brookings Institution Press, 2013), pp. 182–95; "Taiwan's Legislative Yuan: Oversight or Overreach?" transcript of Brookings Institution event, June 23, 2014 (www.brookings.edu/~/media/events/2014/06/23-taiwan-legislative-yuan/23_taiwan_legislative_yuan_corrected.pdf), pp. 1–8, 22–27, 29–50.

28. Marc F. Plattner, "Populism, Pluralism, and Liberal Democracy," *Journal of Democracy* 21 (January 2010), pp. 81–92.

29. Sonny Lo, "Rise of Radical Populism Pitting Hongkongers against Hongkongers," *South China Morning Post,* June 24, 2014 (www.scmp.com/comment/article/1539494/rise-radical-populism-pitting-hongkongers-against-hongkongers).

30. Keith Bradsher and Chris Buckley, "Hong Kong Leader Reaffirms Unbending Stance on Elections," *New York Times,* October 20, 2014 (www.nytimes.com/2014/10/21/world/asia/leung-chun-ying-hong-kong-china-protests.html).

31. Robert J. Barro and Xavier Sala-i-Martin, *Economic Growth,* 2nd ed. (Cambridge, Mass.: MIT Press, 2004), pp. 528–29. The democratization variable is derived from the Freedom House indices of civil and political rights.

32. Stephan Haggard and Robert R. Kaufman, *Development, Democracy, and Welfare States: Latin America, East Asia, and Eastern Europe* (Princeton University Press, 2008), pp. 221–60 (cited passage on p. 256).

33. Richard Wong, "Hong Kong Democracy in Balance as Occupy Movement Nears End," *South China Morning Post,* November 25, 2014 (www.scmp.com/business/economy/article/1648307/hong-kong-democracy-balance-occupy-movement-nears-end).

34. Yun-han Chu and Min-hua Huang, "Solving an Asian Puzzle," *Journal of Democracy* 21 (October 2010), pp. 114–22 (cited passage on p. 117, results on p. 118).

35. World Bank, "What Is Governance," World Governance Indicators (http://info.worldbank.org/governance/wgi/index.aspx#home).

36. Norris, *Making Democratic Governance Work,* pp. 30–34.

37. Samuel P. Huntington, *Political Order in Changing Societies* (Yale University Press, 1968).

38. Francis Fukuyama, *The Origins of Political Order: From Prehuman Times to the French Revolution* (New York: Farrar Straus and Giroux, 2011), and Fukuyama, *Political Order and Political Decay: From the Industrial Revolution to the Globalization of Democracy* (New York: Farrar Straus and Giroux, 2014).

39. Norris, *Making Democratic Governance Work*, p. 33.

40. For more information on the Quality of Government Institute, see http://qog.pol.gu.se/.

41. Norris, *Making Democratic Governance Work,* pp. 58–69.

42. Ibid.. pp. 65–69.

43. One pathology that is a common result in systems that follow a democracy first, state building later sequence is that political parties mobilize support through distributing patronage instead of through programmatic agendas, because the state is not autonomous enough to protect its hiring systems from outside interference. See Francis Fukuyama, "Democracy and the Quality of the State," *Journal of Democracy* 24 (October 2013), pp. 5–16.

44. See David Easton, *A Systems Analysis of Political Live,* 2nd ed. (University of Chicago Press, 1979), especially pp. 363–470.

45. *The Social Science Encyclopedia,* 3rd ed., *s.v.* "Legitimacy."

46. For example, see Richard Stubbs, "Performance Legitimacy and 'Soft Authoritarianism,'" in *Democracy, Human Rights, and Civil Society in South East Asia,* edited by Amitav Acharya, B. Michael Frolic, and Richard Stubbs (Toronto University Joint Centre for Asia Pacific Studies, 2001), pp. 37–53.

47. Daniel A. Bell, "Introduction," in *The East Asian Challenge for Democracy: Political Meritocracy in Comparative Perspective,* edited by Daniel A. Bell and Chenyang Li (Cambridge University Press, 2013), p. 3.

48. Fukuyama, *Political Order and Political Decay,* p. 39.

49. Ibid., pp. 455–524.

50. Website of the World Bank, "Worldwide Governance Indicators," 2015 (http://info.worldbank.org/governance/wgi/index.aspx#home).

51. Wilson Wong, "The Civil Service," in *Contemporary Hong Kong Government and Politics,* 2nd ed., edited by Lam Wai-man, Percy Luen-tim Lui, and Wilson Wong (Hong Kong University Press, 2012), p. 94.

52. Ibid., p. 90.

53. Regina Ip, "Hong Kong Needs a Democratic System That Actually Works," *South China Morning Post,* May 11, 2014 (OSC CHR2014051101506452).

54. Baohui Zhang, "Political Paralysis of the Basic Law Regime and the Politics of Institutional Reform in Hong Kong," *Asian Survey* 49 (March–April 2009), pp. 312–32.

55. Anthony B. L. Cheung, "The Changing Political System: Executive-led Government or 'Disabled' Governance?" in *The First Tung Chee-hwa Administration: The First Five Years of the Hong Kong Special Administrative Region,* edited by Lau Siu-kai (Chinese University Press [Hong Kong], 2002), pp. 44–47.

56. Synergynet, Governance Review Project, "Review of the Governance Performance of the HKSAR Government 2014" (in Chinese) (www.synergynet.org.hk/download/policy-studies-zh/governance-zh/201401153411_b5.pdf), pp. 33–34.

57. Ian Scott, *The Public Sector in Hong Kong* (Hong Kong University Press, 2010) (chapter 12, pp. 289–306, provides an excellent summary).

58. Synergynet, "Review of the Governance Performance of the HKSAR Government 2014," pp. 28–30.

59. Brian C. H. Fong, *Hong Kong's Governance under Chinese Sovereignty: The Failure of the State-Business Alliance after 1997* (New York: Routledge, 2015).

60. For one example out of many, see Yue Chim Richard Wong, *Hong Kong Land for Hong Kong People: Fixing the Failures of Our Housing Policy* (Hong Kong University Press, 2015).

61. Hong Chen, "'Vetocracy' Finds Its Place in Hong Kong," *China Daily (Asia-Pacific)*, March 12, 2014 (OSC CHR2014031203942140).

62. Website of the Legislative Council of Hong Kong SAR Government, "Written Answers to Questions: Judicial Review," Official Record of Proceedings, Wednesday, April 9, 2014 (http://www.legco.gov.hk/yr13-14/english/counmtg/hansard /cm0409-translate-e.pdf#nameddest=wrq01).

63. Andrew Li, "Why a Focus on Proper Procedure Is Essential to Hong Kong's Rule of Law," *South China Morning Post*, December 14, 2015 (OSC CHL2015121410564073).

64. Mike Rowse, "The ICAC Has Been Politicised—but Not by Leung," *South China Morning Post*, September 2, 2013 (www.scmp.com/comment/insight-opinion /article/1301210/icac-has-been-politicised-not-leung).

65. Michael Chugani, "Hong Kong Needs a Dose of Dictatorship, Not Democracy, to Get Things Done," *South China Morning Post*, February 6, 2015 (www.scmp .com/comment/insight-opinion/article/1704271/hong-kong-needs-dose -dictatorship-not-democracy-get-things).

66. "Hong Kong Can Be Both Democratic and Economically Competitive," editorial, *South China Morning Post*, September 22, 2013 (OSC CHR2013092201248786).

67. Dai Yaoyan (Benny Tai), "Yusan Liangzhong guanzhiguan" [Two views of governance under one umbrella], *Hsin Pao*, January 9, 2015 (OSC CHR2015010925118628).

68. Synergynet, "Review of the Governance Performance of the HKSAR Government 2014," pp. 35–37.

69. Johnny Mok, "How Strong Institutions Help Hong Kong Safeguard Its Autonomy," *South China Morning Post*, September 30, 2015 (OSC CHR2015093039532499).

Chapter Eight: Hong Kong's Economy

1. The findings of this chapter benefitted greatly from conversations I had in July 2014 with Ka Mun Chang, Fung Global Initiative; Thomas Chan, Hong Kong University of Science and Technology; Lawrence Lau, Chinese University of Hong Kong; Ming Wai Lau, Bauhinia Foundation; David O'Reare, Hong Kong General Chamber of Commerce; William Overholt, Fung Global Initiative; and members of the Hong Kong American Chamber of Commerce.

2. John Tsang, "Hong Kong Budget Speech by the Financial Secretary 2014–15," February 26, 2014 (www.info.gov.hk/gia/general/201402/26/P201402260264.htm).

3. Qiu Quanlin, "Pearl River Delta Loses Charm with HK Businesses," *China Daily (Asia-Pacific)*, July 19, 2014 (Open Source Center [hereafter: OSC] CHR2014071922270253).

4. Naubahar Sharif, "Innovation and Survival in Guangdong: How Hong Kong Companies Can Succeed," *Hong Kong Journal*, no. 20, January 2011 (www .carnegieendowment.org/hkjournal/archive/2011_spring/5.htm); Qiu, "Pearl River Delta Loses Charm"; Dan Steinbock, "Guangdong Moves into the Future as It Builds a Post-Industrial Society," *South China Morning Post*, January 13, 2016 (OSC CHR2016011354318356).

5. Eddie Lee, "Leading Industrialist Urges Hong Kong Manufacturers to Focus on High Value Added Products," *South China Morning Post*, July 31, 2015 (OSC CHR2015073075955239).

6. Bien Perez and Sophie Yu, "Hong Kong Takes Innovation Lead in Asia, Report Says," *South China Morning Post*, July 18, 2013 (www.scmp.com/news/hong -kong/article/1284972/hong-kong-takes-innovation-lead-asia-report-says); "Hong Kong Losing Ground in Economic Competitiveness," *Want China Times*, July 10, 2013; David Barboza, "China to Test Free Trade Zone in Shanghai as Part of Economic Overhaul," *New York Times*, July 4, 2013 (www.nytimes.com/2013/07/05 /business/global/zone-to-test-renminbi-as-currency-for-trading.html). On the continuing challenge of innovation, see Douglas B. Fuller, *Innovation Policy and the Limits of Laissez-faire: Hong Kong's Policy in Comparative Perspective* (Basingstoke, U.K.: Palgrave Macmillan, 2010).

7. CIA, *The World Factbook*, "Hong Kong," 2015 (henceforth: *World Factbook*, "Hong Kong") (www.cia.gov/library/publications/the-world-factbook/geos/hk .html).

8. World Economic Forum, *Global Competitiveness Report, 2014–2015* (henceforth: WEF, *Global Competitiveness Report, 2014–2015*) (Geneva: World Economic Forum, 2015), p. 4.

9. Ibid., pp. 14, 23–24, 206; World Economic Forum, *The Global Competitiveness Report, 2013–2014, Full Data Edition* (henceforth: WEF, *Global Competitiveness Report, 2013–2014*) (Geneva: World Economic Forum, 2014), p. 16.

10. IMD World Competitiveness Institute, *IMD World Competitiveness: 2014* (henceforth: *IMD World Competitiveness: 2014*) (Lausanne: IMD, 2014), pp. 66–69.

11. World Factbook, "Hong Kong."

12. WEF, *Global Competitiveness Report, 2014–2015*, pp. 22 (quote), 207.

13. *IMD World Competitiveness: 2014*, p. 69.

14. The World Economic Forum conducts a periodic survey of business executives around the world, including Hong Kong, on their business operating environment, but in the 2013 surveys it received only sixty responses for the first survey and sixty-three for the second; WEF, *Global Competitiveness Report, 2014–2015*, p. 88; David O'Rear, Chief Economist, Hong Kong General Chamber of Commerce (a WEF partner institution, author interview, July 2014.

15. "The Basic Law of the Hong Kong Special Administrative Region of the People's Republic of China," (www.basiclaw.gov.hk/en/basiclawtext/images/basiclaw _full_text_en.pdf), p. 34.

16. *World Factbook*, "Hong Kong."

17. Census and Statistics Department, Hong Kong SAR government, "Table 194: Government Spending (General Revenue Account and Funds)" (www.censtatd.gov .hk/hkstat/sub/sp110.jsp?tableID=194&ID=0&productType=8).

18. Ibid., "Table 193: Government Revenue (General Revenue Account and Funds)" (www.censtatd.gov.hk/hkstat/sub/sp110.jsp?tableID=193&ID=0 &productType=8).

19. For a good summary, see Hong Kong Trade and Development Council, "Hong Kong's Simple, Low-Rate Tax System," December 2012 (http://hong-kong -economy-research.hktdc.com/business-news/article/Guide-to-Doing-Business-in -Hong-Kong/Hong-Kong-s-simple-low-rate-tax-system/hkg/en/1/1X000000 /1X073F6L.htm).

20. Tsang, "Hong Kong Budget Speech by the Financial Secretary 2014–15"; Cedric Sam and Alan Yu, "The Visual Hong Kong Budget," *South China Morning Post,* February 26, 2015 (http://multimedia.scmp.com/budget2015/).

21. Richard Harris, "John Tsang's Problem of Plenty," *South China Morning Post,* February 26, 2015 (OSC CHR2015022609384343).

22. Alex Lo, "How Hong Kong's Government Subsidises Those Who Need It Least," *South China Morning Post,* March 27, 2014 (OSC CHR2014032700933247).

23. No information on the study's methodology appears to be available.

24. Tsang, "Hong Kong Budget Speech by the Financial Secretary 2014–15."

25. Ibid.

26. WEF, *Global Competitiveness Report, 2014–2015.*

27. Dan Steinbock, "Guangdong Moves into the Future As It Builds a Post-Industrial Society," *South China Morning Post,* January 13, 2016 (OSC CHR2016011354318356).

28. David Dollar, "Sino Shift," *Finance & Development* 51 (June 2014) (www.imf .org/external/pubs/ft/fandd/2014/06/dollar.htm), pp. 10–13.

29. Census and Statistics Department, Hong Kong SAR government, "The Four Key Industries and Other Selected Industries in the Hong Kong Economy," April 2015 (www.censtatd.gov.hk/hkstat/sub/sp80.jsp?productCode=FA100099), pp. 2–10 (cited passages on p. 2).

30. Ng Kang-chung, "Asian Infrastructure Investment Bank Will Use Hong Kong to Develop Bonds, Says John Tsang," *South China Morning Post,* July 20, 2015 (OSC CHR2015072006018797).

31. Frank Poon (Hong Kong solicitor general), speech at the seminar "Hong Kong—An International Hub for Legal & Arbitration Services," Yangon, August 29, 2014 (www.info.gov.hk/gia/general/201408/29/P201408290681.htm).

32. Eswar S. Prasad, "China's Efforts to Expand the International Use of the Renminbi," report prepared for the U.S.-China Economic and Security Review Commis-

sion, February 4, 2016 (www.brookings.edu/research/reports/2016/02/04-china -efforts-international-use-renminbi-prasad), p. 3.

33. Li Keqiang, "Step Up Cooperation for Development and Prosperity," speech at the Forum on the Twelfth Five-Year Plan and Mainland–Hong Kong Economic, Trade and Financial Cooperation, August 17, 2011 (www.cmab.gov.hk/doc/issues /Document_No1_Li_Keqiang_en.pdf). An example of a new RMB product was RMB sovereign bonds, which the PRC Ministry of Finance has issued in Hong Kong every year since 2009; website of Hong Kong SAR government, "HKSAR Government Welcomes Ministry of Finance's Plan to Issue RMB Sovereign Bonds in Hong Kong in 2015," May 12, 2015 (OSC CHR2015051241422741).

34. William H. Overholt, "Hong Kong's Financial Vitality Continues," *Hong Kong Journal,* no. 21, April 2011 (www.carnegieendowment.org/hkjournal/archive /2011_summer/2.htm).

35. Prasad, "China's Efforts to Expand the International Use of the Renminbi," p. 3.

36. Hong Kong SAR government, "Hong Kong's Population: Characteristics and Trends" (www.info.gov.hk/info/population/eng/pdf/chapter2_e.pdf).

37. Damien Ma, "The Year the Training Wheels Came off China," *Foreign Policy,* December 31, 2014 (www.foreignpolicy.com/2014/12/31/the-year-the-training -wheels-came-off-china-economic/reforms-gdp). The crash of the Shanghai stock market in summer 2015 was a reminder to Hong Kong investors that the PRC government was much more likely to arbitrarily intervene in the operation of markets than was their own government. See Stephen Vines, "Hong Kong's Free Market Stands in Contrast to Mainland China in Wake of Rout," *South China Morning Post,* July 15, 2015 (OSC CHR2015071525817684); Enoch Yiu, "Major Steps in Easing Capital Controls," *South China Morning Post*, November 17, 2014 (www.scmp.com/business /banking-finance/article/1641942/major-steps-easing-capital-controls).

38. "Hong Kong, Mainland Sign New Trade Liberalization Deal," Xinhua, December 18, 2014 (OSC CHR2014121831838155).

39. Benjamin Robertson, "Hong Kong Financial Stocks Up on Cross Border Fund Scheme News," *South China Morning Post,* May 26, 2015 (OSC CHR2015052623717319).

40. "Made in China: Authorities Must Do More to Bring Back Trust in Label," editorial, *South China Morning Post,* October 19, 2015 (www.scmp.com/comment /insight-opinion/article/1869287/made-china-authorities-must-do-more-bring-back -trust-label).

41. John Tsang, in his 2015 budget speech, mentioned product testing and certification merely as one of many areas in which educational opportunities would be increased for Hong Kong residents but otherwise gave it no special emphasis. See Tsang, "Full Text of Financial Secretary's Budget Speech 2015–16," website of Hong Kong SAR government, February 25, 2015 (OSC CHO2015022530556295).

42. Ka Mun Chang, Fung Global Initiative, author interview, July 2014.

43. Tsang, "Hong Kong Budget Speech by the Financial Secretary 2014–15."

44. Ken Davies, "The Reasons Why HK Needs an Industrial Renaissance," *South China Morning Post,* April 27, 2015 (OSC CHR2015042707840176); Denise Tsang, "Now Is the Time for the Return of Made in Hong Kong," *South China Morning Post,* September 24, 2014 (OSC CHR2014092381917662).

45. C. Y. Leung, "2014 Policy Address—Support the Needy, Let Youth Flourish, Unleash Hong Kong's Potential," January 15, 2014 (OSC CHL2014011512164253). In his 2014–15 budget speech, John Tsang recommended acceleration of commercialization of R&D products or services.

46. Ernest Kao, "Hong Kong Still Has What It Takes to Become Research Hub, Says Tech Chief," *South China Morning Post,* September 5, 2013 (www.scmp.com /news/hong-kong/article/1303391/hong-kong-still-has-what-it-takes-become -research-hub-says-tech-chief).

47. Mr. Shangkong [George Chen], "Can Hong Kong Be a Dream City for Start-Ups to Scale Up?" *South China Morning Post,* February 22, 2015 (www.scmp.com /business/companies/article/1721246/can-hong-kong-be-dream-city-start-ups -scale); George Chen, personal communication, July 2015.

48. Alex Lo, "Hong Kong's Hi Tech Reality Is More Low End," *South China Morning Post,* March 27, 2015 (OSC CHR2015032702179337).

49. Alan Lung, "Hong Kong Has the Tools to Be a Leading Knowledge Economy," *South China Morning Post,* June 24, 2013 (www.scmp.com/comment /insight-opinion/article/1267435/hong-kong-has-tools-be-leading-knowledge -economy).

50. Ming Wai Lau, Bauhinia Foundation, author interview, July 2014.

51. Ibid.; Richard Wong, "Health Care Could Account for Almost a Third of HK GDP by End of Century," *South China Morning Post,* August 26, 2014 (www .scmp.com/comment/insight-opinion/article/1580799/health-care-could-account -almost-third-hk-gdp-end-century).

52. Heritage Foundation, "2014 Index of Economic Freedom" (www.heritage.org /index/country/hongkong).

53. Les Gee, "Innovation and Technology Vital to Hong Kong's Future Competitiveness and Productivity," *South China Morning Post,* April 26, 2014 (www.scmp .com/comment/letters/article/1497277/innovation-and-technology-vital-hong -kongs-future-competitiveness); Joyce Ng, "Hong Kong's Planned IT Bureau Heading for Third Delay—until October," *South China Morning Post,* July 18, 2015 (OSC CHR2015071779237099); Mr. Shangkong [George Chen], "Hong Kong Seeks Innovation but Chokes Firms That Can Power Development," *South China Morning Post,* August 16, 2015 (www.scmp.com/business/companies/article/1849976/hong -kong-seeks-innovation-chokes-firms-can-power-development).

54. Lo, "How Hong Kong's Government Subsidises Those Who Need It Least."

55. Kemal Dervis, "The Inequality Trap," *Caijing,* March 12, 2012 (OSC CPP20120313572059). For a similar argument, see Paul Krugman, "Why Weren't the Alarm Bells Ringing?" *New York Review of Books,* October 23, 2014 (www .nybooks.com/articles/2014/10/23/why-werent-alarm-bells-ringing), p. 42.

56. David Madland, "Growth and the Middle Class," *Democracy: A Journal of Ideas*, no. 20, Spring 2011 (www.democracyjournal.org/20/growth-and-the-middle -class.php).

57. Jonathan D. Ostry, Andrew Berg, and Charalambos G. Tsangarides, "Redistribution, Inequality, and Growth," International Monetary Fund Discussion Note 14/2, April 2014 (www.imf.org/external/pubs/ft/sdn/2014/sdn1402.pdf).

Chapter Nine: What Hong Kong Can Do to Improve
Governance and Competitiveness

1. John Tsang, "Hong Kong Budget Speech by the Financial Secretary 2015–16," February 25, 2015 (www.budget.gov.hk/2015/eng/pdf/e_budgetspeech2015-16.pdf).

2. Eddie Lee, "Hong Kong Needs Political Stability and Infrastructure to Reclaim Competitive Top Spot," *South China Morning Post,* May 19, 2015 (Open Source Center [hereafter OSC] CHR2015051872621217).

3. Paul Yip, "Hong Kong Is Falling behind the Innovation Curve," *South China Morning Post,* June 12, 2013 (www.scmp.com/comment/insight-opinion/article /1258583/hong-kong-falling-behind-innovation-curve).

4. Richard Wong, "Hong Kong Democracy Serves to Allay Public Fears over Beijing's Rule," *South China Morning Post,* June 9, 2015 (OSC CHR2015060944447084).

5. Bernard Chan, "Singapore's Leadership Style Will Not Work in Hong Kong," *South China Morning Post,* September 6, 2013 (OSC 2013090602166043).

6. Priscilla Cabuyao, "The Singapore Jobs Market: Data vs. Discontent," Rajaratnam School of International Studies (RSIS) Commentary, no. 022/2015, February 3, 2015 (www.rsis.edu.sg/rsis-publication/cens/co15022-the-singapore-jobs-market-data -vs-discontent/).

7. Benjamin Wong, "Political Meritocracy in Singapore: Lessons from the PAP Government," in *The East Asian Challenge for Democracy: Political Meritocracy in Comparative Perspective,* edited by Daniel A. Bell and Chenyang Li (Cambridge University Press, 2013), pp. 288–313 (cited passage on p. 308).

8. Chan, "Singapore's Leadership Style Will Not Work in Hong Kong."

9. Tsang, "Full Text of Financial Secretary's Budget Speech 2015–16."

10. *The Concise Encyclopedia of Economics*, 2nd ed., *s.v.* "rent seeking" (www .econlib.org/library/Enc/RentSeeking.html).

11. Cannix Yao, "How Taxi Trade Puts Brakes on Changes It Doesn't Like," *South China Morning Post,* August 13, 2015 (OSC CHR2015081272021733); "Is Hong Kong in the Grip of Vested Interests?" *South China Morning Post,* August 13, 2015 (www.scmp.com/comment/insight-opinion/article/1853392/hong-kong-grip -vested-interests).

12. Richard Wong, "Capitalist and Socialist Rent-Seekers Eroding Positive Non-Interventionism," *South China Morning Post,* November 3, 2015 (www.scmp.com /business/markets/article/1875210/capitalist-and-socialist-rent-seekers-eroding -positive-non).

13. World Economic Forum, *Global Competitiveness Report, 2014–2015* (Geneva: World Economic Forum, 2015), pp. 13–14.

14. Ibid., pp. 16–20.

15. Ibid., p. 208.

16. Ng Kang-chung, "Asian Infrastructure Investment Bank Will Use Hong Kong to Develop Bonds, Says John Tsang," *South China Morning Post,* July 20, 2015 (OSC CHR2015072006018797); "Interview: HK Could be Financing Platform for 'One Belt, One Road,' Says Financial Chief," Xinhua, July 19, 2015 (OSC CHR2015071959228459).

17. Sun Kwok, "Hong Kong Has a Part to Play in China's Major Scientific Quests," *South China Morning Post,* May 11, 2015 (OSC CHR2015051106742067).

18. Census and Statistics Department, Hong Kong SAR Government, "Table 10.11: Visitor Arrivals by Country/Territory of Residence," *Hong Kong Monthly Digest of Statistics,* February 2016 (www.censtatd.gov.hk/hkstat/sub/sp140.jsp?productCode =B1010002).

19. Legislative Council Secretariat, "Hong Kong's Tourism Industry," Research Brief, No. 6 (2014–2015), August 5, 2015 (www.legco.gov.hk/research-publications /english/1415rb06-hong-kongs-tourism-industry-20150805-e.pdf).

20. Fung Keung, "It Is Time to Peg the HK Dollar to the Renminbi," *China Daily (Asia-Pacific),* July 15, 2015 (OSC CHR2015071561537528).

21. Richard Wong believes that the current link and the fiscal discipline that goes with it is, on balance, Hong Kong's best option. See Yue Chim Richard Wong, *Hong Kong Land for Hong Kong People: Fixing the Failures of Our Housing Policy* (Hong Kong University Press, 2015), pp. 115–30.

22. Organization for Economic Cooperation and Development, "PISA 2012 Results," 2014 (www.oecd.org/pisa/keyfindings/pisa-2012-results.htm).

23. "Times Higher Education World University Rankings, 2014–2015," November 2014 (www.timeshighereducation.co.uk/world-university-rankings/2015/world -ranking/detailed#/sort/0/direction/asc).

24. Ibid.

25. World Economic Forum, *Global Competitiveness Report, 2014–2015,* p. 208.

26. Alex Lo, "Young People Need the Right Skills to Ensure Hong Kong's Future," *South China Morning Post,* August 5, 2015 (OSC CHR2015080466117463).

27. Ernest Kao, "New Vocational Model Urged to Rid Educational Option of Its Second-Class Status in Hong Kong," *South China Morning Post,* July 7, 2015 (www .scmp.com/news/hong-kong/education-community/article/1833907/new -vocational-model-urged-rid-educational-option).

28. Ernest Kao, "Hong Kong Still Has What It Takes to Become Research Hub, Says Tech Chief," *South China Morning Post,* September 5, 2013 (www.scmp.com /news/hong-kong/article/1303391/hong-kong-still-has-what-it-takes-become -research-hub-says-tech-chief).

29. Kao, "New Vocational Model Urged"; Shirley Zhao, "How to End Class Struggle in Hong Kong," *South China Morning Post,* March 5, 2015 (OSC

CHR2015030474798972); Regina Ip, "Is Hong Kong Dumbing Down Its Education System?" *South China Morning Post,* February 2, 2014 (OSC CHR2014020207534861).

30. Other Asian countries face similar problems. See "Education in East Asia: Overstrained, Outdated and in Need of Reform," *Global Asia* 10 (Summer 2015), pp. 6–53.

31. William Tierney and Gerard Postiglione, "The Vital Role of Academic Freedom in Creating a World Class University," *South China Morning Post,* July 5, 2015 (OSC CHR2015070511123593).

32. Gary Cheung, "Hong Kong and Singapore's Transformations: A Story of Both Rivalry and Partnership," *South China Morning Post,* August 8, 2015 (OSC CHR2015080773551587); "Hong Kong's Door Must Be Opened Wider to Foreign Talent," editorial, *South China Morning Post,* January 24, 2015 (www.scmp.com /comment/insight-opinion/article/1690301/hong-kongs-door-must-be-opened -wider-foreign-talent).

33. "Hong Kong's Door Must be Opened Wider to Foreign Talent."

34. Rachel Chan, "Hong Kong Has Potential to Become Start Up Hub of Asia Pacific Region," *South China Morning Post,* March 13, 2015 (OSC CHR2015031402139764); Tony Chan, "How Our Innovative Youth Can Make Hong Kong Even Greater," *South China Morning Post,* April 27, 2015 (OSC CHR2015042665135083); Hong Liang, "Hong Kong Needs More Tech Start Ups," *China Daily (Asia-Pacific),* July 29, 2015 (OSC CHR2015072903938055).

35. C. Y. Leung, "2014 Policy Address—Support the Needy, Let Youth Flourish, Unleash Hong Kong's Potential," January 15, 2014 (OSC CHL2014011512164253). In his budget speech, John Tsang recommended accelerated commercialization of R&D products and services.

36. Amy Nip, "Inventor Professor Ron Hui Says Free-Thinking Is Vital for Hong Kong's Future," *South China Morning Post,* March 11, 2015 (www.scmp.com/news /hong-kong/article/1734648/inventor-professor-ron-hui-says-free-thinking-vital -hong-kongs-future).

37. Andrew Sheng, Edward Tse, and Sunny Cheng, "Hong Kong Government Must Nurture the Lion Rock Spirit of Innovation," *South China Morning Post,* January 17, 2014 (OSC CHR2014011725515174).

38. Phila Siu, "Regina Ip's Think Tank to Examine Hong Kong's Competitiveness," *South China Morning Post,* May 11, 2015 (OSC CHR2015051106927296).

39. Nip, "Inventor Professor Ron Hui Says Free-Thinking Is Vital."

40. Peter Guy, "Cultivating a Risk Culture Biggest Barrier to Hong Kong's Tech Dreams," *South China Morning Post,* April 12, 2015 (OSC CHR2015041239917791); Jennifer Ngo, "Allow Young the Freedom to Fail, Says Start-Up Founder in SCMP Debate," *South China Morning Post,* July 10, 2015 (www.scmp.com/news/hong-kong /education-community/article/1835557/allow-young-freedom-fail-says-start -founder-scmp).

41. Ngo, "Allow Young the Freedom to Fail."

42. Timmy Sung, "Hong Kong Policy Change Sought to Allow Pearl River Delta Firms to Return to City," *South China Morning Post,* February 11, 2015 (www.scmp

.com/news/hong-kong/article/1709576/hong-kong-policy-change-sought-allow
-pearl-river-delta-firms-return).

43. Mr. Shangkong [George Chen], "Shenzhen Drone Maker DJI Was the Technology Start-Up That Got Away," *South China Morning Post,* June 10, 2015 (www
.scmp.com/business/companies/article/1726929/shenzhen-drone-maker-dji-was
-technology-start-got-away).

44. Cannix Yau, "It's Time to Step out of Our Comfort Zone So Hong Kong
Can Progress, Says Educator," *South China Morning Post,* May 22, 2015 (OSC
CHR2015052172645268).

45. Howard Winn, "World's 'Freest Economy' Accolade Does Hong Kong a
Disservice," *South China Morning Post,* January 28, 2015 (www.scmp.com/business
/economy/article/1694331/worlds-freest-economy-accolade-does-hong-kong
-disservice).

46. Te-Ping Chen, "Hong Kong Law to Bust Cartels? Not Likely," *Wall Street
Journal Blog,* April 12, 2012 (blogs.wsj.com/chinarealtime/2012/04/12/hong-kong
-law-to-bust-cartels-not-likely/); Philip Bowring, "Hong Kong's Professions Must
Not Be Protectors of Their Own Privilege," *South China Morning Post,* January 12,
2014 (OSC CHL2014011200919310). Hong Kong gasoline prices are among the
highest in the world. See "Petrol Prices in Hong Kong Will Be First Big Test for New
Competition Law," editorial, *South China Morning Post,* August 7, 2015 (www.scmp
.com/comment/insight-opinion/article/1847142/petrol-prices-hong-kong-will-be
-first-big-test-new).

47. Chen, "Hong Kong Law to Bust Cartels?" For a legal analysis of the law, see
Kelvin Hiu Fai Kwok, "The New Competition Law: Anomalies and Challenges,"
World Competition 37 (2014), pp. 542–67.

48. Ng Kang-chung, "Hong Kong's Competition Watchdog 'at Risk of Vexatious
Complaints,'" *South China Morning Post,* December 23, 2014 (www.scmp.com/news
/hong-kong/article/1668116/hong-kongs-competition-watchdog-risk-vexatious
-complaints); Ng Kang-chung, "Businesses Fail to Get Watchdog to Tighten Rules on
Anti Competition Complaints," *South China Morning Post,* March 31, 2015 (OSC
CHR2015033062423589).

49. David Dodwell, "Hong Kong's Competition Commission Shaping Up as a
Paper Tiger with Paper Teeth," *South China Morning Post,* December 18, 2015 (www
.scmp.com/print/business/article/1892582/hong-kongs-competition-commission
-shaping-paper-tiger-paper-teeth).

50. Michael Littlewood, "The Hong Kong Tax System: Key Features and Lessons
for Policy Makers," *Prosperitas* 7 (March 2007), p. 10 (http://archive.freedomand
prosperity.org/Papers/hongkong/hongkong.shtml).

51. Ibid., pp. 7–10.

52. Central Intelligence Agency, *World Factbook,* "Country Comparison: Taxes
and Other Revenues" (www.cia.gov/library/publications/the-world-factbook/rankorder
/2221rank.html).

53. Ibid., "Field Listing, Age Structure" (www.cia.gov/library/publications
/resources/the-world-factbook/fields/2010.html#hk). Singapore is the leader in

expenditures for defense at 3.2 percent of GDP, followed by Korea and Taiwan at around 2.5 percent, Japan at 1 percent, and Hong Kong at none. See ibid., "Field Listing, Military Expenditures" (www.cia.gov/library/publications/resources/the-world-factbook/fields/2034.html#sn).

54. A long-time observer of Hong Kong affairs, personal communication, July 2014.

55. Hong Kong Council of Social Service. "Social Indicators of Hong Kong," tables on shares of total household expenditure on housing, food, and transport (http://socialindicators.org.hk/en/indicators/basic_statistics).

56. "Hong Kong Must Reconsider a Broader Tax Base for Fiscal Stability," editorial, *South China Morning Post,* March 2, 2015 (OSC CHR2015030175617818).

57. "Hong Kong's Narrow Tax Base Is Storing Up Trouble for the Future," editorial, *South China Morning Post,* March 1, 2016 (www.scmp.com/comment/insight-opinion/article/1919533/hong-kongs-narrow-tax-base-storing-trouble-future).

58. John Tsang, "Hong Kong Budget Speech by the Financial Secretary 2013–14," February 26, 2014 (www.info.gov.hk/gia/general/201402/26/P201402260264.htm); Jake van der Kamp, "Tsang's Budget Concerns for Hong Kong Ones Most Cities Wish They Had," *South China Morning Post,* January 8, 2014 (www.scmp.com/comment/insight-opinion/article/1397465/tsangs-budget-concerns-hong-kong-ones-most-cities-wish-they).

59. World Bank, "Health Care Expenditures, Public (% of GDP), 2013" (http://data.worldbank.org/indicator/SH.XPD.PUBL.ZS); Tsung-Mei Cheng, "Taiwan's Health Care System: The Next 20 Years," Brookings Institution, Center for East Asia Policy Studies, Taiwan-U.S. Quarterly Analysis, no. 17, May 2015 (www.brookings.edu/research/opinions/2015/05/14-taiwan-national-healthcare-cheng); Tsang, "Hong Kong Budget Speech 2013–14."

60. Pension Funds Online, Wilmington Insights, "Hong Kong" (www.pensionfundsonline.co.uk/content/country-profiles/hong-kong/104).

61. Richard Wong, "Health Care and Home Ownership Most Pressing Concerns for an Ageing Population," *South China Morning Post,* March 3, 2015 (www.scmp.com/business/article/1728344/health-care-and-home-ownership-most-pressing-concerns-ageing-population).

62. Lau Ping Cheung, "Finally, Hong Kong's Housing Policy Is Being Built on Solid Foundations," *South China Morning Post,* January 23, 2016 (www.scmp.com/comment/insight-opinion/article/1903650/finally-hong-kongs-housing-policy-being-built-solid).

63. For the details of Wong's proposal, see Wong, *Hong Kong Land for Hong Kong People,* pp. 191–98.

64. There is a government bond program but its main goal is to develop the local bond market. See website of the Hong Kong SAR, "Government Bond Program" (www.hkgb.gov.hk/en/overview/introduction.html).

65. Website of the Legislative Council of the Hong Kong Special Administrative Region of the People's Republic of China, "Panels and Subcommittees: Fifth Legislative Council (2012–2016)" (http://www.legco.gov.hk/general/english/panels/pan1216.htm).

66. Percy Luen-tim Lui, "The Legislature," in *Contemporary Hong Kong Government and Politics,* 2nd ed., edited by Lam Wai-man, Percy Luen-tim Lui, and Wilson Wong (Hong Kong University Press, 2012), pp. 53–55, 60–61; Percy Luen-tim Lui, author interview, May 2015; author communication, May 2016.

67. Lui, "The Legislature."

68. Ibid., pp. 61–62. My observation about the likely neutrality of the Secretariat is based on my experience working in the U.S. Congress.

69. A Hong Kong political scientist, personal communication to the author, May 2015.

70. Ian Scott, *The Public Sector in Hong Kong* (Hong Kong University Press, 2010), pp. 301–306.

71. Ibid., p. 304.

72. Ibid., p. 305.

73. Brian C. H. Fong, *Hong Kong's Governance under Chinese Sovereignty: The Failure of the State-Business Alliance after 1997* (New York: Routledge, 2014), pp. 250–51 (cited passages on p. 250).

74. Ibid., pp. 251–52.

75. Marilynn Brewer, "Multiple Identities and Identity Transition: Implications for Hong Kong," *International Journal of Intercultural Relations* 23 (March 1999), pp. 187–97.

76. Danny Chan, "Hong Kong's Protesting Youth Seek Freedom of a Different Kind," *South China Morning Post,* June 1, 2015 (OSC CHR5520150615230816).

77. Hong Kong Transition Project, *Constitutional Reform in Hong Kong: Round Three,* June 2013 (www.hktp.org/list/round-3-of-constitutional.pdf), pp. 20–21.

78. Leung Kwok-leung, "Spoiled Young People Are a Menace to Society," *China Daily (Asia-Pacific)*, January 22, 2015 (OSC CHR2015012219081884); John Chan, "Hong Kong's Young Protesters Need Lessons in Civility," *South China Morning Post,* March 9, 2015 (OSC CHR2015030862111559).

79. Eddy Li, "Patriotic Education Will Foster Sense of National Identity," *China Daily (Asia-Pacific),* July 2, 2015 (OSC CHR2015070224033497).

80. Steven Chung Fun Hung, "Civic Education Policy of the Hong Kong Special Administrative Region," *Asian Education and Development Studies* 2, no. 2 (2013), pp. 177–206.

81. Magdalena Mok and Kerry Kennedy, "Discontent Runs Deep: Hong Kong Faces a Real Risk of Losing Its Alienated Youth," *South China Morning Post,* February 24, 2016 (OSC CHR2016022426727465). The concepts of civic and citizenship education include "knowledge and understanding of political institutions and concepts, such as human rights, as well as social and community cohesion, diversity, the environment, communications, and global society"; International Association for the Evaluation of Education Achievement, "International Civic and Citizenship Education Study 2009" (http://www.iea.nl/iccs_2009.html).

82. Yew Chiew Ping and Kwong Kin-ming, "Hong Kong Identity on the Rise," *Asian Survey* 54 (November–December 2014), pp. 1088–112 (cited passage on p. 1110).

83. Elaine Chan and Joseph Chan, "Liberal Patriotism in Hong Kong," *Journal of Contemporary China* 23 (March 2014), pp. 952–72.

84. Kerry Kennedy, "Incivility Reigns in Hong Kong's Civil Society," *South China Morning Post,* November 10, 2015 (OSC CHR2015111024013276).

Chapter Ten: China, Hong Kong, and the Future of One Country, Two Systems

1. Hong Kong SAR Government, "The Basic Law of the Hong Kong Special Administrative Region of the People's Republic of China," hereafter: "Basic Law" (www.basiclaw.gov.hk/en/basiclawtext). Of course, Beijing reserves the prerogative of deciding whether the conditions laid out in article 18 have been met.

2. "Zhanzhong Weijiejue, Jiang 'Yigang Huigui'; Zhonggong Paixi Jie Xiang-gang Wenti Jiaojin" [Jiang Zemin 'reminisces about the return of Hong Kong' before Occupy Central is resolved; the CCP's factions haggle over the Hong Kong issue], *Pingguo Ribao,* December 4, 2014 (Open Source Center [hereafter: OSC] HR2014120422442382).

3. State Council Information Office, "The Practice of the 'One Country, Two Systems' Policy in the Hong Kong Special Administrative Region," Xinhua, June 10, 2014 (OSC CHR2014061013966806).

4. "Basic Law," article 74, p. 25. This provision does allow unrestricted introduction of bills that do not "relate to public expenditure or political structure or the operation of the government."

5. Percy Luen-tim Lui, "The Legislature," in *Contemporary Hong Kong Government and Politics,* 2nd ed., edited by Lam Wai-man, Percy Luen-tim Lui, and Wilson Wong (Hong Kong University Press, 2012), p. 60.

6. "Basic Law," Annex II, section II, p. 60.

7. The prohibition was enacted in the Chief Executive Election Ordinance, a Hong Kong law passed by the Legislative Council.

8. Ma Ngok, "Political Parties and Elections," in Lam, Lui, and Wong, *Contemporary Hong Kong Government and Politics,* p. 161.

9. Li Pang-kwong, "The Executive," in Lam, Lui, and Wong, *Contemporary Hong Kong Government and Politics,* p. 39.

10. Deng Xiaoping, "Speech at a Meeting with the Members of the Committee for Drafting the Basic Law of the Hong Kong Special Administrative Region," *Selected Works of Deng Xiaoping,* April 16, 1987 (https://dengxiaopingworks.wordpress.com/2013/03/18/speech-at-a-meeting-with-the-members-of-the-committee-for-drafting-the-basic-law-of-the-hong-kong-special-administrative-region).

11. Gary Cheung, "How Hong Kong's Electoral System Only Discourages Political Moderates," *South China Morning Post,* November 16, 2015 (OSC CHR2015111632713526).

12. Pippa Norris, *Electoral Engineering: Voting Rules and Political Behavior* (Harvard University Press, 2004), pp. 56–57.

13. Ibid., pp. 68–77; see the table on p. 69.

14. The United States' current lack of decisiveness is not caused by the winner-take-all method but by other aspects of the political system, such as the polarizing way districts are drawn.

15. A PRC scholar made the point more directly to a Hong Kong audience by saying that special representation was necessary to protect the interests of the wealthy. See Johnny Mok, "Nominating Committee's Vital Role in Safeguarding Hong Kong's Interests," *South China Morning Post,* May 5, 2014 (www.scmp.com /comment/insight-opinion/article/1504278/nominating-committees-vital-role -safeguarding-hong-kongs); Michael Forsythe and Keith Bradsher, "On Hong Kong, Democracy and Protecting the Rich," *New York Times,* August 29, 2014 (http:// sinosphere.blogs.nytimes.com/2014/08/29/wang-zhenmin-on-hong-kong -democracy-and-protecting-the-rich/).

16. Man Mun-lam, "Functional Constituencies Help HK's Development," *China Daily (Asia-Pacific),* February 15, 2015 (OSC CHR20150209168494750).

17. Hong Kong Transition Project, *Constitutional Reform in Hong Kong: Round Three,* June 2013 (www.hktp.org/list/round-3-of-constitutional.pdf), p. 119.

18. Tony Cheung, "Hong Kong's Basic Law Could Be More Imaginative and Less Restrictive on the Economy," *South China Morning Post,* September 6, 2015 (OSC CHR2015090715626423).

19. Frank Ching, "Let Political Parties Play a Central Role in 2017 Chief Executive Election," *South China Morning Post,* December 4, 2013 (OSC CHO2013120409230575).

20. Jeffie Lam, "UN Governance Adviser Larry Diamond Suggests Forming Parliament in Hong Kong," *South China Morning Post,* March 10, 2014 (OSC CHR2014031001524438).

21. Alice Wu, "Hong Kong Is Stuck—with or without Political Reform," *South China Morning Post,* March 30, 2015 (OSC CHR2015032962420854).

22. Richard C. Bush, *Uncharted Strait: The Future of China-Taiwan Relations* (Brookings Institution Press, 2013).

23. "Shenme Shi Xianggang di Shenzengzi Wenti?" [What are Hong Kong's deep-seated problems?], *Ta Kung Pao,* December 2, 2015 (OSC CHR2015120227559393).

24. Ibid.

Chapter Eleven: Hong Kong and Taiwan

1. On Beijing's initial proposals on Taiwan, see Richard C. Bush, *Untying the Knot: Making Peace in the Taiwan Strait* (Brookings Institution Press, 2005), pp. 36–38. Policy on Hong Kong was formulated in meetings held in Beijing in December 1981 and January 1982. See Ezra F. Vogel, *Deng Xiaoping and the Transformation of China* (Harvard University Press, 2011), pp. 494–95.

2. Xi Jinping, "Full Text of Remarks by President Xi Jinping at Gathering for Macao SAR's 15th Anniversary," Xinhua, December 20, 2014 (Open Source Center [hereafter: OSC] CHR2014122034233680).

3. Sonny Shiu-hing Lo, "One Formula, Two Experiences: Political Divergence of Hong Kong and Macao Since Retrocession," *Journal of Contemporary China* 16 (August 2007), pp. 259–387.

4. Taiwan's having been a colony of imperial Japan from 1895 to 1945 was something it had in common with British Hong Kong, but the fact that Taiwan was ruled by a rival government to the PRC made its political character very different.

5. Lee Teng-hui, "Answers to Questions Submitted by Former Hong Kong Governor Chris Patten," July 7, 1998, *President Lee Teng-hui's Selected Addresses and Messages 1998* (Taipei: Government Information Office, 1999), p. 102. Contrary to Lee, the Taiwan Foreign Ministry had issued a fairly bland statement on the day of Hong Kong's reversion. See Liang Yu-li, "Establish a Stable and Complete New Taiwan-Hong Kong Structure: Text of the Government's Statement on the Transfer of Sovereignty over Hong Kong," *Chung-Yang Jih-Pao,* July 1, 1997 (OSC FTS19970705000629).

6. There were differences among the three territories. For example, Taiwan had an indigenous military establishment, which Hong Kong and Macau never had. That led Beijing to suggest early on, but without much detail, that the Taiwan armed forces would be preserved after unification as long as they were not a threat to the mainland. See Bush, *Untying the Knot,* p. 38.

7. Website of the Taiwan Mainland Affairs Office, "Act Governing Relations with Hong Kong and Macau" (www.mac.gov.tw/ct.asp?xItem=51261&ctNode =5915&mp=3).

8. Wang Enbao, "The Hong Kong Model and China's Unification," in *Dynamics and Dilemma: Mainland, Taiwan and Hong Kong in a Changing World,* edited by Yu Bin and Chung Tsungting (New York: Nova Science Publishers, 1996), pp. 118–23. Taiwan's Mainland Affairs Council did publish an annual report on Hong Kong developments from 1997, the year of reversion, until 2008. For the last report, see website of Mainland Affairs Council, "Analysis Report: 11 Years After Hong Kong's Handover," September 2008 (www.mac.gov.tw/lp.asp?CtNode=5939&CtUnit =4157&BaseDSD=7&mp=3). Coincidentally, 2008 was the first year of Ma Ying-jeou's administration, which pursued a mainland policy that was more conciliatory than those of his two predecessors.

9. On the sovereignty issue see Bush, *Untying the Knot,* pp. 81–106; Richard C. Bush, *Uncharted Strait: The Future of China-Taiwan Relations* (Brookings Institution Press, 2013), pp. 81–98.

10. Website of New Taiwan Ihla Formsa, "DPP Resolution on Taiwan's Future," May 8, 1999 (www.taiwandc.org/nws-9920.htm). Actually, the DPP's use of the term "jurisdiction" creates ambiguity, because the territory under a state's jurisdiction can be less than what it claims as its sovereign territory. The KMT position effectively employs that distinction. But for practical purposes, the DPP excludes the mainland from Taiwan's sovereign territory.

11. For Beijing's anxiety about Taiwan's democratization, see Bush, *Untying the Knot,* pp. 204–10.

12. Election Study Center, National Chengchi University, "Taiwanese/Chinese Identification Trend Distribution in Taiwan (1992/06~2014/12)" (http://esc.nccu

.edu.tw/course/news.php?Sn=166#). This shift was similar to one that occurred later in Hong Kong (see chapter 5).

13. For a summary of Taiwan's postwar political history, see Bush, *Untying the Knot,* pp. 142–61. The seminal analysis of the formation of Taiwanese identity is Alan M. Wachman, *Taiwan: National Identity and Democratization* (Armonk, N.Y.: M. E. Sharpe, 1994). Blue is the color of the KMT's party flag and green the color of the DPP's.

14. For more on the 1991 position advocating a "sovereign Taiwan Republic," see Shelley Rigger, *From Opposition to Power: Taiwan's Democratic Progressive Party* (Boulder, Colo.: Lynne Rienner, 2001), p. 31. The 1999 position, which was still operative in July 2015, reads as follows: "Taiwan is a sovereign and independent country. In accordance with international laws, Taiwan's jurisdiction covers Taiwan, Penghu, Kinmen, Matsu, its affiliated islands and territorial waters. Taiwan, although named the Republic of China under its current constitution, is not subject to the jurisdiction of the People's Republic of China." See Website of New Taiwan Ihla Formsa "DPP Resolution."

15. Election Study Center, National Chengchi University, "Taiwan Independence vs. Unification with the Mainland Trend Distribution in Taiwan (1992/06~2014/12)" (http://esc.nccu.edu.tw/course/news.php?Sn=167).

16. Shelley Rigger, "Taiwan's Rising Rationalism: Generations, Politics, and 'Taiwanese Nationalism,'" *Policy Studies,* no. 26, 2006 (published by East-West Center, Honolulu, Hawaii).

17. Thomas B. Gold, "Occupy Central/Sunflower: Popular Resistance in Greater China," Foreign Policy Research Institute e-note, October 2014 (www.fpri.org/articles/2014/10/occupy-centralsunflower-popular-resistance-greater-china).

18. Controlling electoral outcomes was not an unknown in Taiwan. During the authoritarian period the KMT created its own mechanisms to ensure that the people it didn't like—mainly native Taiwanese—did not get too much power. Not surprisingly, these anti-democratic arrangements were criticized by democracy advocates both within and outside Taiwan and their termination was the primary focus of political reforms. With the transition to democracy, direct popular elections in the territories under ROC jurisdiction selected the president and members of the legislature.

19. Similarly, anyone who reviewed the membership of the Hong Kong Basic Law Drafting Committee and the low representation from the democratic camp would likewise be concerned by how much say people in Taiwan would have over the drafting of a Taiwan Basic Law.

20. John Lim, "Ma Ignoring HK at Taiwan's Peril," *Taipei Times,* June 26, 2014 (www.taipeitimes.com/News/editorials/archives/2014/06/26/2003593675).

21. Shelley Rigger, "Disaggregating the Concept of National Identity," Asia Program Special Report 114 (Washington, D.C.: Woodrow Wilson International Center for Scholars, August 2003), pp. 17–21.

22. Sonny Lo, "The 'Taiwanization' of Hong Kong Politics," *South China Morning Post,* March 25, 2015 (OSC CHR2015032521909199).

23. Tammy Tam, "Will Taiwan Become a New Hong Kong—or Vice Versa?" *South China Morning Post,* April 7, 2014 (OSC CHR2014040701573896); In Joo Song (Hong Kong University), personal communication to the author, April 15, 2015; Huang Min-hua (National Taiwan University), personal communication with the author, June 2105.

24. This observation is based on an inventory, compiled by Maeve Whelan-Wuest, of coverage of Hong Kong by Taiwan media. Alan Romberg of the Henry L. Stimson Center concluded that because "the majority of people in Taiwan see very little correlation between Hong Kong's situation and their own," the protests had little impact. See "Hong Kong Protests Have Had Little Effect on Taiwan: US Scholars," Central News Agency, December 10, 2014 (OSC CHR2014121026472845).

25. Taiwan contact, personal communication with the author, October 2014.

26. Blue camp scholar, personal communication to the author, August 3, 2015.

27. Website of Democratic Progressive Party, "Press Statement by Chairperson Tsai Ing-wen (Oct. 1, 2014)" (http://english.dpp.org.tw/dpp-supports-democracy-in -hong-kong).

28. "Government Must Learn Hong Kong's Lessons," *Taipei Times,* September 30, 2014 (www.taipeitimes.com/News/editorials/archives/2014/09/30/2003600895).

29. Website of the Office of the President, "President Ma Ying-jeou's National Day Address," October 10, 2014 (http://english.president.gov.tw/Default.aspx?tabid =491&itemid=33376&rmid=2355&sd=2014/10/10&ed=2014/10/11).

30. "Ma Ting Xianggang Xuanpu: Zhongguo Fanpi, Wu Shuosan Daosi" [Ma supports universal suffrage in Hong Kong; China responds with criticism: "Don't say irresponsible things"], *newtalk,* October 10, 2014 (http://newtalk.tw/news/view /2014-10-10/52346).

31. "Liberty Times Editorial: Ma Deaf to Hong Kong's Call to Democracy," *Taipei Times,* September 11, 2014 (OSC CHR2014091065129920). The *Taipei Times* is the sister-paper to the Chinese-language *Tzu-you Shih-pao (Liberty Times).*

32. "Students Join the Fray in Hong Kong," editorial, *Taipei Times,* September 25, 2014 (www.taipeitimes.com/News/editorials/archives/2014/09/25/2003600499).

33. "Liberty Times Editorial: Ma Deaf to Hong Kong's Call to Democracy."

34. Lim, "Ma ignoring HK at Taiwan's Peril."

35. "Government Must Learn Hong Kong's Lessons," editorial, *Taipei Times,* September 30, 2014 (OSC CHR2014092971132314).

36. Tung Chen-yuan, personal communication with the author, July 22, 2015.

37. "United Daily News: 'One Country, Two Systems' Infeasible for Taiwan," Central News Agency, September 8, 2014 (OSC CHR2014090828864827).

38. "'One Country, Two Systems' Is Outdated Policy: Experts," *Taipei Times,* October 10, 2014 (www.taipeitimes.com/News/taiwan/archives/2014/10 /102003601741).

39. "Jiang Rejects Analogy of Taiwan, Hong Kong Fate," *Taipei Times,* October 8, 2014 (www.taipeitimes.com/News/taiwan/archives/2014/10/08/2003601582).

40. I am grateful to an external reviewer of my manuscript for suggesting this perspective.

41. Alan D. Romberg, "Cross-Strait Relations: Setting the Stage for 2012," *China Leadership Monitor,* no. 34, Winter 2011 (http://media.hoover.org/sites/default/files /documents/CLM34AR.pdf), p. 12.

42. Hans Mouritzen, "The Difficult Art of Finlandization," *Foreign Affairs* 89 (May–June 2010), p. 131. See also Hans Mouritzen, *Finlandization: Towards a Theory of Adaptive Politics* (Farnham, U.K.: Gower, 1988).

43. Mouritzen, "The Difficult Art of Finlandization," p. 130.

44. Keith Bradsher and Austin Ramzy, "Taiwan President Backs Hong Kong Protesters While Courting Beijing," *New York Times,* October 31, 2014 (www .nytimes.com/2014/11/01/world/asia/taiwan-president-Ma-Ying-jeou-backs-hong -kong-protesters-while-courting-beijing.html).

45. "Culture Minister Urges Beijing to Win Hearts 'with Civility,'" Central News Agency, September 29, 2014 (OSC CHR2014092932090909).

Chapter Twelve: United States Policy toward Hong Kong

1. U.S. Department of Homeland Security, "Yearbook of Immigration Statistics" (www.dhs.gov/yearbook-immigration-statistics [accessed April 24, 2015]).

2. U.S. Department of State, "The Hong Kong Policy Report," April 10, 2015 (www.state.gov/p/eap/rls/reports/2015/240585.htm); Japan Ministry of Foreign Affairs, "Annual Report of Statistics on Japanese Nationals Overseas," October 1, 2014 (www.mofa.go.jp/mofaj/files/000086464.pdf), p. 36; Consulate General of the Republic of Korea, "Bilateral Relations" (http://hkg.mofa.go.kr/english/as/hkg /bilateral/bilateral/index.jsp).

3. U.S. Department of State, "The Hong Kong Policy Report."

4. Bureau of Economic Analysis, U.S. Department of Commerce, Balance of Payments Section (2)1, December 10, 2015, "U.S. Direct Investment Abroad, U.S. Direct Investment Position Abroad on a Historical Cost Basis" (www.bea.gov /international/datatables/usdpos/usdpos_66.htm and www.bea.gov/international /datatables/usdpos/usdpos_77.htm); Census and Statistics Department, Hong Kong SAR Government, "Table 048: Position and Flow of Inward Direct Investment (DI) of Hong Kong at Market Value by Selected Major Investor Country/Territory" (www.censtatd.gov.hk/hkstat/sub/sp260.jsp?tableID=048&ID=0&productType =8); United Nations Conference on Trade and Development, FDI/TNC database, based on data from the Export-Import Bank of Korea, "Table 2. FDI flows Abroad, by Geographical Destination: Republic of Korea" (http://unctad.org/en/Pages /DIAE/FDI%20Statistics/FDI-Statistics-Bilateral.aspx).

5. Hong Kong SAR Government, Protocol Division Government Secretariat, "Consular Posts and Officially Recognised Representatives: United States of America" (www.protocol.gov.hk/eng/consular/america/usa.htm).

6. U.S. Department of State, "The Hong Kong Policy Report."

7. Unless otherwise indicated, in "Historical Background" I draw on Nancy Bernkopf Tucker, *Taiwan, Hong Kong, and the United States, 1945–1992: Uncertain Friendships* (New York: Twayne, 1994); Chi-kwan Mark, *Hong Kong and the Cold*

War: Anglo-American Relations 1949–1957 (Oxford, U.K.: Clarendon Press, 2004) covers the same ground up through 1957 and reaches similar conclusions.

8. Philip Snow, *The Fall of Hong Kong: Britain, China, and the Japanese Occupation* (Yale University Press, 2003), pp. 142–48, 189–95; Richard C. Bush, *At Cross Purposes: U.S.-Taiwan Relations Since 1942* (Armonk, N.Y.: M. E. Sharpe, 2004), p. 36. Whether Chiang agreed to the free-port idea is uncertain.

9. Snow, *The Fall of Hong Kong*, pp. 229–49.

10. Tucker, *Taiwan, Hong Kong, and the United States*, p. 201.

11. Mark, *Hong Kong and the Cold War*, p. 78.

12. Tucker, *Taiwan, Hong Kong, and the United States*, p. 201.

13. Mark, *Hong Kong and the Cold War*, pp. 32–37; James R. Lilley and Jeffrey Lilley, *China Hands: Nine Decades of Adventure, Espionage, and Diplomacy in Asia* (New York: PublicAffairs, 2005), pp. 83–86.

14. This is the thesis of Mark, *Hong Kong and the Cold War*.

15. Tucker, *Taiwan, Hong Kong, and the United States*, p. 202.

16. Ibid., pp. 203–4.

17. Richard Bush, *The Politics of Cotton Textiles in Kuomintang China: 1927–1937* (New York: Garland, 1982); Siu-lun Wong, *Emigrant Entrepreneurs: Shanghai Industrialists in Hong Kong* (Oxford University Press, 1989).

18. This observation is based on my personal recollections.

19. Tucker, *Taiwan, Hong Kong, and the United States*, p. 219.

20. I was working on Capitol Hill at the time, and my boss, Representative Stephen Solarz, a Democrat from New York, took the lead in this effort.

21. Tucker, *Taiwan, Hong Kong, and the United States*, pp. 222–23, 295n117; U.S. Congress, House of Representatives, Committee on Foreign Affairs, Subcommittee on Asian and Pacific Affairs, *Hearing and Markup: The Political Situation in Hong Kong and Issues Relating to Emigration*, November 14, 1989.

22. Christopher Patten, presentation at the Brookings Institution, May 5, 1993, author's notes.

23. See, for example, U.S. Congress, House of Representatives, Committee on Foreign Affairs, Subcommittee on Human Rights and International Organizations, Subcommittee on Asian and Pacific Affairs, and Subcommittee on International Economic Policy and Trade, *Hearings: Most-Favored-Nation Status for the People's Republic of China*, May 16 and 24, 1990.

24. Governor Chris Patten had a two-part message when he visited U.S. officials and members of Congress in May 1993: Don't cancel China's most-favored-nation status because it would grievously hurt Hong Kong. But do hint to Beijing that a positive approach to the territory's political development would make it easier for the British to argue in favor of most-favored-nation. See Jonathan Dimbleby, *The Last Governor: Chris Patten and the Handover of Hong Kong* (London: Warner Books, 1997), pp. 230–32.

25. Such lobbying continues to this day. See Martin Lee, "Hong Kong's Shaky Democratic Future," *New York Times*, March 17, 2015 (www.nytimes.com/2014/03/14/opinion/hong-kongs-shaky-democratic-future.html).

26. Martin Lee, letter to Congressman Stephen Solarz, April 7, 1991 (in author's collection).

27. *To Establish the Policy of the United States with Respect to Hong Kong after June 30, 1997, and for Other Purposes,* HR 3522, 102nd Congress, 1st session (October 8, 1991), p. 15.

28. Yu Ching, "What Does Some People's Advocacy of 'McConnell Bill' Mean?" *Wen Wei Po,* January 11, 1992, January 13, 1992 (Foreign Broadcast Information Service, FBIS-CHI-92-008).

29. "Pacific Watch: Hong Kong," *Los Angeles Times,* April 27, 1992, p. D-3.

30. *An Act to Establish the Policy of [the] United States with Respect to Hong Kong, and for Other Purposes,* HR 1731, 102nd Congress, 2nd session (May 27, 1992).

31. I did the staff work on the bill for the House Committee on Foreign Affairs.

32. The language of the act leaves unclear what would happen once a presidential determination was made.

33. Rimsky Yuen, "SJ [Secretary of Justice] Speaks on Snowden case (English translation)," Department of Justice, Hong Kong SAR Government, June 26, 2013 (www.doj.gov.hk/eng/public/pr/20130625_pr3.html).

34. Jane Perlez and Keith Bradsher, "China Said to Have Made Call to Let Leaker Depart," *New York Times,* June 23, 2013 (www.nytimes.com/2013/06/24/world /asia/china-said-to-have-made-call-to-let-leaker-depart.html).

35. U.S. Department of State, "The Hong Kong Policy Report." Strangely, the report used the criterion of "autonomy" in judging Hong Kong's performance concerning a treaty when, strictly speaking, the standard in the act is "legal competence."

36. Clifford A. Hart, "Impressions on the U.S.–Hong Kong Partnership: Strong Ties Bring Shared Benefits," speech to the American Chamber of Commerce in Hong Kong, September 24, 2013 (http://hongkong.usconsulate.gov/cg _ch_2013092401.html).

37. Mark, *Hong Kong and the Cold War,* p. 109.

38. Ibid., p. 29.

39. "Full Text: China's Peaceful Development," Xinhua, September 6, 2011 (Open Source Center [hereafter: OSC]) CPP20110906968009).

40. Jiang Rongdiao, "2013 Nian Xianggang Zhengzhi Xingshi Qianxi" [An analysis of the 2013 political situation in Hong Kong], in *Buduan Jinqu* [Strive without stopping], edited by Zhou Tianzhu and Zhang Peimin (Shanghai: Shanghai Dongya Yanjiuso, 2014), p. 193.

41. Keith Bradsher, "Some Chinese Leaders Claim U.S. and Britain Are Behind Hong Kong Protests," *New York Times,* October 11, 2014 (www.nytimes.com/2014 /10/11/world/asia/some-chinese-leaders-claim-us-and-britain-are-behind-hong -kong-protests-.html).

42. "Foreign Countries Backing Occupy: Leung," *The Standard,* October 20, 2014 (OSC CHR2014102001250193).

43. Suzanne Pepper, "For Beijing, Vilifying Foreign Forces Is a Useful Strategy for Hong Kong," *South China Morning Post,* October 21, 2013 (OSC CHR20131100210310172).

44. A Hong Kong business executive, personal communication with the author, summer 2014.

45. "'Democratic Black Hands' Reaching Out to Young Students Must Be Cut Off," editorial, *Ta Kung Pao,* March 20, 2015 (OSC CHR2015032024526670).

46. Xu Shu, *"Caifu* Chuipeng Huang Zhifeng Shuomingle Shemme?" [What has *Fortune's* flattery of Huang Zhifeng explained?], *Wen Wei Po,* March 30, 2015 (OSC CHO2015033021510442). Huang Zhifeng is Joshua Wong.

47. Cheng Chi-tzu, "'Zhanzhong' Yunniang Mei NDI 'Bengshui' Zhangshibei," [To nurture 'Occupy Central,' America's NDI's 'pump-priming' by ten times], *Wen Wei Po,* August 8, 2015 (OSC CHR2015070822343680); an employee of the National Democratic Institute for International Affairs, personal communication with the author, August 2015.

48. Bradsher, "Some Chinese Leaders Claim U.S. and Britain Are Behind Hong Kong Protests."

49. White House, Office of the Press Secretary, "Remarks by President Obama and President Xi Jinping in Joint Press Conference," press release, November 12, 2014 (www.whitehouse.gov/the-press-office/2014/11/12/remarks-president-obama -and-president-xi-jinping-joint-press-conference).

50. Nectar Gan and Stuart Lau, "Hong Kong's Occupy Protest 'Was an Attempt at Colour Revolution': PLA General," *South China Morning Post,* March 3, 2015 (www.scmp.com/news/hong-kong/article/1728027/occupy-central-was-attempt -colour-revolution-pla-general).

51. American scholar, personal communication with the author, June 2015.

52. White House, Office of the Press Secretary, "Press Briefing by Press Secretary Josh Earnest, 9/29/2014," press release, September 29, 2014 (www.whitehouse .gov/the-press-office/2014/09/29/press-briefing-press-secretary-josh-earnest -9292014).

53. White House, Office of the Press Secretary, "Remarks by President Obama and President Xi Jinping."

54. U.S. Congress, Congressional-Executive Commission on China, *Hearings on the Future of Democracy in Hong Kong,* 113th Congress, 2nd session, 2014, "Statement of Congressman Chris Smith," pp. 2–3 (www.cecc.gov/events/hearings/the -future-of-democracy-in-hong-kong).

55. As did the Hong Kong University law professor Michael C. Davis in "Beijing's Broken Promises," *Journal of Democracy* 26 (April 2015), pp. 101–14.

56. U.S. Congress, Congressional-Executive Commission on China, *Hearings on the Future of Democracy in Hong Kong,* "Statement of U.S. Senator Sherrod Brown," November 20, 2014 (www.cecc.gov/events/hearings/the-future-of-democracy-in -hong-kong), p. 1; U.S. Congress, Senate, Committee on Foreign Relations, Subcommittee on East Asia, the Pacific, and International Cybersecurity Policy, *Hearings on Evaluating the Impact of the "Umbrella Movement,"* December 3, 2014 (www.foreign .senate.gov/hearings/120314am).

57. U.S. Congress, Senate, Committee on Foreign Relations, Subcommittee on East Asia, the Pacific, and International Cybersecurity Policy, *Hearings on Evaluating*

the Impact of the "Umbrella Movement," "Testimony of Daniel Russel," December 3, 2014 (www.foreign.senate.gov/download/russel-testimony-12-03-14).

58. U.S. Department of State, "The Hong Kong Policy Report."

59. *A Bill to Reinstate Reporting Requirements Related to United States–Hong Kong Relations,* HR 1159, 114th Congress, 1st session (February 27, 2015) (www .congress.gov/bill/114th-congress/house-bill/1159).

60. In the summer of 2015, the operative provisions of HR 1159 were incorporated into the Senate version of the bill authorizing funds for the State Department, a frequent vehicle for enacting foreign policy measures. See U.S. Congress, Senate, *A Bill To Authorize the Department of State for Fiscal Year 2016, and for Other Purposes,* S 1635, 114th Congress, 1st session (June 18, 2015). On the certification, the text was revised to specify that the "different treatment" was not for Hong Kong in general, but for its citizens. The significance of this change, if there was any, was unclear.

61. The annual report was again required in the omnibus appropriations bill.

62. U.S. Department of State, "The Hong Kong Policy Report."

63. Gary Cheung, "US Urges 'Meaningful Choice' of Candidates for Hong Kong's Leader," *South China Morning Post,* April 23, 2015 (OSC CHR2015042357326942).

64. Clifford A. Hart, Jr., "Independence Day Reception Remarks in Hong Kong," June 30, 2015 (http://hongkong.usconsulate.gov/cg_ch_2015063001.html).

65. Walter Russell Meade, *A Special Providence: American Foreign Policy and How It Changed the World* (New York: Routledge, 2002).

66. Ronald W. Reagan, "Address to Members of the British Parliament" (www .heritage.org/research/reports/2002/06/reagans-westminster-speech).

67. The National Endowment for Democracy's *Journal of Democracy* would become the leading platform for the exchange of ideas on democratic theory and practice and a source of reports on political development of countries around the world.

68. Dimbleby, *The Last Governor,* p. 231.

69. Bush, *At Cross Purposes,* pp. 179–218. The Taiwan regime was quite active in encouraging support for its existing regime within the American political system.

70. White House, Office of the Press Secretary, "Remarks by President Obama and President Xi Jinping."

71. Richard C. Bush, *Perils of Proximity: China-Japan Security Relations* (Brookings Institution Press, 2010).

72. Marco Rubio, "Restoring America's Strength: My Vision for U.S. Foreign Policy," *Foreign Affairs* 94 (September–October 2015), pp. 113–14.

73. Samuel P. Huntington, *The Third Wave: Democratization in the Late Twentieth Century* (Oklahoma University Press, 1991), pp. 109–63.

74. Bush, *At Cross Purposes,* pp. 197–214.

Chapter Thirteen: Conclusion

1. Wm. Theodore de Bary, *Waiting for the Dawn: A Plan for the Prince; Huang Tsung-hsi's Ming-i-tai-fang lu* (Columbia University Press, 1993).

2. In the United States, the statesmen who crafted the 1787 Constitution never abandoned the principles of political freedom and popular rule, yet their principal goal was to create a stronger national government.

3. "Full text of Constitution of Communist Party of China," Xinhua, March 29, 2013 (http://english.cpc.people.com.cn/206972/206981/8188065.html).

4. Because the Hong Kong SAR is not a unit like other subnational units of the PRC system, United Front tactics become particularly important to maintaining control. See Christine Loh, *Underground Front: The Chinese Communist Party in Hong Kong* (University of Hong Kong Press, 2010).

5. Larry Diamond, "Elections without Democracy: Thinking about Hybrid Regimes," *Journal of Democracy* 13 (April 2002), pp. 21–35.

6. Mark P. Lagon, "Beijing's Ruler versus Hong Kong's Heroes," *Freedom at Issue Blog,* September 23, 2015 (www.freedomhouse.org/blog/beijing-s-ruler-versus -hong-kong-s-heroes). Martin Lee, Benny Tai, and Joshua Wong were honored at a Freedom House event in September 2015.

7. On the different purposes of risk taking with respect to Taiwan, see Su Chi, "Su Chi Zhuanlan: Sanying Ma-Xi Hui" [Su Chi exclusive commentary: The Ma-Xi Meeting's triple win], *Chung-kuo Shi-pao (China Times),* November 9, 2015 (www .chinatimes.com/newspapers/20151109000385-260109).

8. Simon-Hoey Lee, "The Pros and Cons of Consensus Politics for Hong Kong," *South China Morning Post,* April 28, 2015 (www.scmp.com/comment/insight -opinion/article/1778726/pros-and-cons-consensus-politics-hong-kong).

9. Francis Fukuyama, *The Origins of Political Order: From Prehuman Times to the French Revolution* (New York: Farrar Straus and Giroux, 2011), and Fukuyama, *Political Order and Political Decay: From the Industrial Revolution to the Globalization of Democracy* (New York: Farrar, Straus and Giroux, 2014).

10. John Fitzgerald, "The Qing Is Dead! Long Live the Qing," *Inside Story,* August 11, 2015 (http://insidestory.org.au/the-qing-is-dead-long-live-the-qing), review of Daniel A. Bell, *The China Model: Political Meritocracy and the Limits of Democracy* (Princeton University Press, 2015). The presumption in the title that China has a meritocracy is belied by the widespread practice of officials' purchasing promotions.

11. I am grateful to one of my external reviewers for bringing this perspective to my attention.

12. On maintaining control over parts of the economy, see Eswar Prasad, "China's Fitful Economic Reforms," *New York Times,* December 2, 2015 (www.nytimes.com /2015/12/02/opinion/chinas-fitful-economic-reforms.html). On adaptation, see David Shambaugh, *China's Communist Party: Atrophy and Adaptation* (Washington, D.C., and Berkeley: Woodrow Wilson Center Press and University of California Press, 2008).

13. J. Stapleton Roy, "Obama-Xi Summit Not Doomed to Fail," *CNN,* September 22, 2015 (www.cnn.com/2015/09/22/opinions/roy-xi-jinping-visit/index.html). For a discussion of the discourse within China about governance, see Qinghua Wang and Gang Guo, "Yu Keping and Chinese Intellectual Discourse on Good Governance," *China Quarterly,* no. 224 (December 2015), pp. 985–1005.

14. "Full Text: CPC Central Committee Decision on Deepening of Reforms," Xinhua, November 15, 2013 (OSC CHO2013111541499182).

15. Sebastian Heilmann, "Policy-Making through Experimentation: The Formation of a Distinctive Policy Process," in *Mao's Invisible Hand: The Political Foundations of Adaptive Governance in China,* edited by Sebastian Heilmann and Elizabeth J. Perry (Harvard University Asia Center, 2011), pp. 62–101; Wang Shaoguang, "Learning through Practice and Experimentation: The Financing of Rural Health Care," in Heilman and Perry, *Invisible Hand,* pp. 102–37.

16. See, for example, website of the Ministry of Foreign Affairs of the People's Republic of China, "President Jiang Zemin's Speech at Ceremony for Establishment of HKSAR," July 1, 1997 (www.fmprc.gov.cn/mfa_eng/ljzg_665465/3566_665531 /t23034.shtml); "Full Text of President Hu Jintao's Speech at Dinner Given by the Hong Kong Special Administrative Region on 30 June 2007," Xinhua, June 30, 2007 (OSC CPP20070701136001); State Council Information Office, "The Practice of the 'One Country, Two Systems' Policy in the Hong Kong Special Administrative Region," Xinhua, June 10, 2014 (OSC CHR2014061013966806).

17. Peter T. Y. Cheung, "Who's Influencing Whom? Exploring the Influence of Hong Kong on Politics and Governance in China," *Asian Survey* 51 (July–August 2011), pp. 713–38 (cited passage on p. 725). See also Sonny Shiu-hing Lo, "The Influence of Hong Kong's Policing on China: Mechanisms of Knowledge Transfer," *Asian Survey* 51 (July–August 2011), pp. 769–84.

18. Website of Transparency International, "Corruption Perceptions Index 2014: Results" (www.transparency.org/cpi2014/results). Denmark ranked the least corrupt, with a score of 96. Somalia ranked the worst, with a score of 8.

19. For a good summary, see James Leung, "Xi's Corruption Crackdown: How Bribery and Graft Threaten the Chinese Dream," *Foreign Affairs* 94 (May–June 2015), pp. 32–38; "James Leung" is a pseudonym.

20. Transparency International, "Corruption Perceptions Index 2014."

21. Melanie Manion, "Lessons for Mainland China from Anti-Corruption Reform in Hong Kong," *China Review* 4 (Fall 2004), pp. 81–97.

22. Ibid., pp. 84–89.

23. Ibid., p. 88.

24. Ibid., pp. 89–91.

25. Xuezhi Guo, "Controlling Corruption in the Party: China's Central Discipline Inspection Commission," *China Quarterly,* no. 219 (September 2014), pp. 611–12.

26. Manion, "Lessons for Mainland China," pp. 91–92.

27. Ibid., p. 33.

28. Ibid., p. 94.

29. Yina Mao, Chi-Sum Wong, and Kelly Z. Peng, "Breaking Institutionalized Corruption: Is the Experience of the Hong Kong Independent Commission against Corruption Generalizable?" *Asia Pacific Journal of Management* 30 (April 2013), pp. 1115–24.

30. Ian Scott, "Institutional Design and Corruption Prevention in Hong Kong," *Journal of Contemporary China* 22 (December 2013), pp. 77–92 (cited passage on p. 92).

31. Ian Scott, "Political Scandals and Accountability of the Chief Executive in Hong Kong," *Asian Survey* 54 (September–October 2014), pp. 966–86.

32. Keith Zhai, "Mainland China Not Ready for Its Own ICAC, Analysts Say," *South China Morning Post,* February 16, 2014 (OSC CHR2014021625199533).

33. Carl Minzer, "Legal Reform in the Xi Jinping Era," *Asia Policy,* no. 20, July 2015, pp. 4–9.

34. Donald Clarke, "China's Legal System and the Fourth Plenum," *Asia Policy,* no. 20, July 2015, pp. 10–17 (cited passage on p. 15).

35. Jacques deLisle, "The Rule of Law with Xi-Era Characteristics: Law for Economic Reform, Anticorruption, and Illiberal Policies," *Asia Policy,* no. 20, July 2015, pp. 23–29.

36. Kjeld Erik Brodsgaard, "Assessing the Fourth Plenum of the Chinese Communist Party: Personnel Management and Corruption," *Asia Policy,* no. 20, July 2015, pp. 30–37.

37. Richard Wong, "Different Legal Traditions Keep Hong Kong and China Apart," *South China Morning Post,* October 6, 2015 (OSC CHR2015100653432323).

38. Marco Rubio, "Restoring America's Strength: My Vision for U.S. Foreign Policy," *Foreign Affairs* 94 (September–October 2015), pp. 113–14.

Index

Craddock, Percy, 33, 36
Cullen, Richard, 84
Cultural Revolution, 9–10
Cyberattacks, 58, 113, 139

DAB. *See* Democratic Alliance for the
	Betterment and Progress of Hong
	Kong
Darwin, John, 10
Davies, Ken, 183
DeGolyer, Michael, 89, 116–17, 144
DeLisle, Jacques, 290
Democracy, 147–59; adversarial
	democracy, 149; balance of power
	restored through, 20; Basic Law on,
	30, 31–34; bureaucratic democracy,
	158; comparative perspective on,
	150–54; and competitiveness, 279;
	and Confucianism, 149; continuum
	of, 275; cultural characteristics
	fostered by, 149; deferral of
	democracy by Britain, 10–12; direct,
	94; dysfunctional systems of, 154–57,
	280; and economic development, 150,
	151, 155, 156; in electoral systems,
	1–2, 3, 16; expansion before and after
	reversion, 34–43; external influences
	on emergence of, 150, 153; factors
	associated with transition to, 150–51,
	270; and governance, 20, 157–59,
	163–67, 279; illiberal, 47–48, 148,
	161; intellectual facilitation of, 272;
	millennial views of, 89–90, 95; and
	modernization, 150, 153; patronage
	democracy, 158; post-reversion,
	29–30, 31–32; public attitudes
	toward, 156–57; and transition
	fatigue, 43; U.S. promotion of, 22,
	243–44, 245, 265–74; value of,
	147–49; waves of democratization,
	209, 270
Democratic Alliance for the Betterment
	and Progress of Hong Kong (DAB):
	in district councils, 79; formation of,

78; in geographic constituencies, 214;
	inter-party collaboration by, 87–88;
	in Legislative Council, 44, 45, 78;
	and United Front, 141, 142
Democratic Party: collaboration with
	pro-establishment parties, 87; on
	electoral reform, 41–42; formation of,
	43; fundraising by, 52; in Legislative
	Council elections, 45, 144; radicalism
	in, 93, 144, 222; and United Front,
	142
Democratic Progressive Party (DPP),
	170, 228, 229, 231, 232–33, 235–36
Demonstrations. *See* Protests
Deng Xiaoping: on democracy, 31;
	economic reform policies of, 10, 25;
	liberalization policies of, 284; on
	national unification mission, 224,
	225; on one country, two systems
	model, 238; on parliamentary
	systems, 214; on political protests, 4;
	on reversion of Hong Kong to China,
	28
Dervis, Kemal, 186
Design Democracy platform, 258, 259
Diamond, Larry, 127, 150, 154–55, 277
Direct democracy, 94
District councils (Hong Kong):
	competitive elections for seats on, 48,
	167; democrats in, 40, 79; formation
	of, 39; functional constituency for,
	41, 42, 80, 89; preservation efforts by,
	70
Document Number 9 (CCP), 103
Domestic workers, rights of, 53–54
DPP. *See* Democratic Progressive Party
Duihua Foundation, 59
Dulles, John Foster, 247

Earnest, Josh, 261
Easton, David, 159
Economic growth: in China–Hong
	Kong complementary
	interdependence, 10, 18, 179, 191–92;

HDI (Human Development Index), 151

Health care services, 67, 180, 181, 184, 200–01

Heritage Foundation, 185

Heung Yee Kuk functional constituency, 84, 86, 134, 204

HKFS (Hong Kong Federation of Students), 4, 95, 113, 123

HKSAR. *See* Hong Kong Special Administrative Region

HKYCA (Hong Kong Youth Care Association), 54

Ho Chun-yan, Albert, 43, 44, 79

Ho Chun-yin, Steven, 85–86

Ho Lok-Sang, 94, 149

Home ownership scheme (HOS), 71–72, 73, 143, 201–02. *See also* Housing

Hong Kong and Macau Affairs Leading Group (HKMALG), 101

Hong Kong as a City-State (Chin Wan-kan), 125, 140

Hong Kong Bill of Rights Ordinance, 98

Hong Kong Federation of Students (HKFS), 4, 95, 113, 123

Hong Kong Human Rights Monitor, 258

Hong Kong Human Rights Ordinance, 37

Hong Kong Independence Party, 125

Hong Kong Land for Hong Kong People (Wong), 71

Hong Kong–Macau Relations Act of 1994, 227

Hong Kong National Party, 137

Hong Kong Special Administrative Region (Hong Kong SAR): British colonization of, 6–7, 8–9, 10–15, 76; Chinese sovereignty over, 1, 14, 56, 211; comparison with Singapore, 188–89; complementary interdependence with Chinese economy, 10, 18, 179, 191–92; consolidation of CCP support

within, 140–42; culture of protest in, 91–95; democracy in a comparative perspective, 150–54; financial crisis in, 15, 72, 91, 173; fragmentation within society, 5; Freedom House assessment of, 48–49; history of, 5–16; Human Development Index on, 151; as hybrid regime, 16–20, 47–49, 63, 148, 277; identity claimed by populations in, 9, 13, 124, 207, 208; independence movements in, 125–26, 137, 278; in international economy, 7, 16–17, 172–74; Japanese occupation of, 7–8, 11; as liberal oligarchy, 48–49, 55, 63, 96, 154; life expectancy in, 174; localist and nativist sentiment in, 124–25, 207; national security in, 105, 136; political development in, 162–63; population growth in, 8, 9, 11; populism in, 155; public satisfaction rates in, 88–90; quality assessment of governance in, 162–69; refugee populations in, 8, 9, 11; SARS epidemic in, 15; social welfare programs in, 9, 11, 155, 200–01; U.S. policies toward, 22–23, 243, 245. *See also* Economic performance; Electoral system; Judicial system; One country, two systems model; Political system; Protests; Reversion of Hong Kong to China; United States policy toward Hong Kong

Hong Kong Transition Project, 88–89, 109, 124

Hong Kong 2020, 112, 130, 140

Hong Kong Youth Care Association (HKYCA), 54

HOS (home ownership scheme), 71–72, 73, 143, 201–02. *See also* Housing

Household workers, rights of, 53–54

Housing: for aging populations, 201; expenditures on, 66, 73; government provisions for, 9, 11, 15; inequality in,